# Direct Reference

# Direct Reference

## *From Language to Thought*

FRANÇOIS RECANATI

BLACKWELL
*Oxford UK & Cambridge USA*

Copyright © François Recanati, 1993

The right of François Recanati to be identified as author of this work has been asserted in accordance with the Copyright, Designs and Patents Act 1988.

First published 1993

Blackwell Publishers
108 Cowley Road
Oxford   OX4 1JF
UK

238 Main Street, Suite 501
Cambridge, Massachusetts 02142
USA

All rights reserved. Except for the quotation of short passages for the purposes of criticism and review, no part of this publication may be reproduced, stored in a retrieval system, or transmitted, in any form or by any means, electronic, mechanical, photocopying, recording or otherwise, without the prior permission of the publisher.

Except in the United States of America, this book is sold subject to the condition that it shall not, by way of trade or otherwise, be lent, resold, hired out, or otherwise circulated without the publisher's prior consent in any form of binding or cover other than that in which it is published and without a similar condition including this condition being imposed on the subsequent purchaser.

*British Library Cataloguing in Publication Data*

A CIP catalogue record for this book is available from the British Library.

*Library of Congress Cataloging-in-Publication Data*

Recanati, François, 1952–
Direct reference : from language to thought / François Recanati.
   p.   cm.
Includes bibliographical references and index.
ISBN 0-631-18154-7
1. Reference (Linguistics)  2. Reference (Philosophy)  3. Thought and thinking.  4. Psycholinguistics.  5. Language and languages – Philosophy.  6. Pragmatics.  I. Title.
P325.5.R44R38   1993
415 – dc20                                   92-29857
                                                CIP

Typeset in 10½ on 12½pt Sabon
by Graphicraft Typesetters Ltd, Hong Kong
Printed in Great Britain by T.J. Press, Padstow

This book is printed on acid-free paper

# Contents

Preface   xi

**PART I: DIRECT REFERENCE IN LANGUAGE AND THOUGHT**   1
Introduction   3

I.1 *De re* communication   5

1  Direct reference and linguistic meaning: rigidity *de jure*   7
    1.1 *Introduction*   7
    1.2 *Rigidity and scope*   7
    1.3 *Rigidity and referentiality*   10
    1.4 *Lockwood's criterion*   13
    1.5 *Type-referentiality*   16
    1.6 *Referentiality, meaning, and psychology*   19

2  Singular propositions and thoughts   26
    2.1 *Truth-conditions, meaning, and propositional content*   26
    2.2 *Content and character: the neo-Russellian theory*   28
    2.3 *Quasi-singular propositions: the neo-Fregean theory*   31
    2.4 *Propositional content and thought*   34
    2.5 *Two basic intuitions*   38

3  The communication of *de re* thoughts   45
    3.1 *Introduction*   45
    3.2 *Singular propositions in a neo-Fregean framework*   46

|       |       |                                                                                   |     |
| :---- | :---- | :-------------------------------------------------------------------------------- | --: |
|       | 3.3   | Interpretation in *de re* communication                                           |  48 |
|       | 3.4   | Communication and subjectivity                                                    |  53 |

## I.2 From language to thought     61

4   Linguistic and psychological modes of presentation   63
    4.1   Introduction   63
    4.2   *Linguistic meaning and narrow content: the Simplified Picture*   66
    4.3   *Two sorts of mode of presentation*   69
    4.4   *Systematic differences between linguistic and psychological modes of presentation*   72
    4.5   Conclusion   76

5   The meaning and cognitive significance of indexical expressions   80
    5.1   Introduction   80
    5.2   *Rebutting the constancy argument*   80
    5.3   *The Simplified Picture again*   84
    5.4   *Immunity to error through misidentification*   87
    5.5   Conclusion   90

## I.3 *De re* thoughts     95

6   *De re* modes of presentation   97
    6.1   Introduction   97
    6.2   *Non-descriptiveness and relationality*   98
    6.3   *Non-descriptiveness and truth-conditional irrelevance*   103
    6.4   *Truth-conditional irrelevance and relationality*   106
    6.5   *Non-descriptiveness as descriptive multiplicity*   109
    6.6   *Non-descriptiveness and iconicity*   112

7   Egocentric concepts vs. encyclopedia entries   119
    7.1   Introduction   119
    7.2   *Indexicality and perception*   120
    7.3   *From 'buffers' to egocentric concepts*   122
    7.4   *Stable and unstable object files*   125
    7.5   Conclusion   129

## I.4 Proper names — 133

**8 The meaning of proper names** — 135
- 8.1 Introduction — 135
- 8.2 The character of proper names — 136
- 8.3 Proper names as indexicals — 140
- 8.4 Indexicality or homonymy? — 143
- 8.5 Localness — 146
- 8.6 The individuation of languages — 149

**9 Answering Kripke's objections** — 155
- 9.1 Introduction — 155
- 9.2 The modal argument — 155
- 9.3 The circularity argument — 158
- 9.4 The generality argument — 161
- 9.5 Conclusion — 165

**10 Proper names in thought** — 168
- 10.1 Introduction — 168
- 10.2 Proper names, sortals, and demonstrative identification — 169
- 10.3 The psychological neutrality of proper names — 172
- 10.4 Descriptive names — 176
- 10.5 Proper names and encyclopedia entries — 181

## I.5 The two-component picture: a defence — 191

**11 Narrow content and psychological explanation** — 193
- 11.1 Neo-Fregeanism and the two-component picture — 193
- 11.2 Alleged arguments for the two-component picture — 197
- 11.3 Narrow content in psychological explanation — 202
- 11.4 The empty case — 206

**12 Externalism and the two-component picture** — 209
- 12.1 Can thoughts be schematic? — 209
- 12.2 The externalist objection — 211
- 12.3 Two forms of environment-dependence: the relative notion of narrowness — 213
- 12.4 Second-order narrow contents: the externalist's dilemma — 218
- 12.5 Holistic Externalism — 222

| | | | |
|---|---|---|---|
| **PART II:** | **THE PRAGMATICS OF DIRECT REFERENCE** | | 227 |
| Introduction | | | 229 |

## II.1  Methodological preliminaries 231

**13  Truth-conditional pragmatics** 233
- 13.1 Enriching the Gricean picture: two sorts of pragmatic explanation 233
- 13.2 Three minimalist principles 240
- 13.3 The Implicature Analysis 244
- 13.4 The Availability Principle 246
- 13.5 Conclusion 250

**14  Primary pragmatic processes** 255
- 14.1 Introduction 255
- 14.2 Can Minimalism be defended? 256
- 14.3 Giving up Minimalism 258
- 14.4 Primary and secondary pragmatic processes 260

Appendix: Availability and the Scope Principle 269

## II.2  Referential/attributive 275

**15  The referential use of definite descriptions** 277
- 15.1 Introduction 277
- 15.2 Donnellan's presentation 278
- 15.3 Improper uses and truth-conditional irrelevance: the intuitive basis of the Naive Theory 281
- 15.4 An alleged argument for the Implicature Theory 284
- 15.5 The Indeterminacy Theory 288
- 15.6 The Synecdoche Theory 293

**16  The descriptive use of indexicals** 300
- 16.1 Introduction 300
- 16.2 Nunberg's counter-examples: *de re concepts in interpretation* 301
- 16.3 Other alleged counter-examples 306
- 16.4 Nunberg's theory: the index/referent distinction generalized 309

|  |  |  |
|---|---|---|
| | 16.5 *The basic level of interpretation* | 312 |
| | 16.6 *Multi-layered pragmatics and direct reference theory* | 316 |

## II.3 Belief reports — 323

17 Belief reports and conversational implicatures — 325
    17.1 *Accounting for opacity* — 325
    17.2 *The Implicature Theory* — 328
    17.3 *What's wrong with the Implicature Theory (1)* — 335
    17.4 *What's wrong with the Implicature Theory (2)* — 341

18 Belief reports and the semantics of 'that'-clauses — 348
    18.1 *Frege's Puzzle and the Relational principle* — 348
    18.2 *Rejecting the Relational principle* — 350
    18.3 *The reference of 'that'-clauses* — 355
    18.4 *The context-sensitivity of 'that'-clauses* — 357

19 Comparison with other accounts — 368
    19.1 *Unitary vs. dualist accounts of belief reports* — 368
    19.2 *The incoherence of dualism* — 370
    19.3 *The combined account* — 375
    19.4 *Schematic belief reports* — 379

20 How ambiguous are belief sentences? — 386
    20.1 *Introduction* — 386
    20.2 *Definite descriptions in belief contexts* — 386
    20.3 *Proper names in belief contexts* — 393
    20.4 *Indexicals in belief contexts* — 397

Bibliography — 403

Index — 413

# Preface

I began working on the theory of direct reference in Oxford, where I spent the academic year 1978–9 as a British Council Scholar. I was struck by the fact that Kripke had not succeeded in providing a satisfactory characterization of the semantic distinction between names and descriptions which was one of the main topics of *Naming and Necessity*. The notion of rigidity was too weak to do the job, as Kripke himself acknowledged. Kaplan's notion of a 'directly referential expression' was stronger than Kripke's notion of a rigid designator. Moreover, Kaplan had put forward a two-tiered analysis of indexicals which seemed to correspond to the crucial distinction between the semantic properties of an expression type and the semantic properties of a token of that expression – a distinction which I found especially important, given that the semantic feature which distinguishes directly referential terms (names or indexicals) from descriptions is a property which directly referential terms must possess as expression *types*. So I turned to Kaplan's work and tried to accommodate his insights, as well as Kripke's, within the multi-layered theory of meaning I had been developing in my earlier work in speech act theory (Recanati, 1979, 1981b, 1987b). The results were fairly encouraging. It turned out to be possible to define directly referential terms as 'indicators' on a par with other indicators such as the imperative mood. In the same way as the imperative mood indicates that a certain type of speech act is being performed, a directly referential term indicates that the truth-condition of the utterance in which it occurs is singular. In this framework the distinguishing property of directly referential terms (*qua* expression types) is a certain feature which they convey as part of their linguistic meaning: the feature REF.

My next step was to defend the theory of direct reference and singular propositions against traditional 'Fregean' objections in terms of cognitive significance. The standard defence rests on the neo-Russellian distinction between the proposition expressed by an utterance and the complete thought associated with it. This led me to the study of *de re* thoughts – a fascinating topic. In this domain I have learnt a lot from the pioneering works of Gareth Evans and John Perry, whose views I found strikingly similar. (In general the difference between so-called neo-Fregeans and neo-Russellians seems to me to have been grossly exaggerated.)

One often takes the theory of direct reference to be the view that some linguistic expressions relate to things directly, without any mediating entity such as the 'meaning' of the expression or the 'concept' it expresses (see e.g. Devitt, 1989). This is not my view. I take directly referential expressions to have a meaning distinct from their reference and to be associated with a certain type of concept. Far from denying that a 'mode of presentation' is involved, I think *two sorts of mode* of presentation are simultaneously at play in direct reference: linguistic modes of presentation, which belong to the meanings of directly referential expressions, and psychological modes of presentation, which belong to the associated thoughts. Direct referentiality as I construe it is not the absence of something otherwise present (a mode of presentation) but the presence of something more (a feature which prevents the mode of presentation from going into the truth-conditions of either the utterance or the associated thought). The meaning of a directly referential expression includes a particular semantic feature, REF, and in quite the same way there is an intrinsic feature of *de re* concepts – the thought-constituents corresponding to directly referential expressions – which distinguishes them from 'descriptive' concepts; what renders direct reference direct is not the alleged fact that no mode of presentation occurs but the fact that the modes of presentation that occur are filtered out and made truth-conditionally irrelevant by virtue of the features in question.

The second half of the book deals with issues in pragmatics. Pragmatics and especially Grice's theory of conversational implicatures plays an important role in direct reference theory: it is commonly used to handle Donnellan's referential/attributive distinction as well as to alleviate the difficulties raised by opaque belief reports. But this appeal to the Implicature Theory is based on mistaken assumptions. In the second part of the book I offer general considerations about pragmatics and its relation to semantics and I put forward what I take to be the proper pragmatic treatment of the referential/attributive distinction and belief reports. The pragmatic mechanism in terms of which I account for referential uses of definite descriptions turns out to be especially important for it is revelatory of the fundamental process at work in *de re* communication: the process of 'synecdoche' through which a descriptive concept such as that conventionally associated with a linguistic expression can stand for a *de re* concept (a dossier of information) to the content of which it belongs.

I have used materials from previously published papers in this book. I wish to thank the editors and publishers of *Mind and Language, Philosophical Studies* and *Noûs* for permission to do so.

Many of the ideas contained in this book were presented at meetings of the 'Friday group' in Paris from 1982 to 1988. Among the participants were Daniel Andler, Scott Atran, Dick Carter, Gilles Fauconnier, Pierre Jacob and Dan Sperber. Fauconnier, Jacob and Sperber deserve special thanks. Four series of lectures were based on earlier versions of this book: two in Paris at the Ecole des Hautes Etudes en Sciences Sociales in 1980–81 and 1989 respectively, one in Liverpool and Sheffield in 1988, and one in Geneva in 1990. I am indebted to many of those who attended my lectures, especially Mark Sacks, with whom I had several stimulating discussions in Liverpool, and Eros Corazza and Jerome Dokic, who attended my lectures in Geneva and sent me comments on an earlier version of the first part. I am heavily indebted to Benoît de Cornulier, who made a number of criticisms and suggestions over the years. I have benefited also from numerous philosophical and linguistic conversations with Mike Harnish, Paul Horwich, Paul Kay, Stephen Neale, Geoff Nunberg and Charles Travis. Like Cornulier, Jacques Bouveresse, Jean-Toussaint Desanti, Oswald Ducrot, and Gilles Granger commented on an earlier version of the book during the defence of my 'doctorat d'Etat' in June 1990. I am pleased to record my debt to them (and especially to Ducrot, who influenced me in many ways). I am grateful also to Gabriella Airenti, Ingar Brink, Robyn Carston, Roberto Casati, Hector Castañeda, François Clementz, Martin Davies, Steven Davis, Marc Dominicy, Jean-Pierre Dupuy, Pascal Engel, Jerry Fodor, Gary Gates, Abel Gerschenfeld, Sam Guttenplan, Jerry Katz, Ruth Kempson, Sam Kerstein, Charles Larmore, Pierre Livet, Brian Loar, Adele Mercier, Michael Morris,

Kevin Mulligan, Jessica Riskin, Albert Newen, Christopher Peacocke, Philip Pettit, Joelle Proust, Stephen Schiffer, John Searle, Julia Tanney, Marcel Vuillaume, Deirdre Wilson, Andrew Woodfield, and Richard Zuber, as well as to my friend Narsov, to my students at the Ecole des Hautes Études en Sciences Sociales, and to my colleagues at CREA.

John Perry considerably influenced my thinking through his own writings and I have greatly benefited from the time we spent at CREA talking together during his sabbatical in 1992. I thank him for those discussions and for his comments on the penultimate version of the book. Thanks also to Kent Bach for the extensive and useful comments he made on the final version.

I began to elaborate my own ideas about those issues under the supervision of John Mackie, whose help was very beneficial to me. At the same time I attended Evans's lectures. Both Evans and Mackie died shortly after I left Oxford. This book is dedicated to their memory.

François Recanati

# Part I

# Direct reference in language and thought

# Introduction

What is it for a singular term, or for a use of a singular term, to be referential in the strong sense, i.e. 'purely' or 'directly' referential?[1] This is the general question I will try to answer in this book. The intuitive (and largely metaphorical) notion of referentiality that is current in the philosophical literature emerges from the following set of statements:

> A (directly) referential term is a term that serves simply to refer. It is devoid of descriptive content, in the sense at least that what it contributes to the proposition expressed by the sentence where it occurs is not a concept, but an object. Such a sentence is used to assert *of* the object referred to that it falls under the concept expressed by the predicate expression in the sentence. Proper names and indexicals are supposed to be referential in this sense; and although definite descriptions are not intrinsically referential, they have a referential use.

That such a notion exists in contemporary philosophy is beyond question. But many philosophers do not like it. I suspect that there are two reasons why this is so. Firstly, it is thought that the intuitive notion of referentiality is too vague and metaphorical to be of any use; secondly, assuming that a definite view does emerge from the set of statements above, it is thought that there are serious objections to this view. I do not share this pessimism. One of my aims in this book is to show that the notion can be satisfactorily defined and the putative objections disposed of.

I will start by providing a theory of direct reference construed as a *linguistic* phenomenon. In so doing I will be concerned with 'type-referentiality', that is, referentiality *qua* semantic property of expression types.[2] It will turn out that there is a parallel feature in thought: *de re* thoughts include constituents, namely *de re* concepts, which are 'referential' in their own way. The nature of *de re* thoughts, and their relation to the semantic properties of utterances containing referential terms, are among the main topics to be investigated.

## Notes

1. Throughout in this book I will use 'referential' and 'referentiality' as short for 'directly referential' and 'direct referentiality'.
2. Referential *uses* ('token-referentiality') will be dealt with in the second part of the book.

# I.1

*De re* communication

# Chapter 1

# Direct reference and linguistic meaning: rigidity *de jure*

## 1.1  Introduction

In this chapter, I will be mainly concerned with defining 'referentiality', the property which proper names and indexicals are often said to have in contrast to definite descriptions.[1] My starting point will be the related notion of rigidity, introduced by Saul Kripke in the philosophical literature. It is perhaps a bit misleading to speak of 'the' notion of rigidity, for there are, as I will try to show, three different notions under that name, all stemming from Kripke's characterization of a rigid designator as a designator that denotes the same object in all possible worlds. The three different notions are: rigidity as a matter of scope, rigidity as a matter of truth-conditions, and rigidity as (pure or direct) referentiality. This last notion, which I shall concentrate upon, is the most interesting, but it is especially hard to characterize in non-metaphorical terms. To provide such a characterization is the task of this chapter.

## 1.2  Rigidity and scope

Let us start, then, with the first sense of 'rigidity'. Many people have said that a rigid designator is simply a designator that (always) takes wide scope in modal contexts. Why have they said so? Because Kripke characterizes a rigid designator as a designator that denotes the same object in all possible worlds, this idea being sometimes expressed, in Kripke's writings, by saying that a rigid designator refers to the same thing whether we use it to talk about what is actually the case or about some counterfactual situation (Kripke, 1971, p. 145 and 1980, p. 77). Now when a designator – say, a definite description – takes wide scope in a modal sentence, i.e. in a sentence used to talk about possible worlds, it does refer to the same object as when it occurs in a sentence used to describe the actual world. In sentence 1 below, for example, the description 'the president of France', when it is given wide scope, refers to the person who is the president of France in the actual world, even though the sentence as a whole describes a counterfactual situation. So it seems that a description designates rigidly when it takes wide scope. The difference between proper names and definite descriptions, on that view, is simply that, contrary to definite descriptions, proper names *always* take wide scope in modal contexts.² This is why, whereas 1 is ambiguous, 2 is not:

1  The president of France might have been tall.
2  Mitterrand might have been tall.

1 means either that France might have had (instead of Mitterrand) a tall man as president, or that Mitterrand himself might have been tall. On this second, 'rigid' reading, the individual who satisfies the description in the actual world is said to be tall in some possible world, whereas in the first reading, the property of being tall in some possible world – say, $w$ – is ascribed to the individual who satisfies the description in $w$ (not in the actual world). Depending on whether the description does or does not fall within the scope of the modal operator, its referent, i.e. the individual satisfying the description, is picked out either in the actual world or in the possible world introduced by the modal operator. There is no such scope ambiguity in the case of 2, which contains a proper name instead of a description.

This view of rigidity, however, is misguided. As Kripke himself has shown (in his preface to Kripke, 1980), rigidity is not simply, and cannot be reduced to, a matter of scope. You cannot say that a designator is rigid if and only if it (always) takes wide scope in modal contexts: this would make the notion of rigidity relevant only to modal contexts, whereas the rigid/non-rigid distinction applies to designators in general, even when they occur in simple sentences like 3 and 4:

3  Mitterrand is small.
4  The president of France is small.

3 and 4, no less than 1 and 2, provide good evidence that 'Mitterrand', contrary to 'the president of France', rigidly designates its referent. To see that, compare the truth-conditions of these two sentences. 3 is true with respect to a world $w$ if and only if, in $w$, Mitterrand is small. In this case, there is a unique individual x such that, for any world $w$, the sentence is true with respect to $w$ if and only if x is small in $w$. But there is no single individual such that, for any world $w$, 4 is true with respect to $w$ if and only if that individual is small in $w$; in a world in which Giscard is the president of France, Giscard's being small makes 4 true, whereas in a world with Chirac as president, the truth of 4 depends on Chirac's being small. No particular individual is involved in the truth-condition of 4: 4 is true with respect to a world if and only if, in that world, there in an individual x such that x is both the president of France and small, but this individual need not be the same with respect to all possible worlds. In the case of 3, on the other hand, the individual whose being small would make the sentence true *is the same in all possible worlds.* We thus find the rigid/non-rigid distinction again, this time at the level of simple sentences, where no scope ambiguity can occur. As Kripke puts it, the rigidity theory 'is a doctrine about the truth-conditions, with respect to counterfactual situations, of (the propositions expressed by) *all* sentences, including *simple* sentences' (Kripke, 1980, p. 12).

Here Kripke's reply ends. But it is possible to go further and conclude from what has just been said that the description in 1 designates non-rigidly not only when it takes narrow scope, but *also* when it falls outside the scope of the modal operator. When it does, 1 says that the man who is president of France in the actual world is tall in some other possible world.[3] (From now on, I'll call this reading of 1 '1a'.) This man, however, is not specified, and it is not necessarily Mitterrand. The sentence, after all, does not tell us *which* world is supposed to play the role of 'the actual world': with respect to any world $w$, 'the actual world' will be that very world $w$.[4] Now suppose a world $w_1$ where Giscard has been elected president instead of Mitterrand. With respect to $w_1$, 1a is true if and only if Giscard is tall in some possible world other than $w_1$. By the same token, with respect to a world $w_2$ where *Chirac* has been elected, 1a is true if and only if Chirac is tall in some possible world other than $w_2$. And, of course, with respect to *our* actual world, where Mitterrand is president, 1a is true if and only if Mitterrand is tall in some other possible world. So we see that the description in 1 designates non-rigidly even when it takes wide scope; for there is no unique individual x such that, with respect to any world *w*, 1a is true if and only if x is tall in some possible world other than *w*. Of course, 1 presents us with two different worlds, one of them playing the role of the 'actual' world; and the description's taking wide scope means that its reference should be picked out in this 'actual' world, notwithstanding the fact that the sentence is used to describe another possible world. But this is not enough to make the designation rigid; for every world is the actual world with respect to itself, so that it will still be possible to change the description's reference simply by changing the world with respect to which the sentence is evaluated. It follows that, even if it was stipulated that a certain definite description always takes maximal scope in modal contexts, this description would still not count as a rigid designator.[5]

## 1.3 Rigidity and referentiality

On Kripke's view, rigidity is a matter of truth-conditions: to say that a designator is rigid is to say that there is an individual such that, with respect to every counterfactual situation, the truth-condition of any sentence containing the designator involves the individual in question. This view was first explicitly put forward by Christopher Peacocke, who gives the following definition (Peacocke, 1975, p. 110):

(R)  *t* is a rigid designator (in a language L free of both ambiguity and indexicals) if and only if:
there is an object x such that for any sentence *G(t)* in which *t* occurs, the truth (falsity) condition for *G(t)* is that <x> satisfy (respectively, fail to satisfy) *G( )*.[6]

Criterion (R), Peacocke claimed, captures Russell's idea that sometimes the reference of a singular term is a constituent of the proposition expressed by the sentence where it occurs. For if a term *t* denoting an object x is a rigid designator by criterion (R), then any sentence *G(t)* will be true if and only if x satisfies *G( )*. In other words, the object x, along with the property *G( )*, is a constituent of the truth-condition of the sentence. What a rigid designator contributes to the truth-condition of the sentence thus is the object itself which it refers to, not an attribute which an object would have to possess in order to be referred to.

Russell's idea is the idea of a purely referential term, a term that serves only to refer. Peacocke, in effect, equates rigidity, in the sense of (R), with referentiality, as the following passage shows:

> This criterion of rigid designation can be seen... as merely a more explicit formulation of an idea variously expressed as that of a term's 'serving... simply to refer to its object' (Quine), 'tagging' an individual (Marcus), or in general of an expression's being 'used to enable... individuals to be made subjects of discourse' (Mill); and the view that proper names are rigid designators in our sense seems a natural elucidation of Miss Anscombe's remark that the proper name contributes 'to the meaning of the sentence precisely by standing for its bearer'. (Peacocke, 1975, p. 111)

This equation of rigidity with referentiality is consonant with Kripke's insistence on the 'Millian' character of proper names, which he takes as paradigm examples of rigid designation. Proper names, Mill says, 'are attached to the objects themselves, and are not dependent on... any attribute of the object' (Mill, 1947, p. 20). It is the function of proper names, according to Kripke, to refer to an object independently of the properties it may have, so as to enable one to refer to *this object* even with respect to possible worlds where it no longer has them. The link between a name and its reference is, for Kripke, 'stipulative' rather than 'qualitative'.

No less than the wide scope view of rigidity, however, the view which equates rigidity (in the sense of (R)) with Millian referentiality is confused. Referentiality is supposed to distinguish proper names from definite descriptions, at least in their non-referential uses. Now some definite descriptions are rigid and satisfy criterion (R). For example, a mathematical description like 'the cube root of 27' denotes 3 in all possible worlds, since '3 is the cube root of 27' is a necessary truth. The rigidity of 'the cube root of 27' can be checked, using criterion (R), at the level of truth-conditions: for any sentence S of the form 'The cube root of 27 is F' (where 'F' stands for a predicate), there is an object x, namely the number 3, such that, with respect to any possible world, S is true if and only if x satisfies the predicate. It is no use saying either that, for S to be true, x must also be the cube root of 27, or that some other number's being both the cube root of 27 and F would verify the sentence as well, for there is no world where 3 is not, or where a number other than 3 is, the cube root of 27.

Like any description, the description 'the cube root of 27' denotes the object which has the property it 'connotes', viz. the property of being a number x such that $x^3 = 27$. The link between the description and its reference is typically 'qualitative' in Kripke's sense. It would be definitely odd to say that the description 'is attached to the object itself, and does not depend on any attribute of the object'. The reference of the description is a function of the concept it expresses, and this concept is what the description contributes to the proposition expressed by the sentence where it occurs. To dramatize this point, consider an attributive use of the description: "The cube root of 27, whatever it is, is F". The proposition expressed by this sentence is clearly not a 'singular' proposition' consisting of an object and the property F. Nobody would be willing to say that the description here is referential, even though it is rigid.

The difference between rigidity and referentiality was pointed out by Kripke himself in *Naming and Necessity*. There is, he says, a difference between a rigid definite description and a proper name, even when the description in question is used to 'fix the reference' of the name:

> π is supposed to be the ratio of the circumference of a circle to its diameter. Now, it's something that I have nothing but a vague intuitive feeling to argue for: It seems to me that here this Greek letter is not being used as *short for* the phrase 'the ratio of the circumference of a circle to its diameter'... It is used as a *name* for a real number... Note that here both 'π' and 'the ratio of the circumference of a circle to its diameter' are rigid designators... (Kripke, 1980, p. 60)

The intuitive difference Kripke has in mind is that 'π', as a name, is purely referential, while the rigid description 'the ratio of the circumference of a circle to its diameter' is not.

There is, of course, a connection between referentiality and rigidity: referentiality *implies* rigidity. A referential term is rigid *'de jure'*; it is, in Mill's terminology, 'attached to the object itself', independently of its properties, and so cannot fail to denote the same object in all possible worlds, since what changes from world to world is not the object itself, its identity, but only its (contingent) properties. By contrast, a mathematical description – or, for that matter, any essential description – is rigid only *'de facto'*: like any description, it denotes the object that falls under a certain concept, but in this case the concept happens to fit the same object in all possible worlds.[7]

The problem is that, whereas rigidity in the sense of (R) is a well-defined notion, referentiality is not. What does it mean to say that a referential term refers to the object 'itself'? One way of understanding this is to say that a referential term is a term wholly devoid of descriptive content, a term whose link to its reference is purely stipulative, as Kripke says. But this is far too strong, for not all referential terms are like proper names in this respect:[8] demonstrative expressions like 'this table' or pronouns like 'I' or 'you' clearly have some sort of descriptive content. Rather than wholly devoid of descriptive content, a referential term is such that what it contributes to the proposition expressed is the object it refers to rather than a concept under which this object falls (even if, at some level, the term does express such a concept). But this cannot be explained, as Peacocke thought, in terms of criterion (R): it is true that, when a term is referential, there is an object such that the truth-condition of any sentence containing the term involves this object. But this criterion is too weak, since it characterizes all rigid expressions, including rigid descriptions, which nobody would want to classify as referential (at least in their attributive uses).

## 1.4 Lockwood's criterion

An obvious solution to the problem at hand is the following. Let us make a distinction between the truth-condition of an utterance and the proposition it expresses. In terms of this distinction, it is possible to define referentiality as opposed to mere rigidity. A rigid expression is an expression such that the truth-condition of any sentence containing it involves a certain object, in conformity to criterion (R). By contrast, when an expression is referential, there is an object such that not only the truth-condition but also *the proposition expressed* involves that object.

Various philosophers have insisted that, to understand the proposition expressed by an utterance where a referential term occurs, it is necessary to know which object has been referred to; it is necessary to identify the reference.[9] (See e.g. Evans, 1982.) This gives a sense in which the proposition expressed includes the very object that is referred to rather than simply a concept under which that object falls. When a term is non-referential the proposition expressed involves only a certain concept; if the term is rigid *de facto*, this concept happens to fit the same object in all possible worlds, but it is not necessary for understanding the proposition to identify the object in question. As Lockwood (1975, p. 488) puts it:

A hearer may be said fully to grasp what statement is being expressed [by 'the cube of 408 has more factors than there are planets'] quite irrespective of whether he knows what the cube of 408 is, or even if he falsely believes it to be, say, 48,914,012. Yet, in the case of a term that is functioning referentially, being able correctly to identify its reference would seem to be a prerequisite of knowing what is being asserted by its aid.

'The cube of 408' being a rigid description, there is an object, viz. number 67,917,302, such that the truth-condition of any sentence containing it involves that object: "the cube of 408 is F" is true, with respect to any possible world, iff 67,917,302 is F. But the number in question is no part of the proposition expressed by the sentence, in the sense that one can understand what is said by an utterance of this sentence without identifying the number that is referred to – and therefore without knowing that the sentence is true iff that number is F. What is part of the proposition expressed is the concept 'cube of 408', not the number that falls under that concept.

The problem is that we don't know exactly, at this stage, what is meant by 'the proposition expressed', as opposed to the truth-condition of the utterance.[10] This, however, is not very important. The notion of proposition expressed as I have just used it is essentially tied to that of understanding, and what counts is precisely the connection between referentiality and understanding. 'The cube root of 27' rigidly designates the number 3, but we can understand the description even if we don't know what number it designates; a referential term, on the other hand, is such that to understand an utterance where it occurs one has to know which object it designates (in a certain sense of 'know which', to be elaborated in due course).

Michael Lockwood has put forward a definition of referentiality in terms of understanding which is intended to capture the connection as well as the difference between referentiality and rigidity. According to (a simplified version of) Lockwood's criterion:[11]

(RR) A term $t$ is referential if and only if there is an object x such that:
 (i) an utterance $G(t)$ is true iff x satisfies $G(\ )$, and
 (ii) to understand the utterance, one must know that it is true iff x satisfies $G(\ )$.

In this framework, a referential term is a rigid designator (this is what clause (i) amounts to), but a rigid designator of a very special sort: it is a rigid designator such that, to understand an utterance where it occurs, one has to know that it designates an object rigidly and which object it so designates (this is what clause (ii) amounts to).[12] More precisely, understanding the utterance involves, according to (RR), *de re* knowledge of the reference: it involves knowing *of* a certain object that the utterance is true if and only if this object satisfies the predicate. (This means that, to understand the utterance, one must form a *de re* thought. On *de re* thoughts, see chapters 6–7.)

I wish to retain Lockwood's insight about the basic nature of referentiality. (RR), however, is not satisfactory as it stands. According to (RR), understanding an utterance with a referential term involves identifying the reference of the term, and this implies that the reference actually exists. Indeed, many philosophers think that when the reference of a referential term does not exist, there is nothing to 'understand', since no proposition is expressed. This I do not wish to dispute. What I think, however, is that identification of the reference is not a necessary condition of *referentiality*: a term may well be referential, and understood by the hearer as referential, without its reference being identified. To understand the utterance 'Ralph Banilla is a midget' involves knowing who Ralph Banilla is, but to understand the *sentence* only involves knowing that the term is referential, that there is an individual that must be identified for an utterance of this sentence to be understood. To be sure, (RR) does not mention identification of the reference as a necessary condition of referentiality; but it says that the existence of the reference, which is a necessary condition for understanding an utterance with a referential term, is also a necessary condition for a term to *be* referential. A term is referential, according to (RR), *only if there is an object* such that to understand the utterance involves identifying this object. But this is too strong: a term can be referential even though there actually is no such object. The term 'Ralph Banilla' is referential, and understood as such, even if for some reason it fails to refer – even if Ralph Banilla does not exist. The category 'referential term' is not different from the category 'proper name' in that respect: 'Raph Banilla' is linguistically a proper name even if, for some reason, it has no bearer. (The very idea that no proposition is expressed when the reference of a referential term does not exist implies that a term can be referential even if its reference does not exist; otherwise, the notion of a referential term without reference would be self-contradictory.)

Something like (RR) was intended by Lockwood as a definition not of referentiality for a term but of referentiality for a use of a term. It may indeed be useful to have a notion of referential use such that a term is 'referentially used' only if there is an object it refers to. But if what we are interested in is the semantic distinction between proper names and demonstrative expressions on the one hand, and definite descriptions on the other, the former being referential and the latter non-referential, we need a notion of referentiality (call it 'type-referentiality') that is independent of extra-linguistic matters such as the existence or non-existence of the reference of the term. We must, therefore, modify the definition accordingly.[13]

## 1.5 Type-referentiality

When the term $t$ in a utterance $G(t)$ is a rigid designator, there is an object such that the utterance is true if and only if this object satisfies the predicate $G(\ )$. In such a case I will say that the truth-condition of the utterance is a *singular truth-condition*. In terms of this notion I think (type-)referentiality can be defined in a fairly straightforward manner. First, however, I must say a few words about sentence-meaning. I take type-referentiality to be a feature of the linguistic meaning of some expressions – the referential terms – and since the linguistic meaning of an expression is its contribution to the linguistic meaning of the sentences where it occurs, it may help to say a few things about sentence-meaning in general.

From the point of view of speech act theory (Searle, 1969; Bach & Harnish, 1979; Recanati, 1987b), the meaning of a sentence is essentially its 'illocutionary act potential'; it consists in indications concerning the illocutionary act the sentence can be used to perform. An illocutionary act is commonly said to have two components: a force and a content, or – in a slightly different framework – a type of satisfaction (e.g. truth or obedience) and a set of conditions of satisfaction (e.g. truth-conditions or obedience-conditions).[14] The meaning of a sentence, therefore, consists in indications concerning both the type and the conditions of satisfaction of the speech act. (Of course, sentence-meaning is related only to the speech act the speaker is supposed to perform 'directly', not to the speech acts that the speaker may perform indirectly.) Needless to say, those sentential indications are insufficient and the 'context' supplies further clues about the speech act being performed. This account is, I admit, oversimplified, but it will do for our present purposes.

Some parts of the sentence – the so-called indicators of illocutionary force, for example the imperative mood – indicate the type of satisfaction of the speech act: they indicate that the utterance is supposed to be *true* or *obeyed* or whatever. Some other elements contribute to indicating the satisfaction-conditions of the utterance; they partially describe a state of affairs such that the utterance is satisfied if and only if this state of affairs obtains. Now my suggestion is that some terms – those that are type-referential – specifically indicate that the truth-condition or, more generally, the satisfaction-condition of the utterance is singular.[15] Here is my definition of type-referentiality:

> (TR)  A term is (type-)referential if and only if its linguistic meaning includes a feature, call it 'REF', by virtue of which it indicates that the truth-condition (or, more generally, satisfaction-condition) of the utterance where it occurs is singular.

The truth-condition of an utterance $G(t)$ is singular if and only if there is an object x such that the utterance is true if and only if x satisfies $G(\ )$. If, therefore, the term *t* is referential, its meaning includes a feature by virtue of which it indicates that there is an object x such that an utterance of $G(t)$ is true or more generally satisfied if and only if x satisfies $G(\ )$.

The feature REF does not exhaust the meaning of a referential term. As I said above, some referential terms are not wholly devoid of descriptive content; they have what Loar calls a 'referential qualifier', Evans a 'referential feature' and Kaplan a 'character'. A referential expression such as 'this table' or the pronoun 'you' somehow characterizes the reference in such a way that it can be identified in context (as a table prominent in the vicinity, or as the hearer). Recall that, when a term is referential, understanding the utterance involves identifying the reference of the term. In his identification of the reference, the hearer is helped by the meaning of the referential term. In some cases at least, a referential term indicates not only (via the feature REF) *that there* is an object such that the utterance is true if and only if this object has a certain property; it also indicates *how* this object can be identified. In other words, a referential term includes as part of its meaning, besides the feature REF, a *mode of presentation* of the reference. Owing both to the feature REF and to the mode of presentation, a sentence $G(t)$ – where *t* is a referential term – indicates that:

There is an object x which is F (= mode of presentation), such that the utterance is satisfied if and only if x satisfies G( ).

For example, "This table is G" indicates that there is a table prominent in the vicinity, such that the utterance is true if and only if it is G; "You are G" indicates that there is a person to whom the utterance is addressed, such that the utterance is true if and only if this person is G and so on. In all those cases, the 'mode of presentation' associated with the referential term makes a certain object contextually identifiable, and the utterance is presented as satisfied if and only if this object has the property expressed by the predicate in the sentence.[16,17]

Although it is part of the meaning of the term, and therefore also of the meaning of the sentence where it occurs, the mode of presentation of the reference is no part of the proposition expressed by the utterance. The proposition expressed by the utterance, in my framework, is *the satisfaction-condition the utterance presents itself as having*.[18] Consider a sentence "α is G", where "α" is a referential term whose meaning includes a certain mode of presentation of its reference; an utterance of this sentence means that there is an object x, possessing a certain property F (= mode of presentation), such that the utterance is satisfied if and only if x is G. In other words, the utterance present itself as true if and only if a certain object x (to be contextually identified) is G. For there to be a definite proposition which the utterance expresses, there must be a definite truth-condition which the utterance presents itself as having, and this presupposes that a particular value has been contextually assigned to 'x'. Suppose, for example, that an object *a* salient in the context of utterance possesses the property F and is such that it is reasonable to ascribe to the speaker the intention to predicate the property G of that object. In this context, the utterance presents itself as 'true iff x is G' *under a particular assignation of value to 'x'*: it presents itself as true iff *a* is G. The utterance therefore expresses the proposition that *a* is G – a 'singular' proposition with the object *a* (and not the concept F) as a constituent.[19] The concept F – the mode of presentation – helps the hearer to understand which object is such that the utterance is satisfied if and only if it has a certain property G, but this object's satisfying the mode of presentation is no part of the conditions of satisfaction the utterance presents itself as having, no part of the proposition expressed – which proposition cannot be grasped unless the object in question is actually identified. In this way, I think we capture the intuitive notion of (pure or direct) referentiality.

## 1.6 Referentiality, meaning, and psychology

Following Peacocke and Kripke, I have defined rigidity (distinguished from the pseudo-rigidity connected with scope) in terms of truth-conditions: a rigid designator is such that the truth-condition of the utterance where it occurs is singular. I have tried to go further and define referentiality as a sort of meta-rigidity – as rigidity reflected in meaning. A referential term *indicates* that the truth-condition of the utterance is singular; it indicates that there is an object x such that the utterance $G(t)$ where it occurs is true iff x satisfies the predicate $G(\ )$. A referential term, therefore, is a designator that signifies its own rigidity.

What characterizes this approach to direct reference is the fact that I take the notion of 'meaning' as primitive. An expression is said to be type-referential if and only if the meaning of this expression (*qua* expression type) includes a certain feature. Token-referentiality, which I mentioned only in passing, is similarly defined in terms of the meaning of an utterance (rather than the meaning of an expression type). The notion of utterance meaning is also that in terms of which I have just characterized the 'proposition' expressed by an utterance, and in particular the singular propositions expressed by utterances containing referential expressions.

Some philosophers might be tempted to argue that my analysis is worthless, precisely because it helps itself to the notion of meaning. The objection I have in mind runs as follows:

> Analysis aims at reducing the more problematic to the less problematic. The notion of 'propositional content' is arguably more problematic than that of truth-conditions, and that of referentiality more problematic than that of rigidity; what makes the notions of propositional content or of referentiality more problematic is the fact that they are more 'intentional' – closer to the paradigmatically intentional notion of 'meaning'. Hence it is legitimate to try to analyse the notion of proposition in terms of truth-conditions, or referentiality in terms of rigidity. This analysis cannot proceed by way of straightforward reduction, for, as this chapter has shown, propositional content is not merely a matter of possible-world truth-condition, and referentiality is not merely a matter of possible-world reference. Some extra factor has

to be added to account for the step from singular truth-condition to singular proposition, or from rigidity to referentiality. This extra factor is what the type of analysis put forward in this chapter was meant to locate. But this analysis turns out to be worthless because the extra factor I had recourse to, namely meaning, is still more 'intentional', hence more problematic, than the notions to be analysed.

This objection raises a number of questions which I do not want to discuss here. The first question concerns the reductive conception of analysis. As Peter Strawson pointed out (Strawson, 1985, chapter 2), this conception is not the only possible one. The second question concerns the naturalistic ideal of dispensing with intentional notions by reducing them to non-intentional ones. This ideal is no more uncontroversial than the reductive view of analysis, but, again, I do not want to discuss these general questions. Rather, I will respond to the objection by making clear what my goal is.

I take for granted the notion of 'meaning', and indeed the whole apparatus used by contemporary linguists and philosophers of language in dealing with semantic and pragmatic phenomena, because I take direct reference itself to be such a phenomenon. I believe that there is a class of expressions in the language which are directly referential, and I think the defining property which expressions in this class have must be characterized using the resources of linguistics (or the philosophy of language — I do not think there is a difference between the two disciplines as far as semantics and pragmatics are concerned). This does not entail that I consider semantic and pragmatic properties to be 'irreducible', whatever that may mean. I believe, with Grice (1989), that meaning properties are to be analysed ultimately in terms of psychological properties. Sentence meaning is to be analysed in terms of utterance meaning, utterance meaning in terms of communicative behaviour, and communicative behaviour in terms of intentions and other psychological states. Then the question arises, how do we account for psychological states? Like utterances, psychological states have content. Can they be analysed in non-intentional terms? This is an interesting question but it is irrelevant to my present purpose. Whether or not intentionality can be ultimately dispensed with is an issue which need not be considered here, for I am concerned only with a local problem, at a local level: how can we account for direct reference *within* the framework of linguistic-*cum*-pragmatic theory?

The study of direct reference, then, must be firmly rooted in the study of language and language use, and may help itself to whatever conceptual resources are available in semantics and pragmatics, including, of course, the notion of meaning (sentence meaning, utterance meaning, and the like). That it is rooted in linguistics does not mean that the study of direct reference is divorced from psychology, however. Firstly, as Grice insisted, the study of meaning itself is rooted in psychology, for meaning properties are ultimately analysable in terms of psychological properties. Secondly, utterances endowed with meaning are used to communicate thoughts, and the connections between utterances and the corresponding thoughts cannot be ignored in a pragmatic approach to meaning and communication (see 3.3). Thus in 1.4 I accepted the Lockwood-Evans claim that understanding an utterance with a referential term involves forming a *de re* thought about the referent. Accordingly the study of *de re* thoughts must be undertaken by anyone attempting to theorize about direct reference. A large part of this book will be devoted to that study.

This issue of the relations between semantics and psychology introduces us to what is in fact the main topic of chapters 2 and 3. The study of direct reference has recently been a battleground between two groups of philosophers, who may conveniently be referred to as the neo-Russellians and the neo-Fregeans. An argument often used by the neo-Fregeans against their neo-Russellian colleagues is that the neo-Russellian picture, with its 'singular propositions' including the reference but no mode of presentation of the latter, has no psychological credibility. Here is one version of the argument:

> The neo-Russellian apparatus may be useful in dealing with the semantic properties of *utterances*, but it is seriously inadequate as far as psychology is concerned. (There may be something like direct reference in speech, but we cannot *think* of an object except under a 'mode of presentation'. We may perhaps *assert* singular propositions, but we cannot *believe* singular propositions: I cannot believe something *of* an object without believing it of that object *under a certain mode of presentation*.) The Fregean apparatus, by contrast, is both semantically and psychologically adequate. Fregean 'thoughts' – including the '*de re* thoughts' of the neo-Fregean – are semantic entities which obey cognitive constraints, while singular propositions are free from such constraints. Now the semantic properties of our utterances are derivative upon the semantic properties of the thoughts which these utterances express. This primacy of the psychological over the linguistic confers

a corresponding primacy to the Fregean framework over the Russellian framework – a primacy which manifests itself in the following disjunction: Either we must dispense with singular propositions and use the neo-Fregean notion of *de re* thought instead, or we must make singular propositions psychologically respectable by reducing them to *aspects* of Fregean thoughts (or to equivalence classes of Fregean thoughts).

This argument can be countered by appealing to the *first* type of connection I have mentioned between the linguistic study of direct reference and psychology, i.e. the fact that the meaning properties of utterances are ultimately to be analysed in psychological terms, along Gricean lines. Owing to these connections, we may grant the primacy of the psychological over the linguistic without accepting the primacy of Fregean thoughts over Russellian singular propositions. Let us assume that the singular proposition of the Russellian is a legitimate and useful notion from a semantic/pragmatic point of view. *Qua* semantic property, the singular proposition expressed by an utterance will have to be reducible to some aspect of a complex Gricean intention, *and this will be sufficient to make it psychologically respectable*; it will not be necessary to reduce the singular proposition expressed by an utterance **u** to an aspect of a Fregean thought also expressed by **u**. This does not mean that I want to use the neo-Russellian notion of singular proposition *instead of* the neo-Fregean notion of *de re* thought. I will argue in chapter 3 that we need both the *de re* thoughts of the neo-Fregean *and* the singular propositions of the neo-Russellian, in a complete (and ultimately psychological) account which deals not only with the thoughts which our utterances express but also with the meaning properties of our utterances themselves.

## Notes

1   That contrast is supposed to hold even though descriptions can be *used* in a referential manner (chapter 15). The sort of referentiality which allegedly distinguishes proper names and indexicals from definite descriptions is a property of expression *types*, not to be confused with a similar property which *uses* of expressions may have. The former property I call 'type-referentiality', the latter 'token-referentiality'. On the sort of view which I want to defend and elaborate, proper names and indexicals are type-referential, in contrast to definite descriptions, which can only be token-referential. Be that as it may, the same sort of contrast that can be found between names and descriptions at the level of types

can be found at the token level between referential and attributive uses of definite descriptions. It is this general contrast which the theoretical framework to be laid down in this chapter is meant to capture.

2 See e.g. Brody, 1977, p. 69, and Devitt, 1981, p. 213 ('the distinction between rigid and non-rigid designators simply *labels* the differing roles of names and descriptions in modal contexts'). See also Cresswell 1985, p. 154.

3 I say: 'in some *other* possible world', because I am assuming that utterances like "It might have been the case that P" are counterfactual and entail that it is not the case that P. This assumption is, of course, controversial (at least under a certain interpretation), but it is not at issue here, and my argument does not rest upon it.

4 This may seem reminiscent of Lewis's Indexical Theory of Actuality and therefore not very Kripkean. But in fact the claim I am making amounts to nothing more than what Peter van Inwagen, in his paper on the Indexical Theory of Actuality, calls the 'Weak Theory', which he says is trivially true (Inwagen, 1980, pp. 410–412). On the other hand, I think one cannot reject the claim according to which even wide scope descriptions are non-rigid without accepting the thesis that a world is a circumstance of utterance, and therefore without accepting something like Lewis's Counterpart Theory (see Inwagen, 1980, pp. 416–417). I cannot elaborate this point here.

5 Stephen Schiffer (1977, p. 31) makes a similar point. He introduces an operator '\*' that transforms a definite description into one that has maximal scope in every sentence in which it occurs, and notes that the proposition expressed by 'It might have been the case that the\* President of the US in 1976 was a lapsed Quaker' is true in a possible world if and only if *whoever in that world is President of the US in 1976* is such that he or she might have been a lapsed Quaker.

6 Belief contexts constitute an obvious objection to criteria such as (R) or (RR) below. On belief contexts and the problems they raise for the theory of direct reference, see chapters 17–20.

7 The distinction between the sorts – or the two sources – of rigidity can be found in various places in the literature, the *locus classicus* being Kaplan's famous monograph on Demonstratives (Kaplan, 1989a); the terminology '*de facto* vs *de jure*' is Kripke's: see Kripke, 1980, p. 21 n.

8 Supposing proper names have no meaning, contrary to indexicals. This issue will be discussed in chapter 8.

9 This requirement will be discussed in chapter 2, 2.5.

10 See 2.1 for an elaboration of this distinction.

11 See Lockwood, 1975, p. 485. A similar view was put forward in Recanati, 1981a, pp. 627–628.

12 Note that the second clause entails the first one (because of the factivity of 'know'). The definition could thus be reformulated with only the second clause.

13 The definition, of course, must also be modified so as to take indexicality into account. (TR) below, contrary to (R) and (RR), works for indexical as well as for non-indexical expressions. As for referentiality for a use of a term ('token-referentiality'), it will be discussed in chapter 15.

14 'Satisfaction' is used here in the Searlean, not the Tarskian sense: truth and obedience are two particular types of 'satisfaction', and truth-conditions and obedience-conditions are varieties of 'satisfaction conditions'. 'Satisfied' will be used in that sense whenever it is an *utterance* or *speech act* that is said to be 'satisfied'. (Note that in the formula below, 'There is an object x such that the utterance is satisfied iff x satisfies G( )', 'satisfy' is used in two different ways.)

15 When a non-referential expression (e.g. a definite description) is used referentially, the context, not the sentence, indicates that the (intended) satisfaction-condition of the utterance is singular. This is what I call 'token-referentiality'.

16 As Dan Sperber has repeatedly pointed out to me, it might be argued that, in the first case, the fact that the relevant object is a table is part of the truth-conditions of the utterance, and not merely a contextual clue helping the hearer to grasp the truth-condition. (By contrast, the fact that the relevant person is the addressee is no part of the truth-conditions of "You are G".) This may be due to the fact that 'table' is a sortal concept necessary for the individuation of the object. See below, note 19.

17 As I said earlier (note 8), the question arises whether all referential terms have an associated mode of presentation, or whether some of them, namely proper names, don't. In chapters 8–9, I will defend the view that proper, names, like ordinary indexicals, have an associated mode of presentation, by virtue of which a sentence G(NN), where "NN" is a proper name, indicates that:

> There is an object x, *called* "NN", such that the utterance is true iff x satisfies G( ).

This theory of the meaning of proper names has been attacked by Saul Kripke, whose arguments I don't find convincing; more on this in chapter 9.

Notice that the notion of 'mode of presentation' that is used here is linguistic and not psychological. The linguistic meaning of a referential term conveys a certain mode of presentation of the reference, but this mode of presentation is not necessarily identical with the mode of presentation of the object referred to in the *thought* expressed by the utterance. (By 'thought', I do not mean the 'proposition' expressed – soon to be defined – but the object of the so-called 'propositional attitudes'. In any theory of Direct Reference, the proposition expressed must be carefully distinguished from the object of the attitudes – here called the thought. See 2.4.) There are, for example, two modes of presentation associated with the pronoun 'I': from a linguistic point of view, the reference is presented as 'the speaker' (or something like that), but the concept that is relevant to the thought being expressed is the concept of 'self' (or something like that). The distinction between the two sorts of mode of presentation will be discussed at great length in chapter 4.

18   See chapter 2, 2.1. In this way, we can distinguish between the propositions expressed by "The cube root of 27 is F" and by "3 is F": both sentences have the same truth-condition – both are true iff 3 is F – but only the second presents itself as true iff 3 is F. Only the second sentence conveys the indication that there is an x such that the sentence is true iff x is F. This is the basis for the distinction between 'the cube root of 27', which is rigid, and '3', which is referential.

19   This should be qualified. A singular proposition is commonly said to include 'the object itself' rather than an individual concept under which the reference falls: but there is nothing like a 'bare' object independent of any mode of identification. As Geach pointed out, identity is *sortal-dependent*. An object can only be individuated according a certain criterion of identity – a criterion telling us what must be the case for something to be *the same thing* as that object. Now there are various criteria of identity depending on the *sort* of object we are talking about. The criterion for individuating water is not the same as that for individuating rivers; the criterion for individuating persons is not the same as the criterion for individuating material objects in general; the criterion for individuating pieces of clay is not the same as that for individuating statues, and so forth. As Geach says, 'the identity of a thing always consists in its being the same X, e.g. the same *man*' (Geach, 1957, p. 69). Identity entails sameness, and sameness 'has no significance unless we say or mean "the same X", where "X" represents a general term ... There is no such thing as being just "the same"' (Geach, 1957, p. 69). Hence, it makes no sense to speak of the object itself if one does not specify what *sort* of object one is talking about. It follows that singular propositions are not 'singular' in the *strong* sense of including 'objects' independent of their classification as tables, statues, persons, material objects, or whatever. They are singular only in the weaker sense that they include *sorted objects* (e.g. tables or persons) independent of the further contingent properties which these objects may possess and which may be used to identify them. (The expression 'sortal-dependency' was coined by David Wiggins in order to distinguish this property of identity from a stronger property, namely the *relativity* of identity. Contrary to Geach, who argues that identity is relative, Wiggins accepts only the weaker claim that it is sortal-dependent. See Geach (1957) and (1962), and Wiggins (1980).)

# Chapter 2

# Singular propositions and thoughts

## 2.1 Truth-conditions, meaning, and propositional content

In this section, I want to clarify a distinction I made in chapter 1 between the linguistic meaning of an utterance, its (possible world) truth-condition, and the proposition it expresses. Let us start with the distinction between the proposition expressed and the truth-condition of the utterance. As is well-known, understanding an utterance involves identifying its truth-condition. However, the truth-condition of an utterance need not be identified in an 'absolute' sense for the utterance to be understood: it may well be the case that (i) the utterance is true iff certain conditions P obtain, (ii) the hearer understands the utterance, yet (iii) the hearer does not realize that the utterance is true if and only if P. For example, 'The cube root of 27 is odd' is true iff 3 is odd, yet the hearer who understands the utterance may not know that this is the case. The hearer who understands the utterance must know its truth-condition *under a certain mode of presentation*, but he may not, and need not, be able to recognize it under another mode of presentation.

The mode of presentation under which the truth-condition has to be identified for the utterance to be understood depends on the meaning of the utterance. The utterance, by virtue of its linguistic meaning, gives indications concerning its truth-condition; it presents its truth-condition in a certain way. For example, directly referential terms convey a semantic feature, REF, by virtue of which they indicate that the truth-condition of the utterance in which they occur is singular; they indicate that there is an object (the reference of the singular term) such that the utterance is true iff that object satisfies the predicate. The meaning of the utterance provides a 'route' to the truth-condition. In order to understand the utterance, what the hearer must grasp is not its truth-condition *simpliciter*, but its truth-condition *as it is presented by the utterance itself*. This – the truth-condition as it is presented by the utterance itself – is what I call the proposition expressed. Thus, the utterance 'The cube root of 27 is odd' presents itself as true iff there is a number x such that $x^3 = 27$ and x is odd; the proposition expressed, therefore, is the (general) proposition that there is a number x such that $x^3 = 27$ and x is odd. The utterance expresses this proposition, rather than the (singular) proposition that 3 is odd, because it does not present itself as true iff 3 is odd – even though it *is* true iff 3 is odd. It does not present its truth-condition as singular, as involving a particular object (in that case, a particular number), but rather as general, as involving a certain concept (the concept of cube root of 27).[1]

The distinction between the proposition expressed and the truth-condition provides the basis for the distinction between rigidity and direct referentiality (or rigidity *de jure*). When the subject-term "α" in a sentence "α is G" is rigid, the truth-condition of the utterance is singular – it includes the reference of "α" as a constituent: there is an object x such that the utterance is true iff x is G. When "α" is a directly referential term, the utterance *presents* its truth-condition as singular: an utterance "α is G" in which "α" is a directly referential term means that there is an object x, possessing a certain property F (= mode of presentation), such that the utterance is true iff x is G. If such an object is actually identifiable in context, the utterance expresses the proposition that it is G. This is a 'singular' proposition, consisting of the reference of "α" and the property expressed by the predicate "G". The proposition expressed by an utterance in which a directly referential term occurs includes the reference of that term as a constituent, in the same way as the truth-condition of an utterance in which a rigid designator occurs includes the reference of that designator as a constituent.

The distinction between the linguistic meaning of the utterance and the proposition expressed is no less important than that between the proposition expressed and the truth-condition. The meaning of the utterance is or includes a set of indications bearing on its truth-condition. These indications provide a route to the truth-condition.

In order to grasp the proposition expressed, it is both necessary and sufficient to identify the truth-condition of the utterance on the basis of the indications conveyed by the sentence, since the proposition expressed *is* the truth-condition of the utterance under the mode of presentation imposed by the meaning of the sentence. But it is possible to understand these indications without actually grasping the truth-condition. Grasping the truth-condition on the basis of the indications provided by the sentence is a contextual matter – it involves more than merely understanding the meaning of the sentence. Consider, again, an utterance of "α is G", where "α" is a directly referential term. One 'understands' the utterance in weak sense when one understands what this utterance *linguistically means*, namely, that there is an object x (possessing a certain property F) such that the utterance is true iff x is G; but to understand the utterance in a stronger sense, that is, to understand the proposition expressed, one must contextually identify the object x such that the utterance is true iff it is G. The first grade of understanding corresponds to an understanding of the sentence type, a token of which is being uttered; the second grade corresponds to an understanding of what is said by uttering this token.

The distinction between the truth-condition of the utterance and the proposition it expresses enables us to define direct referentiality as opposed to mere rigidity. The second distinction, between the meaning of the sentence and the proposition expressed, enables us to recognize as directly referential some terms which, far from being devoid of meaning, clearly convey a certain mode of presentation of their reference. Terms like 'I' or 'this table' are directly referential in my framework, yet they present their reference as possessing a certain attribute (the property F alluded to above). This is possible because the mode of presentation of the reference belongs to the meaning of the sentence, but not to the proposition expressed, which includes only the reference. To define direct referentiality in terms of the proposition expressed, and to distinguish the latter from the meaning of the utterance, therefore makes it possible to bypass Mill's overly strong definition of direct referentiality as straightforward lack of meaning or 'connotation'. To this important issue I now turn.

## 2.2 Content and character: the neo-Russellian theory

It is customary to claim that those terms that are directly referential and whose only function is 'to enable individuals to be made the subject of discourse' (as Mill says) are of necessity meaningless marks, since to endow them with a meaning distinct from their reference would be to ascribe them a descriptive or attributive function over and above their referring function. But this is confusing. A distinction must be made between (i) directly referential terms (or, more simply, referential terms), which contribute to the proposition expressed – to what is said – merely by picking out a certain object, and (ii) non-connotative terms, which have no meaning besides their reference and do not imply any attribute as belonging to the latter. (i) and (ii) would come to the same thing if there were no difference between the linguistic meaning of an utterance and its propositional content. But such a difference exists: there is a difference, for example, between the meaning of the sentence 'I am French' and what is said by an utterance of this sentence (the proposition expressed). Owing to this difference, one may grant that the singular term 'I' has a meaning and 'implies' a certain attribute as belonging to its reference, while insisting that this term is directly referential and contributes to the proposition expressed merely by specifying a certain individual.

By virtue of its linguistic meaning, the pronoun 'I' presents its reference as having the property of being the speaker; yet this mode of presentation is no part of the proposition expressed, no part of the truth-condition the utterance presents itself as having. When Paul says 'I am French', what he says is true (and is presented as being true) if and only if Paul is French. The property of being the speaker is not a constituent of the proposition expressed: it is used only to help the hearer identify the reference, which *is* a constituent of the proposition expressed. As Kaplan says, the mode of presentation of the reference, in such a case, 'should not be considered part of the content of what is said but should rather be thought of as [a] contextual factor ... which help[s] us interpret the ... utterance as having a certain content' (Kaplan, 1978, p. 228). On this view, which I shall henceforth refer to as the 'neo-Russellian theory', the descriptive meaning of a referential term is not reflected in the proposition expressed by the utterance in which it occurs; it remains external to that proposition, which is 'singular' and involves only a particular object. The pronoun 'I', therefore, is both referential and connotative, contrary to Mill's equation of referentiality with non-connotativeness.[2]

Even if one rejects Mill's equation, one must recognize that a non-connotative term – assuming for the moment that there are such terms – can only be referential. If a term refers to an object without implying any attribute of this object, what it contributes to the proposition expressed can be nothing other than its reference. However, in the case of a connotative term, what is contributed to the proposition expressed may be either the reference or the connoted attribute. Kaplan expresses this idea by means of his famous distinction between 'content' and 'character', a distinction which is reminiscent of that made by Austin and Strawson between the linguistic meaning of a sentence and the statement the sentence is used to make. 'Content' is Kaplan's word for a term's contribution to the proposition expressed – the proposition itself being the 'content' of the utterance as a whole; the 'character' of an expression is its linguistic meaning.³ According to Kaplan, the content of a (connotative) term may be either its reference or the mode of presentation of the reference. If the content is constituted by the reference, that is, if the term is referential, the mode of presentation of the reference is external to the proposition expressed and constitutes only the character of the term. If the mode of presentation does not only belong to the character of the expression but also constitutes its content, as happens when the term at issue is not referential, then it is the reference that is external, in the sense that it is only part of the 'world': in this case, it is possible for the utterance to make sense, and to be understood, even if the reference does not exist or cannot be identified. (By contrast, when a term *is* referential, its reference is part of the proposition expressed by the utterance and must be identified for the latter to be understood. More on this in 2.5.) These two possibilities are displayed in table 1.

Table 1

|  |  | *Referential terms* | *Non-referential terms* |
|---|---|---|---|
| (utterance) | Character | Mode of presentation | Mode of presentation |
|  | Content | Reference | Mode of presentation |
| (world) |  | Reference | Reference |

Kaplan has devised an operator, DTHAT, which prevents the mode of presentation of the reference from going into the content, in such a way that the content of an expression within the scope of DTHAT can only be its reference. REF does exactly the same job as DTHAT; the difference between them is simply that I take REF to be a semantic feature of natural language while DTHAT is an operator in an artificial language. *Qua* semantic feature, REF is part of the meaning of some expression types, namely referential expressions (proper names, demonstratives, and the like). Since definite descriptions, as expression types, are not referential, REF is not part of their meaning. However, following Donnellan, I shall argue in chapter 15 that a description can be *used* referentially, so as to express a singular proposition, with the reference of the description as a constituent; the individual concept expressed by the description, in such a case, is external to the proposition expressed. This, I will try to show, is entirely a matter of context, of utterance meaning as opposed to sentence meaning: no feature REF is involved at the level of sentence meaning to impose the referential reading of the description. In other words, descriptions can only be 'token-referential', whereas proper names and demonstrative expressions are 'type-referential'. This is where the difference between REF and DTHAT comes out: for there is nothing to prevent a referential token of a description "the F" from being represented as "DTHAT (the F)" in Kaplanese. (*Any* description can be prefixed with DTHAT in Kaplanese, even if, like 'the first baby to be born in the 21st century' (Kaplan, 1978, p. 241), it could hardly be used referentially.[4]) The presence of DTHAT simply means that a singular proposition is expressed, with the reference, but not the mode of presentation of the reference, as a constituent. The presence of REF means something more: that the 'singular' reading is imposed at the level of sentence meaning, that is, at the level of the expression type.

I shall come back to the difference between type-referentiality and token-referentiality in chapter 15, when discussing the referential use of definite descriptions. As for now, I want to consider an alleged alternative to the neo-Russellian theory, and some of the reasons one might have to prefer it to the neo-Russellian theory.

## 2.3 Quasi-singular propositions: the neo-Fregean theory

It may be argued that the neo-Russellian theory rests on an undefended assumption: that the content of a connotative term must be *either* its reference *or* the mode of presentation of the reference.[5] But why not both? After all, to capture the intuitive distinction between referential and non-referential terms, it may be thought sufficient to say that the proposition expressed by an utterance in which a referential term occurs includes the reference of the term. This does not entail that the mode of presentation itself is external to that proposition, unless one takes for granted the assumption I have just mentioned. If we do not make this assumption, nothing prevents us from saying that the proposition expressed includes not only the reference but *also* the mode of presentation of the reference. This I shall call the 'neo-Fregean theory'. The reference and the mode of presentation jointly constitute the content of the term, on the neo-Fregean theory.[6] One way of expressing this view consists of equating the proposition expressed with an ordered pair, as in the neo-Russellian theory, but an ordered pair whose first member is itself an ordered pair, consisting of the reference *and* its mode of presentation. Schiffer, in 'The Basis of Reference', called this a 'quasi-singular' proposition (Schiffer, 1987, p. 182). I shall retain this name.

Both the neo-Russellian theory and the neo-Fregean theory capture the difference between referential and non-referential terms by introducing the reference into the proposition when a term is referential; and they both take for granted that a referential term may have a meaning and present its reference in a certain way. The difference between the neo-Russellian theory and the neo-Fregean theory is simply the fact that the former takes the content of a referential term to be nothing other than its reference while the latter takes it to be constituted by the reference *under a certain mode of presentation.*[7] On the neo-Fregean theory, there is no inconsistency between the Fregean claim that the proposition expressed (the content of the utterance) must include a mode of presentation of the reference, and the view that the proposition expressed irreducibly involves the reference, whose existence it therefore presupposes.[8]

There are two *prima facie* arguments in favour of the neo-Fregean theory as against the neo-Russellian theory. I will show that neither is compelling. The first argument will be discussed in this section, the second one in 2.4.

The first argument is related to the distinction I made in the first section of this chapter between the proposition expressed and the truth-condition of the utterance. It runs as follows:

# Singular propositions and thoughts

1 I have defined the proposition expressed as the truth-condition of the utterance *under the mode of presentation imposed by the linguistic meaning (the 'character') of the sentence.*
2 The mode of presentation of the reference, which constitutes the character of the subject-term, is a constituent of the global mode of presentation of the truth-condition, which constitutes the character of the whole sentence.
3 Therefore, the mode of presentation of the reference must belong to the proposition expressed, as in the neo-Fregean theory.

This argument cannot be accepted. It is true that the mode of presentation of the reference is (part of) the meaning of the subject-term, which meaning is a constituent of the meaning of the whole sentence; it is also true that the meaning of the sentence consists, at least in part, in a certain mode of presentation of the truth-condition of the utterance, that is, in a set of indications concerning the truth-condition. It follows that the mode of presentation of the reference is a constituent of the mode of presentation of the truth-condition, in the following sense: the sentence indicates, among other things, that the truth-condition of an utterance of this sentence involves a certain object, possessing a certain property – for example, the property of being the person making this utterance. (This property is the mode of presentation of the reference, in the case of the pronoun 'I'.) But it does not follow that the mode of presentation of the reference must be part of the *proposition expressed*, that is, part of *the truth-condition of the utterance as it is presented by the utterance itself.* The meaning of the sentence includes not only the mode of presentation of the reference but also the feature REF, the effect of which is to present the truth-condition of the utterance as *excluding* the mode of presentation of the reference. The sentence indicates both that the truth-condition of an utterance of this sentence involves a certain person, who possesses the property of being the speaker, *and* that this person's having this property is no part of the truth-condition of the utterance. Now, from the fact that the truth-condition is presented as excluding the mode of presentation of the reference, it follows that the mode of presentation of the reference does not belong to the proposition, i.e. to the truth-condition as it is presented by the utterance. So we may grant both premises in the argument, and still reject the conclusion. The mode of presentation of the reference (along with the feature REF) belongs to the meaning of the sentence, the meaning of the sentence presents the truth-condition of the utterance in a certain way, and the proposition expressed is the truth-condition of the utterance under that mode of presentation; all this is consistent with the neo-Russellian theory, which claims that the mode of presentation of the reference does not belong to the proposition expressed.

## 2.4 Propositional content and thought

The second argument against the neo-Russellian theory deserves serious consideration. It is very simple, and very powerful. We may call it the Fregean argument, or the cognitive significance objection:

> The proposition expressed by an utterance is its cognitive significance, that is, the proper object, or content, of our cognitive attitudes towards the utterance. It is what we understand, what we grasp; it is what we believe or disbelieve when we sincerely assent to or dissent from the utterance. Now, our cognitive attitudes are clearly sensitive to the mode of presentation of the reference. I may assent to 'Cicero is bald' and dissent from 'Tully is bald', even though Cicero is Tully; this is because the reference, although identical in the two cases, is presented in two different ways. Likewise, I may believe 'this man is a spy' and 'that man is not a spy' of the same man, if I do not know that the same man is being demonstrated twice. This shows that the proposition expressed, *qua* object of the attitudes, involves a mode of presentation of the reference and not just the reference itself. It follows that the neo-Russellian theory must be rejected, and the neo-Fregean theory adopted in its stead. The neo-Russellian theory holds that the mode of presentation of the reference, which constitutes the character of referential terms, does not belong to their content, which is constituted by their reference alone; the proposition expressed, according to that view, is a singular proposition. But, if really the proposition expressed by sentences in which a referential term occurs was a singular proposition in Kaplan's sense, then in cases such as those I have just mentioned one and the same singular proposition would be assented to and dissented from at the same time: someone who believes 'Cicero is bald' while disbelieving 'Tully is bald' would be entertaining contradictory beliefs. Now, there is a sense in which I am *not* entertaining contradictory beliefs in such a situation, provided I do not know that Cicero is Tully. This sense cannot be accounted for in the framework provided by the neo-Russellian theory. On the neo-Fregean theory, however, this type of example raises no problem. I believe of a certain person under a certain mode of presentation that

he is bald, and I do not believe that of the same person under another mode of presentation. In this case, what I assent to is a quasi-singular proposition, and what I dissent from is *another* quasi-singular proposition.

There is much that is true in this argument, but the truths it contains seem to me perfectly consistent with the neo-Russellian theory. The Fregean argument constitutes a decisive objection to the neo-Russellian theory only if one makes certain assumptions which, precisely for that reason, a defender of the neo-Russellian theory would be foolish to make. The version of the neo-Russellian theory I am defending is pure of these assumptions, and therefore immune to Fregean criticism.

The neo-Russellian theory holds that the mode of presentation of the reference that constitutes the meaning of a referential term is not reflected in the propositional content of the utterance in which that term occurs: the proposition expressed, according to the neo-Russellian theory, is singular and involves only the reference. There are two different claims here:

> (1) the claim that the proposition expressed by a sentence in which a referential term occurs is a singular proposition, i.e. an ordered pair consisting of the reference of the subject-term and the property expressed by the predicate expression; and
> (2) the claim that the proposition expressed does not include what I shall henceforth refer to as the *linguistic* mode of presentation of the reference, i.e. the mode of presentation that constitutes (part of) the linguistic meaning of the referential term.

(1) entails (2), since a singular proposition includes *no* mode of presentation of the reference but only the reference itself. However, (2) may be accepted even though (1) is denied. It is possible to hold that the proposition expressed is a quasi-singular, rather than a singular, proposition, while maintaining that the linguistic mode of presentation constitutes no part of this quasi-singular proposition. Indeed, as I shall argue in chapter 4, the complete content of the attitudes involves a mode of presentation of the reference, as the Fregean rightly emphasizes, but this mode of presentation is different from the *linguistic* mode of presentation, i.e. from the mode of presentation that constitutes the linguistic meaning of the expression. There are two sorts of mode of presentation to be distinguished, and once this distinction is made, the Fregean argument no longer

constitutes an objection to the second claim made by the neo-Russellian. Thus, even if it was conceded to the Fregean that the proposition expressed cannot be a singular proposition, but must include a mode of presentation of the reference, still it could be maintained that the mode of presentation of the reference which constitutes the linguistic meaning of a referential term 'should not be considered part of the content of what is said but should rather be thought of as [a] contextual factor ... which help[s] us interpret the ... utterance as having a certain content' (Kaplan, 1978, p. 228).

This, it may be argued, is not really a defence of the neo-Russellian theory. Even if the neo-Russellian is right to hold (2), the basic difference between the neo-Russellian theory and the neo-Fregean theory is constituted by claim (1), which is the heart of the neo-Russellian theory. Now, it may be argued, the Fregean argument constitutes a straightforward refutation of claim (1). The proposition expressed cannot be a singular proposition, since (i) the proposition expressed is the content of the attitudes, and (ii) the attitudes are sensitive not just to what is being referred to but also to the way the reference is presented. Therefore the neo-Russellian theory must be dropped in favour of the neo-Fregean theory. So the Fregean argument goes.

Certainly, the Fregean argument shows that the *complete* content of the attitudes must include a mode of presentation of the reference. It follows that the complete content of the attitudes cannot be a singular proposition. But who has ever denied that? It would be folly to do so. The only rational position, for someone who holds that the proposition expressed by an utterance in which a referential term occurs in a singular proposition, is to reject (i), the equation of the proposition expressed with the complete content of the attitudes. On this view, the proposition expressed (Kaplan's 'content') is not the complete content of our attitudes: the proposition expressed, which is singular, is apprehended *under a mode of presentation*, and it is this – the proposition under a certain mode of presentation – which constitutes the proper object of the attitudes.[9] Thus, the same (singular) proposition is expressed by 'Cicero is bald' and 'Tully is bald', but this proposition may be apprehended under different modes of presentation. This explains why one may both assent to and dissent from this proposition without irrationality: it is assented to under one mode of presentation and dissented from under another mode of presentation. The complete content of one utterance is distinct from that of the other even though they express the same proposition and have the same 'content' in the Kaplanian sense. The Fregean argument, therefore, does not refute the neo-Russellian theory; it only shows that the neo-Russellian theory implies a distinction between the proposition expressed and the (complete) object of the attitudes.

The distinction between the proposition expressed and the object/content of the attitudes is made by all defenders of the neo-Russellian theory. Even those who, like Nathan Salmon, claim that 'singular propositions are the contents of thoughts and beliefs' (Salmon, 1986a, p. 6), concede that singular propositions are assented to or dissented from only under a mode of presentation (Salmon, 1986a, p. 111).[10] In any event, Kaplan and Perry insist that a singular proposition cannot be the complete content of the attitudes. As Kaplan emphasizes, to believe that my pants are on fire is not the same thing as to believe that this person's pants are on fire, even if this person, whose image I see reflected in the window, turns out to be myself (Kaplan, 1989a, p. 533). Now, for Kaplan, 'My pants are on fire' expresses the same singular proposition as 'His pants are on fire', provided the same person (myself) is being referred to. Kaplan's solution, following Perry, is to say that this proposition may be apprehended under different modes of presentation, different characters:

> A given content may be presented under various characters and ... consequently we may hold a propositional attitude toward a given content under one character but not under another. (For example, on March 27 of this year, having lost track of the date, I may continue to hope to be finished by March 26, without hoping to be finished by yesterday.) (Kaplan, 1989a, p. 532)

Clearly, this amounts to conceding that the complete content of our attitudes involves a mode of presentation and not just a singular proposition. There is no disagreement between the Fregean (or the neo-Fregean) and the neo-Russellian on this score. The difference between them lies elsewhere: contrary to the Fregean, the neo-Russellian draws a distinction between the proposition expressed and the complete content of the attitudes, which from now on I shall call the 'thought'. It is the thought associated with an utterance, not the proposition it expresses, which constitutes its cognitive significance according to the neo-Russellian theory. Owing to that distinction, the neo-Russellian theory is not threatened by the Fregean argument.

## 2.5 Two basic intuitions

I have shown that neither of the two objections to the neo-Russellian theory is compelling. The first one is a non-sequitur, and the second one is based on a premiss which the neo-Russellian rejects. It does not follow that the neo-Russellian theory is right, however. So far, I have put forward no positive argument in favour of the neo-Russellian theory as against the neo-Fregean theory. (Nor have I provided independent justification for the crucial distinction between proposition and thought.) Let us consider whether such an argument can be provided.

I said earlier that both the neo-Russellian theory and the neo-Fregean theory capture the intuitive distinction between referential and non-referential terms. That is not wholly true, though. The neo-Fregean theory as it stands captures only one of the two intuitions on which the distinction between referential and non-referential terms is based.

The first intuition underlying the referential/non-referential distinction concerns what counts as understanding an utterance in which a referring expression occurs. If $t$ is a referential term, a hearer does not understand what is said by an utterance $G(t)$ if she cannot *identify* the reference of $t$. To identify the reference, in the relevant sense, one must go beyond the descriptive content of the referring expression and equate the reference with a certain object about which one has independent information. (This process is what Evans calls '*re*-identification'.)[11] Thus you do not understand what is said by my uttering 'He is a spy' if you do not go beyond the (meagre) indication provided by the word 'he' and identify a certain person, e.g. someone you are currently perceiving, as the person to whom I am referring; likewise, you do not understand what is said by an utterance of 'I am French' if you know only that 'I' refers to the speaker, without knowing *who* the speaker is. Directly referential terms such as 'he' or 'I' prompt the hearer to go beyond the meaning of the sentence and find an object in the world matching the descriptive content of the referring expression What is said cannot be grasped unless that object is identified. By contrast, the reference of an attributively used definite description need not be identified for the utterance to be understood. Even if I have no idea who the Mayor of Paris is, I understand what is said by 'The Mayor of Paris must be a busy man'. The proposition expressed is general and does not involve the reference, but only a certain concept or mode of presentation.

Both the neo-Russellian theory and the neo-Fregean theory capture this fundamental intuition by introducing the reference into the proposition when the term at issue is referential.[12] The neo-Russellian theory and the neo-Fregean theory differ in that the latter maintains the mode of presentation of the reference (along with the reference itself) as a constituent of the proposition expressed, while the former excludes the mode of presentation from the proposition. Now this exclusion, which is an essential feature of the neo-Russellian theory, is meant to capture a second, no less important intuition.

The second intuition concerns the *truth-conditions* of an utterance $G(t)$ containing a referential term $t$. The neo-Russellian theory takes the mode of presentation of the reference of $t$ not to be part of the proposition expressed because the reference's satisfying the mode of presentation is no part of the truth-conditions of what is said. Thus, by virtue of its linguistic meaning, the pronoun 'you' presents its reference as having the property of being the addressee; yet the reference's having this property is no part of the truth-conditions of an utterance in which 'you' occurs. When John says 'You are French' to Paul, what he says is true (and is presented as true) *if and only if Paul is French*. The property of being the addressee is not a constituent of the proposition expressed: it is used only to help the hearer identify the reference, which *is* a constituent of the proposition expressed.

Because it insists on maintaining the mode of presentation of the reference as a constituent of the proposition expressed, it seems that the neo-Fregean theory deprives itself of the means of capturing the second intuition. Hence, it seems that we have an argument in favour of the neo-Russellian theory. This is not really so, however. The argument I have just mentioned no more disposes of the neo-Fregean theory than the Fregean argument disposes of the neo-Russellian theory.

Appearances notwithstanding, it *is* possible to capture the second intuition in the framework of the neo-Fregean theory. One merely has to ascribe a special property to the mode of presentation that is said to figure in the quasi-singular proposition expressed, namely the property of *truth-conditional irrelevance*.[13] A mode of presentation is truth-conditionally irrelevant if it does not affect the truth-conditions of the quasi-singular proposition in which it occurs, that is, if the truth-conditions of the quasi-singular proposition depend only on the reference with which the mode of presentation is associated. Thus, suppose a quasi-singular proposition P with a mode of presentation *m* as a sub-constituent (for example the proposition <<*a,m*>, Φ>, where *a* is the reference and Φ the property predicated of it). If *m* is truth-conditionally irrelevant, you may replace it by another mode of presentation *m'* without affecting the truth-conditions of P, so long as *m'* itself is truth-conditionally irrelevant. To say that the mode of presentation of the reference is truth-conditionally irrelevant provides an easy way of reconciling the neo-Fregean theory (which says that the proposition expressed is quasi-singular and involves a mode of presentation of the reference) with the second intuition (according to which the reference's satisfying the mode of presentation is no part of the truth-condition the utterance presents itself as having).

Consider Kaplan's example ('My pants are on fire'/'His pants are on fire'). A neo-Fregean would say that two different quasi-singular propositions are expressed. The difference between the two quasi-singular propositions consists in their involving two different modes of presentation of the same person. (This difference is what makes it possible to believe one proposition while disbelieving the other.) Still, the neo-Fregean may grant the obvious intuition that the two utterances, as well as the thoughts expressed by them, are true if and only if that person's pants are on fire.[14] The only thing the neo-Fregean has to do to avoid inconsistency is to claim that the modes of presentation involved in Kaplan's example are truth-conditionally irrelevant.

As we have seen, by insisting on the 'non-descriptive' or '*de re*' character of the modes of presentation associated with referential expressions, the so-called neo-Fregeans are able to capture the first of the two basic intuitions I have mentioned. Since *de re* senses are existence-dependent or reference-involving, a thought including such a sense cannot be grasped unless the corresponding reference is identified. (A *de re* sense is a *way of identifying* a reference – this is why it does not exist if the reference does not exist.) But it may be that, when they talk of non-descriptive or *de re* senses, neo-Fregeans have in mind not only the property of existence-dependence but also that of truth-conditional irrelevance. If this is so, then they are able to capture the second intuition as well. In what follows I will apply the principle of charity and take the neo-Fregean view to incorporate the claim that *de re* modes of presentation are truth-conditionally irrelevant (even though the neo-Fregeans do not explicitly discuss this issue). And I will use 'quasi-singular proposition', in a technical sense, to mean a proposition which includes an object and a truth-conditionally irrelevant mode of presentation of the latter.[15]

In chapter 3 we shall see that there is a substantial difference between the neo-Russellian theory and the neo-Fregean theory, despite their overall similarity. That difference will be located in the theory of communication. Having thus distinguished the two views from one another, I will argue that both are justified to a certain extent. The position I will actually defend combines features of both views. In the theory to be put forward in this book, we find both singular propositions and *de re* thoughts which are quasi-singular and include truth-conditionally irrelevant constituents (*de re* concepts).

## Notes

1 I am considering only the so-called 'attributive' use of definite descriptions. 'Referential' uses will be discussed in chapter 15.
2 The neo-Russellian theory is expounded in David Kaplan's famous 1977 monograph, *Demonstratives*, which was published recently, together with Kaplan's 'afterthoughts', in Almog, Wettstein and Perry (eds), *Themes from Kaplan*, Oxford University Press 1989.
3 Kaplan also describes the character of an expression as a function from context to content (i.e. from context to reference, in the case of directly referential expressions). As we shall see (5.2), the linguistic meaning of an expression determines such a function only if the expression is what Kaplan calls a 'pure indexical'.
4 On this example, see 6.3.
5 Unless otherwise indicated, I use 'content' always in the kaplanian sense: the content of an utterance is the proposition expressed (what is said) by that utterance; the content of an expression is its contribution to the proposition expressed. As we shall see later (2.4), there is another, more comprehensive notion of content in the neo-Russellian framework: the 'complete content', which includes more than the proposition expressed. The expression 'complete content' is (I believe) due to Schiffer.
6 Some neo-Fregeans (Evans and McDowell), contrary to others (Peacocke, 1981, pp. 189–90 and 197), do not like this formulation of the neo-Fregean theory; they reject it as inconsistent with Frege's contention that the proposition (or, in Fregean terminology, the

'thought') expressed by an utterance, being the 'sense' of that utterance, must be composed by the 'senses' of its constituents and cannot, therefore, include the reference of a constituent. (See 11.1.) But the difference seems to me mainly terminological. Evans and McDowell hold that the thought expressed by an utterance in which a referential term occurs includes a '*de re* sense', a sense which depends for its existence on the existence of the reference. (A *de re* sense is a 'way of thinking of the reference', in Evans' terms, and as such it presupposes the reference.) McDowell himself seems to admit that such *de re* senses are formally equivalent to ordered pairs consisting of an ordinary mode of presentation and a reference; he says that the latter (the ordered pairs) would 'mimic' the former (the *de re* senses). (See McDowell, 1984, p. 104.) Nevertheless he insists that the resemblance is 'only superficial'. Evans's and McDowell's reasons for rejecting the ordered-pair view will be discussed (and criticized) in chapters 11–12. In the meantime I shall take the equivalence for granted.

7  The neo-Fregean includes modes of presentation into content because, for a neo-Fregean as opposed to a neo-Russellian, the individuation of contents must 'be answerable to facts of cognitive significance' (Peacocke, 1981, p. 197). However, this alleged difference between neo-Fregeans and neo-Russellians will be shown to be mainly terminological (2.4). The neo-Fregean notion of content (or 'thought') is more constrained than the neo-Russellian notion of content ('what is said'); it corresponds to the neo-Russellian notion of *complete* content (note 5) rather than to the neo-Russellian notion of content in the sense of 'what is said'. Since the neo-Russellians admit, indeed insist, that the *complete* content of an utterance includes modes of presentation, there is no conflict (except terminological) between the neo-Russellian theory and the neo-Fregean theory on this score. In chapter 3, however, we shall see that there *is* a genuine (though not a very big) difference between the two views, distinct from the terminological difference I have just mentioned.

8  See Evans, 1982, p. 62.

9  According to John Perry, who did much to elaborate the epistemic consequences of the neo-Russellian theory, there are two distinct relations into which so-called propositional attitudes must be broken (Perry, 1980a): one (e.g. 'belief', in Perry's sense) is a relation between subjects and propositions or states of affairs, while 'acceptance' is a relation between subjects and modes of presentation or 'sentences'. The former relation depends on the latter, on Perry's view: it is by virtue of accepting a certain mode of presentation (a certain 'sentence') that a subject may be said to 'believe' the proposition which this mode of presentation contextually determines or which the accepted sentence contextually expresses. Another way of making the same point consists

in keeping the attitudes unbroken while breaking their objects (their complete contents) into two components, in such a way that the attitudes are said to relate subjects to 'propositions-under-modes of presentation'. I opt for the latter formulation: in what follows, I will talk of attitudes as having 'thoughts' as objects, which thoughts will be analysed as involving states of affairs (or propositions) together with modes of presentation or 'narrow contents'. I believe that nothing hinges on the difference of formulation.

10  In general, the neo-Russellians who take singular propositions to be the contents of attitudes such as belief hold that the binary relation between a subject and a singular proposition which 'belief' consists in holds *by virtue of* another binary relation (Perry's 'acceptance') between the subject and a character or mode of presentation. In other words, the binary relation of 'belief' (with singular propositions as objects) is an *aspect* of a ternary relation between the subject, the proposition and a mode of presentation of the latter. See Salmon 1986a.

11  Evans, 1982, pp. 126–7. Note that this intuition (about what counts as understanding a use of a referential term) is much more congenial to Evans than to Kaplan.

12  Those neo-Fregeans who, like McDowell, do not like this formulation because of the Fregean principle mentioned in footnote 6 capture this intuition by positing '*de re* senses' – senses that are existence-dependent and presuppose the reference. (As I said in note 6, I consider the two formulations as equivalent.)

13  On truth-conditional irrelevance, see 6.3.

14  Kent Bach (1987, p. 18) takes the thought 'His pants are on fire' to be true if and only if *the man who causes the thinker's current visual experience* has his pants on fire. (Searle says similar things in Searle, 1983.) But it seems to me that the thought 'His pants are on fire' could be true even with respect to a world in which the thinker has no visual experience at all. The property of causing the current visual experience of the thinker plays a role in determining the truth-conditional content of the thought, but it is not a part of that content. Bach is well aware of this (see pp. 18–19, especially his note 12, where he criticizes Searle). The 'truth-conditions' he is talking about in this passage are the truth-conditions of (what he would call) the *thought type* 'His pants are on fire' rather than the truth-conditions of a particular token of that thought. This is unfortunate since (as Bach himself recognizes on p. 13) only particular *tokens* of a *de re* thought can be said to have truth-conditions in the ordinary sense. (What I have just called 'the truth-conditions of the thought type' correspond to Perry's 'non-incremental conditions of truth' (Perry, 1990b, 1992); a similar notion will be introduced in 15.5.)

15 Note that a proposition which includes an object and a truth-conditionally *relevant* mode of presentation is nothing other than a *singular* proposition including two properties instead of one (that corresponding to the mode of presentation and that corresponding to the predicate). Such a proposition is true iff the object satisfies both the mode of presentation and the predicate.

# Chapter 3

# The communication of *de re* thoughts

## 3.1 Introduction

Let us take stock. We have two basic intuitions concerning 'direct reference', and two views which capture those intuitions: the neo-Russellian theory and the neo-Fregean theory. On both theories, the first intuition – that about understanding and the necessary identification of the reference – is accounted for by making the reference part of the proposition expressed. The difference between the two views concerns the mode of presentation of the reference. The neo-Russellian theory says that the proposition expressed is singular and does not include the mode of presentation. Since the mode of presentation has obvious cognitive significance, the neo-Russellian theory suggests a distinction between the proposition expressed and the cognitive content of the utterance (the thought). The neo-Fregean does not make such a distinction between proposition and thought; he uses a single notion of 'proposition' or 'thought' corresponding to what the utterance expresses (its semantic content) and insists on maintaining the mode of presentation as a constituent of that proposition or thought. This is consistent with the second intuition – according to which the mode of presentation of the reference is not reflected in the truth-conditions of the utterance – provided the mode of presentation that occurs in the proposition/thought is said to be 'non-descriptive' in the sense of truth-conditionally irrelevant.

At this point we may naturally wonder whether the two theories are substantially different from one another. As we shall see, the neo-Russellian notion of a singular proposition can easily be accommodated within the neo-Fregean framework (3.2). But there remains a substantial difference between the two views. The neo-Fregean equates semantic content and thought; the semantic content of an utterance containing referential terms is taken to be a *de re* thought which the utterance expresses. The neo-Russellian rejects that equation on the grounds that *de re* thoughts are subjective, in contrast to semantic contents; accordingly, he takes the semantic content of an utterance containing a referential term to be a singular proposition rather than a complete thought. In this chapter I will suggest a compromise. I will endorse the neo-Russellian point about the subjectivity of *de re* thoughts and the necessity of distinguishing them from semantic contents (3.3); but, like the neo-Fregean, I will reject the neo-Russellian's alternative proposal, to the effect that the semantic content of an utterance containing a referential term is (nothing other than) a singular proposition (3.4).[1] On the view I will sketch, utterances containing referential terms do express singular propositions, but the semantic content of such an utterance includes more than merely a singular proposition.

## 3.2 Singular propositions in a neo-Fregean framework

The neo-Fregean (like all Fregeans) holds that an utterance $G(t)$ expresses a thought which involves a certain mode of presentation of the reference of $t$. The neo-Russellian accepts this characterization of the *thought* expressed by the utterance. He simply distinguishes the thought from the proposition expressed, which he takes to be singular (if $t$ is a referential expression, e.g. a proper name or a demonstrative). Now this distinction may be interpreted in a way that makes it quite acceptable to a neo-Fregean. Nothing prevents the neo-Fregean from considering that the 'proposition' which the neo-Russellian distinguishes from the thought is merely an aspect of the thought. The neo-Fregean may provide the following, deflationary interpretation of the distinction between proposition and thought:

> Different thoughts may well have the same truth-conditions; in other words, truth-conditions determine *equivalence classes of thoughts*. Those equivalence classes of thoughts are what the neo-Russellian calls 'propositions'. To say that an utterance **u** expresses the singular proposition $P$ is to say that **u** expresses a thought that belongs to a

certain class, namely the class of thoughts that are true if and only if P. On this account, the propositional content of the utterance is nothing other than the truth-conditional content of the thought expressed by that utterance.

In that way, the distinction between propositional content and thought is trivialized and made acceptable to the Fregean. Singular propositions are nothing other than partial aspects of Fregean thoughts.

As we have seen, the neo-Russellian concedes that the thought involves a mode of presentation of the reference, but insists that this mode of presentation is no part of the *proposition expressed*. On the suggested interpretation, this means that the mode of presentation is no part of the truth-conditional content of the thought (by virtue of the equation of the proposition expressed with the truth-conditional content of the thought). Now, *this amounts to saying that the mode of presentation occurring in the thought is truth-conditionally irrelevant*, and this is (part of) what is meant when one says that the mode of presentation occurring in the thought is 'non-descriptive'. Thus there does not seem to be any substantial difference between saying that there is a distinction between the (singular) proposition expressed and the (quasi-singular) thought, only the latter involving a mode of presentation of the reference, and saying that the mode of presentation occurring in the thought is non-descriptive in the sense of truth-conditionally irrelevant.

There still is difference between the two views, though. It concerns the identification of the 'semantic content' of an utterance: that which the utterance expresses and which must be grasped for it to be correctly understood. The semantic content of an utterance is a complete thought, according to the neo-Fregean, but, according to the neo-Russellian, the semantic content of an utterance containing referential terms is a singular proposition, hence *not* a complete thought. When the neo-Russellian claims that the mode of presentation of the reference is no part of the proposition expressed, he means not only that the mode of presentation is truth-conditionally irrelevant (something which the neo-Fregean can accept), but also that it is not part of the semantic content of the utterance. Owing to the latter claim, the neo-Russellian theory and the neo-Fregean theory are *not* equivalent. For the mode of presentation of the reference is part of semantic content, in the neo-Fregean framework.

In the next section I will expound the main reason the neo-

Russellian has for being suspicious of the Fregean equation of thought and semantic content. The notion of semantic content must satisfy various constraints, and among the constraints there is one which concerns *communicability*. The semantic content of an utterance must be a property of that utterance which can be recognized by both speaker and hearer and which remains stable in the process of communication. But there is a sense in which *de re* thoughts are not communicable, insofar as they involve subjective constituents. In chapter 4 we shall see that the thought expressed by the speaker may be different from the thought entertained by the hearer upon understanding the utterance. The sentence means the same thing for speaker and hearer, and the statement that is made – the proposition that is expressed – also is the same for both; but the thoughts which speaker and hearer respectively associate with the speaker's utterance may well be different in type. The thought, when the utterance involves an indexical expression, is subjective (context-relative). Because of this property of subjectivity or egocentricity, the *de re* thoughts which come to be associated with an utterance in the process of communication are unstable – they tend to shift as communication proceeds from speaker to hearer. By contrast, the proposition is what is objectively communicated and it remains constant from one person to the next. This is what makes the neo-Russellian's notion of a singular proposition an arguably better candidate for the status of semantic content than the neo-Fregean notion of a *de re* thought. As John Perry says, 'one reason we need singular propositions is to get at what we seek to preserve when we communicate with those who are in different contexts' (Perry, 1988, p. 4).

## 3.3 Interpretation in *de re* communication

If, as it has just been suggested, subjectivity is inconsistent with communicability, how is the communication of subjective thoughts possible? How can I communicate the thought that I am hungry, if that thought is irreducibly subjective, hence incommunicable? This is a difficult problem which Frege himself had to face (since he acknowledged the subjectivity and incommunicability of first-person thoughts). In 'The Thought', he provides the following answer: what is communicated in such cases is not the subjective thought itself (since it is incommunicable) but something related. This answer is basically correct, and in this section I will elaborate it, using tools from contemporary pragmatics. I will show that subjective thoughts must undergo a process of *interpretation* in order to be communicated; what is communicated is therefore not the subjective thought itself, but an interpretation of that thought. As we shall see, this provides a *prima facie* argument in favour of the neo-Russellian. The neo-Russellian can claim that singular propositions are the output of the interpretation process which makes subjective thoughts communicable, hence that they are what is transmitted in communication. This supports the neo-Russellian equation of semantic content and singular proposition, as opposed to the Fregean equation of semantic content and thought.

Let us first characterize the process of interpretation and its role in communication. In my presentation I will follow Sperber and Wilson who have offered the fullest treatment of this topic I have seen so far (Sperber & Wilson, 1986, p. 226ff).

Sperber and Wilson start with the relation of representing. A propositional representation, e.g. a thought or an utterance, is a representation because it represents something: it represents the state of affairs which would make it true. This is the propositional content of the representation. A different type of representing is achieved through *resemblance* between what is represented and what represents it; thus a cloud in the sky may be used to represent the shape of Brazil. Now among the objects that can be used to represent other objects which they resemble are *propositional representations themselves*: a representation with a certain propositional content may be used to represent something other than its content – it may be used to represent *another representation which it resembles*.

Let us consider only utterances for the moment. An utterance may resemble another utterance on many counts: two utterances may involve the same words, or have the same meaning, or express the same proposition, for example. By virtue of these various sorts of resemblance an utterance can be used to 'represent' another one: this is what happens in direct quotation (where the utterance of a sentence is used to stand for another utterance of the same sentence type), in translation and paraphrase (where the utterance of a sentence is used to stand for an utterance of another sentence with the same meaning), and also in this special sort of paraphrase which aims at preserving the proposition expressed despite changes in the context of utterance (as when I report someone's utterance 'I am fed up with all this' by means of the third-person sentence 'He is fed up with all this').

Sperber and Wilson call 'interpretation' the representation relation which holds between two (propositional) representations by virtue of a resemblance at the propositional level, as in the last example. But they emphasize that a resemblance in propositional content need not involve an *identity* of propositional content, as happens in this example. For two representations to resemble each other at the propositional level, it is sufficient that they share some implications. Sperber and Wilson mention *summaries* and *loose talk* as examples in which a representation (an utterance) represents another representation (another utterance or collection of utterance, or a thought) by virtue of having partly identical implications.

As Sperber and Wilson say, 'the only generally acknowledged interpretive use of utterances is the reporting of speech or thought' (p. 229), but, they argue, 'on a more fundamental level, *every* utterance is used to represent a thought of the speaker' (p. 230):

> We see verbal communication as involving a speaker producing an utterance as a public interpretation of one of her thoughts, and the hearer constructing a mental interpretation of this utterance, and hence of the original thought. (Sperber & Wilson 1986, p. 230)

Thus, in metaphor, the utterance interprets the speaker's thought by virtue of a partial resemblance at the level of content (i.e. by virtue of their sharing some implications), while in ordinary, literal assertion the utterance interprets the speaker's thought by virtue of an identity of content. Identity of content, on Sperber and Wilson's view, is a limiting case of resemblance in content. Likewise, the literal expression of a thought is a limiting case of interpretation.

It might be argued that this puts too much weight on relatively peripheral phenomena such as metaphors and looseness of talk. Some might want to resist Sperber and Wilson's claim that literalness is only a limiting case. I side with Sperber and Wilson in this debate, but the whole debate is irrelevant. For, even if we do not consider phenomena such as metaphor and loose talk, but concentrate on strictly literal assertions, I think we must agree with Sperber and Wilson that *interpretation* plays in linguistic communication the crucial role they ascribe to it. This is so because a great number of our thoughts concern particular objects. Now, when it comes to communicating such thoughts to others, the need for interpretation becomes manifest. For thoughts about particular objects (*de re* thoughts) could *not* be communicated directly, without interpretation. As we shall see, they typically involve 'ways of thinking' or 'modes of presentation' of the objects of thought which crucially depend on certain (contextual) relations between the thinker and these objects. Someone not in the same context cannot entertain the same thoughts about the same objects. Since *de re* thoughts are context-relative and cannot be shared with those in other contexts, what is transmitted in communication cannot be the complete thought of the speaker but only an interpretation of the thought obtained by leaving aside the context-relative constituents of the thought.[2]

Let me spell out how interpretation proceeds in *de re* communication. First, the speaker has a *de re* thought which she wishes to communicate. This thought involves both an 'objective' state of affairs which it represents (i.e. that which would make the thought true), and a (subjective, context-relative) way of thinking of that state of affairs.[3] The state of affairs represented is singular: it consists of an object and a property, or of a sequence of objects and a relation. Being context-relative, the manner in which the thinker thinks of that state of affairs cannot be communicated. But the content – the state of affairs represented – can be communicated: the speaker has only to make an utterance which presents itself as having the singular truth-condition which the thought actually has. Since an utterance *has* the truth-condition which it presents itself as having,[4] the speaker is in a position to 'confer' the truth-conditional content of his thought upon his utterance.

By making an utterance which represents a certain state of affairs (the same as that of her own thought), the speaker invites the hearer to interpret the utterance by forming a thought also representing that state of affairs. The state of affairs in question is singular and involves only a particular object (together with a property), but the hearer's thought must involve a mode of presentation of that object, for a thought cannot be singular, as we have seen. The hearer's thought, like the speaker's thought, will thus involve a singular state of affairs together with a 'way of thinking' of that state of affairs. The state of affairs represented by the hearer's thought is the same as that represented by the speaker's thought, but the ways of thinking are context-relative, hence presumably different for the speaker and the hearer.

To sum up, interpretation as it takes place in normal assertion between the speaker's thought and the proposition expressed, and between the proposition and the hearer's thought, is based on *identity* of truth-conditional content, but it is full-fledged 'interpretation', not replication: for the hearer's thought does not, and could not, replicate the speaker's thought, given the context-relativity of the 'ways of thinking' occurring in *de re* thoughts.

The type of interpretation involved in *de re* communication has been explored by John Perry in the following passage:

> Let us say that to interpret a sentence heard or read or otherwise apprehended is to find a sentence with the same interpretation [i.e. the same propositional content] in one's own situation, as the apprehended sentence had in the utterance of origin.
> We can distinguish several kinds of interpreting.
>
> *Interpreting up.* This is to find an interpreting sentence with a less sensitive meaning. My friend in San Francisco sends me a card on which he has written, 'This city has dilapidated cable cars.' I write in the draft of my travel-guide: 'San Francisco has dilapidated cable cars.' Note that the sentence I find is not insensitive. It has a tense and a proper name. But it is less sensitive than the sentence I read on the card; it has a constant or near-constant interpretation over a wider range of change in the context.
> *Interpreting down.* This is to find a more sensitive sentence with the same interpretation. On a trip to San Francisco I read in my Mobil-Guide, 'San Francisco has dilapidated cable cars'. I write on my notepad, 'This city has dilapidated cable cars.' Or I think it. But I do not get on the cable cars I see.
> *Lateral interpreting.* This is to find a sensitive sentence to interpret a sensitive sentence. My friend shouts,'You are about to be hit by a rock.' I think, 'I am about to be hit by a rock'. (Perry, 1986a, p. 352)

The terminology which Perry introduces in this passage may conveniently be used to summarize what I have said about interpretation in *de re* communication. What is transmitted in *de re* communication cannot be the complete thought of the speaker, but only an impoverished representation which is an interpretation of the thought got by 'interpreting up' (i.e. by leaving aside the context-relative constituents of the thought).[5] Singular propositions with the reference but no mode of presentation of the reference as a constituent can be seen as resulting from this process of interpreting up. Through the process of 'interpreting down' this proposition in its turn yields a complete thought on the hearer's side. As a result, the hearer's thought is related to the speaker's thought by the relation of 'lateral interpreting'.

## 3.4 Communication and subjectivity

We have just seen that the semantic content of an utterance – what it expresses or communicates – is essentially poorer than a thought, for a *de re* thought includes modes of presentation which are private and incommunicable. That is why singular propositions are thought to be better candidates than thoughts for the status of semantic contents of utterances containing referential terms. Singular propositions are *de re* thoughts stripped of their subjective constituents.

Even though I accept the neo-Russellian's objection to the Fregean equation of thought and semantic content, I am suspicious of the neo-Russellian's alternative claim, to the effect that the semantic content of an utterance including referential terms is nothing other than a singular proposition. In this section, I want to defend the neo-Fregean insight that semantic content includes more than merely a singular proposition. The view I will eventually put forward blends features of both the neo-Fregean theory and the neo-Russellian theory.

The first thing to notice, in defence of the neo-Fregean, is that there are cases in which understanding an utterance clearly *requires* thinking of the reference under a certain mode of presentation. Brian Loar gives the following example:

> Suppose that Smith and Jones are unaware that the man being interviewed on television is someone they see on the train every morning and about whom, in that latter role, they have just been talking. Smith says 'He is a stockbroker', intending to refer to the man on television; Jones takes Smith to be referring to the man on the train. Now Jones, as it happens, has correctly identified Smith's referent, since the man on television is the man on the train; but he has failed to understand Smith's utterance. It would seem that, as Frege held, some 'manner of presentation' of the referent is, even on referential uses, essential to what is being communicated. (Loar, 1976, p. 357)

How is the neo-Russellian to account for such examples? If he respects our semantic intuitions, as he should (chapter 13), he will have to admit that semantic content – i.e. what someone must grasp in order to understand the utterance – *sometimes* includes modes of presentation. That move does not necessarily threaten the neo-Russellian position, however, for the neo-Russellian theorist can explain why, in the normal case, the *de re* modes of presentation involved in the communication process are *not* part of semantic content. The obvious explanation is this: the modes of presentation 'man on the train' and 'man on television' are suitably intersubjective, hence they can be communicated. But subjective modes of presentation like that expressed by the first person cannot be part of semantic content.

At this point, however, the neo-Fregean may take a further step and deny the crucial premiss in the neo-Russellian reasoning: the premiss that subjectivity is inconsistent with communicability. Subjectivity, it may be argued, can be made consistent with communicability by distinguishing two forms of communication, a weak one and a strong one. The reason why the speaker's subjective thought cannot be 'communicated' in the strong sense of the term is that the hearer does not come to entertain that thought as a result of the communication process: the hearer does not come to entertain a first-person thought as a result of interpreting a first-person utterance. Still, it may be argued, the speaker's first-person thought is 'expressed' by the utterance and can be recognized as such by the hearer. Even if the hearer's thought is context-relative, hence different from that of the speaker, the utterance may inform the hearer *that* the speaker entertains a certain type of thought, which he himself (the hearer) is unable to entertain. For example, the speaker who says 'I am tired' expresses a first-person thought, to the effect that he himself is tired. The hearer, upon understanding the utterance, forms the thought '*He* is tired'. Contrary to the speaker, the hearer does not think of the referent (i.e. the speaker) in a first-person way. So the hearer's thought is qualitatively different from the speaker's. Yet the hearer who understands the utterance knows that the speaker himself entertains a first-person thought. The utterance 'expresses' such a thought even if the thought is not thereby made available to the hearer. In that way, one may try to defend the Fregean picture by showing that there is a (weak) sense in which subjective thoughts can be communicated.

Not only is it possible to defend the Fregean picture along such lines, but there is a further argument which goes in precisely the same direction. Besides the proposition it expresses, an utterance has a certain linguistic meaning. The distinction between, for example, the meaning of the sentence 'I am tired' and the proposition expressed (what is said) by an utterance of this sentence is hardly controversial. It is also fairly uncontroversial that, in literal communication, the proposition expressed coincides with the truth-conditional content of the speaker's thought: the same state of affairs is represented by the speaker's thought and by the utterance which (literally) expresses that thought. (I call this the Congruence Principle.) Now it seems that *the manner in which this state of affairs is represented in the speaker's thought* – the subjective content of the thought – is expressed by the sentence uttered, by virtue of its linguistic meaning. Thus the speaker S who says 'I am tired' thinks of himself in a first-person way; and it seems that the first-person sentence 'I am tired' precisely expresses this first-person point of view. (A different sentence, for example 'S is tired', could express the same proposition, but it would not capture the subjective content of the thought expressed by 'I am tired'.) When we report someone's thoughts by using *oratio recta*, as when we say 'He thought: "I am too tired for this job",' we take advantage of the systematic correspondence there seems to exist between sentential meanings and subjective ways of thinking. We use a sentence (with a certain meaning) to individuate a thought (with a certain subjective content). In other words, not only does S's utterance 'I am tired' represent the same objective state of affairs as his thought 'I am tired', but the meaning of the sentence 'I am tired' itself seems to correspond to the way S thinks of that state of affairs, i.e. to the subjective content of his thought. If that is true, then the Fregean equation of thought and semantic content is justified: the proposition expressed by the utterance corresponds to the objective aspect of the speaker's thought, and the meaning of the sentence corresponds to its subjective aspect.

This argument is important and interesting, but it raises some difficulties. In chapter 4 we shall *deny* that the subjective mode of presentation which is part of the speaker's thought is conventionally expressed by a certain type of expression (the grammatical first person). The 'modes of presentation' which constitute (part of) the linguistic meaning of indexical expressions will be shown to differ significantly from the 'modes of presentation' which are part of the thought or thoughts associated with the utterance by the speaker and/or hearer. (The former will be called 'linguistic modes of presentation', the latter 'psychological modes of presentation'.) That is not to deny that there are systematic connections between both types of modes of presentation; in chapters 5 and 15 I will acknowledge these connections and attempt to account for them. But that shows that the putative expression relation between indexical sentences and subjective thoughts must be clarified and cannot simply be taken for granted.

The second difficulty is this. How shall we select the point of view which the sentence will be said to express? It seems natural to select the point of view of the speaker, since it is the speaker who entertains a first-person thought when a first-person sentence is being uttered – it is the speaker who expresses the thought that *he himself*\* is tired when uttering 'I am tired'.[6] (The hearer thinks something different, namely 'He is tired'.) Yet there are *also* reasons to select the hearer's point of view. As Evans emphasized, what matters, when we want to individuate semantic content, is what would count as a proper *understanding* of an utterance (Evans, 1982, p. 143n, 171, etc.); now 'understanding' defines the task of the hearer. Thus it is the hearer's point of view which Evans selects; as a result of that choice he is led to deny that the grammatical first person expresses the concept of self: the grammatical first person expresses a demonstrative concept akin to that expressed by the demonstrative 'that man', according to Evans.

To overcome the difficulty, one may try a slightly different route. Instead of making subjective thoughts communicable by selecting a particular point of view (that of the speaker or that of the hearer), we may decide to focus on what is *common* to both points of view. In that way, I think the Fregean picture can be justified to a certain extent. Let me anticipate a bit and show how.

Suppose someone says 'I am tired'. What is common to the thought expressed by the speaker and to that entertained by the hearer upon understanding the utterance? What is common to the thought that *I* am tired and to the thought that *he* (the speaker) is tired? Both the thought of the speaker and that of the hearer include a *de re* mode of presentation having the speaker as reference. The *de re* modes of presentation in question are quite different from each other: the speaker's is a first-person mode of presentation while the hearer's is a third-person mode of presentation. Yet they both are *de re* modes of presentation with their characteristic property of truth-conditional irrelevance. There is a further property which they have in common. In chapters 6–7 *de re* modes of presentation will be construed as dossiers of information. Now both the speaker's and the hearer's dossier or (as Perry says) 'notion' of the reference include a particular piece of information, namely the information that $x$ (the reference) is the utterer. That is part of the speaker's current notion of himself as much as it is part of the hearer's current notion of the speaker: the speaker is conscious of being the utterer, and the hearer also knows that he (the speaker) is the utterer. That information is part of both dossiers, even though one is a first-person dossier and the other a third-person dossier. Now that specific aspect common to both the speaker's and the hearer's notion of the reference is, I suggest, what is expressed by the linguistic expression 'I'. The reference of 'I' is presented as being the speaker (linguistic mode of presentation). That linguistic mode of presentation is intersubjective, unlike the psychological mode of presentation which is subjective (i.e. the notion of *himself*, on the speaker's side, or the notion of *that man*, on the hearer's side); but the former may be construed as an *aspect* or *part* of the latter, an aspect (or part) which is *common* to the speaker's and the hearer's point of view.

If I am right, a referential term *constrains* the *de re* concepts which occur in the thoughts associated with the utterance, and it constrains them in a dual manner. The first constraint bears on the *de re* character of the mode of presentation that occurs in the thought. By virtue of REF, which presents the truth-condition of the utterance as singular, the truth-conditional content of the associated thought must also be singular, hence the modes of presentation occurring in the thought must be truth-conditionally irrelevant (*de re*). The second constraint bears on the content of the *de re* mode of presentation (construed as dossier of information): the linguistic mode of presentation which, together with the feature REF, constitutes the linguistic meaning of the referential term must correspond to some aspect of the information contained in the dossier. I conclude that the semantic content of an utterance, though it cannot include the subjective modes of presentation which occur in the associated thoughts, nevertheless constrains and triggers them in such a way that it can be said to include at least *rudiments* of modes of presentation. In some cases, when it is contextually clear that the hearer is intended to think of the reference in a certain way, the expressed mode of presentation is not even rudimentary. In Loar's example, the mode of presentation which the speaker intends to communicate involves the concept 'man on television' even though the demonstrative pronoun 'he' conveys only the notion of some male person presumably salient. In chapter 16 we shall see other examples in which a fairly specific mode of presentation is expressed as part of the (contextually determined) semantic content of a referential term. All this shows that the Fregean is right to a certain extent: modes of presentation cannot be confined to the realms of the presemantic or the postsemantic; they must be acknowledged as genuine constituents of semantic content.

The fact that we posit more or less rudimentary modes of presentation as part of semantic content is consistent with the neo-Russellian claim that the utterance expresses a singular proposition, however. For the modes of presentation we are talking about are truth-conditionally irrelevant, while the proposition expressed is individuated on a truth-conditional basis. Thus an utterance such as 'He is a stockbroker' (Loar's example) presents its truth-condition as singular, hence it expresses a singular proposition with the referent of 'he' as a constituent, even though the referent in question must be thought of under a particular mode of presentation for the utterance to be correctly understood. In other words, an utterance including referential terms expresses a singular proposition, as the neo-Russellian says, but the latter does not exhaust the semantic content of the utterance. Both the neo-Russellian theory and the neo-Fregean theory turn out to be justified to some extent, in this framework.[7]

## Notes

1  Rejecting that claim is what distinguishes 'critical referentialists' like John Perry or myself from more radical neo-Russellians. 'Critical referentialist' is a term coined by Perry (in conversation). According to Perry, the more radical neo-Russellians include Kaplan's later self, Almog and Wettstein.
2  Sperber and Wilson make essentially this point when they criticize Katz's Effability Principle: 'It seems plausible that in our internal language we often fix time and space references not in terms of universal coordinates, but in terms of a private log-book and an ego-centred map; furthermore, most kinds of reference – to people or events, for example – can be fixed in terms of these private time and space coordinates. Thoughts which contain such private reference [can] only be incompletely represented' by means of natural language sentences. (Sperber & Wilson, 1986, p. 192)
3  This is the 'two-component picture' to be discussed in chapters 11–12.
4  This is so by virtue of a fundamental property of communicative intentions sometimes referred to as their 'self-fulfilling' character (see e.g. Bach & Harnish, 1979 and Recanati, 1986). For an original approach, see Cornulier's book *Meaning Detachment* (Cornulier, 1980).
5  This claim may seem puzzling. For suppose I think 'He is crazy' and express my thought by uttering: 'He is crazy'. The sentence which I utter, and which provides a public interpretation of my thought (as Sperber and Wilson say), is no less indexical and context-sensitive than the thought which it interprets. Why, then, say that the type of

interpretation involved here belongs to the category of 'interpreting up'? For that to be so, the output of the interpretation process would have to be de-indexicalized, which it is not (or so it seems).

I reply, first, that the output of the interpretation process as it is understood here is not the (indexical) meaning of the sentence but the proposition expressed; the sentence, with its meaning, is only a means for expressing the proposition, which is an interpretation of the speaker's thought got by 'interpreting up'. Second, indexical though it is the meaning of the sentence is something 'objective' and context-independent. The sentence means the same thing for speaker and hearer, and the statement that is made – the proposition that is expressed – also is the same for both; but the (types of) thoughts which speaker and hearer respectively associate with the speaker's utterance are essentially tied to their respective viewpoints. It follows that the interpretive step from the thought to the utterance (with its semantic properties: meaning and propositional content) can legitimately be described as a case of interpreting up.

6  I use Castañeda's conventions regarding what he calls 'quasi-indicators' to make clear that the expressed thought is 'reflexive' and involves the concept **Ego**; but, unlike Castañeda, I do not think the natural language expression 'he himself' is a quasi-indicator in his sense, that is, an expression which *conventionally* indicates the occurrence of the concept **Ego** in the reported thought. Whether or not "John believes that he himself is F" serves to ascribe a thought involving the concept **Ego** depends on pragmatic factors, on my view.

7  John Perry makes a similar claim in Perry, 1990b.

# I.2
# From language to thought

# Chapter 4

# Linguistic and psychological modes of presentation

## 4.1 Introduction

Frege used different criteria for individuating the 'senses' or semantic contents of utterances. One criterion was: If S is true and S' is not, S and S' have different contents. By this criterion, it turns out that the constant linguistic meaning – the character – of an indexical sentence such as 'I am hot' cannot be identified with the semantic content of (an utterance of) this sentence. It is obviously possible for an utterance **u** of 'I am hot' to be true and for another utterance **u**' of the same sentence to be false; it follows that their content is different, contrary to the linguistic meaning of the sentence, which is constant. Hence, the content cannot be equated with the meaning of the sentence.

Another criterion Frege used was the cognitive significance criterion, which says, roughly, that two utterances S and S' have different senses, different contents, if their cognitive significance is different, that is, if it is possible for someone who understands S and S' to accept one as true while not accepting the other. This criterion is an essential premiss in the Fregean argument against the neo-Russellian theory (2.4). The Fregean argument says that singular propositions are not acceptable as candidates for the status of semantic contents because they violate Frege's criterion: since it is possible to assent to 'Cicero is bald' while dissenting from 'Tully is bald', these utterances do not have the same content, contrary to what neo-Russellians hold. Two utterances cannot have the same content if they do not have the same cognitive significance.

In order to save the neo-Russellian theory, it is, as we have seen, sufficient to draw a distinction between propositional content and thought. That it is possible to assent to S while dissenting from S' merely shows that different thoughts are associated with S and S', but this is consistent with there being a single proposition that both S and S' express. On this view, the individuation of thoughts and that of propositional contents obey different criteria. It is the thought associated with an utterance, not its propositional content, which is individuated in terms of cognitive significance and must obey Frege's cognitive constraint.

Corresponding to the distinction between the proposition expressed and the thought, there is a similar distinction, more readily acceptable to a Fregean, between the complete thought, whose individuation involves considerations of cognitive significance, and its truth-conditional content. In terms of this distinction, Kaplan's example of the man who sees himself in the mirror with his pants on fire (2.4–5) is analysed as follows: 'My pants are on fire' and 'His pants are on fire' – said when the man believes it is someone else he is seeing in the mirror – are taken to express different thoughts (involving different modes of presentation of the person whose pants are on fire) with the same truth-conditional content (the modes of presentation of the reference being truth-conditionally irrelevant). In other words, the two thoughts represent the same state of affairs, but the latter is apprehended or thought of in two different ways.[1] In this framework also it seems that the two criteria come apart. For it is the way in which a certain state of affairs is represented in thought, rather than the state of affairs which happens to be so represented, which is cognitively relevant and accounts for the subject's behaviour (including verbal behaviour); but it is the state of affairs represented which is relevant for assessing the thought's truth or falsity (Perry, 1977). When two different persons think 'My pants are on fire', they behave in the same way – e.g. by taking off their pants and shouting 'Help!', or by uttering 'My pants are on fire!' – even though the truth-conditional content of their thoughts is different. This is because the mode of presentation (or the type of mode of presentation) is the same. On the other hand, the thoughts expressed by 'My pants are on fire' and 'His pants are on fire' have different behavioural consequences even though they have the same truth-conditional content in Kaplan's example.[2]

So far we have made three main distinctions: between the meaning of the sentence and the proposition expressed, between the proposition expressed and the thought, and between two aspects of the thought: its truth-conditional content and what is sometimes called its 'narrow' content (an expression which I will freely use in what follows, even though it is ambiguous and potentially misleading[3]). This gives us four entities:

(a) the meaning of the sentence,
(b) the proposition expressed by the utterance,
(c) the truth-conditional content of the thought,
(d) the narrow content of the thought.

In literal communication (b) and (c) can safely be equated: the proposition expressed by the utterance coincides with the truth-conditional content of the thought(s) associated with that utterance. This, which I call the Congruence Principle, is definitive of literal communication. As I said in 3.3, the process of interpretation as it takes place in normal assertion between the speaker's thought and the proposition expressed, and between the proposition and the hearer's thought, is based on *identity* of truth-conditional content: the same state of affairs is the truth-conditional content of the thought expressed by the speaker, the truth-conditional content that the utterance attributes to itself, and the truth-conditional content of the thought of the hearer formed by 'interpreting down' the proposition expressed. This chain of content-preserving interpretations characterizes literal communication as opposed, say, to metaphors. This suggests the following picture of (literal) communication:

| Utterance | | Thought |
|---|---|---|
| Linguistic meaning | | |
| vs | | |
| Proposition expressed | = | Truth-conditional content |
| | | vs |
| | | Narrow content |

**Figure 1**

At this point, the question that naturally arises is the following: What relation is there between the two remaining items (a) and (d) – between the meaning of a sentence and the narrow content of the thought expressed by uttering that sentence? That is a very important issue, to which this and the next chapter are devoted.

## 4.2 Linguistic meaning and narrow content: the Simplified Picture

The distinction, within the thought, between its narrow content and its truth-conditional content parallels the distinction between the linguistic meaning of an indexical utterance and the proposition it expresses. There is an important similarity between these two distinctions (Dennett, 1982, p. 15ff). Sentence meaning or 'character', in Kaplan's two-tiered theory, is a function from context to propositional content: the meaning of the sentence 'My pants are on fire' determines that, when Paul utters it at time t, his utterance expresses the proposition that Paul's pants are on fire at t. In the same way, the narrow content of thought has been described as a function from context to truth-conditional content (see e.g. Perry, 1977; Fodor, 1987, pp. 47–8): the narrow content of the thought 'My pants are on fire' determines that, when Paul entertains that narrow content at t, the thought he has on that occasion is true if and only if Paul's pants are on fire at t. And just as the proposition that Paul's pants are on fire can be expressed in different contexts by uttering different, non-synonymous sentences, it is possible to think that Paul's pants are on fire by entertaining different narrow contents in different contexts. (Thus if Paul entertains 'My pants are on fire', he thereby believes that Paul's pants are on fire, but Fred can be said to believe this only if he entertains a different 'narrow content', e.g. 'His pants are on fire'.) What we seem to have is a general distinction between two modes of individuation – 'wide' and 'narrow' individuation – applicable to both meaning and thought (McGinn, 1982; Block, 1986, pp. 618–621).[4] In other words, it seems that there are *indexical* thoughts, in the same way as there are indexical sentences.[5] In both cases, there is a difference between the content the sentence or the thought has independent of context, and the content it has by virtue of its occurrence in a particular context.[6]

Given the close parallelism between the two distinctions – meaning/proposition for utterances, and narrow content/truth-conditional content for thoughts – it is natural and tempting to equate meaning (character) and narrow content, in the same way as we equated the proposition expressed by a literal utterance and the truth-conditional content of the speaker's thought. This equation is suggested, though not explicitly stated, in Perry's and Kaplan's pioneering works on direct reference. On their view, as expounded in Perry (1977) and Kaplan (1989a), it is the character of the utterance rather than its

|           Utterance          |   |        Thought           |
|          Linguistic meaning  | = |     Narrow content       |
|              vs              |   |           vs             |
|        Proposition expressed | = | Truth-conditional content |

**Figure 2**

propositional content that we 'entertain', that we have in mind when we understand an utterance and react to it; it is, in particular, the character that makes us assent to or dissent from the utterance. This is why it is possible to assent to an utterance while dissenting from another one which expresses the same proposition. The speaker himself may be described as entertaining a certain narrow content and selecting a sentence whose linguistic meaning captures that narrow content. Thus the speaker who thinks 'I will be finished by Friday' utters 'I will be finished by Friday'. What he thinks is what his sentence means. The (singular) proposition expressed by his utterance may well be the same as that which another utterance, e.g. 'I will be finished by tomorrow', would express (assuming that Friday is the next day), still the second utterance may not correspond to what the speaker 'has in mind'. This will be so if the speaker does not realize that Friday is the next day. The same proposition is presented differently, under different characters, in the two cases, and it is the mode of presentation that counts from a cognitive point of view.

In this picture, which I call the 'Simplified Picture', the narrow content of the thought expressed by an utterance *is* the meaning of the uttered sentence (figure 2): the meaning of the sentence is what is 'in the head' and accounts for the cognitive (and behavioural) significance of the utterance. By thus 'entertaining' a certain meaning in a certain context, one apprehends a certain objective content – the truth-conditional content of the thought – in the same way as, by uttering a certain sentence in a certain context, one expresses a proposition.

In accordance with figure 2, Kaplan and Perry used 'character' (or equivalent expressions such as 'sense' and 'role') interchangeably to mean the meaning of the sentence or the narrow content of the thought expressed by the utterance. Equating narrow content with linguistic meaning enables one to account for the observation that our cognitive attitudes are sensitive to the mode of presentation of the reference. As we have seen, the meaning of a directly referential term such as 'I', which is the contribution made by that term to the meaning of the whole sentence, is a certain mode of presentation of its reference. To say that the narrow content of the thought is the meaning of the sentence therefore entails that the narrow content of the thought involves a mode of presentation of the reference. Hence, the observation which the Fregean argument presents as an objection to the neo-Russellian theory can be straightforwardly accounted for within the latter, given the equation of narrow content with linguistic meaning (character).

The Simplified Picture arises most naturally out of the neo-Russellian theory. There are two levels of semantic analysis in this theory: content and character. Since cognitive significance cannot be equated with propositional content, it was natural and tempting to equate it with character. In this framework, the divergence between Frege's two criteria of individuation for 'senses' is particularly neat. Contents, but not characters, satisfy the first criterion, while characters, but not contents, satisfy the second one. Characters are the bearers of cognitive significance, whereas contents are that for which the question of truth arises (Perry, 1977).

The Simplified Picture is supported by an observation I made earlier (3.4), concerning the use of *oratio recta* in the reporting of thoughts. As I pointed out in footnote 4, we may use *oratio recta* or *oratio obliqua* both in reporting speech and in reporting thoughts. Thus we have the following contrasts:

|  | *Oratio recta* | *Oratio obliqua* |
|---|---|---|
| Speech: | He said: 'I am tired' | He said he was tired |
| Thought: | He thought: 'I am tired' | He thought he was tired |

Now when we use *oratio recta* in the reporting of thoughts, we use a meaningful sentence (that which occurs within the quotation marks: 'I am tired') to represent the subjective content of the reported thought, i.e. what runs through the thinker's mind. As I said in 3.4, 'we take advantage of the systematic correspondence there seems to exist between sentential meanings and subjective ways of thinking. We use a sentence (with a certain meaning) to individuate a thought (with a certain subjective content).' This correspondence is straightforwardly accounted for on the Simplified Picture.

In this chapter, I will argue *against* the Simplified Picture.[7] I will show that the meaning of a sentence is distinct from, and cannot be considered as a conventional expression of, the narrow content of the thought expressed by uttering that sentence. I will make this point by showing that there are crucial differences between the mode of presentation of the reference that constitutes the meaning of a directly referential term and the mode of presentation of the reference which the Fregean argument shows to be a constituent of (the narrow content of) the thought.

## 4.3 Two sorts of mode of presentation

As I have just said, Kaplan and Perry in their early works use a single label ('character' for Kaplan, 'role' or 'sense' for Perry) to cover two quite different things. They start by defining the character/role of a word like 'I' as follows: it is a rule which, given a context, determines the reference (the semantic value, the content) of that term in that context. Thus the character/role of 'I' is the rule that 'I' refers to the speaker, i.e. to the person who utters this token of 'I'. By virtue of this linguistic rule, the reference of 'I' is presented as being the speaker. The character/role of a word like 'I' can therefore be described as a certain mode of presentation of the reference. Since this mode of presentation is determined by linguistic rules, I call it the *linguistic* mode of presentation of the reference. It has the following properties:

1. It is conventionally determined by the rules of the language. The way the reference of 'I' is presented (viz. as being the speaker) is determined by the linguistic rule that 'I' refers to the speaker. Kaplan (1989a, p. 505): 'The character of an expression is set by linguistic conventions and, in turn, determines the content of the expression in every context. Because character is what is set by linguistic conventions, it is natural to think of it as meaning in the sense of what is known by the competent language user.'

2. As a consequence of 1, the linguistic mode of presentation is constant and does not vary from context to context, contrary to the reference. Perry (1977, p. 479): 'When we understand a word like "today", what we seem to know is a rule taking us from an occasion of utterance to a certain day. "Today" takes us to the very day of utterance, "yesterday" to the day before the day of utterance, "I" to the speaker, and so forth. I shall

call this the role of a demonstrative. (...) The object a demonstrative takes us to in a given context, I shall call its value in that context or on that occasion of use. Clearly, we must grant "today" a role, the same on both occasions of use. And we must, as clearly, give it different values on the two occasions.'

3   In the case of indexical or 'token-reflexive' words such as 'I', the reference of a token of the expression is presented as bearing a certain relation to this token: the reference of 'I' is presented as being the utterer of this token, the reference of 'you' as being the person to whom this token is addressed, the reference of 'now' as being the time at which this token is uttered, and so on (see Reichenbach, 1947, para. 50).

Now, as we have seen, Perry and Kaplan emphasize that the singular proposition which they take to be the content of an utterance containing a directly referential term cannot be the object of the attitudes, since the latter are sensitive to the mode of presentation of the reference. The object of the attitudes is not the content, they say, but the content 'under the character' imposed by the meaning of the sentence. The character thus plays an important role in the individuation of the attitudes. I may believe that Cicero is bald without believing that Tully is bald, even though 'Cicero is bald' and 'Tully is bald' express the same singular proposition; this is possible because the same proposition may be expressed under different characters.

Although Kaplan and Perry use 'character', 'role' or 'sense' indiscriminately for both, it seems to me that the mode of presentation which is crucially involved in the individuation of the attitudes is very different from the mode of presentation which has the properties 1, 2 and 3 mentioned above. In what follows, I shall argue that the mode of presentation of the reference which is involved in the individuation of the attitudes is a *psychological* mode of presentation − or mode of identification − of the reference, *distinct from* what I have just called the linguistic mode of presentation. Distinguishing between these two types of mode of presentation amounts to rejecting the claim that narrow content can be equated with character in the original sense, that is, with linguistic meaning.

Consider, again, Kaplan's example. Suppose that, looking at the window and seeing there the reflected image of a man whose pants are on fire, I say: 'His pants are on fire'. Unbeknown to me, this man happens to be myself. Corresponding to my utterance, there is a certain belief which I entertain – the belief that this man's pants are on fire. If I am mean and selfish, I may laugh at the situation, instead of doing something to help the poor man. When I realize that I am the man whose image I see in the window, I exclaim: 'My pants are on fire!' Corresponding to this utterance, there is another belief – the belief that *my* pants are on fire. That this belief is different from the first one is shown by the fact that it results in a different sort of behaviour – I immediately start doing something to stop the fire. In such a case, according to Perry and Kaplan, the same (singular) proposition is apprehended under different modes of presentation. This proposition involves a certain person – the person whose pants are on fire, namely, myself – who is thought of under different modes of presentation, a first-person mode of presentation in one case and a third-person mode of presentation in the other. The mode of presentation of the reference is not reflected in the proposition expressed, that is, in the content of the utterance (the same in both cases), but it plays a crucial role in the explanation and prediction of behaviour and therefore in the individuation of the belief expressed by the utterance.

Can we equate the first-person mode of presentation of myself that occurs in my belief that my pants are on fire with the linguistic mode of presentation associated with the first person in English? I do not think so. The linguistic mode of presentation associated with 'I' (or more generally with the first person) is something like 'the person who utters T', where 'T' names the token of 'I' that is being uttered. Now, I might possibly believe that the pants of the person who utters T are on fire, without realizing that I am the person who utters T, and therefore without behaving as I do when I realize that *my* pants are on fire. (A situation in which I do not realize that the person uttering a token is in fact me is not a very common situation, of course, but I take it not to be impossible.[8]) This shows that the psychological mode of presentation that occurs in my belief that my pants are on fire – i.e. the way I think of myself when I think that my pants are on fire – differs from the linguistic mode of presentation associated with the word 'I'. I think of myself as *myself*, not as the utterer of such and such a token. Yet, if we turn from the thought expressed by the utterance to its linguistic meaning, we have no reason to deny that the reference of 'I' is presented as being the speaker, by virtue of the linguistic rule that a token of 'I' refers to the person who utters this token. All this raises no problem if we accept that the mode of presentation of the reference in the thought (psychological mode of presentation) is different in principle from the mode of presentation of the reference at the level of linguistic meaning (linguistic mode of presentation).

## 4.4 Systematic differences between linguistic and psychological modes of presentation

If we focus on the *psychological* modes of presentation associated with indexical expressions, we see that it is not obvious they have *any* of the three properties listed above as properties of linguistic modes of presentation. In particular, they do not have the third property, that of 'token-reflexivity'. A mode of presentation is token-reflexive when the reference is presented as bearing a certain relation R to the current token of the expression whose reference it is. Now, in the case of 'I' or other indexical expressions, it is intuitively clear that the psychological mode of presentation is not token-reflexive in this sense.[9] There certainly are objects which I identify only indirectly, by their relations to something else, but it is paradoxical to claim that I identify *myself* (or the present time, or the present place) in that indirect way, as whatever bears a certain relation to an independently identified object. Even Russell, who went so far as to claim that we know material object only by description, maintained that he was directly acquainted at least with *himself*. In general, there is something ludicrous in the suggestion that we think of the objects of our indexical thoughts as 'whatever bears such and such relation to the present token', for it implies that we think of these objects only 'by description', instead of being directly acquainted with them; a very paradoxical consequence, since the objects of our indexical thoughts are precisely the objects with which it seems that we are 'directly acquainted', if there is anything like direct acquaintance.

The claim that psychological modes of presentation are token-reflexive would entail not only that the objects of our indexical thoughts are identified indirectly, by description, but also that they are identified in an objective (rather than a subjective) manner. As many philosophers have insisted after Castañeda (1966, 1967), we think of ourselves under an essentially subjective or *first-person* perspective: for any objective (i.e. third-person) description of *myself* as the F, it is possible for me not to realize that I am the F. In the same way, for any objective description of the present time (or of the present place) as the F, I might not realize that the present time (now) is the F, or that the present place (here) is the F. Given this fact, the psychological modes of presentation associated with indexical expressions such as 'I', 'now' or 'here' *cannot* be token-reflexive, for token-reflexive modes of presentation appeal to *objective* relations between the token of the word and the reference of the token.

The psychological modes of presentation associated with indexical expressions can no more have the second property of linguistic modes of presentation than they can have the third property, that of token-reflexivity. As we have seen, the linguistic mode of presentation associated with an indexical expression does not vary from context to context, contrary to the reference of the expression; since it is set by conventions and belongs to the linguistic meaning of the expression, the linguistic mode of presentation of the reference is constant from one occurrence of the expression to the next. What about psychological modes of presentation? Are they also constant from context to context? My answer is that they are not, and cannot be, given (i) their subjectivity, and (ii) their role in psychological explanations.

Let us start with a simple observation concerning the word 'I'. That linguistic modes of presentation are constant entails in particular that the linguistic mode of presentation conventionally associated with the word 'I' is the same for the speaker and the hearer, as it is for any user of English. The constant meaning of 'I' is simply the rule that 'I' refers to the speaker; by virtue of this constant meaning, the reference of a token of 'I' is always presented as being the speaker. But the psychological mode of presentation of the reference, that is, the way the reference of 'I' is thought of, is not constant like the linguistic mode of presentation. As I pointed out earlier, when I utter 'I am tired', I think of *myself* as being tired; the psychological mode of presentation in this case is a first-person mode of presentation. But when *you* hear me say 'I am tired', you do not think of the reference under a first-person mode of presentation. Rather, you think: '*He* is tired'. The linguistic mode of presentation ('the speaker') is the same for speaker and hearer, but the psychological mode of presentation, that is, the mode of presentation of the reference that occurs in the thought associated with the utterance, is different for the thought expressed by the speaker and for the thought the hearer forms upon understanding the utterance. This form of non-constancy goes along with the *subjectivity* of psychological modes of presentation.

To be sure, it would be possible to maintain that the psychological mode of presentation associated with 'I' is constant, merely by 'selecting a point of view' (3.4) and defining the psychological mode of presentation associated with an expression as *the mode of presentation of the reference in the thought of the speaker*, or alternatively as *the mode of presentation of the reference in the thought of the hearer who understands the utterance* (Evans, 1982). Certainly, I think of myself under the same first-person mode of presentation when I say 'I' as you do when *you* say 'I': in this sense, the psychological mode of presentation associated with 'I' can be said to be constant. But the linguistic mode of presentation associated with 'I' has a stronger, unrelativized form of constancy. Two people, A and B, associate the same linguistic mode of presentation with the word 'I', no matter which one utters it. From A's point of view, the reference of a token of 'I' is linguistically presented as being the speaker even if it is B who utters this token. On the other hand, A does not think of the reference of a token of 'I' as being *himself* if it is B who utters this token.

In any event, it cannot be maintained that psychological modes of presentation are constant even in the weaker, relativized sense. The linguistic meaning of the expression 'this ship', and therefore the linguistic mode of presentation of the reference, is constant from occurrence to occurrence: the reference is always presented as being a ship salient in the context of utterance.[10] But the psychological mode of presentation is not constant. In fact, it cannot be. Consider the utterance 'This ship <pointing to a ship through one window> is a steamer but this ship <pointing to a ship through another window> is not a steamer' and suppose that, unbeknown to the speaker, the same, very long ship is being demonstrated twice.[11] The speaker is not irrational even though she says of the same ship both that it is and that it is not a steamer. She is not irrational because she does not realize that there is only one ship; and she does not realize this because she thinks of the ship under two different (psychological) modes of presentation. In other words, we have to posit two different (psychological) modes of presentation of the reference, one corresponding to each token of the expression 'this ship', in order to make sense of the utterance. But there is only *one* linguistic mode of presentation, the same for both tokens of this expression. This provides us with a powerful argument to support the distinction between linguistic and psychological modes of presentation – an argument that can be formulated in quite general terms.

Psychological modes of presentation are needed to make sense of our attitudes – e.g. to make sense of the fact that we believe 'Cicero is bald' while disbelieving 'Tully is bald'. In order to play this role, psychological modes of presentation must obey what Schiffer (1978, p. 180) calls 'Frege's Constraint':

> Necessarily, if $m$ is a mode of presentation under which a minimally rational person $x$ believes a thing $y$ to be F, then it is not the case that $x$ also believes $y$ not to be F under $m$. In other words, if $x$ believes $y$ to be F and also believes $y$ not to be F, then there are distinct modes of presentation $m$ and $m'$ such that $x$ believes $y$ to be F under $m$ and disbelieves $y$ to be F under $m'$. Let us call this *Frege's Constraint; it is a constraint which any candidate must satisfy if it to qualify as a mode of presentation.* . . . In effect, Frege's Constraint provides *the* motivation for the introduction of modes of presentation.

Frege's Constraint provides the motivation for the introduction of *psychological* modes of presentation. But linguistic modes of presentation do not have to satisfy Frege's Constraint. In the ship example, there is only one linguistic mode of presentation: both tokens of 'this ship' have the same linguistic meaning, by virtue of which they present their reference as a ship salient in the context of their utterance. However, Frege's Constraint dictates that there be two different psychological modes of presentation involved in this example. Since the speaker is not irrational yet believes of a certain ship both that it is and that it is not a steamer, there must be two different (psychological) modes of presentation of this ship, $m$ and $m'$, such that the speaker believes the ship to be a steamer under $m$ and believes it not to be a steamer under $m'$. It follows that there is a difference between linguistic and psychological modes of presentation. Linguistic modes of presentation are constant from occurrence to occurrence, and do not necessarily satisfy Frege's Constraint; psychological modes of presentation satisfy Frege's Constraint, and are not necessarily constant from occurrence to occurrence.

What about the first property of linguistic modes of presentation, namely conventionality? Are psychological modes of presentation conventionally associated with linguistic expressions? A negative answer to this question follows immediately from what I have just said. If psychological modes of presentation are not necessarily constant from context to context, that is, if the same linguistic expression may be sometimes associated with a certain psychological mode of presentation of the reference and sometimes with another, then psychological modes of presentation are not conventionally associated with linguistic expressions; for if they were, they would be constantly associated with those expressions. Thus it seems that psychological modes of presentation have none of the three characteristic properties of linguistic modes of presentation.

## 4.5 Conclusion

It is important to realize that the wide/narrow distinction applies to both utterances and thoughts. As I said in 4.2, to realize this is to realize that there are *indexical* thoughts, in the same way as there are indexical sentences. My purpose in this chapter was not to defend the analogy between thoughts and indexical sentences, however. (I shall do that in chapters 11–12.) Rather, taking this analogy for granted, I have tried to show that it should not be pressed too far. If I am right, we must resist the temptation to *equate* the narrow content of an indexical thought and the linguistic meaning (the 'character') of the sentence used to express that thought. When the sentence includes an expression that we would classify as directly referential, for example a pronoun such as 'I' or 'you', or a demonstrative such as 'this ship', both the linguistic meaning of the sentence and the narrow content of the thought involve a mode of presentation of the reference. But this cannot be used to support the equation of linguistic meaning and narrow content, for I have argued that in *de re* communication the linguistic mode of presentation that is part of the meaning of the sentence is crucially different from the psychological mode of presentation that is part of the narrow content of the thought associated with this sentence. The linguistic mode of presentation is essentially descriptive, whereas the psychological modes of presentation involved in *de re* thoughts are non-descriptive.

This fundamental heterogeneity of linguistic and psychological modes of presentation must be overcome for language to connect up with thought in communication. A connection must be established between the descriptive mode of presentation which is linguistically encoded and the non-descriptive, psychological mode of presentation which is a constituent of the communicated thought. How is that connection established? This is one of the main issues to be dealt with in chapter 5.

## Notes

1 In the same way as a given content or state of affairs can be apprehended under different modes of presentation, different contents can be apprehended under the same mode of presentation (or the same sort of mode of presentation). Thus it can hardly be denied that there is something common to our thoughts when we both think something that we might express by uttering 'My pants are on fire'. This common element cannot be the truth-conditional content of the thought, since our thoughts have different truth-conditional contents (my thought is true if and only if *my* pants are on fire, yours is true if and only if *your* pants are on fire). What is common can only be the mode of presentation, or the sort of mode of presentation, under which these different contents are apprehended.

2 As many people pointed out (e.g. Peacocke, 1981, para. 2; Evans, 1982, p. 203; McCulloch, 1989, pp. 210–5), it would be a mistake to claim that *only* 'narrow' contents – i.e. what I have just called 'modes of presentation' as opposed to the truth-conditional contents of thoughts – can be used in psychological explanations of behaviour. Psychological explanations of (object-involving) actions typically mention 'wide', truth-conditional contents. (This is so in particular when there is no divergence between what is done and the subject's representation of what is done.) This remark, which I fully accept, paves the way to a radical critique of the two-component analysis of thoughts into narrow content and truth-conditional content – a critique which I will discuss in chapter 11. Arguably, the two-component analysis is justified only if narrow contents *can* be singled out by their special role in psychological explanations. If they cannot, the notion of narrow content has no role to play in the theory, and we cannot move from the distinction between the complete thought and its truth-conditional content to the more controversial distinction between two *components* of the thought. Thus there are two versions of the neo-Fregean theory: one which accepts the two-component analysis of thought and one which does not. The latter view, held by neo-Fregeans such as Evans and McDowell, is closer to Fregean orthodoxy than the former, since it rejects the claim that Frege's two criteria come apart: on this view, the only psychologically relevant notion is that of thought (i.e. the complete thought), and the thought is *both* what is true or false and what accounts for behaviour. I shall discuss this view in chapter 11. In the meantime, the two-component analysis of thoughts will be taken for granted, and the only version of the neo-Fregean theory to be considered will be that which incorporates the two-component analysis.

3 As I shall argue in chapter 12, 'narrow content' can be understood either in an absolute sense or in a relative sense. What I am calling

'narrow content' in this chapter is not narrow in the absolute sense but in a relative sense; hence my theory is consistent with Externalism, the thesis that there is no 'narrow content' in the absolute sense. More on this in chapter 12.

4   In both cases the wide/narrow distinction can be made salient by contrasting two types of report. In reporting speech as well as in reporting thought, one can use *oratio recta* or *oratio obliqua*. In *oratio obliqua*, what is reported is the (wide) content of speech or the (wide) content of thought; in *oratio recta*, what is reported is the way that content is presented (i.e. the meaning of the uttered sentence in a case of reported speech, or the narrow content of thought in a case of reported thought).

5   Of course 'thought' is not taken in Frege's sense when I say that there are indexical thoughts. In 6.2 I shall distinguish two senses of 'thought': thought$_1$ and thought$_2$. It is only thoughts$_1$ that can be said to be indexical.

6   Obvious though it may now seem, this analogy between utterances and thoughts has not always been recognized. It has too often been suggested that indexicality characterizes natural language sentences *qua* communicative devices, as opposed to thoughts. Thoughts were traditionally taken to be much more like so-called eternal sentences than like the ordinary, heavily context-dependent sentences of natural language. The contextual dependence of thoughts was acknowledged as a result of, *inter alia*, Castañeda's insistence on the irreducible subjectivity of first-person thoughts and Putnam's 'twin-Earth' thought-experiments. It is John Perry, however, who systematically explored the analogy (in a series of papers on what he called the 'circumstantial relativity' of the attitudes). Some philosophers, well aware of the analogy, think it must be resisted; I shall discuss their view in chapters 11–12.

7   I am not the first to criticize the Simplified Picture. My predecessors include Evans (1981, pp. 300–3) and Wettstein (1986). Related ideas are to be found in Peacocke (1981, p. 195) and Taschek (1987). The issue of *Noûs* 24 (1990) in which a first version of this chapter was published also contains a critique of the Simplified Picture by Ruth Millikan. As for Perry, although (to my knowledge) he never explicitly criticized the Simplified Picture, it is clear from his more recent work that he no longer holds it, if he ever did. Kaplan himself expresses dissatisfaction with the Simplified Picture in his 'Afterthoughts' (Kaplan, 1989b, pp. 597–9).

8   Peacocke describes such a situation: 'An utterance can occur and I be its producer without my knowing that I am its producer. I and my twin brother may be in the same room, and both of us may try to utter the same sentence. If the vocal cords of one of the two of us are inoperative – we do not know which – and the normal forms of

feedback which would tell one of us that he and not the other had produced the utterance have been severed, then neither of us will know whether he issued the utterance; but one of us did' (Peacocke, 1983, p. 134). This type of situation was originally imagined by Nozick (1981, p. 72).

9  It may perhaps be said to be token-reflexive in another sense. As we shall see in chapter 6, *de re* modes of presentation are essentially relational: they are 'mental indexicals' (as Bach says) whose reference is determined relationally, as the reference of a token-reflexive expression. On token-reflexivity in thought, see Searle, 1983; Peacocke, 1983; Perry, 1992.

10 Strictly speaking, the linguistic mode of presentation associated with a demonstrative expression like 'this ship' is poorer. We need not suppose that it includes the property of being 'salient' in the context of utterance in order to explain the fact that this property is involved in the interpretation process. Its being involved is sufficiently accounted for once we notice that the reference of a demonstrative is *linguistically underdetermined* (18.3): it is determined on *pragmatic* grounds as the most 'salient' (or 'relevant') object satisfying the linguistic mode of presentation. On underdetermination in general, see Sperber & Wilson, 1986; on the underdetermination of demonstratives, see Bach, 1987, pp. 176–79.

11 I borrow this example from Perry (1977, p. 483) and Evans (1986, p. 84). Wettstein (1986, pp. 195–6) uses the same type of example to show that cognitive significance cannot be accounted for in terms of linguistic meaning. See also LePore & Loewer 1986, pp. 602.

# Chapter 5

# The meaning and cognitive significance of indexical expressions

## 5.1 Introduction

In chapter 4 I criticized the Simplified Picture, according to which the linguistic meaning of an indexical sentence is or constitutes the narrow content of the thought which such a sentence can be used to express. I have shown that there are systematic differences between the modes of presentation of the reference we find at the level of linguistic meaning (linguistic modes of presentation) and the modes of presentation of the reference which occur in thought (psychological modes of presentation). But I have not said anything of the relation between the two sorts of mode of presentation. If psychological modes of presentation are not an aspect of the conventional meaning of linguistic expressions, if they are distinct from linguistic modes of presentation, how do they come to be expressed? How does language connect up with thought? This is an essential question, and a difficult one indeed. In this chapter, I will provide only the beginning of an answer (5.5). A fuller answer will become available only after we have investigated the nature of psychological modes of presentation (chapters 6 and 7).

## 5.2 Rebutting the constancy argument

Let me first sketch a possible defence of the Simplified Picture criticized in chapter 4. The defence I have in mind is based on a rebuttal of the constancy argument presented in 4.4. According to this argument, an expression such as 'this ship' has a constant linguistic meaning but is associated with different psychological modes of presentation whenever a subject is in a position to think "this ship is F but this ship is not F". It follows that psychological modes of presentation are to be distinguished from those modes of presentation to be found at the level of linguistic meaning (linguistic modes of presentation). In contrast to the former, which are contextually variable, the latter are 'constant' in the sense that the same expression always presents the reference in the same way. So the argument goes.

The constancy argument, it might be objected, can be dismissed on the grounds that the example I used ('this ship') involves a demonstrative rather than a 'pure indexical' (Kaplan, 1989a, pp. 490–1). According to Kaplan, pure indexicals like 'I', 'here', 'now', and so forth, are semantically complete in a sense in which demonstratives like 'he' or 'this ship' are not. Their conventional meaning fully determines (indeed constitutes) a 'character', that is, a function from context to content, whereas in the case of true demonstratives a character is attached not to the expression in isolation, but to the expression *in conjunction with a demonstration*.[1] Now if, following Kaplan, we take the demonstrative-*cum*-demonstration, rather than the demonstrative in isolation, to be the relevant semantic unit (i.e. what possesses a character), we can no longer analyse the ship example by saying that the psychological mode of presentation varies from occurrence to occurrence, for in that example we do not have two occurrences of the *same* demonstrative-*cum*-demonstration. The demonstrative (i.e. the linguistic expression) is the same, but the demonstration (the pointing) has changed. (See Wettstein, 1986, p. 196n.)

This point is well-taken, but what exactly does it show? One of the things it shows is that Kaplan himself acknowledges the divorce between *linguistic meaning* (distinct from character, in the case of demonstratives) and psychological mode of presentation, when demonstratives are concerned. Thus, Kaplan and I agree that psychological modes of presentation may vary from one occurrence of the demonstrative (*qua* linguistic expression) to the next, while linguistic meaning remains constant.

Kaplan's distinction raises an important issue, however. For it is not obvious that in the case of pure indexicals the psychological mode of presentation may vary from one occurrence of the linguistic expression to the next. Let us try to find an example, similar to the ship example but involving a pure indexical rather than a demonstrative. In Recanati (1990, p. 721) I offered the following example:

A friend and I, visiting a foreign city, stop by a restaurant in the morning and my friend says: 'It would be nice to have dinner here'. I agree. Later on, we stop by the same place, and my friend says again: 'It would be nice to have dinner here'. But I don't recognize the place and I disagree. Again, we have two utterances of the same sentence ('It would be nice to have dinner here') which express the same proposition under the same character. Since what is involved is 'here', a pure indexical by Kaplan's standards, it is not possible to argue that the character has changed even though the sentence is the same. Yet the cognitive significance of one utterance is different from that of the other, as witnessed by the fact that I assent to one while dissenting from the other.

I used that example to argue that the psychological modes of presentation associated with a pure indexical such as 'here' may vary from one occurrence of the expression to the next. However, as Christopher Peacocke pointed out to me, this example involves judgements made at different times, and this feature may be thought sufficient to account for the case without having to posit two different psychological modes of presentation: it may be argued that a change in the knowledge base (in the background beliefs of the subject), rather than a difference in the psychological mode of presentation of the place referred to, is what accounts for the conflicting judgements in this example. This is a tricky issue, for in a certain sense I have *not* changed my mind between the two judgements: at the time of the second judgement I still agreed with what my friend had said the first time (I still thought it would be nice to have dinner *there*).[2] Still, Peacocke is right to point out that on a strict reading, Frege's constraint must be understood as saying that two distinct psychological modes of presentation $m$ and $m'$ are involved whenever a rational subject judges *at the same time* that an object is F and that it is not F. On this strict reading of Frege's constraint, one need not posit two distinct psychological modes of presentation associated with a single linguistic expression in the restaurant example, since the conflicting judgements are made at two different times.

I must confess that, although I tried hard and asked many friends (and students) to help me in the task, I have been unable to find a convincing example of a pure indexical such that a rational subject can think at the same time "$\alpha$ is F" and "$\alpha$ is not F". What is possible with demonstratives turns out not to be possible with pure indexicals. It seems that I cannot at the same time think of two different places as 'here', or of two different persons as 'me';[3] nor can I be deceived into *believing* that there are two distinct places or two distinct persons which I am simultaneously thinking of as 'here' or as 'me'. It follows that the constancy argument works only for demonstratives. Psychological modes of presentation are not constant from one occurrence of a demonstrative to the next, hence we cannot equate linguistic and psychological modes of presentation in the case of demonstratives; but there is no reason to deny that psychological modes of presentation are constant from one occurrence of a pure indexical to the next.

Even in the case of demonstratives, it may be argued that the constancy argument is not as damaging as I suggested in 4.4. To see that, let us consider an argument offered by Colin McGinn to the effect that there must be, associated with every indexical expression, a thought-constituent which does not vary from one occurrence of the expression to the next. McGinn's argument is a priori; it runs as follows (McGinn, 1983, pp. 64–6):

> The first and fundamental consideration is the constancy of the linguistic meaning of indexicals from occasion to occasion. No theory of sense which entails denying this semantic constancy can be correct, and any theory which acknowledges it is compelled to discern a parallel constancy at the level of thought, since thoughts must have common conceptual elements if their linguistic expression does... The naive view suggested by indexical word meaning is thus that in thinking of items under 'I', 'now', 'here' one applies a single constant concept – the concept of oneself, of the present, and of the spatial vicinity – and not variable occasion-relative concepts... None of this is to say – what is patently untrue – that different thinkers employing indexical concepts do not commonly associate different bodies of information with their indexically identified objects of thought: that is, I am not saying that you and I have the same conception of ourselves, in the sense that we associate the same information with our respective uses of 'I'. Neither am I saying that successive times identified as 'now' are cognitively indistinguishable for the temporal thinker; and similarly for 'here'. My claim rather concerns the conceptual content directly expressed by indexicals, not other associated beliefs a person may have about his objects of reference.

McGinn's argument essentially relies on the claim that 'thoughts must have common conceptual elements if their linguistic expression does'. This I shall call the thesis of psycho-semantic parallelism.[4] It entails that two utterances with 'here' or with 'this ship' must express two thoughts that have some element in common – some concept that corresponds to the expression 'here' or 'this ship'. For pure indexicals the concept in question may be straightforwardly equated with the psychological mode of presentation *qua* satisfier of Frege's constraint. For demonstratives, the constant thought-constituent cannot be the psychological mode of presentation, but it can be a *type* of psychological mode of presentation. In the ship example, the same expression 'this ship', whose linguistic meaning is constant, is associated with two distinct psychological modes of presentation, but these two psychological modes of presentation may be said to fall under the same 'type', and the latter may be said to be constantly associated with the linguistic expression.[5]

## 5.3 The Simplified Picture again

At this point, it seems that the proponent of the Simplified Picture is in a position to regain much of the ground that was lost in 4.4. For, he may argue, there no longer is any reason to deny that psychological modes of presentation are *conventionally* associated with linguistic expressions – either directly, as in the case of indexicals, or indirectly, by falling under types which are conventionally associated with linguistic expressions (as in the case of demonstratives). On the contrary, there is a good reason to assume that there are conventions associating linguistic expressions with psychological modes of presentation (or with types of psychological mode of presentation, in the case of demonstratives), for this allows one to account for the constant character of the link between linguistic expressions and psychological modes of presentation (or types of psychological modes of presentation).

Once we have taken this step, it may be argued that we *must* endorse the Simplified Picture, according to which there is no difference between linguistic and psychological modes of presentation. For the claim that psychological modes of presentation are conventional comports badly with the distinction between linguistic and psychological modes of presentation: if one accepts the former, one had better reject the latter. To accept both would be to accept that there are two sets of conventions (since linguistic modes of presentation are by definition convention-constituted): those which determine linguistic modes of presentation, and those associating referring expressions with psychological modes of presentation (or types of psychological modes of presentation). For example, there would be two conventions governing the use of 'I': the convention that 'I' refers to the speaker, and the convention that 'I' expresses the egocentric concept **Ego** (i.e. the concept, or psychological mode of presentation, that is common to my thoughts about myself and to your thoughts about yourself). Or, in the case of 'here', there would be two conventions, the convention that 'here' is used to talk about the place where one is, and the convention that 'here' expresses what McGinn calls the 'concept of spatial vicinity'. Now, if this is not multiplying conventions beyond necessity, what is? Certainly, it would be more attractive to have only *one* set of conventions. One obvious way to achieve that aim precisely consists in dropping the distinction between psychological and linguistic modes of presentation and endorsing the Simplified Picture. On this view, referring expressions are conventionally associated with (types of) psychological modes of presentation, and the linguistic meaning of a referring expression consists in this association: there is no linguistic mode of presentation over and above the (type of) psychological mode of presentation with which a referring expression is conventionally associated. The psychological mode of presentation *is* the linguistic mode of presentation, on this view.[6] Thus, instead of taking the linguistic convention governing the use of 'I' to be the rule that 'I' refers to the speaker, one would take it to be the rule that 'I' is used to express the sui-generis concept **Ego**. In this framework, there is only one type of convention, the convention that pairs linguistic expressions with (types of) psychological modes of presentation.

The view I have just sketched is not to be dismissed on *a priori* grounds. It is a serious theoretical possibility, which deserves to be considered. But I am far from sure that it can be worked out in a satisfactory way. How, for example, will it be extended so as to account for the mode of presentation of the reference of 'you'? Is there a communication-independent concept of **Alter-ego** that the word 'you' could be said conventionally to express, in the same way as 'I' expresses the communication-independent concept of **Ego**? In general, the problem with this version of the Simplified Picture is that it forces us to abandon the classical view of the meaning of indexical expressions and leaves us with only the promise of a new theory. According to the classical, token-reflexive view, the meaning of an indexical like 'I', 'you' or 'here' is constituted by a reference rule governing the use of that indexical – the rule that 'I' refers to the speaker, 'you' to the addressee, 'here' to the place of utterance, and so on. This rule determines the linguistic mode of presentation associated with a token of the expression – for example, the rule that 'I' refers to the speaker determines that a token $t$ of 'I' presents its reference as being the utterer of $t$. No one has ever fully stated the alternative meaning theory for indexicals, with its alternative conventions. It is not even clear whether or not, in the alternative theory, the senses of indexicals could be displayed be reference rules, as they are in the classical theory.

What I would favour is a theory which simultaneously satisfies the following constraints:

1. it enables us to preserve the classical, token-reflexive analysis of indexical expressions;
2. it does not posit more than one set of conventions governing the use of indexical expressions;
3. it accounts for the observation that indexical expressions like 'I', 'now' or 'here' are constantly associated with the egocentric concepts of oneself, of the present, of spatial vicinity (psychological modes of presentation).[7]

It is difficult to satisfy the three constraints simultaneously. To satisfy 3 one is tempted to posit conventions associating psychological modes of presentation (egocentric concepts) with indexical expressions; since linguistic modes of presentation are by definition conventional, this means that we sacrifice 2 and posit two sets of conventions. Alternatively, to avoid sacrificing 2, we may give up the distinction between linguistic and psychological modes of presentation and reduce the former to the latter, but this means sacrificing 1, as we have seen.

In what follows, I shall put forward a view which satisfies the three constraints. In order to satisfy 1, I suggest that we maintain a sharp distinction between linguistic and psychological modes of presentation. Linguistic modes of presentation, on my view, are what the classical, token-reflexive analysis says they are: the reference of 'I' is presented as the speaker, the reference of 'you' as the addressee, and so forth. These modes of presentation are very different from the psychological modes of presentation (e.g. the egocentric concept **Ego**, in the case of 'I'), as I emphasized in 4.4. In order to satisfy 2, I suggest that we reject the claim that psychological modes of presentation are conventionally associated with linguistic expressions. On my view, there is only one set of conventions, those associating linguistic expressions with linguistic modes of presentation (which are *distinct from* psychological modes of presentation). In order to satisfy 3, we must account for the constant link between indexical expressions and egocentric categories without assuming that the latter are conventionally associated with the former. To provide such an account is the task of the next section.

## 5.4 Immunity to error through misidentification

On the view I am going to sketch, psychological mode of presentation are not *conventionally* associated with referring expressions, and the only conventions there are associate the latter with linguistic modes of presentation, which are *not* identical to psychological modes of presentation. As far as 'I' is concerned, the only relevant convention is the convention that 'I' refers to the speaker; this convention determines the linguistic mode of presentation associated with 'I' ('the person who utters this token'), and the linguistic mode of presentation, in turn, *non-conventionally* determines that a certain (type of) psychological mode of presentation is expressed.[8]

The problem, with this view, consists in making sense of the claim that the expression of a particular psychological mode of presentation is non-conventionally determined by the linguistic mode of presentation. Something has to be said about how this is done. Peacocke, who believes that the only convention governing 'I' is the rule that 'I' refers to the speaker, suggests the following mechanism. The concept **Ego** is expressed by a use of 'I' because normally the speaker who uses 'I' fully realizes that *he* (= **Ego**) is the speaker and intends to refer to *himself* (= **Ego**) by using an expression which designates the speaker. Since it is manifest that the speaker fully realizes that he is the speaker and intends to refer to himself by saying 'I', an utterance in the first person is naturally and correctly taken as 'an expression of the first-person way of thinking' (Peacocke, 1983, p. 138). There is no more than that to the association between 'I' and the concept **Ego**.

I think this solution is basically correct, but it raises a problem. If psychological modes of presentation are not conventionally associated with linguistic expression, how are we to account for the intuition that they are 'directly expressed' by indexical expressions, as McGinn says? There seems to be a very intimate relationship between an indexical expression and the egocentric concept (psychological mode of presentation) associated with that expression.

This seems hardly consistent with the view under discussion. According to this view, the utterance 'I am French' means that *the speaker* is French, and expresses the first-person thought that **Ego** is French merely because (it is manifest that) the speaker thinks 'the speaker = **Ego**'. The association between the first person and the category **Ego** is only *normal*, on this view: it depends on the speaker's realizing that he or she is the speaker. To be sure, the speaker normally realizes that he or she is the speaker, but it is possible for him or her not to realize this, as we saw earlier. Thus, far from capturing the intimate relationship between the first person and the concept **Ego**, the view under discussion makes the tie between the expression and the associated psychological mode of presentation rather loose and shaky.

I think the intimate connection between indexical expressions and egocentric concepts can be accounted for within the theory of *de re* modes of presentation to be put forward in chapters 6 and 7. We shall see that *de re* modes of presentation, of which egocentric concepts are a particular variety, are best conceived of as dossiers of information. Egocentric concepts are distinguished by their specific function: they are used to register information *gained in a certain way*. An egocentric concept is associated with a particular way of gaining information, and serves as a repository for information gained in that way. Now the fact that a given piece of information is gained in a certain way, and registered as such by being filed into an egocentric concept, makes certain thoughts 'immune to error through misidentification' (Schoemaker, 1968). This is so because the way the information is gained determines what it is about. Thus there is a first-person way of gaining information, and information gained in the first-person way can only be about oneself. Hence a thought to the effect that some information (gained in the first-person way) is about oneself is immune to error through misidentification. The information may be mistaken (it may be misinformation), but the thinker cannot be wrong when he takes it to be information (or misinformation) *about himself*. It is that property of immunity to misidentification which, I believe, accounts for the intimate link between indexical expressions and egocentric concepts. Let us see how the explanation proceeds.

Criticizing Wittgenstein, who implicitly restricted the notion of immunity to misidentification to self-ascriptions of mental properties, Evans has shown that it also applies to self-ascriptions of *physical* properties. Beliefs such as 'My legs are crossed', when they are acquired in the normal, kinaesthetic way ('from the inside', as one might say), *are* immune to error through misidentification, in the following sense: the information that someone's legs are crossed (i.e. the information that the predicate ξ*'s legs are crossed* is instantiated) is not given independently of, and cannot be dissociated from, the information that *I* am the person whose legs are crossed; hence it does not make sense to ask: 'Someone's legs are crossed, but is it I whose legs are crossed?' As Evans says, 'there just does not appear to be a gap between the subject's having information (or appearing to have information), in the appropriate way, that the property of being F is instantiated, and his having information (or appearing to have information) that *he* is F' (Evans, 1982, p. 221). To be sure, the same belief will not have the property of immunity to error through misidentification if it is *not* formed in the normal way. If, when anaesthetized, I see my legs in a mirror and discover that they are crossed, I gain the belief that my legs are crossed, but this belief may be erroneous through misidentification: I may have misidentified the person whose legs are crossed (I may have been right in forming the belief that someone's legs were crossed, but wrong in equating that person with myself). In that case, there is a gap between the information that the predicate is instantiated and the information that it is I who instantiate the predicate. Yet in the other case (when the belief is formed in the normal way, 'from the inside'), there is no such gap. If it turns out that I was mistaken in believing that *my* legs were crossed, I have no longer any reason to believe that *anyone's* legs are crossed. As Evans (1982, p. 221) puts it:

> We cannot think of the kinaesthetic and proprioceptive system as gaining *knowledge* of truths about the condition of a body which leaves the question of the identity of the body open. If the subject does not know that *he* has his legs bent (say) on this basis . . . , then he does not know *anything* on this basis. (To judge that *someone* has his legs bent would be a wild shot in the dark.)

The same thing can obviously be said of the belief that I am the person uttering the words now being uttered. When it is acquired in the normal way, this belief is immune to error through misidentification. The information that someone is uttering this token is not given independently of (and cannot be dissociated from) the information that *I* am uttering this token. Hence, the concept of 'utterer of this token' (i.e. the linguistic mode of presentation of the reference of 'I') cannot be dissociated from that of **Ego** (i.e. from the corresponding psychological mode of presentation), in a normal situation. This is so from the point of view of the speaker, of course; but it is manifest that this is so, hence it is manifest that an utterance in the first person expresses a thought involving the concept **Ego**.

The property of immunity to misidentification accounts for the intuition that psychological modes of presentation are directly expressed by indexical expressions. That intuition comes from the fact that, in a normal situation, there is 'no gap' between the concept that constitutes the linguistic mode of presentation (e.g. that of utterer of this token) and the concept that constitutes the psychological mode of presentation (**Ego**). The linguistic mode of presentation is conventionally associated with the expression, and there is no gap between the psychological mode of presentation and the linguistic mode of presentation; it follows that the association between the expression and the psychological mode of presentation is as direct as possible (from the speaker's point of view) – as direct as it would be if it were conventional, even though it is *not* conventional.

What I have just said can be generalized to the various psychological modes of presentation associated with indexical expressions. In the same way as the belief that I (**Ego**) am uttering these words is immune to error through misidentification when it is acquired in the normal way, the belief that this token is being uttered now (**Nunc**), or here (**Hic**), is also immune to error through misidentification when it is acquired in the normal way: there is no gap between the information that this token is uttered and the information that it is uttered here and now. (If it turned out that I were wrong in forming the latter belief, I would have no reason to retain the former.) This shows that in a normal situation the egocentric concepts, or psychological modes of presentation, **Hic** and **Nunc** are indissociable from the linguistic modes of presentation 'place at which this token is uttered' and 'time at which this token is uttered', in the same way as the concept **Ego** is indissociable from the linguistic mode of presentation 'utterer of this token'.

## 5.5 Conclusion

As I said in conclusion of chapter 4, there is a fundamental heterogeneity of linguistic and psychological modes of presentation in *de re* communication: linguistic modes of presentation are essentially descriptive, while psychological modes of presentation are non-descriptive. (The sense in which the psychological modes of presentation involved in *de re* communication are non-descriptive will be elaborated in chapter 6). That heterogeneity must be overcome for language to connect up with thought. In the second part of this book, using tools available from linguistic pragmatics, I will consider how it is overcome. I shall elaborate the view that, in *de re* communication, the linguistic mode of presentation corresponds to some information contained in the dossier which constitutes the psychological mode of presentation. Thus the relation between the two modes of presentation will turn out to be the part-whole relation, and the connection between them will be described as established through a pragmatic process of synecdoche.

In this framework two interesting distinctions can be made:

1  When an expression conveys the feature REF as part of its meaning, the pragmatic process of synecdoche is mandatory because it is 'marked' at the level of linguistic meaning. But the same process may also take place without being linguistically triggered. The referential use of definite descriptions will thus be analysed as involving an *optional* process of synecdoche taking the interpreter from the descriptive concept expressed by the description to a *de re* concept – a dossier – which includes the descriptive concept as constituent (chapter 15).
2  The dossier may be either an egocentric concept or an encyclopedia entry (7.4). If the dossier is an egocentric concept, and the linguistic mode of presentation corresponds to information gained through the 'fundamental epistemic relation' on which the concept is based, then the concept (or rather the 'category' which it instantiates) is associated with the expression in a very intimate manner. It is this special case which I dealt with in this chapter. The nature of the egocentric concepts which are associated with indexical expressions through the mechanism described in this chapter will be explored in chapter 7.

## Notes

1  Or in conjunction with an appropriate manifestation of intention on the part of the speaker, as Kaplan acknowledges in his 'Afterthoughts' (Kaplan, 1989b, p. 582ff).

2  The sort of issues which this example raises are discussed by John Perry in his article, 'A Problem about Continued Belief' (Perry, 1980b).
3  The reason why this is so cannot be expounded at this stage of our enquiry, for we have not yet established the nature of *de re* modes of presentation (see chapters 6–7). Let me anticipate a bit, however. We shall see in chapter 7 that the mental counterpart of a pure indexical is an egocentric concept, that is, a concept based on what Perry calls a fundamental epistemic relation between the subject and the objects which fall under that concept. Now to account for the impossibility mentioned in the text it is sufficient to note, which Christopher Peacocke (1981, pp. 195–6), that the egocentric concepts associated with pure indexicals have the following property: the fundamental epistemic relation on which such a concept is based uniquely determines an object, in the sense that one cannot bear that relation to different objects at the same time.
4  McGinn claims that we cannot afford to reject this thesis, because to do so would be to 'sever the tie between the structure of thoughts and the structure of sentence meaning' (McGinn, 1983, p. 65). There is some exaggeration here. What cannot be denied, without severing the tie between sentence meaning and thought, is that there must be something common to all the thoughts expressed by uttering a sentence with a given expression like 'I'. But, one might argue, that common element need not be a common *conceptual* element – a constituent of the thought. What is common to all thoughts expressed by 'I' *might* be the mere fact that these thoughts are all about the person who utters the sentence; this is something common to all these thoughts, but is it a common 'conceptual' element, i.e. something internal to the thought? I can imagine someone arguing that it is not. In any event, whether or not we accept the thesis of psycho-semantic parallelism construed as an a priori principle, what McGinn calls the 'naive view suggested by indexical word meaning' sounds intuitively correct at least as far as pure indexicals are concerned. It seems that there are ways of thinking which correspond to linguistic expressions such as 'here', and which are constant from one occurrence of the expression to the next.
5  Note that what I am calling psychological modes of presentation are already 'types' in some sense. I said earlier that 'I think of myself under the same first-person mode of presentation when I say "I" as you do when you say "I"' (4.4). Psychological modes of presentation in this sense clearly are types, not tokens. Like the narrow contents of which they are constituents, they are not tied to a particular context. They acquire a 'semantic value' (determine a reference) only with respect to a particular context, however. In this respect they are very different from Fregean senses. It is only particular *tokens* of a psychological mode of presentation which resemble Fregean senses, in this respect. (On the

type/token distinction with regard to psychological modes of presentation, see Peacocke (1981, para. 1); see also below, 6.2.) Thus there are three things to distinguish: (i) psychological modes of presentation are like Fregean senses in that they satisfy Frege's constraint but, unlike them, they do not determine a reference (a semantic value) independent of context. They are narrowly individuated, like the narrow contents of which they are constituents. Psychological modes of presentation in this sense are constantly associated with pure indexicals. (ii) Demonstratives may perhaps be said to be constantly associated with *types* or *sorts* of psychological modes of presentation in the sense of (i), which types or sort do not satisfy Frege's constraint. (iii) Particular *instances (tokens)* of psychological modes of presentation in the sense of (i) satisfy Frege's constraint *and* determine a semantic value (a reference). Like the complete thoughts of which they are constituents, token modes of presentation can be given a two-component analysis, as Peacocke suggested: they involve a psychological mode of presentation (in the sense of (i)) plus a contextually determined semantic value.

This threefold distinction is still not sufficient, however. As McGinn rightly pointed out in the passage quoted, we must make a further distinction between psychological modes of presentation, for example the concept of spatial vicinity (i.e. the concept constantly expressed by 'here'), and our *conception* of the place where we are on a particular occasion. What McGinn calls our 'conception', that is, the 'body of information' which we associate with our indexically identified object of thought (together, presumably, with the indexical notion under which that information falls) is what varies from one occurrence of 'It would be nice to have dinner here' to the next in the example discussed above. We are to imagine two utterances of this sentence which are made in reference to the same place but which are believed to be made in reference to two different places. The same person assents to the first utterance but dissents from the second one. In this situation, Frege's constraint does not dictate that there be two distinct psychological modes of presentation of the place referred to, because the judgements are made at different times. Still, we may say that two distinct 'conceptions' are involved: there are two distinct bodies of information which the person who makes the two conflicting judgements associates respectively with the two tokens of 'here', which bodies of information turn out to be about the same place. Although I cannot elaborate this point here, I believe that McGinn's 'conceptions' are not the same thing as token psychological modes of presentation (although they involve token modes of presentation). In chapter 7 I will make a distinction between egocentric categories (which are psychological modes of presentation in the sense of this chapter), egocentric concepts (which are token modes of presentation), and a third thing, namely 'egocentric concepts saturated by information'. The latter correspond to McGinn's 'conceptions'.

6 Insofar as it is identical to the (type of) psychological mode of presentation, the linguistic mode of presentation would not possess the property of token-reflexivity; but it would retain the two other properties – constancy and conventionality.
7 Note that the intimate connection which exists between indexical expressions and egocentric categories has no obvious counterpart in the demonstrative domain. As we saw, the way the reference of 'this ship' is thought of undergoes considerable variations from context to context, and there is no determinate psychological mode of presentation (i.e. no satisfier of Frege's constraint) which the demonstrative 'this' expresses in the sense in which, say, 'now' expresses the concept of the present. It is an open question whether or not a more abstract *type* of psychological mode of presentation can be said to be associated with a demonstrative expression (as I suggested earlier), while I take it to be a fact that pure indexicals are associated with egocentric categories. It is the latter fact which the theory to be put forward in the next section is intended to account for.
8 This is, roughly, the view held by Evans (1982, pp. 313–15) and Peacocke (1983, pp. 137–9). In his paper 'Demonstrative Thought and Psychological Explanation' (Peacocke, 1981), Peacocke still defended the view that psychological modes of presentation are conventional.

# I.3

## *De re* thoughts

# Chapter 6

# *De re* modes of presentation

## 6.1 Introduction

By a 'non-descriptive' or '*de re*' thought I mean the type of thought expressed by an utterance in which a referential expression occurs, e.g. the thought that Paul is crazy, or the thought that I am crazy, or the thought that this is crazy. (Of course, these thoughts need not be verbally expressed; they exist whether or not they are expressed.) Such a thought has two dimensions: an objective, truth-conditional content and a subjective, narrow content.[1] The truth-conditional content of a *de re* thought is a singular proposition – indeed, it is the singular proposition expressed by the utterance which literally expresses the thought (Congruence Principle). It thus involves an object – the object which is thought about – rather than a mode of presentation of that object. The thought nevertheless involves a psychological mode of presentation of the reference, as the Fregean argument establishes, but this mode of presentation occurs only in the narrow content of the thought; it affects the thought's cognitive significance but not its truth-conditions. The mode of presentation of the reference which occurs in the narrow content of a *de re* thought I call a non-descriptive or *de re* mode of presentation.

So far I have not said much about non-descriptive or *de re* modes of presentation. The only property I ascribed to them is that of truth-conditional irrelevance (i.e. the fact that they do not affect the truth-conditions of the thought in which they occur). I have also indicated how they come to be non-conventionally associated with indexical expressions, via the linguistic modes of presentation conventionally expressed by the latter (chapter 5). But what exactly are non-descriptive modes of presentation? Is truth-conditional irrelevance their only defining characteristic? Are there other non-descriptive modes of presentation besides those that are associated with indexical expressions? These are some of the questions I want to address in this and the next chapter.

I will start by discussing Evans's and McDowell's objections to the notion that non-descriptive modes of presentation occur at the level of 'narrow content'. On their view, non-descriptive modes of presentation are 'object-dependent' modes of presentation which cannot be narrowly individuated. I will try to show that this view is not significantly different from that which it rejects, and which I will take for granted. Beyond these notational differences, the central feature of non-descriptive modes of presentation is, I shall argue, their *relational* character. I will then enquire into the relationship between this and two other features: truth-conditional irrelevance and iconicity. In the next chapter, I will make a distinction between two types of *de re* modes of presentation: egocentric categories (i.e. the psychological modes of presentation associated with indexical expressions) and encyclopedia entries. Egocentric categories, I shall argue, are essentially tied to perception.

## 6.2 Non-descriptiveness and relationality

Evans's and McDowell's non-descriptive modes of presentation or '*de re* senses', as they call them, are Fregean senses: they are thought-constituents and they determine an object as their corresponding reference. Their distinctive feature is their *object-dependence*: they would not exist if the corresponding reference did not exist.[2] Intuitively a *de re* sense can be characterized as a mode of donation of the reference, a manner in which the reference is given to the thinker. Perception is an example: through perception an object is given to us, and the perception of the object, which is the way it is given to us, would not exist if the object itself did not exist. When no object is given – when, for example, the thinker is hallucinating and there is no object he is actually perceiving, contrary to what he believes – there can be no 'manner in which the object is given': no reference entails no (*de re*) sense. In the hallucinatory situation, there is no thought (since a *de re* thought, i.e. a thought including a *de re* sense, inherits the object-dependence of the latter), but only an illusion of thought. By contrast, a descriptive mode of presentation is such that the thought in which it occurs is not affected by the non-existence of the reference. The thought that the actual King of France is F does not depend for its existence on the existence of an actual King of France.

There is another notion of non-descriptive or *de re* mode of presentation current in the philosophical literature, which (for reasons that will become apparent) we may call the 'narrow' notion. It can be found in the writings of e.g. Peacocke, Perry, McGinn, Bach and Searle. In my discussion of this notion I will mostly use Kent Bach's lucid presentation (Bach, 1987).

Bach's *de re* modes of presentation are thought-constituents, but they do not determine an object, like genuine Fregean senses. A *de re* mode of presentation determines a reference *only with respect to a context*, according to Bach. On this view, *de re* modes of presentation themselves (and the *de re* thoughts of which they are constituents) are context-independent. This means in particular 'that they can (and should) be individuated narrowly, without mention of their objects' (Bach, 1987, p. 12). Thus if I perceive an apple in front of me and think that it is green, there occurs in my thought a (perceptual) mode of presentation which is the same whether the apple I perceive is apple A or apple B, provided they are qualitatively indistinguishable; the apple which I perceive is part of the context, and my thought, narrowly construed, is independent of the context. My thought, narrowly construed, is not affected if (unbeknown to me) one apple is substituted for the other while I am thinking 'This apple is green'. The thought is also the same if there actually is no apple and I am hallucinating.

What, then is the difference between descriptive and *de re* modes of presentation, on Bach's account, if *de re* modes of presentation are not object-dependent? According to Bach, the difference between descriptive and *de re* modes of presentation is this:

> The object of a descriptive thought is determined SATISFACTORILY, [hence] the fact that the thought is of that object does not require any connection between thought and object. However, the object of *de re* thought is determined RELATIONALLY. For something to be the object of a *de re* thought, it must stand in a certain kind of relation to that very thought.... *De re* modes of presentation function as mental indexicals. They determine the contextual relation that something must bear to a thought to be the object of that thought. (Bach, 1987, p. 12)

Let us see to what extent the two notions really differ. For one thing, Bach's *de re* modes of presentation are types, not tokens. A mode of presentation is said not to determine the reference because, as a type, it does not determine the reference: it does so only as a token, i.e. with respect to a context. So it is with *tokens* of *de re* modes of presentation *à la* Bach that *de re* senses *à la* Evans and McDowell must be compared. *Qua* tokens, Bach's *de re* modes of presentation do determine an object, like genuine Fregean senses. And, *qua* tokens, it might be argued that they are object-dependent (in a certain sense). Suppose a situation in which I perceive a certain apple in front of me. According to Bach, there occurs in my thought a token τ of the *de re* mode of presentation 'this apple'. Other tokens of this mode of presentation might have occurred in thoughts caused by other apples as well as in hallucinatory thoughts caused by no apple, but, *qua* token, it might be argued that τ is individuated in part by the apple of which it is the perceptual representation, i.e. by the apple which is actually perceived (say apple A). Had another, qualitatively indistinguishable apple been perceived instead of A, it is not clear that τ itself could be said to have existed. On these lines, it can be argued that τ is object-dependent, contrary to the type of which it is a token.

The object-dependence I have just mentioned is fairly weaker than that which Evans and McDowell talk about, however. Let us assume that the token τ is indeed object-dependent: *qua* token, it would not have existed had the perceived object been numerically different. Not all tokens of a *de re* mode of presentation in Bach's sense are object-dependent in this way: it is only the tokens that are actually caused by their objects in perception that depend on these objects for their individuation. But think of the hallucinatory situation: there we have a token of the *same* (type of) *de re* mode of presentation which is not caused by its object since it has no object in reality. Not having an object, the token cannot be object-dependent.[3] The fact that some tokens at least are not object-dependent shows that object-dependence in this framework is not an essential feature of *de re* modes of presentation. *Qua* types, *de re* modes of presentation in Bach's sense are individuated narrowly, without mention of their objects, nor even of the fact that they have an object. But a type (a 'sort') of *de re* sense for Evans and McDowell is a *class* of *de re* senses all of which have the property of object-dependence: it is a property of a sort of *de re* sense that a sense of this sort is object-dependent.[4]

Because of what I have just said, we cannot identify tokens of *de re* modes of presentation in Bach's sense with Evans's and McDowell's *de re* senses. In hallucination, there is no *de re* sense (because there is no *res*) but there is a token of *de re* mode of presentation in Bach's sense. But we might be tempted to identify Evans's and McDowell's *de re* senses with *successful* tokens of *de re* modes of presentation in Bach's sense. A *de re* mode of presentation in Bach's sense determines the contextual relation that something must bear to a token of that mode of presentation to be the object (the reference) of that token; let us say that a token is 'successful' just in case there is an object which actually bears that relation to the token. A successful token, by definition, has a reference; it is therefore object-dependent.

On the view I have just sketched, it seems that a *de re* mode of presentation in Bach's sense (henceforth to be called a 'mental indexical', for clarity's sake) is simply an aspect of what Evans and McDowell call a *de re* sense. A mental indexical is the subjective component of a *de re* sense. The other component is objective and contextual: it is the fact that a certain relation holds between the mode of presentation (token) and an object. If the contextual component is lacking, the mental indexical is not successful.

McDowell would not accept this way of putting the matter. He rejects the idea that a *de re* sense can be analysed in terms of a mode of presentation narrowly construed (a mental indexical) together with contextual factors. He does not deny that there may be something common to a thought involving the perception of an apple and to the pseudo-thought of a *Doppelgänger* who hallucinates a qualitatively indistinguishable apple, but he denies this putative element the status of a thought-constituent: it is not 'an *aspect* or *ingredient* of content', he says, but 'a putative *bearer* or *vehicle* of content' (McDowell, 1984, p. 103n). In this framework, a mental indexical is nothing more than a mental *symbol* which expresses a *de re* sense with respect to a certain type of context and which expresses nothing with respect to other types of contexts (the hallucinatory case). To say that a mental indexical is successful is to say that it occurs in a context with respect to which it expresses a content (a *de re* sense). But the mental indexical is not an ingredient, an aspect of content, any more than a linguistic expression is part of the Fregean sense which it may contextually express.

I will criticize McDowell's main reason for rejecting the two-component analysis of *de re* senses in chapter 12. This reason is McDowell's fear of what he calls 'the Cartesian danger' (McDowell,

1986, p. 161). I will show that accepting mental indexicals as genuine ingredients of content does not commit us to Cartesianism, so that McDowell's fear is unfounded. Be that as it may, even if McDowell is right to hold that a mental indexical cannot be considered as an *ingredient* of a *de re* sense, this does not prevent one from analyzing *de re* senses in terms of successful mental indexicals. A *de re* sense can be straightforwardly equated with what a successful mental indexical expresses. So it seems that the two views are more or less intertranslatable ('notational variants', as Evans says[5]).

McDowell (1984, p. 104n) claims that there is a substantive issue at stake, however. He approvingly quotes McGinn who situates it as follows:

> The question is whether [the sense of a (token) indexical, i.e. what determines reference] can be construed as a conceptual content or whether appeal must be made to extra-conceptual (i.e. contextual) factors. The thrust of Perry's position, which Evans takes himself to be criticizing, is precisely that indexical thoughts differ from descriptive thoughts inasmuch as conceptual content determines reference in the latter case but not in the former. Unless the issue is seen in this light, the dispute between supporters and critics of Frege will degenerate into an uninteresting verbal quarrel about the word 'sense'. (McGinn, 1983, p. 68 n.17)

Thanks to the distinction between thought-*symbols* which express content and the thought-*content* which is thereby expressed, McDowell is able to save Frege's thesis that *content (sense) determines reference* even in the non-descriptive case. Appeal must be made to contextual factors only at a prior level, that of thought-symbols. A sequence of thought-symbols, if it includes a mental indexical, expresses a complete thought-content only with respect to a context, but the content in question does not need to be relativized to a context in order to determine reference. Those who criticize Frege because they believe his framework cannot accommodate non-descriptive thoughts are guilty of a conflation, that between thought-content (which by itself determines reference) and thought-symbols (which may need a context to express a complete content).

But I do not see why this is not a verbal issue. The philosophers who say that a *de re* thought determines a reference only with respect to a context use 'thought' or 'conceptual content' in the sense of 'mental sentence'. What McDowell points out is that such 'thoughts' in the sense of mental sentences (= thoughts$_1$) are not thoughts by

Fregean standards (thoughts$_2$)⁶: they are putative vehicles of thought, and the fact that they need a context in order to determine a reference (i.e. in order to express a genuine thought$_2$ which will in turn determine a reference) raises no problem for the Fregean picture, contrary to what Burge, Perry and others mistakenly believe. This point is well-taken, but, again, it is a verbal point concerning the meaning of 'thought' or sense' in Frege's theory. Once this exegetical problem is set aside, nothing prevents one from saying that a *de re* thought$_1$ determines a reference only with respect to a context, contrary to a descriptive thought$_1$ (Burge, 1977). This is a no less satisfactory characterization of the distinction everybody is trying to capture than the neo-Fregean characterization of *de re* thoughts$_2$ as object dependent-thoughts$_2$ (McDowell, 1984). For an object dependent-thought$_2$ is a thought$_2$ which requires a context for its expression: an object-dependent thought$_2$ can be expressed by a thought$_1$ only with respect to a particular context (a context which includes the reference), contrary to an object-independent thought$_2$.

On the whole, the difference between the two views seems to me as thin as that between those theoretical frameworks in which truth and falsity are ascribed to the propositions expressed by sentence tokens and other theoretical frameworks in which they are directly ascribed to these tokens themselves. Be that as it may, I am more interested in what is common to the two views than with their difference.⁷ What is common seems to me this: a *de re* mode of presentation – be it a successful mental indexical or a *de re* sense – involves a certain *relation to* the reference. A *de re* thought$_2$ (or a successful *de re* thought$_1$) is empirically related to what it is about.⁸ The apple causes the perception of the apple, and this must be so for there to be a perception of the apple. There is no such empirical relation between descriptive modes of presentation and the reference: there need be no causal connection between the strongest man in the world and my thoughts about the strongest man in the world.⁹

## 6.3 Non-descriptiveness and truth-conditional irrelevance

Besides relationality (i.e. the relational determination of reference), there is another characteristic feature of *de re* modes of presentation: truth-conditional irrelevance. I am now in a position to characterize the latter notion somewhat more explicitly than I did when it was first introduced.

Let us first draw a distinction between the conditions of satisfaction of a representation and its conditions of reference. The latter determine the reference of the representation (what is represented), while the conditions of satisfaction are the conditions which an object must satisfy in order to 'match' the representation, that is, in order to be as depicted by the representation. A photograph is a type of representation characterized by the possibility of a divergence between these two sorts of conditions. The conditions of reference of a photograph involve a causal relation, in the sense that the photograph cannot be of an object unless a certain causal relation holds between the photograph and the object in question. But the conditions of satisfaction of the photograph involve a similarity relation, and it may be that whatever bears the right sort of similarity to the photograph is not causally related to it in the way required for being the reference. All this of course is well-known.

If what I said in the previous section is correct, it is a general fact about non-descriptive representations that they involve a relational, extrinsic condition of reference distinct from the intrinsic condition of satisfaction of the representation. And it is a property of descriptive representations that the two sets of conditions coincide: the conditions of reference of a descriptive representation are its conditions of satisfaction. Thus in order to match the description 'the strongest man in the world', that is, in order to be as depicted by the description, an object must be the strongest man in the world – in the same way as, in order to be as depicted by a certain photograph, an object must possess certain features. But in order to be the reference of the description 'the strongest man in the world', the *same* condition must be satisfied: being the strongest man in the world is the reference determining condition for the description, while the conditions of reference of a photograph do not coincide with its conditions of satisfaction, as we have seen. The two sets of conditions diverge whenever the reference is determined 'relationally' rather than 'satisfactionally', as Bach says.

The divergence between the two sets of conditions associated with non-descriptive representations makes the notion of truth-conditional *ir*relevance somehow equivocal. Descriptive representations are truth-conditionally relevant in the following sense: the condition which is both the condition of satisfaction and the condition of reference of the representation is clearly part of the truth-conditions of the thought where it occurs. For the thought "The strongest man in the world is F" to be true, the condition 'being the strongest man in the world' must be satisfied by someone; this thought cannot be true with respect to a world in which there is no strongest man. However, the claim that non-descriptive representations are truth-conditionally irrelevant may be understood in different ways, as there are two sets of conditions to be distinguished. A non-descriptive representation may be said to be truth-conditionally *ir*relevant either because the condition of satisfaction of the representation is not among the truth-conditions of the thought in which the representation occurs, or because the condition of reference is not among the truth-conditions.

Despite what I have just said, I do not think there is a real need for two distinct notions of truth-conditional irrelevance, for *both* the condition of satisfaction and the condition of reference of a representation are external to the truth-conditions of the thought in which the representation occurs, when the latter is non-descriptive. Take our standard representation of Jonah. It includes the feature 'man having being swallowed by a fish'. However, the thought that Jonah was a vegetarian may be true even though Jonah was never swallowed by a fish. Having been swallowed by a fish is a condition of satisfaction of our representation of Jonah – it is an internal feature of our representation – but it is not among the truth-conditions of the thoughts in which that representation occurs, as Kripke has shown (Kripke, 1980, p. 67). That, I think, is obvious. What is perhaps less obvious is the fact that the relational condition of reference (i.e. 'being the causal source of Jonah-related (mis)information') *is not among the truth-conditions either*. That Jonah was a vegetarian is the content of the thought that Jonah was a vegetarian; now it might be true that Jonah was a vegetarian even if no information concerning him had ever reached us. There are possible worlds in which Jonah was a vegetarian and the Bible was never written, and still other worlds in which Jonah was a vegetarian but we do not exist. With respect to such worlds, the thought that Jonah was a vegetarian is true even though, in those worlds, he is *not* the causal source of any information or misinformation in our possession.

Many philosophers have trouble realizing that the conditions of reference of a non-descriptive representation are not among the truth conditions of the thoughts in which that representation occurs because the conditions of reference of the representation clearly *determine* the truth-conditions of the thought in which the representation occurs. The conditions of reference of the representation determine its reference, and the reference of the representation is part of the truth-conditions of the thought. The conditions of reference thus determine the truth-conditional content of the thought, but, I maintain, they are not an *aspect* of this truth-conditional content – they are not conditions that have to be satisfied for the thought to be true, but conditions that have to be satisfied for the thought in question (in the non-Fregean sense: 'thought$_1$') to have the truth-conditions which it actually has, or for the thought in the Fregean sense ('thought$_2$') to be expressed, had or entertained. The important point is that it is perfectly possible for a *de re* thought to be true 'with respect to' (or 'of') a world in which the relational condition of reference is not satisfied. The thought "This apple is F" is true if and only if the apple in question – say, A – is F, whether or not it causes the subject's perception of A, indeed whether or not the subject in question exists.

Truth-conditional irrelevance can now be defined. For the representation of an object to be truth-conditionally irrelevant, the truth-conditions of the thought in which that representation occurs must be singular and involve the object itself (the reference) *independent of its satisfying either set of conditions*. Neither the conditions of satisfaction of the representation nor its conditions of reference are among the truth-conditions of the thought, when the representation is truth-conditionally irrelevant. I take truth-conditional irrelevance thus understood to be a fundamental property of non-descriptive modes of presentation.

### 6.4 Truth-conditional irrelevance and relationality

Is it possible for a mode of presentation to be truth-conditionally irrelevant without essentially involving a relation to the reference? If that were possible, we would have to make a distinction between two varieties of non-descriptiveness: a strong variety, characterized by the conjunction of relationality and truth-conditional irrelevance, and a weak variety characterized by the latter feature alone. David Kaplan apparently thinks that such a distinction is in order, for he writes:

> I was mistaken in 'Quantifying In' in thinking that the most fundamental cases of what I might now describe as a person having a propositional attitude (believing, asserting, etc.) toward a singular proposition required that the person be *en rapport* with the subject of the proposition. It is now clear that I can assert *of* the first child

to be born in the twenty-first century that *he* will be bald, simply by uttering: *Dthat ['the first child to be born in the twenty-first century'] will be bald.* (Kaplan, 1978, p. 241)

According to Kaplan, the reference of "Dthat (the F)" is determined satisfactorily, not relationally – it is whatever satisfies the enclosed description – but the descriptive condition which fixes the reference is not among the truth-conditions of the utterance; the truth-conditions involve only the referent and the property of being bald. If this is right, then we can have truth-conditional irrelevance without relationality: it is *not* necessary for a mode of presentation to be truth-conditionally irrelevant that the reference be determined relationally. On this view, there are two varieties of non-descriptiveness: the standard variety, characterized by the conjunction of relationality and truth-conditional irrelevance, and a weaker variety characterized merely by truth-conditional irrelevance. The thought expressed by the utterance 'Dthat (the first baby to be born in the twenty-first century) will be bald' is non-descriptive or *de re* only in the weaker sense, in Kaplan's framework.

Kaplan's example is very similar to what Evans calls 'descriptive names'.[10] A descriptive name is a proper name whose reference is fixed by means of an attributive definite description – e.g. 'Julius' as a name given to whoever invented the zip ('Jack the Ripper' and 'Neptune' are real life examples of this phenomenon). Insofar as proper names are directly referential expressions which we use to say something *of* an object (thereby expressing a singular proposition), Evans's descriptive names give rise to the same sort of paradox as 'Dthat'-expressions with an attributive description enclosed; in both cases it seems that the mode of presentation of the reference must be descriptive and non-descriptive at the same time. On the one hand the expression (whether a proper name or a 'Dthat'-expression) is directly referential, and this entails that the mode of presentation under which the reference is thought of is truth-conditionally irrelevant (since the truth-conditions of an utterance including a directly referential expression must be singular). On the other hand the mode of presentation is 'descriptive' in the sense that the reference is thought of as whatever satisfies the associated description. In order to avoid the contradiction it seems that one has to make a distinction between the two sorts of non-descriptiveness: that based on truth-conditional irrelevance, and the stronger variety based on relationality.

I will show later (10.4) that there is another way of disposing of the problem raised by descriptive names, so that we do not really need the distinction between the two sorts of non-descriptiveness. This is fortunate for the claim that the mode of presentation of the reference of 'Julius' is non-descriptive in some sense strikes me as very implausible. It is implausible because the thought expressed by "The inventor of the zip, whoever he is, is F" is clearly descriptive in the fullest possible sense: the mode of presentation in this case is neither relational nor truth-conditionally irrelevant. Now it is implausible to suggest that one's thought can be significantly changed simply by changing the way it is expressed – simply by coining a name for whoever invented the zip. Thus I am in complete agreement with Evans when he writes:

> The thought expressed by 'Julius is F' may equivalently be expressed by 'The inventor of the zip is F'... Someone who understands and accepts the one sentence as true gets himself into exactly the same belief state as someone who accepts the other. Belief states are distinguished by the evidence which gives rise to them, and the expectations, behaviour, and further beliefs which may be derived from them (in conjunction with other beliefs); and in all these respects, the belief states associated with the two sentences are indistinguishable. We do not produce new thoughts (new beliefs) simply by 'a stroke of the pen' (in Grice's phrase) – simply by introducing a new name into the language. (Evans, 1982, p. 50)

Kaplan may be right as far as *utterances* are concerned; it may be that someone who *says* "Julius is F" in the envisaged situation says *of* Julius that he is F, thereby asserting a singular proposition. However, we should by all means refrain from extending this view to *thoughts*. For someone who *thinks* "Julius is F" (or, for that matter, 'Dthat [the inventor of the zip] is bald') can only be entertaining a fully descriptive thought, namely the same thought as he would be entertaining if he thought "The inventor of the zip is F". The mode of presentation of the reference is in both cases the same, and this provides a good reason for insisting that it is straightforwardly descriptive, hence neither relational nor truth-conditionally irrelevant. I conclude that we need not make a distinction between two varieties of non-descriptiveness.[11] We do not have strongly non-descriptive modes of presentation characterized by the conjunction of relationality and truth-conditional irrelevance and weakly non-descriptive modes of presentation characterized merely by the property of truth-conditionally irrelevance. The two properties go together and cannot be separated. Non-descriptive modes of presentation have both, and descriptive modes of presentation have neither.

## 6.5 Non-descriptiveness as descriptive multiplicity

Another attempt can be made to show that there is a weaker notion of non-descriptiveness which does not involve the property of relationality. Consider, again, descriptive names like 'Julius'. In chapter 10 I shall argue that such a name is created in anticipation of a time at which it will be possible to think of its reference non-descriptively: when we create such a name, we suppose that we shall come to know the reference and be in a position to entertain *de re* thoughts about it. This is what happened, for example, in the case of 'Neptune', when the referent of the name was actually discovered. When such a 'discovery' occurs, the name is no longer a descriptive name; it becomes an ordinary name for the thing in question. Now, the question I want to ask is this: When – at which stage in the process of its becoming an ordinary name – are we entitled to say that the reference of a descriptive name has ceased to be thought of in a *purely* descriptive manner? Not only, one is tempted to reply, when the thinker has got 'acquainted' with the referent, i.e. when she is able to think of the referent under a *de re* mode of presentation involving an empirical relation to the referent. For the referent to be thought of non-descriptively, it seems to be sufficient that the thinker acquire what Grice calls a 'dossier' for the definite description used to fix the reference.

In Grice's framework, 'X has a dossier for a definite description δ if there is a set of definite descriptions which includes δ, all the members of which X supposes . . . to be satisfied by one and the same item' (Grice, 1969, p. 140). Suppose the speaker has acquired such a dossier for the definite description used to fix the reference of a descriptive name; suppose she has acquired the information that Julius – the inventor of the zip – is also the first president of a certain bank, the man who married the author of *Tu l'as dit, petit* (Strasbourg, 1920), and the satisfier of a number of other descriptions. Suppose, further, that this information has come to be associated with the name 'Julius' in such a way that the description 'the inventor of the zip' has lost its privileged status of (unique) referent-fixer. The name 'Julius' is now a name for the man about whom there exists a certain dossier of information, which includes (but is not limited to) the description 'the inventor of the zip'. At this stage, *an utterance such as "Julius is F" is no longer associated with the descriptive thought expressed by the same utterance in which 'Julius' is replaced by 'the inventor of the zip'*. For any description *d* in the dossier, *including the description 'the inventor of the zip'*, the thinker may come to think that *d* is a misfit in the dossier, i.e. that it 'is not, after all, satisfied by the same item' as that which satisfies the majority of, or each member of a specially favoured subset of, the descriptions in the dossier' (*ibid.*, p. 142); and he may, as a result of this thought, come to think that Julius was not, after all, the inventor of the zip. Such a thought would have been contradictory in the earlier phase, when 'Julius' was a descriptive name associated, not with a complete dossier, but with a single description used to fix its reference. It is no longer contradictory once there is a dossier.

In the situation I have described, the thinker is not acquainted with the referent; she knows Julius only 'by description(s)'. Nor has a causal link necessarily got established between the thinker and the referent in order for her to gather the descriptions constituting the dossier: we may suppose she got them through magic or divination. Nevertheless, in the situation I have described, the introductory, reference-fixing description gets subordinated to the dossier and loses its privileged status: the name becomes associated with the dossier rather than with the description which initiated it. As a result of this subordination, the truth-conditions of a thought "Julius is F" no longer involve the satisfaction of the description 'the inventor of the zip' (nor, it may be argued, does it involve the satisfaction of any particular description in the dossier), and it makes sense to think that, perhaps, it was not Julius who invented the zip (or, for some other description in the dossier, to think that Julius does not after all fit that description). This certainly gives a sense in which Julius is thought of non-descriptively in this situation, even if the thinker is not acquainted with Julius. *Non-descriptiveness, here, seems to arises from sheer descriptive multiplicity.*[12]

Does this example really show that it is possible for a mode of presentation to be non-descriptive without involving a relation to the reference? I can imagine two ways of resisting this conclusion. First, one can maintain that the mode of presentation in this example is descriptive, and argue that the description which fixes the reference and which occurs in the truth-conditions is not any one of the descriptions in the dossier, but rather a meta-description such as

'Whatever satisfies most of the descriptions in the dossier'. I do not find this line of argument very promising, so I shall leave it aside.[13] But there is another counter-argument which I find rather convincing. It consists in denying that the reference of 'Julius' in the envisaged situation is determined in a purely 'satisfactional' (rather than 'relational') manner. This enables one to block the conclusion that there is a weak form of non-descriptiveness which does not involve the property of relationality, without having to deny that the mode of presentation of the reference is non-descriptive in the dossier example.

The structure of the argument is as follows:

1 The reason why the reference seems to be thought of in an essentially 'non-descriptive' manner in this example, even though the thinker knows the referent only 'by description', is that none of the descriptions which are available to the thinker (i.e. none of the descriptions in the dossier) occurs in the truth-conditions of the thought "Julius is F".

2 The reason why none of the descriptions in the dossier occurs in the truth-conditions of the thought is the fact that they may all be considered as potential misfits (i.e. for every description $d$ in the dossier, it is conceivable that Julius is not $d$).

3 To be considered as a potential misfit a description has to be taken as *informative* rather than *reference-fixing*; and the reference of an informative (as opposed to a reference-fixing) description is precisely *not* determined in a purely satisfactional manner.

Let me say, first, what I mean by 'informative' and 'reference-fixing'. The reference of an informative description is its *target*: the object it purports to describe, and which is determined independently of its satisfying the description. When a description is informative, it may incorrectly describe its purported reference, and constitute a 'misfit'. But a reference-fixing description has no other reference than the object, if any, which satisfies it; hence there is no possibility of a divergence between what satisfies the description and its purported reference.[14]

In the original situation, when the name 'Julius' is introduced by means of the reference-fixing description 'the inventor of the zip', there is no possibility of misfit. When other descriptions are introduced into the dossier, there are two possibilities: these further descriptions may be taken as reference-fixing (like the first one) or as informative. If the former, the reference – the object corresponding to the dossier – will be determined in a purely satisfactional manner, as whatever satisfies every description in the dossier. In such a case *there is no object corresponding to the dossier unless every description in the dossier is satisfied by one and the same object*; the dossier amounts to nothing other than a long, conjunctive reference-fixing description, and leaves no room for misfit. But some of the new descriptions may also be taken as informative. In this case the reference is considered as fixed and the new descriptions are intended to describe it. If, as it should be, those descriptions are independent from the reference-fixing description – if they cannot be inferred for it – then the grounds for holding them true of the referent can be only this: the referent, i.e. what satisfies the reference-fixing description, has been somehow identified (or is thought to have been identified), and what the other descriptions provide is (or is intended to be) information derived from this object. In other words, for there to be informative rather than mere reference-fixing descriptions in the dossier, *contact must be made with the referent*. To be sure, the contact in question may be very indirect, as when a chain of informants is involved, and it may also be spurious: it may be a pseudo-contact yielding only pseudo-informative descriptions (e.g. descriptions of Julius gathered through magic or divination). But whether or not they are genuinely informative, these descriptions are *intended* to be grounded in the reference itself, and they serve as putative anchors for the whole dossier, by relating it to the object from which the information is supposed to derive. This informative anchoring explains why the initial, reference-fixing description can be freed from its reference-fixing role and be considered as a potential misfit, like any informative description. For what determines the reference is now relational in nature: the referent is, basically, that from which the information derives. I conclude that even those cases in which non-descriptiveness apparently arises from the sheer multiplicity of descriptions are cases in which a relation to the reference is crucially involved.

## 6.6 Non-descriptiveness and iconicity

Besides relationality and truth-conditional irrelevance, are there other important characteristics of non-descriptive or *de re* modes of presentation? The study of perception, the most perspicuous case of non-descriptive thinking, suggests a third important characteristic, namely *iconicity*. Iconic representations are not, or not wholly, conceptual. They include a pictorial element which makes them 'non-descriptive' in a straightforward sense.

The iconicity of perceptual representations may be analysed in terms of three characteristic properties. First, the representation is perspectival: the object is presented from a certain point of view, namely the point of view of the perceiving subject. Second, there is a significant degree of isomorphism between the representation and its object.[15] Third, the representation is analogic in Dretske's sense (Dretske, 1981, p. 135ff). An information about an object is coded in analog form in this sense when it is conveyed by means of a signal which also carries additional information about the represented object.[16] Thus an image of an apple does not merely convey the information that what it pictures is an apple: it also conveys something about e.g. the colour or shape of the apple.

It turns out that there are two sources of non-descriptiveness in perceptual representations, iconicity on the one hand, truth-conditional irrelevance and relationality on the other hand. What is the relation between the two sets of properties? Are they necessarily coinstantiated, as relationality and truth-conditional irrelevance are? I do not think so. Iconic representations are certainly involved in imagination, but the representations in question apparently lack the two properties of truth-conditional irrelevance and relationality. Suppose I imagine (or, for that matter, dream of) a certain car, with extraordinary features. If my representation refers to anything at all, it is to whatever satisfies the content of the representation, i.e. to whatever is a car and has the features possessed by the imagined car. (Thus if I come across a car which matches the imaginary car of my dream, I may say: This is the car I dreamt of last night – or even better: This is *exactly* the car I dreamt of last night.) The 'reference', if there is such a thing here, is determined satisfactionally rather than relationally. The case is very similar to that of an attributive description, except that the representation is not descriptive, but iconic. As in the case of an attributive description, the reference determining condition is part of the truth-conditions of the thought: the truth-conditions of my imaginative thought about the extraordinary car – the conditions under which this thought would come true – certainly involve the satisfaction of the condition which determines what the representation is about, e.g. the condition 'being a car, and having such and such extraordinary features (as in the image)'. In other words, the representation is truth-conditionally relevant even thought it is not 'descriptive' in the most straightforward sense.

If what I have just said is right (and even if it is false – see below), we must distinguish between two senses of 'descriptive' and 'non-descriptive'. In the first sense, which I have just called the most straightforward sense, 'descriptive' is opposed to 'iconic' and is more or less equivalent to 'symbolic' (in the Peircean terminology). A non-descriptive representation in this sense is a representation with the three features I mentioned in connection with iconicity: perspectivalness, isomorphism and analog coding. In the second sense, a non-descriptive representation is a representation with the two characteristic properties of relationality and truth-conditional irrelevance. In perception, the representations involved are non-descriptive in both senses, but this should not obscure the fact that the two varieties of non-descriptiveness may be disjoined, as in imagination. (In order to forestall misunderstanding, I shall henceforth use the label '*de re* representations' when talking about those representations which are non-descriptive in the second sense, i.e. relational and truth-conditionally irrelevant.)

What I have said about imagination is fairly controversial, however. It might be argued that *de re* representations are involved in imagination in the same sense in which *de re* representations are involved in hallucination. Hallucination is parasitic on perception, and this is what makes hallucinatory representations *de re* in some sense: they belong to the category of representations which are normally *res*-involving, hence, considered as representation *types*, they are *de re* even though (*qua* unsuccessful tokens) they are associated with no *res*. At the level of narrow content, they are indistinguishable from standard *de re* representations. In the same way, one might argue, imagination is parasitic on perception and imaginary perceptions *qua* representation types may also be considered as *de re* (that is, the narrow content of the imaginary representation of the extraordinary car may be classified as belonging to the same type as the narrow content of the perception and/or the hallucination of such a car).

I shall not try to settle this issue here. Whatever one thinks of imagination in its relation to perception and hallucination, the distinction between two varieties of non-descriptiveness is forced upon us by the 'dossier' example, which shows that a representation may be non-descriptive in the sense of *de re* without being non-descriptive in the sense of 'iconic' or 'non-symbolic'. The information about Julius which the subject has in the situation I have depicted is purely descriptive in the sense of symbolic: the only thing she knows is that Julius satisfies a certain set of definite descriptions. What makes her way of thinking of him non-descriptive (in the other sense, i.e. *de re*) is the mere fact that those descriptions, *qua* pieces of *information*, ultimately derive (or are intended to derive) from Julius: this is sufficient to establish the relation to the referent which makes a mode of presentation non-descriptive in the sense of *de re*. Still, the situation is different from that in which the information about the referent is non-descriptive 'in the first place', as we might say, i.e. does not consist of *descriptions* of the referent (but consists of perceptions or memories of it). In other words, a distinction must be made between non-descriptive and descriptive information, even if descriptive information, *qua information*, introduces a crucial element of non-descriptiveness into the modes of presentation which are based on it. It follows that the non-descriptive character of modes of presentation based on *non-descriptive* (perceptual) information is somehow overdetermined, as Evans rightly pointed out (Evans, 1982, pp. 132–6). Thus I suggest that we distinguish, within *de re* modes of presentation, between two sub-categories: perception-based modes of presentation, whose non-descriptive character in overdetermined, and *de re* modes of presentation based on descriptive information 'from' the object. The former are strongly non-descriptive while the latter are only weakly so.

In terms of this distinction I think it is possible to provide a characterization of the psychological difference between proper names and indexicals. As I shall argue in chapter 10, the reference of a proper name has to be thought of non-descriptively, under a *de re* mode of presentation, but need not be thought of under a strongly non-descriptive, perception-based mode of presentation. Indexicals, by contrast, are associated with the specific category of perception-based mode of presentation. That is the main thesis of chapter 7.

## Notes

1 A defence of the two-dimensional analysis will be offered in chapters 11–12.
2 *De re* senses were first introduced by McDowell in his paper 'On the sense and reference of a proper name' and opposed to Frege's 'senses', which were supposed to be object-independent (McDowell, 1977,

pp. 172–4). Evans later proposed an interpretation of Frege according to which Frege's senses are *de re* senses (Evans, 1981 and 1982, ch. 1), an interpretation which McDowell endorsed (see e.g. McDowell, 1984, p. 98 and McDowell, 1986, pp. 143–5).

3   Peacocke (1981, pp. 189–90, 197) defines a token mode of presentation in such a way that, if there is no reference, there is no token either. In Peacocke's framework, token modes of presentation cannot fail to be object-dependent in the strong sense. What Peacocke calls a 'token' is what I shall refer to below as a 'successful token'. Peacocke's position is intermediate between that of Evans-McDowell and that of Perry-Bach-McGinn: he accepts 'type modes of presentation' which are narrowly individuated, but his token modes of presentation are strongly object-dependent.

4   On 'sorts of *de re* senses', see 11.2.

5   Evans, 1981, pp. 299–300. McDowell says this is 'a slip on Evans's part' (McDowell, 1984, p. 104n).

6   McDowell holds that they are not thoughts by ordinary standards either.

7   I shall go back to the debate between 'wide' and 'narrow' conceptions of modes of presentation in chapter 11.

8   It may be argued that a Fregean sense, *qua* Platonic entity, cannot enter into causal relations with objects. For this reason a Fregean would rather say that the *thinker* of a *de re* thought is related to the reference. (This characterization raises another issue, that of *de re* thoughts about abstract objects; an issue which I will leave aside in this book.)

9   It may be objected that neo-Fregeans like Evans precisely reject the 'photograph model' according to which what determines reference is not the content of the thought but the contextual, causal relations between the thought and its objects (Evans, 1982, pp. 76–9). In a similar vein McDowell expresses dissatisfaction with the claim that '[in some cases] what matters is not the object's fitting a specification in the content of the thought but its standing in some suitable contextual relation to the episode of thinking' (McDowell, 1986, p. 162). But these critiques have to be properly understood. It is the *sufficiency* of a bare causal relation for determining reference which Evans casts doubt upon; in order to determine an object as what a thought is about the relevant relation must put the thinker in a position to *discriminate* the object in thought. Far from denying that *de re* thoughts, or the thinkers who grasp them, are empirically related to the objects of these thoughts, in contrast to what happens in the descriptive case, Evans and McDowell merely emphasize that these relations between thought (or thinker) and object are *constitutive* of the *de re* thoughts themselves, in such a way that the relational determination of the reference which characterizes *de re* modes of presentation no longer undermines Frege's

principle that *intentional content* determines reference (nor, thus understood, does it undermine Russell's principle, that in order to have a thought about an object you must have discriminating knowledge of that object). In other words, what the neo-Fregeans reject is not the satisfactional vs. relational distinction which theorists in the anti-descriptivist tradition rightly use to characterize *de re* thoughts as opposed to descriptive thoughts; but merely the claim that what determines reference is something *external* to the thought. (Notice that nothing I have said so far entails acceptance of this claim: in the neo-Russellian framework I have sketched, the referent is part of the truth-condition of the *de re* thought; this, together with the view that truth-conditional content is an integral aspect of the thought, entails that the relational determination of the reference is constitutive of the thought.)

10   The issue of descriptive names will be discussed at length in chapter 10.
11   This is not to deny that there *is* a distinction to be made, as far as utterances are concerned, between the 'Julius' type of case, in which the speaker is not in a position to entertain the *de re* thought which he purports to express by using a directly referential expression, and normal cases in which the subject is suitably related to (*en rapport* with) the object she directly refers to. I shall return to this issue in chapter 10, when discussing descriptive names.
12   The view I have just sketched bears an obvious similarity to the Wittgenstein-Searle line about proper names.
13   One reason why I do not find this line of argument promising is this: it assumes without argument that a cognitive system lacking the relevant meta-representations could not be in the envisaged situation. This strikes me as implausible.
14   The distinction between informative and reference-fixing descriptions corresponds to Donnellan's 'referential/attributive' distinction. The latter will be discussed in chapter 15.
15   As many people have insisted, the relevant isomorphism 'should be sought – not in the first-order relation between (a) an individual object, and (b) its internal representation – but in the second-order relation between (a) the relations between alternative external objects, and (b) the relations among their corresponding internal representations' (Shepard & Chipman, 1970, p. 2, quoted in Peacocke, 1989, p. 305; see also Bach, 1970).
16   Peacocke (1983, p. 315) raises the following objection to Dretske's definition of 'analog' and 'digital': 'On this definition, . . . the recording of a particular sentence of the form "John is a bachelor" [would] carry the information that John is a man in analog form'. But Dretske's definition could perhaps be satisfactorily reformulated in terms of what he calls 'primary representation' (Dretske, 1981, p. 160). The definition would thus become: 'A signal which gives primary representation to

the information that *s* is F carries this information in *digital* form if and only if the signal carries no additional information about *s*, no information that is not already nested in *s*'s being F'. In Peacocke's counter-example, the information that John is a man is not given primary representation in Dretske's sense, so it cannot be said to be carried in analog form on the revised definition.

# Chapter 7

# Egocentric concepts vs. encyclopedia entries

## 7.1 Introduction

From what I said in chapter 6 it follows that the general category of *de re* modes of presentation is best characterized in terms of the notion of information: for something to be thought of under a *de re* mode of presentation, the subject must possess information about it. This information may be purely descriptive, provided it is information. (Here I rely on standard accounts of information, according to which there is no information without a causal link between the information-bearer and that which the information concerns.) A *de re* mode of presentation may thus be conceived of as (a pointer to) an information file. *De re* modes of presentation so characterized have two properties: their reference is determined (in part) relationally, as that from which the information derives, and the reference-determining condition is not among the truth-conditions of the thought (truth-conditionally irrelevance). As I have argued at length, there is no weaker notion of *de re* mode of presentation than this.

There is, however, a stronger notion, corresponding to a particular species of *de re* modes of presentation whose non-descriptive character is overdetermined: they are non-descriptive in the sense of *de re*, but they are also non-descriptive in the sense that they essentially involve non-descriptive (iconic) information. Since iconic information is typically information derived from perception, the stronger notion is that of a 'perception-based' mode of presentation. In this chapter, I want to argue that perception-based modes of presentation are the psychological modes of presentation expressed by indexicals. I will call such modes of presentation 'egocentric concepts', in contrast to another type of *de re* modes of presentation, which I will call 'encyclopedia entries'.

## 7.2 Indexicality and perception

The claim I have just made may seem surprising. For the psychological modes of presentation with which indexicals are associated (**Ego, Hic, Nunc**, and so forth) do not seem to be very much like the perceptual representations described in 6.6. An iconic representation of the reference seems to be involved when we think of an object demonstratively, e.g. when we think '*this dog* is bizarre', but it is not clear that the same sort of analysis is appropriate in the case of indexicals proper. Is a perceptual representation necessarily involved when we think of a place as 'here', or when we think of ourselves in the first-person way? The obvious and immediate answer seems to be 'No'. So how can it be maintained that the psychological mode of presentation of the reference associated with an indexical expression is a perception-based mode of presentation?

There is, I think, an obvious reason for tying indexicality to perception. Our perceptual experience is irreducibly egocentric. This is what in 6.6 I called the *perspectival character* of perception: perception is essentially from a point of view, namely the point of view of the perceiving subject, who serves as origin for what Evans calls 'egocentric space'. This egocentricity of our perceptual experience can only be captured using indexical expressions. Thus we see that the thing *over there* moves very fast, that it gets closer to *us*, and so forth. (Our plans for action, being themselves based on our perception of the world in which we act, inherit this perspectival or egocentric character: we intend to pick up the box of matches *over there*, and so forth.)[1] The natural conclusion is that egocentric concepts such as those mentioned in chapters 4–5 are constitutive of perception-based thoughts: perception-based thoughts *are* egocentric thoughts.

It does not follow that all egocentric thoughts are perception-based, though. On the contrary, it seems that egocentric thoughts can be had in the absence of any perception. Thus Elizabeth Anscombe describes the following case:

> Imagine that I get into a state of 'sensory deprivation'. Sight is cut off, and I am locally anaesthetized everywhere, perhaps floated in a tank

of tepid water; I am unable to speak, or to touch any part of my body with any other. Now I tell myself 'I won't let this happen again!' (Anscombe, 1975, p. 58)

This example shows that one can have an *I*-thought in the absence of any perception. (One may complicate the case and imagine, with Evans, that the anaesthetized subject is also amnesiac: this does not prevent her from entertaining *I*-thoughts). Similar examples can be found, showing that one can entertain *here*-thoughts or even *this*-thoughts in the absence of any perceptual information about the place or the object thought about (Evans, 1982, pp. 161, 169).

The sensory deprivation cases oblige us to make a distinction between two sorts of egocentric thought. Perception-based thoughts involve egocentric concepts; they are egocentric thoughts. Not all egocentric thoughts are perception-based thoughts, however. What distinguishes perception-based thoughts within the *genus* of egocentric thoughts is that they are 'saturated', as Evans says, by perceptual information (Evans, 1982, p. 122). Thus when I think 'That bear is getting closer to me' I have a perception-based thought, i.e. an egocentric thought saturated by the perception of the bear as it moves. But I may also have an egocentric thought in the absence of any perceptual information, as in the sensory deprivation examples. Such an egocentric thought unsaturated by perceptual information may be called a 'pure egocentric thought', as opposed to a perception-based one.

Appearances notwithstanding, one need not sever the link between egocentric concepts and perception in order to account for pure egocentric thoughts. Egocentric thinking, it may be maintained, requires that the subject be perceptually connected to the object of her thought. The sensory deprivation cases do not constitute a counter-example to this principle if the required perceptual connection is allowed to be *dispositional* (Evans, 1982, p. 161). On this construal, 'the informational connection still obtains even if the subject's senses are not operating' (Evans, 1982, p. 161n): it obtains provided the subject's thought is *in principle* sensitive to perceptual information from the object. This type of sensitivity to perceptual information, which may exist even if it is not actualized, is what Evans takes to be constitutive of egocentric thinking. Thus 'it is essential, if a subject is to be thinking about himself self-consciously, that he be disposed to have such thinking controlled by information which may become available to him' in perception, especially through proprioception and kinaesthesis (p. 216). In the same way, 'it is difficult to see how we could credit a subject with a thought about *here* if he did not appreciate the relevance of any perception he might have to the truth-value and consequences of the thought...' (pp. 161–2). All egocentric thoughts may thus be said to involve perception in the sense at least that it is constitutive of such thoughts to be 'controlled' by the deliverances of the perceptual system *if there are any*. Pure egocentric thoughts are, as it were, *counterfactually* controlled by perception: in the sensory deprivation type of example there is no perception, but if there were, the thought, insofar as it is egocentric, would be controlled by it.

To be sure, not any type of perceptual information is relevant to any type of egocentric thought. The type of perceptual information which is relevant to a particular egocentric thought depends on the egocentric concepts which occur as constituents of the thought. As Evans and Perry both emphasized, egocentric concepts are associated with particular ways of gaining (perceptual) information, based on particular relations to the object of one's thought. (I shall present the Evans-Perry view in the next section.) This suggests that perceptual information is relevant to a given egocentric concept only to the extent that it is gained in the special way associated with that concept.

## 7.3 From 'buffers' to egocentric concepts

In perception we gain information about objects by virtue of standing in certain relations to those objects. Thus by watching an object, or by holding it in my hand, I gain (visual or tactile) information about that object; by standing in a certain place, I gain information about what is going on at that place; by being a certain person, with a certain body, I gain information about that person and that body. In each case there is, corresponding to the particular relation (or set of coordinated relations)[2] in which the subject stands to that which the information concerns, a special way of gaining information about it. There is a particular way of gaining information about ourselves which depends on our being ourselves: we can gain information in this way (the first-person way) about no one other than ourselves. Similarly, there is a special way of gaining information about an object which is accessible only to those who are in a position to perceive the object and 'track' it in egocentric space; there is a special way of gaining information about a place which depends on our occupying the place in question; and so forth.³ Following Evans and Perry, I suggest that egocentric concepts are associated with special ways of gaining information, based on 'fundamental epistemic relations' to the object of one's thought.⁴ Thus **Hic** (the concept we express by the indexical 'here') is associated with what Evans describes as 'the special way of gaining knowledge which we have in virtue of occupying a place' (Evans, 1982, p. 153); the concept **Ego** is associated with the special way of gaining information about a person which we have in virtue of being that person; and so forth. It follows that the information which is relevant to (i.e. may 'control' or 'saturate') my first-person thoughts is the type of information which I gain 'from the inside', as when I feel that the wind blows my hair about, or that I have a toothache, or that I am blushing; the information which is relevant to my *here*-thoughts is whatever information I gain in virtue of occupying the place where I am; and so forth.

Instead of talking of perceptual information as saturating, controlling or being relevant to the thoughts involving a given egocentric concept, we may, following Perry, construe egocentric concepts as 'buffers' the role of which is to serve as repository for information gained in the special ways mentioned above.⁵ The buffer **Hic**, on this proposal, is the repository for that information about places which one gains in virtue of occupying the places in question; thus, when I gain some information about a place *p* by virtue of occupying *p*, that information is fed into the buffer **Hic**. Similarly the buffer **Ego** is the repository for information gained about a person by virtue of being that person.

Egocentric concepts, however, cannot be reduced to 'buffers' in the sense which has just been glossed. For something to be a genuine *thought*-category (a concept) it must obey a basic constraint, which Evans calls the Generality Constraint: 'If a subject can be credited with the thought that *a* is *F*, then he must have the conceptual resources for entertaining the thought that *a* is *G*, for every property of being *G* of which he has a conception' (Evans, 1982, p. 104). In the case of egocentric concepts such as **Ego**, **Hic**, and so forth, one must be able to entertain not only the thought that **Ego** is *F*, where *F* is some predicate knowledge of whose instantiation can be gained in the special way relevant to the buffer **Ego**, but also the thought that **Ego** is *G*, where *G* is some predicate knowledge of whose instantiation *cannot* be gained in the relevant way. In other words, someone who has the concept of himself must be able to entertain not only the thought that *he* (**Ego**) has a headache, but also the thought that he was born in 1952, or the thought that he will die in a car accident in the distant future. Now, precisely because this type of information (that the subject was born in 1952, or that he will die in a car accident) cannot be gained in the first-person way, as the information that one has a headache, but only in a third-person way, the concept **Ego** must be exercisable in connection with information which does *not* belong to the type of information which is fed into the buffer **Ego** (that is, the type of information which is derived in the 'special way' associated with the buffer **Ego**). If this is true, then an egocentric buffer becomes a genuine thought-category only when, and to the extent that, it can be exercised outside its narrow informational domain so as to satisfy the Generality Constraint.

These is an obvious reason why egocentric concepts must satisfy the Generality Constraint, and it is related to the holistic character of thought. By this I mean, simply, that *something is not a thought if it cannot be integrated to our general thought-system*. Now predicates like 'born in 1989' are such that their instantiation cannot be detected through perception. One perceives that a baby is being born now, but one does not perceive that it is being born in 1989: one has to infer this using an additional premiss such as 'Now = 1989'. This type of premisses I shall refer to as 'bridging thoughts'. As John Perry emphasized, they are necessary to integrate perception-based knowledge (involving egocentric concepts) to our general world-knowledge. For example, it is part of my general knowledge that 1989 is the year of the Bicentenary of the French Revolution. Knowing that this baby is being born now, and believing that now = 1989, I am in a position to conclude that this baby's birth coincides with the Bicentenary of the French Revolution. Without the bridging thought 'Now = 1989', my general world-knowledge and my knowledge derived from perception could not be inferentially integrated. It is, therefore, a condition for the integration of perception-based thoughts (hence for their status as genuine thoughts) that the egocentric concepts which occur in those thoughts be able to occur also in bridging thoughts, i.e. *in connection with non-perceptual information*. Again, we reach the conclusion that egocentric concepts must be exercisable outside their narrow domain, that of perception.

To sum up, the difference between egocentric concepts and their ancestors, the 'buffers', is that only perceptual information (of the right sort) can be fed into egocentric buffers, while egocentric concepts are hospitable to any type of information: like their perceptual ancestors, they serve as repository for perceptual information, but they can also host descriptive information, as happens when I entertain the thought that I had a Bulgarian grandfather, or the bridging thought that it is now six o'clock. (As we shall see in 7.4, there is another important difference between egocentric buffers and egocentric concepts: the latter, but not the former, satisfy a second constraint on concepts which I call the Objectivity Constraint.) In this framework, the possibility of 'pure' egocentric thoughts, that is, the possibility of exercising egocentric concepts outside perception, straightforwardly follows from the latter's being genuine concepts.

## 7.4 Stable and unstable object files

The general picture which emerges is the following.[7] There are three levels to be distinguished. The *bottom level* is that of perception, which we share with animals. At this level, perceptual information, whose iconic character has been stressed in 6.6, is fed into various proto-categories (the 'buffers') corresponding to various aspects of the perceptual situation. The *top level* consists of what I called our general thought-system or world-knowledge. It may be represented as a network of concepts or notions, that is, as an encyclopedia, each node in the network being an 'entry' into the encyclopedia. Now there is an *intermediate level* where we find concepts, as in the encyclopedia, but concepts which closely correspond to the proto-categories of the bottom level.

Many problems remain to be solved, in this framework. Let us start with the most obvious. What exactly is the difference between the two types of (*de re*) concepts or modes of presentation I have distinguished – the egocentric concepts of the intermediate level, and the encyclopedia entries of the top level? We cannot say that the difference is located in the *type of information* involved, for it has just been established that egocentric concepts can host any type of information, perceptual or non-perceptual. Now, the same thing obviously holds of standard encyclopedia entries. My concept of Ronald Reagan may contain any type of information, perceptual or otherwise. What, then, is the difference between the two types of concept?

From what has been said so far, the following response emerges:

It is constitutive of egocentric concepts that they serve as repository for perceptual information, hence it is a necessary condition for an egocentric concept that it be at least sometimes exercised in perception; there is no such condition for other concepts, like the concept of Ronald Reagan. If perceptual information is fed into the latter concept, this is a purely contingent matter.

As the words 'constitutive', 'necessary', and 'contingent' indicate, this is a modal claim. Perceptual information is said to be *essential* to egocentric concepts in a way in which perceptual information is not essential to standard encyclopedia entries. To make sense of this modal claim, I must introduce two new notions: that of an 'object file' and that of an object file 'dominated by non-descriptive information'.

There is something which egocentric concepts and encyclopedia entries have in common in contrast to buffers: they are *object files*, while buffers are role-oriented, not object-oriented. The unity of an object file stems from the unity of its reference, i.e. from the object which the file concerns. But the unity of a role-oriented file does not stem from its reference, for the simple reason that there is no unity of reference, no single object which the file concerns. For example, the content of the buffer 'here' includes whatever information I am currently gaining through the special avenue of knowledge (mode of acquaintance) based on the fundamental epistemic relation: *being at place p*. At time t this mode of acquaintance provides information about location l, but at t' it provides information about another location l' (on the assumption that I am moving). The unity of content comes not from the object but from the *mode of acquaintance* itself: the content is not a file about an object, but a file for whatever information is gained in a certain mode.

We may nevertheless consider that, at a given moment t, the buffer's content provides information about an object, namely, the object which at t figures as the *relatum* in the 'fundamental epistemic relation' which underwrites the mode of acquaintance. So we may consider that the buffer's content constitutes an object file *with respect to* a given context, with time fixed. The relativization to a particular context can thus be seen as a precondition for there to be a genuine object file, characterized by the unity of reference. This is what I call the Objectivity Constraint. Besides this constraint, we saw in 7.3 that a second condition (Generality) must be fulfilled for the object file in question to be a genuine concept: the file must be open to any type of information, not necessarily gained in the special mode, not even necessarily through acquaintance. When these two conditions are satisfied – when a context is fixed to guarantee the unity of reference, and when information is added from other sources than the relevant mode of acquaintance – we have the type of concept which I call an egocentric concept. Satisfaction of the two conditions (Objectivity and Generality) can thus be seen as turning buffers into egocentric concepts.

Let us now consider the distinction between egocentric concepts and encyclopedia entries. Both egocentric concepts and encyclopedia entries are object files which may include any type of information. The difference between them, I suggest, is that non-descriptive information based on fundamental epistemic relations is *dominant* in egocentric concepts. I mean that the file exists only inasfar as the subject, in virtue of the fundamental epistemic relation, is in a position to gather non-descriptive information from the object. When the fundamental epistemic relation no longer holds between the subject and the object the file is about, the subject ceases to be in a position to receive non-descriptive information from the object and the file is destroyed, even if descriptive information about the object is still available.

The dominance of non-descriptive information thus entails the essential *instability* of egocentric concepts. Non-descriptive information about an object is made available to us in virtue of a fundamental epistemic relation holding at time t between us and this object. When, at a later time t', the relation ceases to hold, this type of information is no longer available. This means that the object file which that information dominates (i.e. the object file which is the content of the category at t) is destroyed at t', while another object file is created, concerning the object, if any, which figures as the new *relatum* of the fundamental epistemic relation at t'. Egocentric concepts thus are *temporary* object files.[8] They do not last very long.

In contrast to egocentric concepts, which are unstable, an encyclopedia entry is a *stable* object file, because it is not dominated by non-descriptive information. Since non-descriptive information is not dominant, the object file is made independent of the 'context of acquaintance' (i.e. the set of fundamental epistemic relations, with their relata). The existence of the file is no longer relativized to a particular context of acquaintance.

Consider, as an example, two simple object files, the egocentric concept 'That man who keeps staring at me' and the encyclopedia entry 'My sister's piano teacher'. Unless I believe that the man who keeps staring at me is my sister's piano teacher, the respective contents of the two files will clearly differ. In the first file we shall not find information related to my sister's piano teacher, nor, in the second file, shall we find information about the man staring at me. A further difference between the two files is the fact that non-descriptive information (viz. the information made available by my perception of the man as he keeps staring at me) is dominant in the first file, but, we may suppose, not in the second.

In order to see what the dominance of non-descriptive information consists in, let us suppress the first difference between the two files, by supposing that the man staring at me *is* recognized (re-identified) as my sister's piano teacher. Then, *information in both files is transferred into the other file*. Information about the piano teacher is fed into the file 'That man staring at me', while information about the man in question is fed into the file 'My sister's piano teacher'. The informational content of the two files in now the same, yet the two files remain distinct. In the file 'That man staring at me' we find (i) non-descriptive (visual) information derived through fundamental epistemic relations to the object x the file is about, namely the information that x is a man, that x is staring at me, that x is wearing a white shirt, and so forth, and (ii) information not derived through fundamental epistemic relations but through 're-identification' of the object by means of the bridging thought 'This man = my sister's piano teacher', for example the information that x is my sister's piano teacher, that x is a lunatic, that x's lessons are rather expensive, and so forth. In the second object file (i.e. the file labelled 'My sister's piano teacher'), we find exactly the same information as in the first one, with the following difference: while the non-descriptive information acquired through fundamental epistemic relations is dominant in the first file, whose existence therefore depends on the continued existence of the fundamental epistemic relation, is it not dominant in the second file. As a result, the first file is opened only 'on a short-term basis', as Bach says (Bach, 1978, p. 36); it is the cognitive reflex of the fundamental epistemic relation to the reference, which it does not survive. But the second file survives the current perceptual encounter.

To say that the file is destroyed is not to say that the information in the file is lost. As has just been noted, a process of information transfer takes place as a result of my re-identifying the man staring at me as my sister's piano teacher. This process is all-important precisely because it is what enables the information in the temporary file to be preserved by being fed into the stable file.⁹

## 7.5 Conclusion

There are two sorts of *de re* modes of presentation: egocentric concepts, on the one hand, and encyclopedia entries on the other hand. Egocentric concepts are information files which presuppose acquaintance with the reference of the file, that is, a particular type of relation to the reference which Perry calls a *fundamental epistemic relation*: a relation (or set of relations) to the object which puts the thinker in a position to acquire non-descriptive information from it. Egocentric concepts serve as repository for non-descriptive (perception-based) information. Standard encyclopedia entries do not presuppose acquaintance, even though they presuppose an information link to the reference. Qua thought-categories, both egocentric concepts and encyclopedia entries satisfy the constraint of Generality, hence both are hospitable to any type of information, perceptual or otherwise. But perceptual information is *dominant* in egocentric concepts, while it is not dominant in standard encyclopedia entries.

The dominance of non-descriptive information gained through acquaintance goes together with the particular status of egocentric categories as intermediate between perceptual buffers and encyclopedia entries. Buffers are role-oriented, not object-oriented. They register whatever is detectable on the basis of acquaintance, independently of which object that information concerns. In encyclopedia entries what is stored is primarily information *about objects*. Egocentric categories are intermediate: with respect to a given context, their content is an object file like that of an encyclopedia entry, but there is no one-one correspondence between egocentric categories and object files. With respect to a context C, an egocentric category has for content an information file (or 'egocentric concept') about the object which enters into the relevant epistemic relations at C. But another object enters into the relevant relations at a later time t', in such a way that a new object file (a new egocentric concept) replaces the first one.[10] The informational content of an egocentric category is therefore referentially unstable, like that of perceptual buffers. This instability stems from the dominance of context-sensitive (perception-based) information.

Whatever their difference, a central feature common to egocentric concepts and encyclopedia entries is their *de re* character, that is, the constraint they bring to the truth-conditions of the thoughts in which they occur. *When such a concept or mode of presentation occurs in a thought, the referent itself is part of the truth-conditions* of the thought. (Hence no complete thought is expressed unless this individual exists.) It is supposed that there is an object outside the mind from which the subject receives information – either by virtue of some specific relation, as in the case of egocentric thinking, or by any channel available – and this object is that which is relevant to evaluating the thought's truth or falsity. Direct reference in language merely reflects this 'referential' feature of our thought about the world.

What I have just called the referential feature of our thought about the world may also be termed 'intentionality' (in the strong sense): that by virtue of which thought points to something outside thought. On the present conception, intentionality is an intrinsic feature of thought, in the same way in which direct reference is an intrinsic feature of language (1.5). It is a feature which some of our concepts – our *de re* concepts – possess. There necessarily are concepts under which we think of objects when we think about the world; in this sense, we cannot think about objects 'directly': we cannot think of objects without a conceptual mediation. But, in another sense, it is possible to think about objects directly, thanks to the special nature of *de re* concepts. They are such that *the thought in which they occur is intended to characterize the reference itself independently of its satisfying the very concept which is used to think of it.* This property of truth-conditional irrelevance which characterizes *de re* modes of presentation is the mental counterpart of the feature REF in language. It is achieved by means of a simple architectural trick: putting our conceptions of an object in an informational file supposed to derive from the object makes it the case that a thought containing a pointer to that file is about the object itself.

## Notes

1  This wrongly suggests that action is secondary with respect to perception. But, as Perry constantly emphasizes after Gibson (1968), perception itself can hardly be dissociated from the ability to move and act.

(This point is already made in Condillac; on Condillac and Gibson, see Morgan, 1977, pp. 164–5.) Perception and action are thus best seen as two aspects of a unified, complex system, which we might call the 'egocentric system'.

2   This qualification is needed to account for 'tracking'. Tracking is a fundamental epistemic relation involving a set of more basic relations. Demonstrative concepts based on the 'tracking' relation will be briefly considered in chapter 10 (10.2 and 10.5).

3   The existence of these 'special ways of gaining information' accounts for the phenomenon of immunity to error through misidentification (see 5.4). A special way of gaining information is such that a piece of information gained in that way can only be about an object to which the subject stands in a certain relation – the relation on which the special way of gaining information is based. It follows that information gained in that way can only be about an object bearing that relation to the subject. If there is only one such object, there can be no mistake as to which object the information concerns. Thus information gained in the first person way can only be about the subject (the relevant relation being identity). It may turn out to *mis*information, but it cannot be about something other than the subject herself.

4   'Fundamental epistemic relations' is Perry's phrase (Perry, 1990a, 1992). In Perry's framework, fundamental epistemic relations are closely tied to fundamental pragmatic relations which concern action and are also part of what I earlier called the egocentric system.

5   Even though I use Perry's term I do not try to be faithful to his own usage, which tends to change as he makes progress on this topic. What Perry now calls 'buffers' (in 1992) is quite different from what he used to call 'buffers' a couple of years ago (in 1990), when I took the term from him. As Perry *now* uses the term, 'buffers' satisfy the Objectivity Constraint stated below. Thus the contrast to be drawn in 7.4 between 'buffers' and 'egocentric concepts' would not hold if 'buffers' were understood in Perry's new sense.

6   Perry calls them 'orienting sentences': see Perry, 1986a, p. 353.

7   Here I am adapting (and modifying) Perry's three-tiered picture as sketched in Perry 1986a, 1986c and 1990a.

8   See Bach (1987, p. 36): 'Files labelled with names ... are relatively permanent ones, stored in long-term memory, but we have temporary files as well ... Demonstratives and indexicals often serve to create temporary files'. See also Millikan (1984, p. 172): 'Each of us possesses certain very general abilities ... that allow us to coin temporary inner terms for almost any item that we may perceive ... These abilities allow us to re-identify a thing that we are 'tracking' as we compound information about it ... These general abilities yield temporary concepts of individual things in the environment. But such concepts do

not last longer than the tracking process.' On temporary files, see also the quotation from Anne Treisman in 10.2.

9   Information from a temporary file may be preserved even if the subject is unable to re-identify the reference of a temporary file, hence unable to find a pre-existing stable file into which to feed the newly acquired information. To save that information in this type of situation it is always possible to create a special-purpose (stable) object file concerning whichever object x made such and such a perceptual impression on the subject at time t. Such a file is context-independent; it is not dominated by non-descriptive information. The move, here, consists in making descriptive information out of non-descriptive information, by explicitly representing the context in which the latter is acquired (Smith, forthcoming). This type of move is needed not only to transfer information from temporary files when no pre-existing stable file is available, but also to preserve non-descriptive information within encyclopedia entries when the fundamental epistemic relation which makes that information available no longer holds.

10  As some readers will have already noted, what I am calling here an egocentric 'category' as opposed to an egocentric 'concept' is what I earlier called a psychological mode of presentation as opposed to its particular 'instances'. See 5.2, note 5.

# I.4

## Proper names

# Chapter 8

# The meaning of proper names

## 8.1 Introduction

Proper names are often considered the prototype of directly referential expressions. The reason why this is so is the following. Indexicals are directly referential in the sense that what they contribute to the proposition expressed is their reference, not a mode of presentation of the latter. Still, they do present their reference in a certain way, by virtue of the semantic rules of the language. (This mode of presentation constitutes their 'character', not their 'content'.) Moreover, there is also a particular way the reference of such an expression is thought of. For example, the utterer thinks of the reference of the first-person pronoun as being *himself* or *herself*. I have insisted on the distinction between this psychological mode of presentation (the concept **Ego**, in this example) and the linguistic mode of presentation ('the utterer of this token'). There are three levels to be distinguished, not two: the cognitive content of an utterance (the thought) can no more be reduced to the meaning of the sentence than it can be reduced to the proposition expressed. Both the meaning of the sentence and the thought expressed by the utterance involve a mode of presentation of the reference, whereas the proposition expressed is singular and involves only the reference. Now the reason why proper names are considered 'more' directly referential than indexicals is that, in their case, it can be argued that no mode of presentation is involved, whether at the level of meaning or at the level of thought. Proper names are often said to have no meaning, and to be associated with no particular way of thinking of their reference.

In this chapter, I will address the first issue, that of the meaning of proper names. Do proper names have senses? The discussion will centre around four particular claims, which have been repeatedly put forward as possible answers to this question:

1 Proper names have no meaning.
2 Proper names are not part of the language.
3 A proper name NN means 'the entity (thing, person, etc.) called NN'.
4 The meaning of a proper name is its reference.

In 8.2, I will present reasonable interpretations of 1 and 2 – that is, weak versions of 1 and 2 – and show that they pave the way for 3. In 8.3 I will say more about the 'indexical view', based on 3. The next two sections will be devoted to the conflict between the indexical view and an alternative view – the 'homonymy view' – based on 4. In the next chapter, the indexical view will be defended against Kripke's objections.

## 8.2 The character of proper names

The main reason why proper names are often said to have no meaning is this. In order to be denoted by an ordinary word, e.g. by a common name such as 'table', an object must possess certain characteristics associated with this word. Thus an object will not fall under the denotation of the word 'table' unless it is has the characteristics of a table. I am not free to call any object I want a 'table': certain conditions have to be satisfied. But I am free to confer any proper name I want on my cat. I may call her 'Table' if I so wish (in so far as this is a proper name).[1] In the same way, I am allowed to call a person 'you' only if I am addressing that person, because of the linguistic rule that 'you' refers to the addressee; but I may confer the proper name 'You' on anything I like, provided I make my intention sufficiently clear. This is supposed to show that a proper name lacks a meaning, not only in the sense of (conceptual) 'content', but also in the sense of 'character' (understood as linguistic mode of presentation). If this is true, then proper names are more directly referential than other directly referential expressions, like indexicals, which have a character even though they lack a conceptual content.

## The meaning of proper names

Even if this is true, I cannot accept a strong interpretation of claim 1, according to which proper names have *no meaning at all*. For I have defined directly referential expressions by saying that they convey the feature REF as part of their meaning; it follows that proper names, *qua* directly referential expressions, must have a meaning. But it may be argued – and this is a weaker, more interesting interpretation of claim 1 – that proper names have no meaning over and above the feature REF. On this view, proper names have no 'character': by virtue of REF, they indicate that there is an entity x such that the utterance where they occur is true iff x satisfies the predicate, but they do not present this entity in a particular way – they do not say how this entity is to be contextually identified. I shall refer to this weak interpretation of 1 as 1*:

1*   The meaning of a proper name if nothing over and beyond the feature REF. By virtue of its meaning, a proper name NN indicates that there is an entity x such that an utterance S (NN) is true iff x satisfies S ( ), but it does not present this entity in a particular way. Hence a proper name has no 'meaning' in the sense of a (linguistic) mode of presentation of the reference.

1* can also be interpreted in two different ways. On the stronger interpretation, 1* implies that all proper names are equivalent: they all indicate, and indicate only, a referential intention on the part of the speaker, without providing any hint as to the particular entity to which the speaker intends to be referring. Clearly, this is not acceptable: all proper names are certainly not equivalent, and it makes a big difference whether I utter 'Cicero was bald' or 'Aristotle was bald'. There may be 'names' (or rather pseudo-names) which indicate only a referential intention on the part of the speaker without providing any hint as to the intended reference: 'Thingumbob' and 'What's-his-name' could be taken as examples of such a category of pseudo-names (although there is a gender feature in the case at least of 'What's-his-name'). But in the case of 'Cicero' or 'Jones' or 'Aristotle', it hardly makes sense to say that these names give no clue concerning the identity of the intended reference. The name does provide a way of identifying the reference, because there is a convention associating the name with the reference.[2] In the case of 'Thingumbob' or 'What's-his-name', there is no such convention: these names are not conventionally used to designate a particular person, but can be used to designate anybody.

The other interpretation of 1* does not assume that all proper names are equivalent; it recognizes that there are conventions associating genuine proper names such as 'Jones' or 'Cicero' with particular individuals. By virtue of these conventions, a proper name provides a substantial piece of information concerning the individual the speaker is referring to. 1* nevertheless holds because the information which the proper name thus conveys is not conveyed *by virtue of its meaning*. The only indication *linguistically* conveyed is that corresponding to REF – namely, the indication that there is an entity such that the utterance is true iff this entity satisfies the predicate. On this interpretation, the information which a proper name conveys by virtue of the convention associating it with the reference is not linguistic, hence not part of the meaning of a proper name, because the convention itself is not linguistic. It is a social convention, which belongs to the extralinguistic context. This interpretation of 1* I call 1**:

1**    By virtue of its meaning, a proper name NN indicates only that there is an entity x such that an utterance S(NN) is true iff x satisfies S( ). NN also indicates *which* entity y is such that y = x, but this indication is not part of the meaning of the name: it is conveyed by the name by virtue of an extralinguistic convention, namely the convention which associates NN with its bearer.

1** embodies a crucial assumption, namely 2*:

2*    The conventions assigning bearers to proper names are not linguistic conventions. They are part of the context rather than part of the language.

I call this assumption 2* because it corresponds to a possible interpretation of claim 2 – the claim that proper names are not part of the language. To be sure, proper names *are* part of the language in the minimal sense that they form a grammatical category;[3] but the conventions by virtue of which proper names are assigned to this or that entity are not linguistic conventions: this is what 2 may be taken to mean, on a reasonable interpretation. I shall consider only this interpretation in what follows, since it is the only one worth discussing, according to me. One reason to find 2* reasonable is that it does not seem necessary to know the bearers of all proper names to be linguistically competent, as far as natural languages are concerned. This issue will be discussed below (8.4–5). As for now I will show that, even if we take 2* for granted, 1** is not satisfactory as it stands.

Let us call 'name-conventions' the conventions assigning bearers to proper names. The problem with 1** is the following. Even if 2* is right and name-conventions are extralinguistic, the fact that *there are* such conventions has to be treated as somehow a linguistic fact. The fact that a proper name has a 'bearer' – a semantic value directly assigned by virtue of a convention, e.g. the convention that 'Cicero' refers to Cicero – is part of what *defines* the category of proper names, in contrast to other categories of singular terms, such as pronouns. It is not necessary to know the bearer of a name to be linguistically competent, but it is necessary to know what a proper name is, and this involves recognizing that a proper name is supposed to have a 'bearer'. If this is true, then REF does not exhaust the meaning of a proper name. A proper name NN indicates not only that there is an entity x such that an utterance S(NN) is true iff <x> satisfies S( ), it also indicates – simply by virtue of the fact that it is a proper name – *that x is the bearer of the name NN*, i.e. that there is a social convention associating x with the name NN.[4]

This is the gist of the indexical view, based on 3. According to the indexical view, a proper name conveys not only the feature REF but also a mode of presentation of the reference, a 'character'. In the same way as the reference of 'I' is presented as being the speaker by virtue of the linguistic convention that 'I' refers to the speaker, the reference of a proper name NN is presented as the bearer of NN by virtue of the linguistic convention that a proper name refers to its bearer.[5] This convention can be spelled out as follows:

> For each proper name there exists in principle a social convention linking that name to a definite individual, called its bearer. This individual is the referent of the name.

This linguistic convention is a general convention, the same for all proper names. It gives a general rule which enables the hearer to determine in context the reference of a proper name. The linguistic convention refers to a social convention associating the name with an object, and says that this object is the reference of the name. Note that, contrary to the linguistic convention, which is general and applies to all proper names, a specific social convention is involved for each proper name (and sometimes more than one convention, as when a name has more than one bearer). Each time a proper name is used, the linguistic convention is appealed to, and a social convention is thereby invoked, viz. a convention linking the name to some definite individual.

In this framework, a proper name refers by linguistic convention to whoever (or whatever) happens to be the bearer of that name; but who (what) is the bearer of the name is a contextual, non-linguistic matter, a matter of social convention. The reference of the name thus depends on a contextual factor, as the reference of an indexical expression does.

## 8.3 Proper names as indexicals

On the view I have just sketched proper names are very much like indexicals. (This is why I call it the indexical view.) An indexical expression $t$ in an utterance $S(t)$ indicates that:

> There is an object x which is F (= linguistic mode of presentation), such that the utterance is true if and only if x satisfies $S(\ )$.

The mode of presentation which is one aspect of the meaning of $t$ makes a certain object contextually identifiable, and the feature REF, which is another aspect of the meaning of $t$, presents the utterance as true if and only if this object has the property expressed by the predicate in the sentence. For example, "You are G" indicates that there is a person to whom the utterance is addressed (linguistic mode of presentation), such that the utterance is true if and only if this person is G. In the same way, if the indexical view is right, a proper name NN occurring in an utterance "NN is G" indicates that there is an entity x, called NN (linguistic mode of presentation), such that the utterance is true iff x is G.

Slightly more precisely, the linguistic meaning of an indexical expression refers the hearer to a relation R which is supposed to hold in context between the expression and the reference. To know that this relation holds is what enables the hearer to identify the reference: the reference is the object (or *an* object)[6] which contextually stands in that relation to the expression. For example, the reference of 'I' is the person who utters 'I'. Proper names are only a special case of this phenomenon, on the indexical view: the meaning of a proper name NN refers the hearer to a relation which holds in context between the name and its reference, namely the name-bearer relation. The reference of NN is the entity which is called NN in the context of utterance.

There are differences between proper names and ordinary indexicals, though. Ordinary indexicals are 'token-reflexive' in the sense that the relevant relation R is an empirical relation which holds, or is supposed to hold, between the expression-*token* and the reference (Reichenbach, 1947, para. 50). A token of 'I' refers to the utterer of this token, not to the utterer of the world 'I' in general. But in the case of proper names, R is a conventional relation which holds between the reference and the proper name as expression *type*. A token of NN refers to the entity which, in the context of utterance, has the property of bearing the name type NN (not to the entity which bears *this token* of NN: that would be viciously circular as a way of determining the reference of the token[7]). To be sure, if different persons, say A and B, bear the same name, the reference of the name will possibly vary from one token to the next: one token will refer to A, another to B. But this does not show that A and B are not bearers of the name *type*. As I have described the case, they must bear the name type, for it is only the name type that they may be said to share. What happens in this sort of situation is that there are two distinct name-conventions associating the same name type, say 'Gareth Evans', with particular persons (the regretted British philosopher and an Australasian politician). These conventions are not appealed to in the same contexts of utterance, and this is why the reference may vary from one token to the next. The reference of a particular token of 'Gareth Evans' is the person who is related to the name type 'Gareth Evans' by a name-convention operative in the context of utterance of this token.

Given what I have just said, this difference between proper names and ordinary indexicals turns out not to be essential. Proper names *may* be considered as 'token-reflexive', i.e. as referring the hearer to a relation holding in context between the reference and the current *token* of the name, even though the crucial relation is the name-bearer relation which holds between the reference and the name type. For there are two distinct relations: the name-bearer relation, and the relation which holds between a token of the name and an entity iff that entity is related to the name by a name-convention operative in the context of utterance of this token. The former is a relation between the reference and the name type, but the latter relates the reference to the current token of the name, hence it makes the name token-reflexive. Many indexicals (in the broad sense, which includes demonstratives) are no more token-reflexive than this: for example 'this N' is token-reflexive only in the sense that a token of this expression is used to refer to an N salient in the context of utterance of this token. Proper names are token-reflexive in exactly the same sense: a token of the name NN refers to an entity which bears that name in the context of utterance of this token.

Another, more important difference between proper names and ordinary indexicals in this. An ordinary indexical is associated with a particular relation R by the semantic conventions of the language. For every expression type belonging to the category of ordinary indexicals, there is a specific relation R, such that the reference of a token of the expression is the object (or an object) which stands in that relation to the token. Different indexicals are thus paired with different relations by the semantic rules of the language. But it seems that all proper names are associated with the same relation R by the semantic rules of the language: the reference of a proper name, in all cases, is the entity which bears that name. In other words, while there is a single semantic rule for each indexical (the rule that 'I' refers to the speaker, 'you' to the addressee, 'this' to an entity contextually salient, and so forth), there is a single semantic rule for all proper names, namely the rule that a proper name refers to its bearer. Thus it seems that all proper names have the same meaning, consisting of the feature REF and the mode of presentation 'bearer of that name'.[8]

This difference between proper names and ordinary indexicals raises a difficulty if we want to go further than merely stressing the analogy between them – if we want to say that proper names *are* a category of indexicals. For indexicals are individuated partly by their meaning, while proper names all have the same meaning and are individuated only by their form, on the indexical view.[9] Faced with this difficulty, someone who wishes to maintain that proper names are indexicals may say either that they constitute a special category of indexicals which are not individuated by their meaning but only by their form, or – if we insist that indexicals are to be individuated by their meaning – that there is a single abstract indexical, call it PN, corresponding to all proper names, or to the general category of proper names. Every proper name would be an instance of this abstract indexical, which could thus be defined by the following rule: an instance of PN refers to the bearer of that instance.

Whether or not one insists on considering proper names as a category of indexicals, they have much in common with them, on the indexical view. In particular, the reference of a proper name is contextually dependent: the same proper name may refer to different objects in different contexts. To use a proper name is to invoke a name-convention, a convention of using that name to talk about a given individual. Now there may be, in a given linguistic community (e.g. in the English-speaking community), different conventions involving the same name; two different individuals, for example, may be called 'John Smith', 'Ralph Banilla' or 'Aristotle'. What is referred to by a particular use of the name depends on which convention happens to be invoked, and which convention happens to be invoked depends on the context of utterance. In some contexts, the relevant convention is the convention of using 'Aristotle' to name a philosopher, whereas in other contexts it is the convention of using 'Aristotle' to name a shipowner. Therefore a proper name is referentially context-dependent, exactly as an ordinary indexical. This is true, in principle, of all proper names, including those which, as a matter of fact, are involved in only one name-convention and give rise to no ambiguity.

## 8.4 Indexicality or homonymy?

The indexical view is based on 2*, the claim that name-conventions are part of the context rather than part of the language. But there is an alternative view, which corresponds to claim 4 above. It holds that the meaning of a proper name is its reference, exactly as the meaning of a predicate expression is the property or relation it denotes.[10] On this view, the convention associating a proper name with its bearer is a linguistic convention. It follows that there are two homonymous names 'Aristotle' rather than a single one. They count as two distinct names, although they share the same phonological form, because they participate in two different linguistic (semantic) conventions: one which associates the form 'Aristotle' with a certain person, the other which associates the same form with another person. In this framework, to specify the name-convention which is invoked in a particular context *is* to specify the name ('Aristotle'$_1$ or 'Aristotle'$_2$) which is used in that context. A proper name is individuated not by its form alone, but by its form-and-bearer, as Jonathan Cohen says (Cohen, 1980, p. 140).[11]

How are we to choose between these two alternative views – the indexical view and the homonymy view, as I shall call it? What reasons can we have for accepting or rejecting 2*, the claim that name-conventions are part of the context rather than part of the language? I already mentioned the main argument in favour of 2*. Name-conventions do not seem to be *linguistic* conventions because it is not necessary to know the bearer of a name such as 'Aristotle' or 'Ralph Banilla' in order to master the language. If by 'language' we mean something like English or French, the only thing that has to be known in order to master the language is that 'Aristotle' or 'Ralph Banilla' is a proper name. I understand the English sentence 'Ralph Banilla is a midget' even if I do not know who Ralph Banilla is – even if I do not know the convention which links the name 'Ralph Banilla' to a certain person. This gives *prima facie* support to the indexical view as against the homonymy view. For if the name-convention which relates the name to its bearer was a linguistic convention, knowledge of that convention would be required for linguistic competence.

The homonymy theorist has an easy reply to this argument, however. He may point out that language is a social phenomenon, which allows for a division of labour. This 'division of linguistic labour' makes it possible for an ordinary speaker of English not to know the difference between e.g. an elm and a beech (Putnam, 1975; 1988). An ordinary speaker may know only *that there is* a difference between the two trees respectively named by the nouns 'elm' and 'beech', a difference which a more expert speaker might tell. The morals of this example is this: the community, as a whole, distinguishes elms from beeches, and this distinction is reflected in the community's language, which involves two distinct words. But an individual member of the community need not be able to make the distinction to be considered a member of that linguistic community. In other words, *only a partial mastery of the communal language is expected of an ordinary member of the linguistic community*. A distinction therefore has to be made between full mastery of a language and linguistic competence in the weaker sense of membership in the linguistic community.

In light of this distinction, let us reconsider the fact adduced in favour of the indexical view: the fact that it is not necessary to know the bearer of the name 'Aristotle' or 'Ralph Banilla' to be linguistically competent. Owing to the distinction between full mastery of the language and ordinary linguistic competence, the fact in question no longer supports the indexical theory. Knowledge of the reference of a proper name is not necessary for membership in the linguistic community – I may be an ordinary speaker of English and not know who Aristotle or Ralph Banilla is; but knowledge of the references of proper names might be considered necessary for *full* mastery of the communal language. To be sure, nobody knows the references of all proper names in use in the linguistic community (i.e. of all proper names ever used by English speakers), but all this shows is that *no individual* can be expected to have a full mastery of the language of the community; the latter can be mastered only collectively.

Note that, if we considered the actual language of the individual – his or her idiolect – rather than the language of the community, which the individual only partially masters, we would not be so reluctant to consider name-conventions as linguistic conventions. If I have no idea who Ralph Banilla is, there is a sense in which the proper name 'Ralph Banilla' does not belong to my idiolect; it is foreign to me, as the word 'sofa' is foreign to me if I do not know what it means. In this sense the names that belong to my idiolect are the names which I fully master, i.e. the names whose references are known to me. The homonymy theory generalizes this point: it holds that, if a proper name NN belongs to a given language L, then someone with a full mastery of L must know the convention which pairs NN with a particular individual. This seems counterintuitive to us only because we consider the *individual's* (partial) command of the *communal* language instead of the individual's mastery of her own idiolect or the collective mastery of the communal language.

If this defence of the homonymy view is correct, proper names are not as special as many have thought. As Burge has emphasized after Putnam, 'much of our vocabulary is taken over from others who, being specialists, understand our terms better than we do' (Burge, 1979, p. 80; see also Putnam, 1975, p. 242). Some people know some aspects of the world better than other people who are mostly concerned with other aspects. Not surprisingly, someone who has extensive knowledge of a certain aspect of the world masters the words related to it better than someone who does not know this aspect of the world very well. In particular, someone who knows Ralph Banilla or Aristotle is in a better position to understand the words 'Ralph Banilla' or 'Aristotle' than someone who has no idea who they are. This does not show that proper names are not part of the language, or that the conventions pairing proper names and individuals are not linguistic conventions, any more than incomplete mastery of the word 'sofa' by some speakers shows that this word is not part of the language, or that the convention associating it with a certain piece of furniture is not a linguistic convention.

The problem with this defence of the homonymy view is that proper names do seem special, in a way. They are essentially *local*, and this provides an argument for the indexical view as against its rival.

## 8.5 Localness

The special character of proper names was pointed out by Putnam in the very paper in which he introduced the division of linguistic labour (Putnam, 1975). The division of linguistic labour means that some people (the 'experts') know more about some aspects of the world, hence more about the extension of certain words, than other people. The experts are in a better position to fix the reference of terms in their domain of expertise than ordinary speakers are. But this does not mean that an ordinary speaker need not know *anything* about the extensions of the terms she uses. An ordinary speaker knows less than the experts, but she knows something. Putnam uses the word 'stereotype' to refer to what the ordinary speaker of a language knows – or has to know – about the extension of a given term. The social division of linguistic labour means that the experts' knowledge of the reference of a term goes beyond the stereotype associated with this term by an ordinary speaker of the language. Now what is special about proper names is that they have no associated stereotype, according to Putnam. An ordinary speaker need not know *anything* about the reference of a proper name, except that it is called by that name:

> It is instructive to observe that nouns like 'tiger' or 'water' are very different from proper names. One can use the proper name 'Sanders' correctly without knowing anything about the referent except that it is called 'Sanders' . . . But one cannot use the word 'tiger' correctly, save *per accidens,* without knowing a good deal about tigers, or at least about a certain conception of tigers. (Putnam, 1975, pp. 246–7)

If Putnam is right, there is something which distinguishes proper names from other terms in the language even if we take the division of linguistic labour into account. In the general case, full mastery of a term (in the sense of an ability to determine the reference) is not required for ordinary linguistic competence; but something, namely knowledge of the stereotype, is required. In the case of proper names, nothing (beyond knowledge that the reference is the bearer of the name) is required for ordinary linguistic competence. Thus a competent user of English must know at least that a sofa is a kind of seat. But she need not even know that Banilla is a man (rather than, say, a cat or a car); all a competent user of English has to do is recognize the word 'Banilla' as a proper name for some object.

It could be argued that, in a certain sense, one does not count as having a given proper name in one's repertoire unless one is able at least to place the reference in a given ontological category. On this view, someone who does not know whether Banilla is a man, a cat or a car would no more count as having the proper name 'Banilla' in her repertoire than someone who does not know that a tiger is an animal counts as having the word 'tiger' in her repertoire. Even if this is true, however, it can be maintained that a competent user of the language need not know whether Banilla is a man, a cat or a car, if only because *a competent user of the language need not have the name 'Banilla' in her repertoire* (in the fairly strong sense which has just been glossed). On the other hand, a competent user of English is required to know that a tiger is a certain type of animal, with stripes, etc., because this is part of the stereotype associated with the word 'tiger' and a competent user of English is required to have the word 'tiger' in her repertoire.

This difference between proper names and other names is related to another difference Putnam noticed between e.g. 'tiger' on the one hand and 'elm' on the other:

> Speakers are *required* to know something about (stereotypical) tigers in order to count as having acquired the word 'tiger'; something about elm trees (or anyway, about the stereotype thereof) to count as having acquired the word 'elm'; etc. . . . The nature of the required minimum level of competence depends heavily upon both the culture and the topic, however. In our culture speakers are required to know what tigers look like (if they acquire the word 'tiger', and this is virtually obligatory); they are not required to know . . . what an elm tree looks like. English speakers are *required by their linguistic community* to be able to tell tigers from leopards; they are not required to be able to tell elm trees from beech trees. (Putnam, 1975, pp. 248–9)

What Putnam is saying is that the stereotype of elm is 'weaker' (as he says) than the stereotype of tigers. This is an important remark. In general the stereotype associated with a word is more or less extensive, depending on factors such as the frequency of the word: the more widespread a word is, the more extensive its stereotype. Let us characterize a word as 'local' when its stereotype is poor, generally as a result of its low frequency. Among Putnam's examples, 'molybdenum' is a local word, but 'water' is not (it is widely used, and its stereotype is fairly extensive). It is not only that the stereotype associated with the word 'molybdenum' is poor, but knowledge of the word itself is not required for ordinary linguistic competence. This is what happens with many technical terms, which are unknown to ordinary speakers. Thus there is a continuum: some words are unknown to the average user of the language; other very local words may be known to exist, but the average speaker knows virtually nothing about their extension; in still other cases, something is known of the extension of the word, but this knowledge (the stereotype associated with the word) is very poor and so on. At the other end of the spectrum, when a word is central rather than local, the associated stereotype is fairly rich.

What is special about proper names, I would claim, is their essentially *local* character: they fall at the 'poor' end of the continuum. Proper names such as 'Putnam' or 'Banilla' are like specialized technical terms: an ordinary user of the language is not required to know anything about the extension of such words – she is not even required to know that they exist.[12]

It may be argued that what is true of ordinary proper names such as 'Putnam' or 'Banilla' is not true of famous proper names such as 'Ronald Reagan'. The average user of the language knows a good deal about the reference of such a name. However, even famous proper names tend to be more local than ordinary words. Ronald Reagan is now well-known in the English-speaking community. Yet there was a time when English was English but Ronald Reagan was unknown to the average English speaker. At an earlier time Ronald Reagan and the proper name 'Ronald Reagan' did not even exist. 'Ronald Reagan' came into existence as a local proper name for Ronald Reagan when the latter was born, and became famous when the latter became famous. Some day, perhaps, Reagan and his name will no longer be famous, or as famous: many English speakers will not remember who Reagan was. In general, the lifetime of a proper name (construed as individuated by its form and bearer) is shorter than that of an ordinary word. Famous proper names are *temporally* local, as it were.

# The meaning of proper names

The local character of proper names provides a reason to favour 2*. The fact that virtually no knowledge of the reference of a proper name is required of a competent user of English provides evidence that the conventions pairing proper names with their bearers are not among the semantic rules constitutive of this language. We may view them as constitutive of *a* language, if we like, but then we have to recognize that this language is not English in the ordinary sense; it is an extension of English, constituted by the conventions of English plus some further conventions (the relevant name-conventions). In the same sense, we distinguish ordinary English from the language of, say, (English-speaking) computer scientists, which consists of English plus a set of technical words unknown to the ordinary user of English.[13]

## 8.6 The individuation of languages

The local character of proper names constitutes an argument in favour of the indexical view only if a certain decision is made concerning the type of language we are willing to consider. We may follow the homonymy theorist, and consider name-conventions as part of the language, if the language we have in mind is some local sub-language rather than the language of a wide community; but if we have in mind a natural language such as English, widespread both is space and time, it is better to view name-conventions not as part of the language but as part of the context, as the indexical view suggests. The argument in favour of the indexical view is therefore conditional. The indexical view is preferable *if* we are talking of natural languages understood in the ordinary way, e.g. English or French.

Because it is conditional, this argument cuts both ways. It could be argued, on behalf of the homonymy theory, that the ordinary individuation of English as a single language raises too many problems to be taken for granted in a scientific enquiry. This is what Chomsky says:

> We speak of Chinese as a language, whereas Spanish, Catalan, Portuguese, Italian, and the other Romance languages are different languages. But the so-called dialects of Chinese are as varied as the Romance languages. We call Dutch a language and German a different language, but the variety of German spoken near the Dutch border

can be understood by speakers of Dutch who live nearby, though not by speakers of German is more remote areas. The term 'language' as used in ordinary discourse involves obscure sociopolitical and normative factors. It is doubtful what we can give a coherent account of how the term is actually used. This is not a problem for the ordinary use of language... But in pursuing a serious enquiry into language, we require some conceptual precision and therefore must refine, modify, or simply replace the concepts of ordinary usage, just as physics assigns a precise technical meaning to such terms as 'energy', 'force', and 'work', departing from the imprecise and rather obscure concepts of ordinary usage. (Chomsky, 1988, pp. 36–7)

This type of consideration might lead one to give up the ordinary individuation of natural languages, and in particular that of English as a single language. This brings grist to the mill of the homonymy theorist. As we have just seen, we may consider name-conventions as part of the language if by 'language' we mean some local sub-language rather than a natural language such as English. Now if, for some reason independent of the debate over proper names, it turns out that so-called natural languages, such as English, are scientifically less respectable than the local sub-languages of the homonymy theorist, then the conditional argument I have just presented for the indexical view turns out to support the homonymy view.

The issue is more complicated than that, however. To avoid the problems mentioned by Chomsky it would not do merely to split English into a great number of local sub-languages, for there are problems with the individuation of *any* public language, unless it is the language of an ideal, entirely homogeneous community. Chomsky suggests that we focus on *idiolects*, which are less intractable as far as individuation is concerned. At first sight this individualistic stragegy seems to support the homonymy view, for I said earlier that in a certain sense a person's idiolect includes only the names which that person fully masters; it follows that the name-convention assigning a bearer to a particular name is constitutive of, rather than external to, the idiolect to which that name belongs. However, if we follow Chomsky and decide to consider *only* idiolects, it will not be possible to maintain that the idiolect of a person includes only the proper names which this person fully masters; for that view would not allow us to account for the social aspects of language. If we exclude from my idiolect the names which I do not fully master (i.e. the names whose references I am unable to fix), how shall we account for my involvement in the communal practice of using this proper name? How for example shall we account for my understanding of a name such as 'Feynman', if I do not know who Feynman was? For Chomsky, a person's idiolect may include many terms which the person does not fully master; this is how he accounts for the social nature of language within a strict individualistic framework:

> The study of language ... conducted within the framework of individual psychology allows for the possibility that the state of knowledge attained may itself include some kind of reference to the social nature of language. Consider, for example, what Putnam (1975) has called 'the division of linguistic labour'. In the language of a given individual, many words are semantically indeterminate in a special sense: The person will defer to 'experts' to sharpen or fix their reference. Suppose, for example, that someone knows that yawls and ketches are sailing vessels but is unsure of the exact reference of the worlds 'yawl' and 'ketch', leaving it to specialists to fix their reference. In the lexicon of this person's language, the entries for 'yawl' and 'ketch' will be specified to the extent of his or her knowledge, with an indication that details are to be filled in by others, an idea that can be made precise in various ways but without going beyond the study of the system of knowledge of language of a particular individual. (Chomsky, 1986, p. 18)

Chomsky's way of dealing with the social aspects of language within an individualistic framework would, if applied to the problem of proper names, yield something closer to the indexical theory than to the homonymy theory. Following Chomsky's suggestion, we would take as constitutive of the entry 'Feynman' in my idiolect two items of knowledge, namely my incomplete knowledge of the reference on the one hand and my knowledge that there is something more to be known on the other hand. Nothing prevents the first item to be merely the knowledge that the reference is a person called by that name. In any event, the name-convention pairing the name 'Feynman' with a particular person is no more constitutive of my idiolect, on this view, than it is constitutive of English. Hence Chomsky's individualistic approach to language provides no comfort to the homonymy theorist.

In any case, I shall continue to talk of natural languages in the ordinary sense in this book. I admit that such languages cannot be clearly delineated, but I think this fuzziness is something to be accounted for rather than an obstacle to scientific theorizing. The graded notion of localness which I put forward is intended to capture one aspect of the fuzziness of natural languages. My concern with natural languages in the ordinary sense does not mean that I do not share Chomsky's individualistic concern, however; my hope is that some day it will be possible to characterize natural languages such as English or French in terms of idiolects (understood in Chomsky's manner) within a communication-theoretic framework. Meanwhile, I shall use the ordinary idiom and talk of 'the language' in the usual sense. In this sense of 'language', I maintain that it is more illuminating to construe name-conventions as part of the context rather than as semantic rules constitutive of the language.

## Notes

1   See Rundle (1979, pp. 79–80): 'Unlike a general term, a proper name does not have a meaning which must be respected when we are proposing to confer that name on a person or thing, a meaning fixed in advance of any such christening... Lack of meaning – the fact that we must have non-linguistic knowledge of what is intended, and cannot derive this from an interpretation of the name – explains the inclination to say that names are not part of the language.'
2   Before the convention exists – as when a proper name is introduced for the first time to refer to a given object – the name by itself provides no way of identifying the reference; the latter is identified on a purely contextual basis. (However, even in this type of case, there is a convention in the offing, namely the convention which the speaker intends to be initiating by his use of the name.)
3   The existence of a stock of standard proper names can also be used as evidence that they are part of the language, but this is more controversial.
4   This is true even if the convention in question is one the speaker intends to be initiating by his use of the name.
5   This is consistent with the observation that I may confer any proper name I want on my cat (see the first paragraph of 8.2). This observation seems to entail that there are no constraints on the use of proper names, hence that the latter have no 'characters', but there is another possible interpretation: the only constraint is that there be a convention pairing the name with its bearer, and this constraint is satisfied, or at least intended to be satisfied, when a proper name is first introduced, since this introduction is supposed to initiate the convention in question.

6 This qualification is made necessary by the fact that the linguistic mode of presentation of the reference does not always uniquely determine the reference, even with respect to a context of utterance. In other words, the linguistic mode of presentation of the reference is not always a complete 'character' in Kaplan's sense – a function from context to content (see 5.2). When the linguistic mode of presentation is 'incomplete' in this sense, a powerful pragmatic mechanism involving something like Grice's maxims of conversation is required to determine the reference on the basis of the indication provided by the expression itself. The pragmatic literature is full of suggestions concerning this mechanism (see, in particular, Sperber & Wilson, 1986).

7 Some people think that the account provided by the indexical view, according to which a proper name refers to the bearer of that name, is circular in any case. I shall discuss this objection to the indexical view in 9.3.

8 One might argue that different proper names do not convey exactly the same mode of presentation: the name 'Aristotle' presents its reference as the bearer of 'Aristotle', whereas the name 'Plato' presents is reference as the bearer of 'Plato'. But this cannot be used to show that different proper names have different meanings. For different tokens of 'I' also present their references in slightly different ways: a token $\alpha$ of 'I' presents its reference as the utterer of $\alpha$, while a token $\beta$ presents its reference as the utterer of $\beta$. This is no sufficient reason to say that different tokens of 'I' (or, for that matter, different proper names) do not have the same linguistic meaning.

9 An alternative view will shortly be considered, according to which proper names are individuated by their forms *and* their bearers (8.4).

10 This is another possible interpretation of claim 1 above: to say that the meaning of a proper name is its reference is a way of saying that it has no meaning in the standard sense (that is, no meaning over and beyond its reference).

11 Far from endorsing the view in question Cohen subjects it to detailed (and persuasive) criticism in his paper.

12 This last remark – that a competent user of the language is not required to know that a given proper name exists – is controversial; it may be true of some unfamiliar proper names, but other proper names are very common (in a given language) and may be considered as part of the vocabulary. (See Cohen, 1980, pp. 143–4 and Kaplan, 1990, p. 113.) Even if the remark was true in its full generality, however, that would not entail that proper names 'are not part of the language', for the reason I mentioned earlier: A competent user of the language would still be required to know that there are proper names (and to know what a proper name is). In other words, the *category* of proper names would still be part of the language.

13  In general, local words are said to belong to the dialects of local groups of language users rather than to the language of the wider community with respect to which they turn out to be local. Technical words are not the only example. Some words are local because they are spoken (with a certain meaning) only in certain places, for example England or the USA; these local words, which may by unknown to a competent speaker of English who does not live in the right area, are said to belong to American English or to British English rather than to English simpliciter. For the same reason other words, which are temporally local (i.e. widespread among English speakers only at a certain time), are said to belong only to a certain period of English – to modern English, say, or to the language of the seventies.

# Chapter 9

# Answering Kripke's objections

## 9.1 Introduction

The view according to which the sense of a proper name NN is something like 'the bearer of NN' has appealed to a number of people, including Bertrand Russell, Alonzo Church, Roman Jakobson, William Kneale, and in more recent times Brian Loar, Jerry Katz, Gareth Evans, Kent Bach, and Jerry Fodor, to mention only a few.[1] Yet this 'metalinguistic' view of the meaning of proper names has fallen into general discredit as a result of Kripke's attack on it in *Naming and Necessity* and elsewhere. In this chapter I will consider Kripke's arguments and show that they do not threaten the indexical view, which is my version of the metalinguistic view.

Three main arguments against the metalinguistic view can be derived from Kripke's remarks on the topic: the modal argument, the circularity argument, and the generality argument. Let us consider them in turn.

## 9.2 The modal argument

The modal argument is a general argument levelled by Kripke against all 'description theories', that is, all theories which ascribe descriptive meanings to proper names. The metalinguistic view, according to which a proper name NN means 'the bearer of NN', is only a particular case, to which the modal argument can be applied:

> *Modal argument* (as applied to proper names):
> If a proper name such as 'Socrates' meant 'the bearer of "Socrates"', 'Socrates is the bearer of "Socrates"' would be analytic, hence

necessary. But it is not a necessary truth that Socrates is the bearer of 'Socrates': Socrates might have been called differently. It follows that 'Socrates' does not mean 'the bearer of "Socrates".'

This argument is based on the following assumption:

[A] If the meaning of a referring expression *e* is constituted by a certain concept F, in such a way that the reference of *e* is presented as being F, then "*e* is F" is analytic, hence necessary.

I reject this assumption. Indexicals are obvious counter-examples: 'I' means something like 'the utterer of this utterance', but 'I am the utterer of this utterance' is not necessary. In some other possible world, I would not have uttered this utterance. 'I am the utterer of this utterance' can perhaps be said to be 'analytic' in a *weak* sense; but in this sense analyticity does not entail necessity. Utterances such as 'I am the utterer of this utterance' or 'I am here now' are true by virtue of their meaning, hence a priori – someone who graps the meaning of the utterance knows that it expresses a truth – but the truths they express are nonetheless contingent. In other words, their 'necessity' is purely epistemic.[2]

The distinction between (epistemic) a prioricity and (metaphysical) necessity is, of course, Kripke's. Kaplan has shown that it parallels his own distinction between content and character. The content of 'I am here now' – the proposition expressed by this utterance – is contingent; but the character of this utterance is such that it demonstrably expresses a truth in every context (although not the same truth in all contexts). By virtue of this last feature, 'I am here now' is a logical truth, even though the truths it expresses are contingent:

> A truth of the logic of demonstratives, like 'I am here now', need not be necessary ... The bearers of logical truth and of contingency are different entities. It is the *character* (or, the sentence, if you prefer) that is logically true, producing a true content in every context. But it is the *content* (the proposition, if you will) that is contingent or necessary. (Kaplan, 1989a, pp. 538–9)

Given the distinction between content and character, and the corresponding distinction between necessity and a prioricity, assumption [A] must be replaced by either [A1] or [A2]:

[A1]  If the *content* of a referring expression *e* is constituted by a certain concept F, in such a way that the reference of *e* is presented as being F, then "*e* is F" is *necessary*.
[A2]  If the *character* of a referring expression *e* is constituted by a certain concept F, in such a way that the reference of *e* is presented as being F, then "*e* is F" is *a priori*.

The modal argument can only be based on [A1], since [A2] does not involve necessity at all. But [A1], together with modal intuitions, can be used only against theories which ascribe a certain conceptual *content* to proper names. It is only if an expression *e* is said to have the concept F as content that it will be possible to infer the necessity of "*e* is F". But the indexical view holds that the *character* of 'Socrates' is constituted by the concept 'bearer of "Socrates".' The content of a proper name – or of any referential expression, for that matter – is its reference, on the indexical view. Proper names are said to resemble indexicals for two reasons: (1) like indexicals, they are referential expressions (they convey the feature REF), hence their content is their reference; (2) like indexicals, they have a certain meaning by virtue of which they present their reference in a certain way. On this view, the reference of 'Socrates' is presented as being the bearer of 'Socrates' *in exactly the same way as* the reference of 'I' is presented as being the speaker. In both cases, the mode of presentation of the reference constitutes the character of the expression, not its content.

From the claim that the concept 'bearer of "Socrates"' constitutes the character of the name 'Socrates', all that can be concluded (via assumption [A2]) is that 'Socrates is called "Socrates"' is a priori. But this consequence of the indexical view cannot be used against the latter, for it is far from obvious that it is false; on the contrary, it seems to be true. 'Socrates is called "Socrates"' seems no less a priori than 'I am here now'. Kripke himself says so about a very similar example: 'Anyone who knows the use of "is called" in English ... knows that if "quarks" means something then "quarks are called 'quarks'" will express a truth' (Kripke, 1980, p. 69). In the same way, 'Socrates is called "Socrates"' is known a priori to be true, even though the truth expressed by this utterance is contingent. As I said above, the contingent status of this truth shows that the concept 'being called "Socrates"' is not part of the *content* of the proper name 'Socrates' (i.e. not part of the name's contribution to the possible-world truth-condition of the utterance), but this is consistent with the indexical view.

## 9.3 The circularity argument

The second argument against the metalinguistic view is the circularity argument. It is based on premiss [B] which Kripke calls the 'non-circularity condition':

> [B] *Non-circularity condition*
> A theory of reference – a theory which tells us under what conditions a given expression refers to a given object – must not be circular, in the following sense: the conditions in question 'must not themselves involve the notion of reference in a way that it is ultimately impossible to eliminate'. (Kripke, 1980, p. 68)

The problem with the metalinguistic view, according to Kripke, is that it violates the non-circularity condition:

> As a theory of reference [the metalinguistic view] would give a clear violation of the non-circularity condition. Someone uses the name 'Socrates'. How are we supposed to know to whom he refers? By using the description which gives the sense of it. According to Kneale, the description is 'the man called "Socrates"'. And here, (presumably, since this is supposed to be so trifling!) it tells us nothing at all. Taking it in this way it seems to be no theory of reference at all. We ask, 'To whom does he refer by "Socrates"?' And then the answer is given, 'Well, he refers to the man to whom he refers'. If this were all there was to the meaning of a proper name, then no reference would get off the ground at all.
> So there's a condition to be satisfied; in the case of this particular theory it's obviously unsatisfied... Obviously if the only descriptive senses of names we can think of are of the form 'the man called such and such', 'the man called "Walter Scott"', 'the man called "Socrates"', then whatever this relation of *calling* is is really what determines the reference and not any description like 'the man called "Socrates"'. (Kripke 1980, p. 70)

I agree that a theory of reference must not be circular. So I grant premiss [B]. But as an objection to the metalinguistic view the circularity argument involves two further claims – the claim that the metalinguistic view is (intended as) a theory of reference, and the claim that it is circular. A defender of the metalinguistic view may choose to deny either of these claims. Katz, for example, presents a version of the metalinguistic theory which is explicitly circular but draws a sharp distinction between a theory of meaning and a theory of reference; he then argues that the metalinguistic view is perfectly acceptable as a theory of meaning for proper names even though it is circular, hence inacceptable, as a theory of reference (Katz, 1990). Other philosophers deny that the metalinguistic view is circular, or, rather, they offer what they take to be non-circular versions of the metalinguistic view. Thus Loar presents a version of the view which involves, he claims, 'no definitional or explicative circularity' (Loar, 1980, p. 85). On this version of the view, the reference of the name 'Socrates' is not fixed by the description 'the man *the speaker* calls "Socrates"', but by the description 'the man who *is called* "Socrates"', where 'is called' involves a reference to (past) uses of the name by experts distinct from the speaker.

As far as I am concerned I tend to favour a mixture of the two lines of defence. I would not go as far as Katz when he radically disjoins the theory of meaning and the theory of reference, but I follow him in denying the first of the two assumptions on which the circularity objection is based:[3] that the metalinguistic view is intended as a fully-fledged theory of reference. The indexical view, which is my version of the metalinguistic view, is not intended as a *complete* theory of reference, but as a partial one. It is a theory about the character of proper names, and the character of an expression is only a partial determinant of reference. If it were presented as a complete theory of reference, it could perhaps be said to be circular or at least empty, for it would explain reference in terms of reference. But as a partial theory of reference, it is not circular, for the reasons given by Brian Loar: it accounts for a certain sort of reference (namely the reference of a proper name token – e.g. the reference of the name 'Socrates' as used by me now) in terms of another sort of reference (the reference of the name type in the community or sub-community to which I belong, i.e. the individual who *is called* 'Socrates' in the context of utterance).[4] This is not a complete theory of reference, since the relation of 'calling' is left unexplained. To get a complete theory of reference, one must say under which conditions an individual may be said to be called 'Socrates'. However this is done, I agree with Kripke that 'whatever this relation of *calling* is is really what determines the reference' of a token of the name, since the reference of a token of a name depends on which entity is called by that name, on the indexical view. But this constitutes an objection to the indexical view only if the latter is construed as a complete theory of reference.

The indexical view as I construe it provides only the first stage of an account of reference by names, by making the reference of a particular use of a name dependent on the reference of the name type in the community.[5] The second stage in the account must provide an analysis of the latter notion; it must tell us what it means to say that an object is *called* NN. And here it will not do to say that an individual is called 'Socrates' in a group if the members of this group generally refer to this individual when they utter the name 'Socrates', for the notion of reference of a token of the name has already been explained in terms of the relation of calling, which cannot therefore be explained in terms of the former without obvious circularity. So the relation of calling must be explained otherwise. According to Loar and Evans, whose position on these matters is not substantially different from Kripke's, who or what 'is called' by a given name in a given community is determined by the practice of 'a class of past and present users of that name whose use *sustains* the general use and whose reference *determines* the general reference' (Loar, 1980, p. 87). They are the 'producers' of the name, in Evans' terminology (Evans, 1982, p. 376), or the (causal) 'sources' of its use in the community, in Loar's terminology. So the *first stage* in the account describes the reference of the name as used by an ordinary speaker as dependent upon the reference of the name in the community, and the *second stage* describes the reference of the name in the community as causally dependent on the practice of the producers.

But, it may be asked, what is the point of having a two-stage account of the reference of proper names? Why not forget the first stage and directly offer the second stage as a theory of reference for proper names? Because, as Putnam has emphasized, two different things must be considered and accounted for: individual competence, on the one hand, and the social factors which play a role in the determination of reference, on the other hand. The meaning of an expression – what is 'in the head' of the competent language user – is not sufficient to determine its reference; it is only a partial determinant of reference. The first stage in the account is intended to capture this determinant of reference. If the indexical view is correct, what a competent user of the language knows (and has to know, in order to be a competent user of the language) is merely that a proper name NN refers to an entity called NN. It is an essential characteristic of proper names that they can be used by people who do not know the name-conventions pairing the names with their bearers. The reference of the name as used by such people is determined by the reference of the name in the community, and the reference of the name in the community is determined by the practice of other, more expert people who know the name-conventions.

## 9.4 The generality argument

The third (and most serious) objection raised by Kripke to the metalinguistic view is the generality objection. Kripke denies that 'being called NN' is part of the meaning of a proper name NN, for the following reason: If we say that being called NN is part of the meaning of the proper name NN, then, by parity of reasoning, we shall have to say the same thing of all denotative words in the language – we shall have to say, for example, that 'being called "alienist"' is part of the meaning of 'alienist', or that 'being called "red"' is part of the meaning of 'red'. But this is absurd. It follows that a proper name NN does not mean 'entity called NN'.[6]

The generality objection as I have reconstructed it relies on two premisses:

[C]  If a proper name NN includes 'bearer of NN' as part of its meaning, then (by parity of reasoning) a word such as 'alienist' includes 'called "alienist"' as part of its meaning.

[D]  'Called "alienist"' is not part of the meaning of 'alienist'.

In what follows I shall grant premiss [D]. There is a sense in which the concept of an alienist – which is what the word 'alienist' is associated with by virtue of the semantic rules of English – does not involve the feature 'called "alienist"'.[7] What I want to discuss is not premiss [D] but premiss [C]. Why is it not possible to dissociate proper names from other words? What does 'by parity of reasoning' mean in this particular case?

According to [C], the reasons a defender of the metalinguistic view has for saying that 'Socrates' means 'bearer of "Socrates"' would be also reasons for saying that 'alienist' means 'called "alienist"'. What are these reasons? First, there is the fact that 'Socrates is called

"Socrates"'" is a priori – a fact which Kneale adduces in favour of the metalinguistic view. As Kripke rightly points out, if the a priori character of this utterance is used as an argument supporting the view that 'Socrates' means 'called "Socrates"'", then the same conclusion must be reached in the case of 'alienist' or of any other word, since 'alienists are called "alienists"'" is no less a priori that 'Socrates is called "Socrates"'":

> Kneale gives an argument for [the metalinguistic view]. 'Socrates' must be analysed as 'the individual called "Socrates"', because how else can we explain the fact that it is trifling to be told that Socrates is called 'Socrates'? In some cases that's rather trifling. In the same sense, I suppose, you could get a good theory of the meaning of any expression in English and construct a dictionary. For example, though it may be informative to tell someone that horses are used in races, it is trifling to tell him that horses are called 'horses'. Therefore this could only be the case because the term 'horse' means in English 'the things called "horses"'. Similarly with any other expression which might be used in English. Since it's trifling to be told that sages are called 'sages', 'sages' just mean 'the people called "sages"'. Now plainly this isn't really a very good argument, nor can it therefore be the only explanation of why it's trifling to be told that Socrates is called 'Socrates'. (Kripke, 1980, p. 69)

Another, closely related reason for holding the metalinguistic view of proper names is a tendency to equate what a competent user of the language has to know concerning a given word and the meaning of that word. As I emphasized in the previous chapter, what a competent user of the language knows (and has to know) as far as proper names are concerned is merely that a proper name NN refers to an entity called NN. Concerning a word such as 'tiger', more has to be known; a competent user of the language must know something over and above the fact that the noun 'tiger' denotes entities called 'tigers'. Nevertheless, this fact undoubtedly belongs to what a competent user of the language knows, in the case of 'tiger' as in the case of proper names. (This is why 'tigers are called "tigers"'" is no less trifling than 'Socrates is called "Socrates"'".) Hence, if the proper name 'Socrates' is said to include 'called "Socrates"'" as part of its meaning, it seems that the noun 'tiger' must also include 'called "tiger"'" as part of its meaning. On the other hand, if the equation between the meaning of a word and what a competent user of the language has to know concerning that word is rejected, then there is no more reason to hold that 'Socrates' means 'called Socrates' than to hold that 'tiger' means 'called "tiger"'.

So far, the generality objection is justified. If the reasons mentioned above were the only reasons in favour of the metalinguistic view of proper names, the very fact that they also support a metalinguistic view of ordinary words would constitute a *reductio* of the metalinguistic view of proper names, given [D]. Even if there were other reasons to hold the metalinguistic view of proper names, the generality objection would stand if those reasons were also reasons to believe that 'alienist' means 'person called "alienist"', 'sages' means 'people called "sages"', and so forth. Kripke's objection in its most general form assumes that this is so – it assumes that *any* reason given in support of the metalinguistic view of proper names would also support a similar view concerning ordinary words. This corresponds to premiss [C] above, as expressed by Kripke's very general statement that 'there is no more reason to suppose that being so-called is part of the meaning of a name than of any other word' (Kripke, 1979, p. 274).

As far as I am concerned, however, I deny [C]. It is because I hold 2*, the thesis that name-conventions are not linguistic conventions (8.2), that I hold the indexical view, which is a particular version of the metalinguistic view. Now this reason works only for proper names: it does not support a metalinguistic view of words such as 'red' or 'alienist'. On the contrary, as I will now show, 2* is both what supports the indexical view of proper names and what prevents one from extending the view to other words such as 'red' or 'alienist'. Hence there are *more* reasons to believe that being so-called is part of the meaning of a proper name than of any other words.

Let me mention, first, something that is common to proper names and words like 'alienist' or 'red'. A proper name, say 'Socrates', conventionally refers to a certain individual. In the same way, the word 'red' is conventionally associated with a certain colour, and the word 'alienist' is conventionally associated with the concept of an alienist. The relevant conventions may be stated as follows:

(i)  This man [pointing to Socrates] is called 'Socrates'.
(ii) This colour [pointing to a sample of red] is called 'red'.
(iii) Pychiatrists are called 'alienists'.

The three conventions relate the words 'Socrates', 'red', and 'alienist' to something else, which I will call the relatum.

The difference between proper names and words like 'red' or 'alienist' is that, according to 2*, the first convention is not a linguistic convention, whereas (ii) and (iii) *are* linguistic conventions. *Qua* semantic conventions of the language, (ii) and (iii) fix the meaning of the words 'red' and 'alienist' by pairing them respectively with the colour red and the concept of an alienist. The meaning of a word is what the relevant semantic convention pairs this word with. In the case of 'red' or 'alienist', the meaning of the word is what I called the relatum. By contrast, the *relation* between the word and the relatum (i.e. the fact that the relatum is conventionally associated with the word) is not part of the meaning of the word. The word 'alienist' expresses the concept of an alienist, not the concept of 'person called "alienist"' or of 'concept expressed by "alienist"'. The situation is very different in the case of (i), however. Since (i) is not a semantic convention of the language, it does not fix the meaning of the proper name 'Socrates' *qua* word of the language. The meaning of the name *qua* word of the language can only be determined by a *linguistic* convention. What is this convention? I have suggested that it is the general convention that a proper name refers to its bearer. This is a semantic convention of the language, and it relates the word 'Socrates' to the conventional relation between this name and its bearer. Hence it is the latter (the relation 'being so-called' or 'bearer of this name') rather than the relatum (the individual who is so-called) which constitutes the meaning of the name 'Socrates'. To sum up, it is the relation, not the relatum, which constitutes the meaning of a proper name, while it is the relatum, not the relation, which constitutes the meaning of words such as 'red' or 'alienist'. This difference is entirely due to the fact that (i) is not a linguistic convention, contrary to (ii) and (iii).

I conclude that [C] cannot be assumed in an argument against the metalinguistic view without begging the question. The indexical view, which is my version of the metalinguistic view, is based on 2*, the claim that name-conventions are contextual rather than linguistic (if the language we are talking about is English). Suppose 2* is right: then there is a difference between proper names and ordinary words like 'alienist' or 'red', and this difference provides a good reason for saying that proper names do, while other words do not, include 'being so-called' as part of their meaning. On the other hand, suppose 2* is wrong and there is no such difference between proper names and other words: then Kripke may be right to say that 'there is no more reason to suppose that being so-called is part of the meaning of a name than of any other word'. But this cannot be used as a premiss in an argument against the indexical view, since it presupposes the falsity of a claim central to the indexical view.

## 9.5 Conclusion

In this chapter, I have shown that the theory of proper names argued for in Chapter 8 stands against Kripke's objections. Hence I maintain that proper names behave like indexicals. On my view, the main difference between proper names and indexicals is the fact that all proper names have the same linguistic meaning, in contrast to indexicals.[8]

When I say that proper names behave like indexicals, I mean that they do so from a *linguistic* point of view. This is consistent with there being an essential difference between indexicals and proper names at some other level or from some other point of view. In Chapter 10 we shall be concerned with thought rather than with linguistic meaning; we shall study proper names from a psychological point of view. Proper names will turn out to be very different from indexicals in this respect. As we shall see, the psychological difference between them corresponds to the distinction I made in chapter 7 between two varieties of non-descriptive or *de re* modes of presentation: indexical concepts and encyclopedia entries.

### Notes

1  See Russell, 1981, p. 221; Church, 1956, p. 6n; Jakobson, 1957, para. 1.3; Kneale, 1962, p. 630; Loar, 1976 and 1980; Katz, 1977, 1979, 1986 and 1990; Bach, 1981, 1987; Evans, 1982, p. 312n; Fodor, 1987, pp. 85–6.
2  In this sense of 'necessity', Descartes says that 'I exist' is a necessary truth (Descartes, 1647, p. 22).
3  As the second part of this paragraph will show, I deny the second assumption as well.
4  If only one person is called 'Socrates' in the context, this person is the reference; if more than one person are known as bearers of the name 'Socrates' in the context, the most 'relevant' is the reference (see Sperber & Wilson, 1986 for an account of relevance).

5 The distinction between the reference of a use of the name and the reference of the name type may be misleading, for there are *three* different things (Kaplan, 1990, p. 108, 111): the name type *qua* word of the language, for example the name 'Putnam' in English (a 'generic name', in Kaplan's terminology); the name type *qua* word of a dialect or sublanguage, for example the language of the local community to which I belong, in which a particular person is called 'Putnam' (an 'individual name', in Kaplan's terminology); and a particular token of the (individual) name, for example the name 'Putnam' as used by me now. The notion of 'reference of the name type' makes sense only with respect to a particular community in which there exists a practice of using this name to refer to a particular object. [In Kaplan's terminology: 'the generic name doesn't name anyone', contrary to individual names which 'have a semantic function' (Kaplan, 1990, p. 111); hence the reference of the name type can only be the reference of the individual name, *not* the reference of the generic name of which the individual name is an instance.] So when I say that the reference of a token of the name depends on the reference of the name type in the community, I do not mean the English-speaking community, but a *local* community. In different local communities the name 'Putnam' names different persons. (As we shall see, the reference of a name in a community is causally dependent on the reference of the name as used by the persons who are the 'sources' of its use in the community). The role of the context of utterance is to select the community – the 'name-using practice', in Evans's terminology – with respect to which the name type may be said to have a reference. To say that a token of a name refers to an object called by that name in the context of utterance is to say that the reference of the token is an object called by that name in a community determined by the context of utterance.

6 This objection (like the circularity objection) was originally raised by Searle. 'It is no answer at all to the question of what if anything is the sense of a proper name X to say its sense or part of its sense is "called X". One might as well say that part of the meaning of "horse" is "called a horse"' (Searle, 1969, p. 171). See also Geach, 1957, pp. 71–2.

7 In the same sense, the concept of an elm does not involve the feature 'called "elm"', as Putnam emphasized:

> That elms are called 'elms' is not part of the concept of an elm, it is simply something very important to me as an English speaker. Few things could be more important, in fact, to an English speaker who wants to talk about the species than to know its name; but the importance of the fact doesn't make it part of the meaning of the name 'elm' that these trees have this name in English. An important part of the purpose of the notion of *meaning* is precisely to

*abstract away from* the phonetic shape of the name. To say that the phonetic shape of the name ('elm', or 'Ulme', or 'orme') is essential to the meaning is to confuse precisely what we want to abstract away from in meaning talk. (Putnam, 1988, p. 27)

8   This aspect of the indexical view, dealt with in 8.3, has been noted by Ruth Millikan in her forthcoming piece, *White Queen Psychology*.

# Chapter 10

# Proper names in thought

## 10.1 Introduction

In chapter 8 I considered the question whether proper names can be said to have meaning. Although I found much truth in the view that proper names have no meaning and are not even part of the language, a reasonable interpretation of these claims led me to the view that proper names resemble indexicals on many counts. In particular, there is a mode of presentation of the reference associated with a proper name by virtue of its meaning – a linguistic mode of presentation, in the terminology of chapter 4.

In the case of indexicals such as 'I', 'now', 'here' and so forth, there is not only a linguistic mode of presentation but also a psychological mode of presentation associated with the expression (chapters 4–5). This psychological mode of presentation is the contribution made by the expression to the narrow content of the thought expressed by the utterance in which it occurs. We saw in chapter 7 that the psychological modes of presentation associated with indexical expressions form a particular class, that of *egocentric categories*. Now the question that arises is this: Is there a particular class of psychological modes of presentation associated with proper names, in the same way in which egocentric categories are associated with indexicals? More generally, is there a particular way in which the reference of a proper name must be thought of?

## 10.2 Proper names, sortals, and demonstrative identification

It is often said that proper names are associated with no particular way of thinking of their reference. This claim may be understood in two different fashions. On one interpretation, it means that there is no unique mode of presentation (or no unique sort of mode of presentation)[1] such that, whenever a proper name is used, its reference is thought of under this mode of presentation (or under a mode of presentation of this sort). This is consistent with the view that, whenever a proper name is used, *there is* a mode of presentation, although not always the same one, under which its reference is thought of. It is the unicity of the mode of presentation, not its existence, which is denied on this interpretation. But there is a stronger interpretation, according to which it is possible to refer to an object by means of a proper name without thinking of that object under any particular mode of presentation. Suppose, for example, that I overhear the utterance 'What will happen to Globos?', without having the least idea who or what 'Globos' is. I may comment: 'John wonders what will happen to Globos.' No particular psychological mode of presentation of the reference seems to be involved here.

I said in chapter 2 that a thought about an object necessarily involves a way of thinking (a mode of presentation) of that object. I see no reason to depart from this commonsensical view. Examples such as 'Globos' can be handled in two ways: either (i) by saying that the speaker entertains a descriptive, metalinguistic thought about whatever is referred to by 'Globos', rather than a genuine *de re* thought about a particular object; or (ii) by saying that the speaker does not express a *complete* thought, but rather what Sperber (1982, pp. 69–80) calls a 'semi-propositional' thought – a thought with a gap in it. In any case, as Evans used to insist, there is a difference between the thought (or tentative thought) which the speaker actually entertains and the thought which *must* be entertained in order to count as understanding the utterance.[2] The speaker himself, in the Globos example, would not count as genuinely understanding his own utterance. This phenomenon is not specific to proper names; it may occur with all sorts of linguistic expression. Thus someone might utter 'John went to the taxidermist', without knowing what a taxidermist is. In such a case the speaker does not entertain the thought which his utterance may perhaps be said to express, but only an incomplete, schematic thought such as 'John went to the . . .'. He entrusts the hearer with the task of supplying the missing thought-constituent.

One reason why a thought about a particular object must involve a mode of presentation is that there is nothing like a 'bare' object independent of any mode of identification. As I pointed out earlier, following Geach and Wiggins, an object can only be individuated according a certain criterion of identity — a criterion telling us what must be the case for something to be *the same thing* as that object (chapter 1, note 19). Geach made this point in connection with proper names:

> If an individual is presented to me by a proper name, I cannot learn the use of the proper name without being able to apply some *criterion* of identity; and since the identity of a thing always consists in its being the same X, e.g. the same *man*, and there is no such thing as being just 'the same', my application of the proper name is justified only if . . . I keep on applying it to one and the same *man*. (Geach, 1957, p. 69)

As against this, Dretske recently argued that one *can* refer to an object, or think of an object, without knowing what sort of object it is. He gave the following examples:

> Perceptual beliefs of a certain sort — what philosophers call *de re* beliefs (e.g. *that* is moving) — are often as silent as gauges about what it is they represent, about what topic it is on which they comment, about their reference. Clyde can see a black horse in the distance, thereby getting the information about a black horse (say, that it is near the barn), without getting the information that it is a black horse — without, in other words, seeing *what* it is. Just as a gauge represents the gas level in my tank without representing it as the amount of gas in my tank, Clyde can have a belief about (a representation *of*) my horse without believing that it is (without representing it *as*) my (or even *a*) horse. (Dretske, 1988, p. 73)

It may be that Dretske's examples of demonstrative thoughts concerning unidentified objects conflict with the claim that a *de re* thought about an object must involve a 'sortal concept' corresponding to the object in question; for the 'sortal concepts' Geach and Wiggins talk about are fairly specific. But Dretske's examples in no way establish that one could have a *de re* thought about an object without having *the least idea* what it is — without being able to say whether it is abstract or material, for example. Only thoughts that are satisfactionally related to objects – descriptive thoughts – could possibly have this property. Thus I may entertain a descriptive thought about 'whatever Jonathan talked about in his last speech' without having the faintest idea what it is that Jonathan talked about. In the same way, I may entertain a descriptive thought about whatever is referred to by 'Globos'. But when a thought is directly (i.e. non-descriptively) about an object, as in Dretske's examples, it seems obvious that there is a minimal sense in which the thinker *has to know what sort of object it is he is thinking of*. Dretske's example, 'That is moving', is not a counter-example to this principle because something *like* a sortal concept is involved in this example also (although the concept in question is too general to count as a genuine sortal in the sense of Geach and Wiggins). The thinker does not know that what he sees is a horse, but at least he knows that it is perceptible and occupies a certain portion of space.[3]

The mode of presentation involved in Dretske's example is one which plays a central role in human cognition according to some psychologists (Kahneman & Treisman, forthcoming; Treisman, 1992). Treisman argues for the following picture of what goes on in the process of e.g. perceiving a black horse. Firstly, at the pre-attentional level, various features of the perceptual situation (such as the presence of black, of curves, and so forth) are detected by specialized modules working in parallel. Secondly, as attention is focussed on a particular area (that where the black horse is), some of the features detected at the prior level are integrated as belonging to one and the same object occupying this position in space. At this level a 'file' is created, corresponding to the putative space-occupier. This file makes it possible to group the features together even though the nature of the object to which the properties thus detected belong is still unknown. The nature of the object is discovered at the next level by comparing the conjunction of features in the file with memories of familiar objects. The output of this process of comparison is the identification of the object as e.g. a black horse.

If Treisman is right, two distinct levels of identification are involved in perception: an object is first identified – or rather localized – as a space-occupier, and then identified as a certain type of object (a plane, say, or a bird, or a black horse). The first, demonstrative type of identification enables one to think of the object – and to give it a proper name, if one wishes to do so – prior to any identification of it in the second, stronger sense.[4] This type of identification 'plays an important role by enabling us to keep an impression of continuity and preserved identity when an object moves or when its features change. We may watch something which looks like a distant plane, see it flip its wings and land on a tree, without any interruption of its unity and perceptual continuity. The only thing that abruptly changes is the identity of the object (its label: the name we give it). The plane *becomes* a bird; it is not *replaced* by a bird' (Treisman, 1992, p. 187).[5] Thus if we associate the proper name 'Bozo' with the temporary file corresponding to the first level of identification, we may discover that *Bozo was not a plane, after all, but a bird*. Such a discovery would not make sense if Geach was right, that is, if it was constitutive of a proper name such as 'Bozo' to be associated with a specific sortal such as 'bird' or 'plane'.[6] Such sortals are available only at the second stage of identification, but to think of an object, and to dub it, only the first level of identification is required. It follows that we must reject the claim that *de re* thoughts about an object necessarily involve specific 'sortals' in the sense of Geach and Wiggins. But one may reject this claim without also rejecting the commensensical view that a *de re* thought about an object must involve a mode of presentation of that object.

I conclude that there is no reason to accept the strong interpretation of the claim that proper names are associated with no particular way of thinking of their reference. In the next section, I will consider the weaker interpretation, according to which there is no *unique* mode of presentation such that, whenever a proper name is used, its reference is thought of under this mode of presentation. Thus interpreted, I think the claim is true to a large extent.

## 10.3  The psychological neutrality of proper names

The mechanism by which psychological modes of presentation come to be associated with indexical expressions was explained in 5.4. Indexicals are governed by rules of use (such as: 'I' refers to the speaker, 'here' to the place of utterance, etc.). By virtue of these rules, the reference of 'I' is conventionally presented as the utterer, the reference of 'here' as the place of utterance, and so forth. These are the linguistic modes of presentation of the reference. Contrary to them, psychological modes of presentation are not conventionally associated with linguistic expressions, but they are nonetheless expressed by them because of the very close tie between the linguistic mode of presentation, which is conventionally expressed, and the psychological mode of presentation. The linguistic mode of presentation is a concept F (e.g. the concept of utterer of the current token) and the close tie between this concept and a psychological mode of presentation $\Phi$ (e.g. the concept **Ego**) is due to the fact that the information "$\Phi$ is F" (e.g. '**Ego** is the utterer of this token') is immune to error through misidentification, given the way it is (normally) acquired.

We have seen that the linguistic mode of presentation of the reference of a proper name NN is the concept: bearer of NN. For there to be a psychological mode of presentation expressed by the proper name NN in accordance with the mechanism we found at work in the case of indexicals, there must be a concept $\Phi$ and a way of acquiring information $w$ such that the information that $\Phi$ is the bearer of NN is immune to error through misidentification if it is acquired in the way $w$. Can we find such a pair $<\Phi,w>$?

I must confess that I can imagine no such pair, unless $\Phi$ is a descriptive concept. Let us consider only non-descriptive concepts for the moment. For any non-descriptive $\Phi$, it seems that there is no way of acquiring the belief that $\Phi$ is the bearer of NN which does not leave open the possibility of error through misidentification. Suppose I think '*This man* is the bearer of NN', in such a way that the words 'this man' correspond to a non-descriptive psychological mode of presentation of a certain man (for example a perceptual representation of the man in question). I may have acquired the belief 'This man is the bearer of NN' in many different ways – for example, I may have heard that a certain person was called NN and identified this man as the person in question; or, more directly, I may have witnessed this man being referred to or addressed as NN. In all those cases, the belief 'This man is the bearer of NN' can be seen as the result of two distinct beliefs, namely a belief of the form '$a$ is the bearer of NN' together with a second belief of the form 'This man = $a$'. Precisely because it rests in part on the second belief, which Evans calls the 'identification component' (Evans, 1982, p. 180), the resulting belief is open to error through misidentification, for the second belief may turn out to be false. This is quite obvious in the first case: I may be mistaken in thinking that this man is the man whom I heard of as the bearer of NN. Although less obvious, the same pattern is discernible also in the second example. Even if some man is being referred to or addressed as NN right in front of me, the belief that this man is being referred to or addressed as NN still rests on the combination of two independent beliefs, namely the belief that *this man is the person now being addressed (or referred to)* together with the belief that *someone is now being addressed (or referred to) as NN*. The resulting belief is open to error through misidentification, for the 'identification component' (i.e. the first of the two component beliefs) may turn out to be false: I may be mistaken in thinking that *this man* is being addressed (or referred to). Perhaps there is another man, hidden behind him, who is the true referent or the true addressee.

What if the relevant Φ is a descriptive concept? Then, I think, there is a possibility for the belief "Φ is the bearer of NN" to be immune to error through misidentification. Suppose I overhear the utterance: 'Mr Banilla, there is a phone call for you!', without having the faintest idea who the addressee is. Upon hearing this utterance, the following thought passes through my mind: 'This guy is called "Banilla"; an Italian, certainly.' Here, 'this guy' stands for the descriptive concept 'whoever is now being addressed'.[7] In this situation there is no gap between the information that the predicate 'being called Banilla' is instantiated, and the information that *the person now being addressed* is called Banilla, since I acquire the former information (that someone is called Banilla) by acquiring the information that someone is now being addressed as Banilla. Given this way of acquiring the information that the predicate is instantiated, the belief that it is the person now being addressed who instantiates this predicate seems to be immune to error through misidentification. So there is at least one concept Φ such that the information that Φ is the bearer of NN is immune to error through misidentification if it is acquired in a certain way.[8]

Be that as it may, I think descriptive concepts are not to be taken into consideration. Assuming that proper names are directly referential expressions, the possibility that a proper name expresses a descriptive mode of presentation at the level of thought is ruled out by the Congruence Principle, the substance of which was introduced in 3.3 and 4.1:

*Congruence Principle*:
In literal communication, the proposition expressed by an utterance coincides with the truth-conditional content of the thought expressed by that utterance. Hence, *if an utterance expresses the proposition that P, the thought it expresses must be true if and only if P.*

# Proper names in thought 175

From this principle, it follows that the psychological mode of presentation of the reference of a directly referential expression (the way the reference of such an expression is thought of) cannot be a descriptive mode of presentation. This is so because the proposition expressed by an utterance including a directly referential expression is a *singular* proposition, with the reference of the expression, but no mode of presentation of the reference, as a constituent. In virtue of the Congruence Principle, this entails that the truth-conditional content of the thought expressed by the utterance must itself be singular: the truth-conditions of the thought cannot involve the satisfaction of a mode of presentation, they can only involve the reference itself. Now, when an object is thought of under a *descriptive* mode of presentation *m, the satisfaction of* m *is one of the truth-conditions of the thought* (6.3). It follows that the psychological mode of presentation of the reference of a directly referential expression cannot be descriptive – it can only be *non*-descriptive (truth-conditionally irrelevant).

It turns out that the mechanism by means of which indexicals, or at least some of them, come to be associated with particular psychological modes of presentation (viz. egocentric categories) does not work in the case of proper names. The mode of presentation under which the reference of a proper name is thought of cannot be a descriptive mode of presentation (by virtue of the Congruence Principle), and we have seen that, for any non-descriptive mode of presentation $\Phi$, there is no way of acquiring the belief "$\Phi$ is the bearer of NN" which renders this belief immune to error through misidentification. It follows that proper names do not express particular psychological modes of presentation in the way indexicals do. There are particular psychological modes of presentation of the reference, namely the egocentric categories **Ego**, **Nunc** and **Hic**, associated with indexicals such as 'I', 'now' and 'here', but there is no particular psychological mode of presentation of the reference associated with a proper name such as 'Banilla'.

The conclusion we have just reached will have to be qualified in 10.5, but there is an interpretation of it which must immediately be rejected as too strong. On a certain reading, it is inconsistent to hold both (i) that proper names are not associated with particular ways of thinking of their referents, and (ii) that the reference of a proper name cannot be thought of descriptively. If the reference of a proper name can only be thought of non-descriptively, as I have said, then there is a sense in which it is not true that proper names are not associated with particular ways of thinking of their referents. I agree that there is a virtual inconsistency here, and I suggest the following, suitably weak interpretation of my conclusion concerning the psychological neutrality of proper names:

> Proper names, like all referential expressions, require that their referent be thought of non-descriptively; but while there are referential expressions which express a specific non-descriptive mode of presentation, proper names are not associated with anyone in particular.

## 10.4  Descriptive names

I have just said that the mode of presentation under which the reference of a proper name is thought of cannot be a descriptive mode of presentation, by virtue of the Congruence Principle. This consequence of the Congruence Principle raises an obvious difficulty, for in certain cases it seems that the utterance includes a referential term (e.g. a proper name or a demonstrative), but it also seems that the reference of the term is thought of descriptively. One example of this phenomenon is provided by what Evans called 'descriptive names' (see 6.4): proper names whose reference is fixed stipulatively by means of a definite description, e.g. 'Julius' as a name for whoever invented the zip. It seems that the reference of such a name is thought of descriptively; but the Congruence Principle entails that the reference of a referential term cannot be thought of descriptively. Faced with this difficulty, one may either deny that descriptive names are genuine proper names (hence deny that they are directly referential) or deny that the reference of such a name is thought of descriptively. As I will indicate, neither solution seems to me satisfactory.

It seems very hard to deny that the reference of a descriptive name such as 'Julius' is thought of descriptively. We suppose a situation in which we have no further information about the inventor of the zip – a situation in which the only thing we know is that someone or other invented the zip. In such a situation, we may refer to this person using the description 'the inventor of the zip' attributively, or using a descriptive name 'Julius' introduced stipulatively by means of that description. Now, whether we use the description or the descriptive name, whether we say "Julius is F" or "The inventor of the zip is F", the only thought available to us is a thought about *whoever invented the zip* – it is a thought with a descriptive mode of presentation as a constituent. *The same descriptive thought is involved whether we use the description or the name, because this thought is the only one available to the thinker.* As Evans puts it, 'someone who understands and accepts the one sentence as true gets himself into exactly the same belief state as someone who accepts the other... We do not produce new thoughts (new beliefs) simply by a "stroke of the pen" (in Grice's phrase) – simply by introducing a name in the language' (Evans, 1982, p. 50). I conclude that the reference of a descriptive name is thought of descriptively.

The fact that this is so provides a *prima facie* reason to hold that descriptive names are not genuine proper names, given the Congruence Principle. But this conclusion is not easy to accept. Russell, for one, held that ordinary proper names were not 'genuine' proper names; they were, he thought, definite descriptions in disguise. It is this view, restricted to descriptive names, which the Congruence Principle seems to force upon us.

The problem is that, even restricted to descriptive names, the Russellian type of approach has a normative flavour that no longer seems attractive. Contemporary philosophers of language study language as it is rather than language as it ought to be; when it comes to proper names, they try to capture the characteristic features of those words which *are* called 'proper names' rather than the features of the words which *deserve* to be so-called. Now descriptive names such as 'Julius' fall into the category of proper names in the ordinary sense of the word. Not only do they behave like other proper nouns from a narrow grammatical standpoint; semantically also they have much in common with ordinary proper names. If what I have said in chapter 8 is right, proper names are characterized by the fact that there is a convention pairing them with an object (the bearer of the name). The convention is of the form: 'The bearer of NN is...', what fills the blank being the specification of an object. Nothing prevents the specification in question from being descriptive: 'The bearer of "Julius" is whoever invented the zip'.

Another reason to resist the conclusion that descriptive names are not genuine names is that there are demonstratives which behave in much the same way as descriptive names (chapter 16). Schiffer mentions the sentence 'He must be a giant', uttered in reference to an enormous footprint on the sand. We cannot say that the pronoun 'he' in 'He must be a giant' is not a genuine demonstrative, for it is the familiar demonstrative pronoun; but the thought in the mind of the speaker seems to be the descriptive thought that *the man, whoever he might be, whose foot made that print must be a giant* (Schiffer, 1981, p. 49). So it seems that directly referential expressions in general can be used to express descriptive thoughts.

There is a third solution, though. It consists in showing that, despite appearances, the existence of genuine proper names (or demonstratives) whose reference is thought of descriptively is consistent with the Congruence Principle. After all, the Congruence Principle only applies to *literal* communication (3.3). When the reference of a directly referential expression is thought of descriptively, all the Congruence Principle permits one to conclude is that the thought of which the descriptive mode of presentation is a constituent is not the sort of thought which might be said to be literally expressed by the utterance, or the sort of thought the forming of which would constitute genuine understanding of the utterance. In other words, the Congruence Principle states a constraint on literal communication: it says what the thought(s) must be like in literal communication if the utterance expresses a singular proposition. In particular, it entails that the reference of a proper name *must* be thought of non-descriptively, but this, suitably understood, is consistent with the existence of descriptive names. For there is a crucial distinction between the way the reference of a proper name *is* thought of (*de facto*) and the way it has to be thought of (*de jure*).

*De facto* the referent of 'Julius' is thought of descriptively, because it is known only by description; but this is consistent with the fact that, *qua* proper name, 'Julius' *requires* that its referent be thought of non-descriptively. As I said above (10.2), we must distinguish the actual thought in the mind of the thinker in the envisaged situation from the type of thought which someone who fully understands the utterance would have to form upon hearing or uttering it. The only thought that *is* available to the thinker in the envisaged situation is not the type of thought which the utterance, insofar as it includes a (genuine) proper name, requires one to form upon understanding it, namely, a thought including a *non-descriptive* mode of presentation of the reference.[9] On this view, the Congruence Principle tells us what 'must' be the case, what type of thought is to be associated with an utterance with a proper name, in virtue of its status as a referential term, but it does no tell us what is the case as a matter of fact, hence it does not rule out the possibility of names whose reference is thought of descriptively.

It is worth noting that Russell himself was attracted by a similar view concerning ordinary proper names. Along with the well-known view that ordinary proper names such as 'Bismarck' are not genuine proper names, because genuine proper names require direct acquaintance with their referents (a type of acquaintance possible only with oneself and one's sense data), Russell seems to have held a slightly different view, namely: that 'Bismarck' *is* a genuine proper name, but that we are unable to entertain the thoughts which our utterances including this name are meant to express. The thought we think when we hear or say 'Bismarck was an astute diplomatist' is not the thought this utterance purports to express, Russell claimed, because this thought is unavailable to us; it is available only to Bismarck himself.[10] It is because ordinary proper names such as 'Bismarck' *are* genuine proper names, on this view, that they require their users to be acquainted with their referents (a condition that is not fulfilled when someone other than Bismarck uses the name 'Bismarck'); this is also why an utterance including a name such as 'Bismarck' is meant to express a singular thought – a thought which an ordinary user of the name is unable to entertain.

In the framework I have just sketched, a proper name is a word which *must* be used in a certain way, even though it may happen to be used in other ways.[11] A genuine proper name is defined (normatively) by what it demands; Russell thus speaks of 'the direct use which (a proper name) *always wishes to have*'[12] (my emphasis). In the case of 'Julius', as in the case of 'Bismarck' (in Russell's framework), there is no reason to deny that the name itself is a genuine proper name, which requires that its reference be thought of non-descriptively. This is perfectly consistent with the fact that the reference of the name *happens* to be thought of descriptively.[13]

But, it may be replied, a descriptive name is *defined* by the fact that its reference is known only by description. It would be misleading to say that the reference of such a name is thought of descriptively as a matter of contingent fact (in opposition to what the name itself would normally require), because *it is the essential purpose of such a name to name an object which is known merely by description*. The descriptive nature of the mode of presentation under which the reference of such a name is thought of is built into the name-convention which governs the uses of the name ('Let us call "Julius" whoever invented the zip'). Hence it is far from obvious that descriptive names, like other proper names, 'require' their reference to be thought of non-descriptively. What characterizes descriptive names seems to be precisely the fact that they do not.

This objection presupposes a highly doubtful claim: that the type of information available concerning the bearer of a name – for example, the fact that we know the bearer of 'Julius' merely by description – can be used to *individuate* the name in question. This claim is doubtful because a proper name such as 'Julius' does not become a different name if more comes to be known concerning its referent – if we discover who invented the zip and continue to call this person 'Julius'. Thus 'Neptune' once was a descriptive name, in the sense that its referent was known only by description. One day astronomers became acquainted with Neptune and continued to use the name.[14] The claim I am criticizing entails that there are two distinct homonymous names 'Neptune' (or 'Julius'), one belonging to the category of descriptive names and the second to the category of ordinary names. I see no reason to accept this. It seems to me – as it does to common sense – that there is only one name, which was first introduced when its referent was known merely by description. Thus we cannot say that a name such as 'Julius' is *defined* by the fact that its referent is known merely as whatever satisfies the description 'the inventor of the zip'. Nor can we say that it is the 'essential purpose' of such a name to name an object which is known merely by description. The name-convention 'Let us call "Julius" whoever invented the zip' simply *fixes the reference*, as Kripke says, and it does so by means of the only information that is available to us concerning the latter. But what counts as far as name individuation is concerned is the link between the name and the object, not the piece of information which is used in establishing the link.

I conclude that it is a mistake to think of a descriptive name such as 'Julius' as being essentially (or intrinsically) descriptive. The fact that its referent is known only by description is purely contingent. Far from being essentially descriptive, a name such as 'Julius', like any other proper name, demands that its referent be thought of non-descriptively. If we use a descriptive *name* rather than a description, this is precisely because we look forward to a richer state of knowledge in which we will be able to think of the referent non-descriptively. A descriptive name such as 'Julius', 'Neptune', or 'Jack the Ripper' is created only in the expectation that more information about the bearer will accumulate, thus eventuating in the possibility of thinking of the latter non-descriptively. This possibility is simply *anticipated* by the use of a descriptive name.[15]

## 10.5 Proper names and encyclopedia entries

In chapter 7 I argued that there are two sorts of *de re* mode of presentation: egocentric concepts on the one hand and encyclopedia entries on the other hand. My first example of an encyclopedia entry in chapter 7 was my concept of Ronald Reagan, associated with the proper name 'Ronald Reagan'. Since egocentric concepts, or at least egocentric categories, are associated with indexical expressions (though not on a conventional basis), we might expect the same type of association to hold between proper names and encyclopedia entries. It is very natural indeed to construe proper names as labels for or pointers to encyclopedia entries in the minds of the language users. But what I have said about proper names in this chapter might be construed in such a way that it would forbid this sort of move. For encyclopedia entries are a specific sort of *de re* mode of presentation, as opposed to another sort, namely, egocentric concepts. So, if proper names are associated with encyclopedia entries, it is not true that they are not associated with any particular sort of *de re* mode of presentation, contrary to what I claimed in 10.3.[16]

I have to admit that the conclusion of 10.3 – namely, that proper names are not associated with any particular sort of *de re* mode of presentation – was exaggerated, at least on a certain interpretation. What was actually shown in that section was that the mechanism at work in the case of indexicals (i.e. the mechanism which crucially involves the property of immunity to error through misidentification) did not work in the case of proper names. But what the mechanism in question does, when it works, is associate a linguistic expression with an *egocentric concept*; for it is only egocentric concepts which give rise to the phenomenon of immunity to error through misidentification (see 7.3, note 3). So the only thing that could have been legitimately concluded was that proper names are not associated with egocentric concepts. Since proper names are associated with *de re* modes of presentation (because of the Congruence Principle, which rules out descriptive modes of presentation), this leaves two possibilities open: either proper names are associated with encyclopedia entries, or they are not associated with any particular sort of *de re* mode of presentation. These two possibilities are illustrated by figures 3 and 4 respectively. In figure 3, proper names are associated with encyclopedia entries; in figure 4, they are not associated with any particular sort of *de re* mode of presentation, but only with the generic category of *de re* mode of presentation.

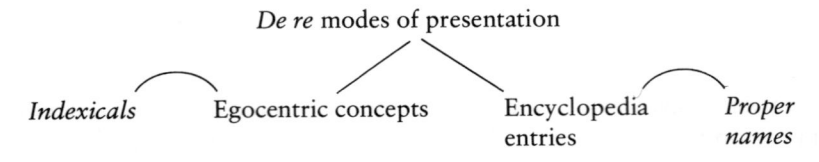

```
                De re modes of presentation
              ╱         ╱        ╲
    ╱────╲   ╱                    ╲       ╱────╲
  Indexicals   Egocentric concepts   Encyclopedia   Proper
                                        entries    names
```
**Figure 3**

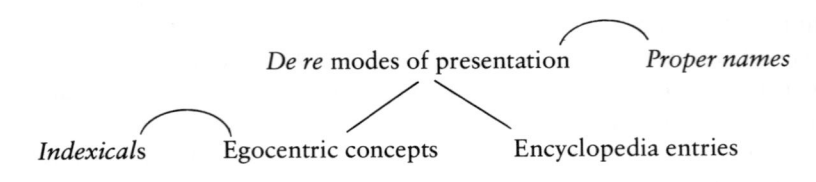

```
                                              ╱────╲
                De re modes of presentation    Proper names
              ╱         ╱        ╲
    ╱────╲   ╱                    ╲
  Indexicals   Egocentric concepts   Encyclopedia entries
```
**Figure 4**

Something which I said earlier seems to support the view illustrated by Figure 4 – the view that proper names are not associated with any particular sort of *de re* mode of presentation, not even with encyclopedia entries as opposed to egocentric concepts. Treisman's 'temporary files' mentioned in 10.2 are egocentric concepts; they are based on the subject's ability to 'track' objects in the perceptual environment. As Treisman points out, two distinct levels of identification are involved in perception: an object is first localized, then recognized as a certain type of object (a plane, say, or a bird). The first level is that of *demonstrative* identification: an object is perceived as occupying a certain position in (egocentric) space, and information gained via the subject's perceptual relation to that object is fed into a temporary file whose existence does not require an identification of the object in the second, stronger sense. Now I have suggested that we can associate a proper name, say 'Bozo', with the temporary file corresponding to the first level of identification; thus we may see something moving in the sky, call it 'Bozo', assume that it's a plane, and later discover that *Bozo was not a plane, after all, but a bird.* If that is true, then it seems that proper names can be associated with egocentric concepts as well as will encyclopedia entries.

The sort of evidence I have just adduced should not be given too much weight, however. For we have seen that there is a sense in which proper names can be 'associated with' even *descriptive* concepts: we may decide to call whoever invented the zip 'Julius'. Still, the view that proper names require a non-descriptive mode of identification of their referent can be maintained. When an object known only by description is given a proper name (as in the 'Julius' case), a situation in which that object will come to be known in a more direct manner is anticipated (10.4). The same sort of thing might be true of the 'Bozo' case, where a proper names is given to an object identified on a purely demonstrative basis. That may also be a case of anticipation of a further state of knowledge in which the object will be identified in a more stable manner, via an encyclopedia entry.[17] From such examples, not much follows concerning the psychosemantics of proper names.

Although I keep an open mind on this issue, I tend to favour the view illustrated by figure 3. Egocentric concepts, in general at least, are temporary files: they serve as repository for information got through acquaintance with objects, and do not last more than the acquaintance relation itself (7.4–5). Encyclopedia entries are stable files; they are the the sort of file into which information got through acquaintance with the object has to be stored in order to be preserved. Now, we do not use a proper name for an object unless we *expect* our mental file about that object to last more than the time of the encounter with the object. For that very simple reason, I think proper names are associated with encyclopedia entries in a fairly close manner.

Proper names have two functions in relation to encyclopedia entries: they can be used to initiate them or to access them. Let us consider the initiating function first. A mental file, whether an encyclopedia entry or an egocentric concept, is created on the basis of specific pieces of information which serve as a 'peg' for clustering further information about the object that information concerns. Suppose I acquire the information that a certain person is my new neighbour. The concept 'my new neighbour' (or rather, the information that someone satisfies that concept) can be used to cluster information about the person whom I take to be my new neighbour in a way that reflects the putative fact that it is all information about a single person. The information which plays the initiating role I call the 'initiating label' of the file. It is part of the informational content of the file, along with whatever information comes to be stored in the file (table 2). Note that, although certain pieces of information play a special role in initiating files, *any* information in the file can

**Table 2** An encyclopedia entry with its initiating label

*My new neighbour*
man met in the staircase on January 1st, 1992
has a beard
Englishman
wears glasses
member of the Labour party
called 'Peter Jones'
reads *Mind and Language*
has a daughter called 'Sarah'
...

be used to access the file, through the process of synecdoche alluded to earlier (5.5; more on this in 15.6). I will come back to that issue in a moment.

In order to initiate a file, a concept must be (putatively) identificatory of an object; in order to initiate an *encyclopedia entry* as opposed to an egocentric concept it must be so in a stable manner: it must identify the referent in a way that does not depend upon a perceptual relation to it. Both definite descriptions and proper names express concepts which have the required property. Definite descriptions such as 'my new neighbour' or 'the man I met in the staircase on January 1st, 1992' express concepts which stably identify some object the subject has information about. 'Peter Jones' expresses the concept 'called "Peter Jones"', and that concept, too, stably identifies some object the subject has information about. (This is one sense in which proper names are very much like definite descriptions.) In contrast, 'that man' expresses a demonstrative concept which identifies an object in a non-stable manner, typically through perception.

Suppose I meet someone who tells me 'I am Judith.' By telling me her name, she provides me with what I need for creating an encyclopedia entry about her. If she says 'I am the new Professor of Botany', that will work too. Both types of information about the (demonstratively identified) referent can be used to create a stable encyclopedia entry about her which will enable me to preserve information gained through acquaintance with her (7.4).

I said earlier that any information in a file can be used to *access* the file. Thus if someone tells me he has met an Englishman in coming to my place that will probably call up the concept of my new neighbour, since the latter contains the information 'is an Englishman' (and is made contextually salient by the reference to my place). The expressed concept of an Englishman calls up my notion of my new neighbour by virtue of the part/whole relation in which the former stands to the latter. If the speaker asks me 'Do you know Peter Jones?', that will also call up my notion of my new neighbour, since it contains the information 'called "Peter Jones"' (i.e. the very concept which the proper name expresses). That is the second function of proper names: they serve to call up encyclopedia entries including the information that the referent bears a certain name. That function of proper names is very similar to that of indexicals, as I shall now emphasize: in communication the relation between proper names and encyclopedia entries is the same as that between indexicals and egocentric concepts.

In order to communicate successfully and enable the hearer to re-identify the object he is referring to, the speaker must express a concept – a linguistic mode of presentation – which (i) fits the object he wants to talk about, and (ii) corresponds to some information the hearer has in his dossier for that object. In other words, the linguistic mode of presentation must correspond to some information which both the speaker and the hearer possess about the referent. But quite often the speaker and the hearer know different facts about the referent. Now the speech situation *creates* facts about various objects involved in the speech situation itself, and those facts are automatically known to both speaker and hearer *qua* participants in that situation. Thus both the speaker and the hearer (in a normal conversational setting) know that the speaker – say John – is the speaker, that the hearer – say, Jim – is the hearer, and so forth. This enables the speaker to use these mutually manifest facts in referring to the speaker, the hearer and other aspects of the speech situation. *The linguistic modes of presentation conventionally expressed by indexicals correspond to facts about their referents which are created by the speech situation itself and are therefore mutually manifest to participants in the speech situation.* What is so special about reference by means of indexicals is that the facts exploited for identificatory purposes are not facts which exist independently of communication, but facts which are created in the very process of communication (Benveniste, 1956).

The same sort of thing is true of proper names. The fact that someone is called 'Peter Jones' does not exist independently of communication: it is a fact which is created in order to make communication about (and with) Peter Jones easier. Calling a man 'Peter Jones' in a speech community C is a way of conventionally introducing a certain piece of information in the dossiers which members of C have for Peter Jones, thereby making successful communication possible.

We saw in 3.4 and 5.5 that the linguistic modes of presentation expressed by indexicals (e.g. the concept of the utterer of this utterance, expressed by the first person) correspond to particular pieces of information contained in the egocentric concepts which constitute the 'psychological modes of presentation' associated with those indexicals. Contrary to the linguistic modes of presentation, which are the same for speaker and hearer, the psychological modes of presentation are different: the speaker thinks of himself as *himself*, while the hearer thinks of the speaker as *that man*. But there is something common to the speaker's and hearer's respective egocentric concepts (the speaker's notion of himself, and the hearer's notion of the man he is talking with). It is part of John's notion of himself that he is uttering this utterance, and it is also part of the hearer's notion of the man he is talking with that that man is uttering this utterance. That common constituent is what the ndexical conventionally expresses and which enables it to (non-conventionally) stand for both the speaker's and the hearer's respective egocentric concepts, through a pragmatic process of synecdoche.[18] In the same way, the speaker and the hearer may have very different encyclopedia entries about Peter Jones – they may know different facts about him – but there is a fact which their belonging to the same (local) speech community guarantees they both know: the fact that Peter Jones is called 'Peter Jones'. That common constituent of their respective encyclopedia entries about Peter Jones, namely the concept 'called "Peter Jones"', is what the proper name 'Peter Jones' conventionally expresses and which enables it to stand for the speaker's and the hearer's respective encyclopedia entries.

The two functions of proper names I have talked about in this section, namely the initiating function and the accessing function, are not specific to them. Like proper names, definite descriptions – or rather the concepts they express – can be used to initiate encyclopedia entries; and any information in an encyclopedia entry (including non-individuating information of the sort expressed by indefinite descriptions) can be used to access or call up the latter. What characterizes proper names is the fact that these functions are essential to them: it is constitutive of proper names that they fulfil that sort of function. To put it slightly differently, proper names have a secondary character: the concept which a proper name conventionally expresses – the concept of being called by a certain name – does not correspond to 'primary' information about the referent, like the concept of being my new neighbour, but has an organizing function with respect to information of the latter sort. To know that someone is called by a certain name is a practical or formal bit of knowledge which makes it possible (i) to store whatever primary information we gain about that person under an entry labelled by that name and (ii) to communicate with others about that person even though the (primary) facts they know about her are different from those we know.

## Notes

1. This qualification will often be implicit in what follows. By 'mode of presentation' I generally mean 'mode of presentation *or* sort of mode of presentation'.
2. Evans, 1982, p. 92 and 143n. A similar distinction will be elaborated later (10.4).
3. Wiggins insists that 'to fulfil its office and constitute an answer to the *what is it* question, a genuinely sortal predicate must stand for a concept that implicitly determines identity, persistence and existence conditions for members of its extension' (Wiggins, 1980, p. 62). The concept of space-occupier is not such a genuinely sortal predicate, according to him (Wiggins, 1980, p. 63), because some spatio-temporal continuants are more tolerant of intermittent manifestation than others (Wiggins, 1980, p. 50): it follows that the notion of spatio-temporal continuity *per se* is too general to determine a genuine principle of individuation. Wiggins, however, concedes that in certain situations, 'it does no matter very much to know more than roughly what the thing in question is' (Wiggins, 1980, p. 122n). Hence it might be argued that *for practical purposes* the concept of space-occupier may serve as a sortal concept even though it is not a genuine one for theoretical purposes. This would amount to making a distinction between the sortal concept necessary for effective individuation (i.e. the sortal concept which is truth-conditionally relevant) and the sortal concept which is actually used by the thinker (i.e. the sortal concept which is cognitively relevant). See Wiggins's reply to Ayers in Wiggins, 1980,

pp. 217–19. See also below (10.4–5) the distinction between the actual cognitive state of the name-user and the cognitive state 'required' and 'anticipated' by the use of a name.
4 See Evans, 1982, pp. 178–9.
5 Contrast this with what Aristotle says in the passage of *De Generatione et Corruptione* quoted (with approval) by Wiggins (1980, p. 61n).
6 This conclusion could be qualified by appealing to the distinction alluded to at the end of note 3. See below 10.4–5.
7 Such 'attributive' uses of indexicals will be discussed below (10.4); see also chapter 16.
8 The possibility of immunity to error through misidentification in connection with descriptive concepts has been noticed by Evans (1982, pp. 180–1).
9 If I am right, we cannot accept Evans's words at face value when he says that 'someone who understands and accepts the one sentence [e.g. "Julius is F"] as true gets himself into exactly the same belief state as someone who accepts the other [e.g. "The inventor of the zip is F"] . . .' (Evans, 1982, p. 50). What is true is this: in the envisaged situation, the same belief state corresponds to both utterances, as Evans rightly insists. But it is not true that the thinker in this situation fully understands the utterance with the name 'Julius'. To fully understand this utterance, one would have to think of the referent non-descriptively – something that is simply not possible in the envisaged situation. It is precisely because the thinker does not fully understand the utterance with a proper name in it that he forms the same belief in connection with both utterances. (To be sure, the thinker in the envisaged situation fully understands the *sentence* 'Julius is bald'; but that is another issue.)
10 'Knowledge by acquaintance and knowledge by description', in *Mysticism and Logic*, p. 218.
11 Gilles Granger once objected to this account that it is normative rather than descriptive, contrary to the intention I expressed earlier in this section (when I said that we contemporary philosophers of language study language as it is rather than language as it ought to be). I reject this charge. The normative element which plays a crucial role in my account of descriptive names does so only because it is integral to 'language as it is'. This element is *mentioned* in my account, but the latter is not thereby rendered normative.
12 *Op. cit.* p. 216.
13 Using Gardiner's terminology, we might characterize the *uses* of a proper name as being 'congruent' or not (Gardiner, 1932): a proper name would be said to be 'used congruently' if and only if the conditions set up by the word itself (*qua* proper name) are fulfilled as a matter of fact.

## Proper names in thought

14  On this example see Kripke, 1980, p. 79n.
15  What I have said of descriptive names can also be said, I believe, of 'descriptive demonstratives' of the sort mentioned by Schiffer (see the giant footprint example). The most interesting descriptive uses of demonstratives to be discussed in chapter 16 belong to a different category, however.
16  The conclusion of 10.3 might still be defended, though. It was formulated thus: Proper names, like all referential expressions, require that their referent be thought of non-descriptively; but while there are referential expressions which express a specific non-descriptive mode of presentation, proper names are not associated with anyone in particular. This might be defended as follows: Even if proper names are associated with encyclopedia entries, they are not associated with specific (types of) encyclopedia entries, whereas indexicals such as 'I' or 'now' are associated with specific indexical categories, viz. the indexical category **Ego** or the indexical category **Nunc**.
17  The same strategy might be used in defence of the claim that the use of a proper name 'requires' the ability to think of its referent under a specific 'sortal'. See 10.2.
18  See 15.6.

# I.5

# The two-component picture: a defence

# Chapter 11

# Narrow content and psychological explanation

## 11.1 Neo-Fregeanism and the two-component picture

It was shown in 2.5 that the neo-Russellian theory which posits singular propositions is supported by two basic intuitions, and also that these intuitions can be accounted for in a broadly 'Fregean' framework, that is, in a framework which considers the propositions/thoughts expressed by utterances to be answerable to facts of cognitive significance (whence it follows that they cannot be singular but must include modes of presentation of the referents). The neo-Fregean theory which accounts for both intuitions incorporates theses 1 and 2:

1. *World-involvingness:* the thought expressed by an utterance with a directly referential expression involves the reference in the sense that (i) if there is no reference, there is no thought, and (ii) if the reference cannot be identified, the thought cannot be grasped.
2. *Truth-conditional irrelevance:* the reference, not the way it is presented or thought of, is what is relevant for assessing the thought's truth or falsity.

These two theses constitute a serious departure from Frege.[1] It is unlikely that he would have accepted anything like World-involvingness, or anything like Truth-conditional irrelevance. Be that as it may, contemporary neo-Fregeans do accept these theses, or at least the first one. Their view is therefore very similar to that of contemporary neo-Russellians like Kaplan and Perry. In chapter 2 and 3 I tried to show that the two views agree to a large extent, and the theory I put forward in this book blends features of both. But neo-Fregeans such as Evans or McDowell, while accepting the claim that the two pictures *as I have described them* are more or less equivalent, would deny that the allegedly neo-Fregean theory I sketched in chapters 2 and 3 corresponds to their own position. There is, they would argue, an essential difference.

According to the view I sketched, the complete thought can be decomposed into two ingredients: the truth-conditional content of the thought, on the one hand, and the mode of presentation under which it is thought of, on the other hand. If we consider not the thought, but the thought-constituent which corresponds to a directly referential expression (i.e. the *sense* of that expression), this decomposition is particularly manifest since the complete sense of a referential term was represented in chapter 2 as an ordered pair consisting of an object and a mode of presentation. But neo-Fregeans such as Evans and McDowell hold that neither thoughts nor the thought-constituents corresponding to referential terms are decomposable in this way (Evans, 1982, pp. 200–4; McDowell, 1986, pp. 158–67).

The view that the complete thought associated with an utterance in which a directly referential expression occurs can be decomposed into two ingredients in the manner indicated I call *the two-component picture*.[2] It was prompted by the observation that such thoughts are indexical in much the same sense in which indexical utterances are. Here is a standard statement of the two-component picture:

> The truth-conditions of an utterance of an indexical sentence depend not only on the intrinsic meaning of the sentence but also on objective properties of the context of utterance. In the same way, the truth-conditions of the thought 'It's cold in here' depend not only on the intrinsic content of the thought but also on the context of the thought-episode: my *Doppelgänger* and I may think of two different places as 'here', and think of those places in exactly the same way (i.e. we may entertain the same representations of the places in question – what goes on in our head when we think 'It's cold in here' may be exactly the same thing) yet there is a difference between our thoughts at the level of reference and truth-conditions – my thought is about the place where *I* am, my *Doppelgänger*'s about the place where *he* is. As Putnam was able to show, the same thing holds of thoughts about

natural kinds. Such thoughts can be decomposed into a subjective, internal component and an objective, truth-conditional component.

*Prima facie* evidence in favour of the two-component analysis is provided by the fact that two thoughts which have the same objective truth-conditions may not have the same significance for the thinker. As David Kaplan pointed out, I may assent to 'I will be finished by Friday' and dissent from 'I will be finished by tomorrow', even though tomorrow is Friday (Kaplan, 1989a, p. 532). The thought that I will be finished by Friday and the thought that I will be finished by tomorrow have the same truth-conditional content, but not the same cognitive or subjective significance: their common truth-conditional content is not presented (thought of) in the same way. Two thoughts may also have the *same* subjective significance while differing in truth-conditions. If I perceive a certain apple and think that it is green, while my *Doppelgänger* perceives a qualitatively indistinguishable apple and thinks that it is green, our thoughts differ in truth-conditions (one is true iff apple A is green, the other iff apple B is green) but there is a sense in which they are 'the same thought', as shown by the fact that they are prompted by the same sensory stimulations and prompt the same cognitive or behavioural reactions (Perry, 1977, p. 494). What is common to our thoughts in this case is their 'narrow' content: the subjective, internal aspect of the thought. Together with a context, the narrow content yields a complete thought (a 'wide' content),[3] with both a subjective component and an objective component (the truth-conditions, as jointly determined by the narrow content and the context). In certain cases, as when my *Doppelgänger* hallucinates an apple qualitatively indistinguishable from that which I perceive, the narrow content fails to determine truth-conditions. In this particular case, no complete thought is entertained, but only a narrow content.

So far I have considered only one version of the neo-Fregean theory, namely that which incorporates the two-component picture. But there is another version, advocated by Evans and McDowell, which *rejects* it. Note that the latter version is closer to Fregean orthodoxy than the former. For accepting the two-component picture entails giving up two principles which play an important role in Frege's theory:

3  Senses can only have senses, not objects, as constituents.
4  A single entity, the thought, plays the role of cognitive content (content of propositional attitudes, as used in psychological

explanations of behaviour) and the role of (absolute) truth-value bearer.

The first principle is inconsistent with the analysis of *de re* senses as ordered pairs consisting of an object and a mode of presentation, and of *de re* thoughts as quasi-singular propositions involving *de re* senses so analysed. The neo-Fregean who wants to preserve 3 will therefore refrain from saying that *de re* senses have objects as constituents; he will rather say that they 'involve' the reference in the sense that they depend on it for their very existence and individuation, without literally *including* it. On this view, *de re* senses *cannot* be analysed into two components, the reference and a narrowly individuated mode of presentation, and the same thing can be said of *de re* thoughts.

But, one might ask, why should we want to maintain Frege's principle 3? According to Peacocke, there is nothing sacrosanct about that principle. Frege's principle, Peacocke says, 'was not for him an underived axiom; rather, he thought it followed from the requirement that the individuation of senses be answerable to facts about cognitive significance. If we can build a theory which accepts this requirement while rejecting the conclusion which Frege drew from it, that theory will be Fregean in accepting his underlying principles' (Peacocke, 1981, p. 197). Much more important, from this point of view, is the departure from Frege involved in giving up principle 4. If one accepts the two-component picture, one is led to claim that the two criteria which Frege used for individuating thoughts actually diverge (4.1–2): the truth-conditional criterion individuates the objective component of thought while the cognitive significance criterion individuates the narrow component.[4] The fact that there is such divergence is the main reason why the two-component picture was introduced in the first place. But Evans and McDowell deny the divergence; they remain Fregean in this respect.

The two-component picture has been more or less taken for granted in the first part of this book. Before turning to the second part I want to consider the reasons which have led neo-Fregeans such as Evans and McDowell to reject that picture. There are, I believe, two basic reasons. The most important one, to be dealt with in chapter 12, is what McDowell calls 'the fear of Cartesian danger': the notion of narrow content is taken to imply a Cartesian view of the mental, a view which we have good reasons to reject. The other reason, to be dealt with in this chapter, is the feeling that the notion of 'narrow content' has no role to play in the theory, since the role which is ascribed to it by its proponents – that of *explanans* in psychological explanations – is actually played by the (complete) thought.

## 11.2 Alleged arguments for the two-component picture

Let us start by considering a couple of arguments in favour of the two-component picture and the responses which someone who rejects the picture can make. These responses I find basically correct. This does not mean that I concur with those who reject the two-component picture: I accept it, as I hope the next sections (and the next chapter) will show.

The *first argument* in favour of the two-component picture is this:

> We need the distinction between the (complete) thought, which includes a mode of presentation of the reference, and the truth-conditional content of the thought, in order to account for truth-conditional irrelevance. The only way to even describe the phenomenon of truth-conditional irrelevance is by saying that the truth-conditional content of the thought is singular even though the thought itself includes a mode of presentation of the reference. How could we make that point, without the two-component picture?

The response, I think, is obvious. The neo-Fregean who rejects the two-component picture because he does not want to give up 4 need not have any scruple *accepting* the distinction between the (complete) thought, which includes a mode of presentation of the reference, and the truth-conditional content of the thought. To be sure, the very expression 'truth-conditional content' is not one which a strict neo-Fregean would use. The alleged 'truth-conditional content' of the thought, for him or her, is nothing other than the *truth-conditions* of the thought. The distinction between the complete thought, which includes a mode of presentation of the reference, and the (singular) truth-conditional content of the thought reduces to the unmysterious distinction between the thought and its (singular) truth-conditions. Such a distinction does *not* prevent the neo-Fregean from adhering to Frege's principle 4. It is the thought which *has* truth-conditions, he or she may argue, and the thought is also what has cognitive significance, that is, what serves as *explanans* in psychological explanations.

To sum up, what the opponent of the two-component picture rejects is not the distinction between the thought and its truth-conditional content (i.e. its truth-conditions), but the view, suggested by the unhappy expression 'truth-conditional *content*', that the complete thought can be *decomposed* into the 'truth-conditional content' plus something else, namely a 'narrow content'. There is only one sort of content, for the single-componentist, namely the thought itself. The thought has, or determines, truth-conditions, but the truth-conditions do not constitute a 'part' of the thought, the substraction of which would yield the other part, namely the narrow content.

The *second argument* in favour of the two-component picture invokes McGinn's observation that 'in thinking of items under "I", "now", "here" one applies a single constant concept – the concept of oneself, of the present, and of spatial vicinity – and not variable occasion-relative concepts' (McGinn, 1983, p. 65). It runs as follows:

> The rejection of the very idea of narrow content has unwelcome consequences. If, as the single-componentist insists, there is nothing like narrow content, there cannot be anything like 'modes of presentation' in the *narrow* sense, that is, modes of presentation which remain constant through changes of reference (as when we say that you and I both think of ourselves under the *same* mode of presentation). Now this conflicts with McGinn's fairly intuitive claim that e.g. every first-person thought involves the same concept of self, whose constancy corresponds to the constant linguistic meaning of 'I' (5.2).

McDowell has responded to that objection. The single-componentist need *not* deny that there is an abstract concept of self, which everybody uses in his first-person thoughts. He must only deny this concept the status of a genuine sense or mode of presentation. A *de re* sense or mode of presentation is individuated in part by the object of which it is a mode of presentation (this is how Evans and McDowell account for world-involvingness); hence there is nothing like a 'narrow' mode of presentation independent of reference. In the case of 'I', the first-person thoughts which different thinkers entertain necessarily include *different* modes of presentation, since the referents are different.[5] This does not debar the single-componentist from recognizing that there is something common to my first-person thoughts and to yours, namely, the fact that they both are first-person thoughts. The single-componentist may acknowledge this by saying that all first-person thoughts involve the same *type* or *sort* of sense or mode of presentation. As McDowell says in explicit reference to McGinn's claim:

> Particular *de re* senses, each specific to its *res*, can be grouped into sorts. Different *de re* senses (modes of presentation) can present their *res* in the same sort of way: for instance, by exploiting their perceptual presence. And the univocity of a context-sensitive expression can be registered by associating it with a single sort of *de re* sense. (McDowell, 1984, p. 103)

At this point the question arises, whether the two views are substantially different, or whether the difference is mainly terminological. What, one might ask, is the difference between modes of presentation 'narrowly individuated' and McDowell's 'sorts' of mode of presentation? The step from tokens to 'sorts' means that we abstract from context, hence that we individuate the mode of presentation 'narrowly'. What, in this framework, prevents us from analysing reference-involving modes of presentation into two components: the type or sort of mode of presentation involved, and the reference? In the same way, what prevents us from analysing a *de re* thought into two components: the type or sort of thought involved, and the truth-conditions?

What prevents us from reinstating the two-component picture with 'types' or 'sorts' of mode of presentation (or thought) as narrow components is a constraint which types must satisfy if the type/token terminology is understood strictly.[6] The constraint is this: *A type or sort is instantiated only if a particular token of the type occurs.* This constraint is precisely not satisfied by the narrow component in the two-component picture. The narrow component is supposed to be available even if the objective component if lacking (as in hallucination). But on the Evans-McDowell view, the 'type' of mode of presentation is something like a *class* of reference-dependent modes of presentation or *de re* senses. Such a type is instantiated only if there occurs a token, that is, a reference-dependent mode of presentation, and a reference-dependent mode of presentation is, by definition, not available if there is no reference. No *res* entails no *de re* sense, and no *de re* sense (no token) entails no 'sort' of *de re* sense (no type). I conclude that there *is* a substantial difference between the two-component picture and the Evans-McDowell view; it concerns the analysis of hallucinatory situations and other 'empty' cases in which the objective component is not available. The two-component theorist maintains that, in such cases, the narrow component *is* available. This feature can indeed be used to define narrow content. But for the single-componentist, there is no such thing as a narrow content defined by its availability in the empty case.

The *third argument* I want to discuss is the standard argument offered in support of the two-component picture. We are to imagine a subject and his qualitatively indistinguishable twin on a qualitatively indistinguishable twin-Earth. Whatever passes through the mind of one (say, A) also passes through the mind of the other (say, twin-A); for example, if one thinks 'I am hungry' at t, the other also thinks 'I am hungry' at t. The argument proceeds along the following lines:

> There is a clear sense in which A's and twin-A's thoughts can be said to be 'the same'. Yet their thoughts have different truth-conditions: A's thought 'I am hungry' is true iff A is hungry at t, while twin-A's thought 'I am hungry' is true iff twin-A is hungry at t. This difference, however, is not relevant as far as psychology is concerned. For the aspect of thought which matters for psychology is that which plays a role in explaining action. Now A's behaviour is exactly the same as twin-A's: both open the fridge at t', as a result of their thinking 'I am hungry' at t. So there is a distinction to be made between two aspects of thought: one aspect is common to A and twin-A, and this aspect – the narrow component of thought – is what accounts for their common behaviour. The other aspect – the truth-conditional aspect of the thought – is irrelevant for psychological explanation although it is relevant for assessing the thought's truth or falsity. Accordingly there are two modes of individuation for thoughts. From the psychological point of view, thoughts are individuated 'narrowly', in such a way that A's and twin-A's thoughts count as the same. But their thoughts may also be individuated 'broadly', so as to take the objective, truth-conditional aspect into consideration. Thus individuated, A's and twin-A's thoughts count as different, even though they involve the same 'narrow' component, because the other component crucially depends upon the environment.

This argument has been criticized as question-begging; and indeed it is. A thought-content common to A and twin-A is posited to account for their common behaviour. 'If the *explanandum* (the behaviour) is the same in the case of A and twin-A, the *explanans* (the psychological state) must be the same also, hence we need a narrow notion of content, that is, a thought-content common to A and his twin' – so the argument goes. But, as Peacocke and Evans made perfectly clear, it cannot be taken for granted that twin-A's behaviour is the same as that of A. Their behaviour is 'the same' only under a description which abstracts from the different environments in which that behaviour takes place. Under a less abstract description, the behaviour is not the same: A opens A's fridge, twin-A opens twin-A's fridge. Different actions are performed on different objects. To be sure, it is the same type of action, prompted by the same type of thought. But what causes, hence explains, A's particular action is A's particular thought (*distinct* from twin-A's particular thought), and this particular thought involves a particular fridge (distinct from twin-A's particular fridge). It follows that we need not depart from Frege; we need not reject principle 4 and endorse the two-component picture. The complete, particular thought is both psychologically explanatory and truth-evaluable, as Frege had suggested.

I fully agree with Evans and Peacocke that the standard argument in favour of the two-component picture begs the question when it takes for granted that A's behaviour is the same as that of twin-A. Hence the conclusion of the argument – that only 'narrow' contents common to A and his twin are relevant for psychological explanation – must be rejected. Broad contents do play a role in psychological explanation of actions, for the obvious reason that actions themselves are, in general at least, individuated 'broadly', in terms of the particular objects which they involve. Thus we might provide the following psychological explanation: 'Mary said "Goodbye" to John because she thought he was leaving.' In this explanation, the action and the thought which is offered as *explanans* are both individuated broadly, in terms of the particular person (John) whom they involve. The thought that *John* is leaving is offered as an explanation of the action of saying 'Goodbye' to *John*. Mary's *Doppelgänger* could not entertain this thought nor perform this action, but only a similar thought, and a similar action, concerning John's *Doppelgänger*.

It does not follow that we do not need the notion of narrow content, however. It might well be that the notion of narrow content *has* a role to play in psychological explanation, even if it is not the sole notion that plays such a role – even if broad contents also are psychologically explanatory. Peacocke himself (in contrast to Evans) acknowledged this when he said, 'the claim that attitudes to Fregean thoughts [i.e. to thoughts broadly individuated] are not psychologically inert [i.e. play a role in psychological explanation] does not rule out the view that what it is to have such an attitude has some division into environmental and non-environmental components' (Peacocke, 1981, p. 203). The question that must be asked, then, is this: Do we need narrow contents at all in psychological explanations, and why?

## 11.3 Narrow content in psychological explanation

We need to posit a psychological state common to A and twin-A only if among the *explananda* is some behaviour common to A and twin-A. Now it is clear that A's behaviour is the same as that of twin-A if the kind of 'behaviour' we have in mind is their bodily behaviour physically described. But that is not what ordinary psychological explanations seek to explain. As I said above, ordinary psychological explanations explain actions or tentative actions, and the latter are individuated 'broadly', in terms of the objects which they involve. Even so, there is enough similarity between A's and twin-A's actions for us to find some common *explanandum* on the action side, thereby justifying the postulation of a common *explanans* on the mental side. Clearly, the *type* of action which A and twin-A perform – e.g. the generic action of opening the fridge – is the same in both cases, and it is perfectly legitimate to account for this by positing a type of thought which is also the same for A and twin-A.

As we noted earlier, McDowell fully accepts talk of 'sorts' of *de re* thought. It is, I believe, uncontroversial that sorts of *de re* thought may be used to explain sorts of action. The only thing which Evans and McDowell can reasonably deny is that psychological explanations *must* be conducted at the level of sort – that is, at the level at which A's and twin-A's behaviour and thought may be said to be 'the same'. But they have no reason to deny that psychological explanations *can* be conducted at this level. Consider, for example, the following passage from Evans (1982, pp. 203–4):

> Suppose $S$ thinks there is a cat where he is, and $S'$ (his Doppelgänger) thinks there is a cat where he is. $S$ may be, for instance, disposed to search $p$; $S'$ will not be at all disposed to search $p$, but will be disposed to search $p'$. $S$'s belief, then, will explain one kind of behaviour, searching $p$; $S''$s belief will explain a different kind of behaviour,

searching *p'*... Now this place-specific disposition no doubt results from (*S*'s) having a more general disposition, in the spelling out of which one would mention no specific place, and which [*S*] share [s] with [his] Doppelgänger... But what arguments are there for holding that mental states must be identified with, or individuated in terms of, dispositions of the general sort rather than dispositions of the specific sort? (Evans, 1982, pp. 203–4)

In this passage Evans rightly rejects the view that mental states *qua* explanatory of behaviour *must* be individuated narrowly, i.e. 'in terms of dispositions of the general sort rather than dipositions of the specific sort'. But this does nothing to show that mental states *qua* explanatory of behaviour *cannot* be individuated narrowly. It seems that *both* particular, object-involving thoughts *and* object-independent types of thought can be used in psychological explanations: the former explain particular actions, the latter explain types of action. As Mark Sainsbury points out in his review of Evans's book, 'substantial disagreement would occur if the dual component theorist were to hold that only [types of thought, individuated in terms of "general dispositions"] count as genuinely mental' (Sainsbury, 1985, p. 137), but, precisely, the two-component theorist need not maintain that *only* narrow contents play a role in psychological explanation. He may grant the Evans-Peacocke point that truth-conditional differences between our thoughts are not 'psychologically inert' (Peacocke, 1981, p. 202) while maintaining the need for a notion of narrow content which we can use in psychological explanations at a higher level of generality.

At this point the single-componentist may reply by strengthening his case and pointing out that *only* broadly individuated particular thoughts play a causal role in bringing about actions on the part of the thinker. Here is a possible argument in support of this conclusion:

> 'Types' of thought are abstractions devoid of causal efficacy. For pragmatic reasons we may, when we explain an action, abstract from some aspects of the particular thought which causes it and mention only the *type* of thought which it instantiates. Still it is the particular thought which causes the action. As Davidson says, 'we must distinguish firmly between causes and the features we hit on for describing them' (Davidson, 1967, p. 155). The fact that we describe the cause of a certain effect incompletely, by mentioning only some of its properties which we consider more relevant than others, does not entail that the

properties in question are the true causes. The true cause is the particular event which we incompletely describe in terms of some of its properties. For example, the cause of A's action of opening the fridge is the particular thought which A entertains at t, to the effect that he (A) is hungry. This thought is different from twin-A's thought, also entertained at t, to the effect that twin-A is hungry. The two thoughts cause two different actions: A's action in the first case, twin-A's action in the second case. It may well be that, in *describing* these actions and the thoughts which cause them, we focus on some property which they share: we may describe both A's and twin-A's actions as *the action of opening the fridge*, and we may describe both thoughts as *the thought that one is hungry*, thereby abstracting from the environmental differences between A's and twin-A's thoughts and actions. Even so, the genuine effect is a particular action (not a generic one) and the genuine cause is a particular thought (not a type of thought).

This argument in support of the view that environment-independent 'types' of thought have no role to play in psychological explanation I find quite unconvincing, for it defeats itself. It makes use of Davidson's distinction between the true cause of an event – what Mill calls the 'producing cause' – and what we might call the 'explanatory cause', i.e. what we actually mention when we provide causal explanations of the event.[7] The producing cause, Davidson says, is a singular event, with all its properties, but the *explanatory* cause consists of (a particular subset of) properties of the event, or of the fact that the event in question has the properties in question. Now this very distinction can be used to show that the abstract type which the thought instantiates has a crucial role to play in psychological explanation, namely that of explanatory cause, even if the thought itself, *qua* particular event, is the producing cause. It may well be conceded that the action to be explained is the particular action performed by A upon his fridge, and the cause of this action the particular thought entertained by A (but not by twin-A); still, in *explaining* the action, we describe it abstractly as the subject's entertaining the thought that he is hungry. At this abstract level, *characteristic of psychological explanation*, A's and twin-A's thoughts and actions are 'the same'. Davidson's distinction between actual causation and causal explanation therefore justifies the two-component theorist in maintaining that the abstract types instantiated by A's and twin-A's thoughts and actions play a special role in psychological explanation.

I have just said that the abstract level of types is characteristic of psychological explanation. Why is this so? Because there is no causal explanation, thus no psychological explanation of an action as caused by a thought, without a 'covering law' – a law which, in the psychological case, we use to back the postulated causal relation between the effect (the action) and the cause (the thought). Causal explanation has an ineliminably nomological character. Now the laws in question, insofar as they are laws, can only be *general*; in the case at issue, the covering law can only relate *types* of thoughts to *types* of action.[8] Psychological explanations of an action proceed by (implicitly or explicitly) invoking such a law and pointing out that the particular thought mentioned as the putative cause and the particular action to be explained respectively instantiate the types of thought and action specified in the law. I conclude that the two-component theorist is right to maintain that psychological explanations are essentially conducted at the level of 'sorts' or 'types', even though it is *particular* thoughts and actions that enter into causal relations.

To legitimate the two-component picture, more needs to be said about the types or sorts involved in psychological explanation. For any aspect of a thought (or action) might be abstracted from so as to yield a 'type' of thought (or action). In defence of the two-component picture, it must be shown that the types in question result from abstracting *from the environment* and considering only what is common to e.g. A and twin-A. Now it all depends on the sort of psychology we are talking about. A distinction must be made between human psychology and, for example, the psychology of a particular person. The laws of human psychology must be species-wide; this demands that the types which occur in the laws be environment-independent: they cannot be specific to a particular subject (or class of subjects), nor specific to a particular context. It follows that we need mental states narrowly individuated for the purposes of human psychology.[9] The situation would be different if the psychology talked about was not human psychology but the psychology of a particular person. Imagine we are interested in the (idiosyncratic) psychology of John. The laws of this psychology involve types of thought and action specific to John. They relate types of John-thoughts to types of John-actions. But the psychology which, *qua* theorists, we are mainly interested in *is* human psychology, and in this particular case the laws involve environment-independent types of thought and action.

## 11.4 The empty case

Having gone this far, the two-component theorist has to face a crucial objection which we have already considered (11.2). The thought types which have just been shown to play a central role in psychological explanation are arguably still distinct from the 'narrow contents' of the two-component theorist, because of the constraint on types which was mentioned earlier: *Types, contrary to narrow contents, cannot be available in the empty case.*

The objection shows that narrow contents cannot be straightforwardly equated with types of *de re* thought. But they may be equated with more abstract types of thought. Suppose that A thinks 'This fridge contains food'. Twin-A also thinks 'This fridge contains food'. Their thoughts are different in the sense that they involve two different fridges, namely the fridges they are respectively looking at. But they instantiate the same type of *de re*, fridge-involving thought. By contrast, consider another possible *Doppelgänger*, Twintwin, who hallucinates a fridge and thinks, 'This fridge contains food'. Twintwin's thought is not a *de re*, fridge-involving thought. Since it involves no *res*, Twintwin's thought does not instantiate the *de re* type of thought which both A's and twin-A's thoughts instantiate. Nevertheless there is a significant degree of similarity between Twintwin's type of thought and the type of thought which A and twin-A entertain. Functionally there is much in common between the three thoughts (or mental episodes): as a result of their entertaining their respective thoughts, A, twin-A and Twintwin are all disposed to entertain further thoughts such as the thought that there is a food-containing fridge in front of them, and they are all diposed to act in such a way that, if there were a fridge in front of them, their behaviour would constitute the opening of the fridge in question. (In the case of A and twin-A, there *is* a fridge in front of them, and their behaviour *does* constitute the opening of a fridge.) The functional similarity between Twintwin's thought and those of A and twin-A suggests that there is a type of thought which they all instantiate. Such a type is available in the empty case, contrary to types of *de re* thought.

The types I have just introduced are the types which a species-wide psychology requires. Consider, for example, 'laws' L1 and L2:

L1: If a subject $S$ wishes to eat and thinks a certain fridge he sees in front of him contains food, then, if certain conditions are satisfied, $S$ opens the fridge in question.

L2: If a subject *S* wishes to eat and thinks 'This fridge in front of me contains food', then, if certain conditions are satisfied, *S* behaves in a tentatively fridge-opening way (that is, in such a way that, if there actually is a fridge in front of him, *S*'s behaviour constitutes the opening of the fridge).

A law which, like L1, relates a type of *de re* thought to a type of *res*-involving action applies only to subjects who are contextually in a position to entertain the relevant *de re* thoughts and accomplish the relevant *res*-involving actions; it does not apply to subjects who are not in the appropriate contextual relations to the relevant *res*. Thus both A's and twin-A's thoughts and actions can be subsumed under the types which occur in L1, but Twintwin's thought and action cannot: for there is no fridge such that Twintwin thinks of that fridge that it contains food (nor is there a fridge such that Twintwin opens it). L2, by contrast, is more general. It can be used to explain not only A's and twin-A's behaviour, but also Twintwin's behaviour.

The relation between L2 and L1 is similar to that between L1 and L:

L: If John wishes to eat, and if he thinks a certain fridge he sees in front of him contains food, then, if certain conditions are satisfied, John opens the fridge in question.

L is a law of John-psychology, not a law of human psychology. L, however, can be derived from L1 by existential instantiation. In the same way, L1, which applies only to subjects who find themselves in a certain context, could in principle be derived from L2 by means of appropriate analysis of (the second conjunct in) its antecedent clause.

Whatever we think of 'impure' psychological laws which, like L and L1, can be derived from 'pure' psychological laws like L2, my point is that the latter do not involve types of *de re* thought but more abstract types of thought which (contrary to types of *de re* thought) *are* available in the empty case. The notion of narrow content is thereby vindicated – at least as far as its role in psychological explanation is concerned. We must now consider the other objection raised by neo-Fregeans like Evans and McDowell to the notion of narrow content: the 'externalist objection', as I will call it.

### Notes

1   Or at least from Frege as traditionally interpreted. The non-Fregean nature of the two basic intuitions was acknowledged by McDowell

(1977) and Peacocke (1981), but Evans has convinced his fellow neo-Fregeans that Frege was much more 'Russellian' than had traditionally been thought. See chapter 6, note 2.

2  The two-component picture has been put forward by Putnam and Perry. A good statement of the view is to be found in McGinn (1982). See also Dennett (1982).

3  'Wide' and 'broad' will be used interchangeably in what follows.

4  Peacocke (1981) thinks he can have it both ways: he thinks he can maintain that a single entity (the Fregean thought) plays both roles, *and* accept the two-component analysis of this entity (or of what it is to have an attitude toward this entity). But I understand Frege's claim that the same entity plays both roles in such a way that it cannot be reconciled with the two-component analysis. On my interpretation, to say that a single entity plays both role is to say that the entity in question cannot be analysed into two components, each playing one of the two roles.

5  Here again, the single-componentist is closer to Frege than the two-componentist; for Frege takes the mode of presentation to *determine* the reference, and this makes it impossible for one and the same mode of presentation to correspond to different objects.

6  McDowell criticizes Peacocke for using the type/token terminology even though the constraint is not satisfied (McDowell, 1984, p. 14, note 14).

7  Davidson does not use 'explanatory cause' in contrast to Mill's 'producing cause' but he distinguishes the relation '*x* causally explains *y*' from the relation '*x* causes *y*' (Davidson, 1967, pp. 161–2). What I call the 'explanatory cause' is what fills the first argument place in the former relation; the producing cause is what fills the first argument place in the latter relation.

8  Of course, such 'laws' relating types of thought to types of action are not strict; they are *ceteris paribus* laws (whatever that may mean). This raises a host of well-known issues which I do not want to consider here.

9  This point is made (and ascribed to Fodor) in Adams *et al.* (1990, p. 222): 'If the laws that explain Al's behavior are different from the laws that explain Twin-Al's – because they feature different broad contents – then *no single* belief-desire psychology would apply to both Al and Twin-Al. However, since Al and Twin-Al are brain-identical, it is reasonable to expect that they fall under the same psychology. And if they do, it would have to be in virtue of sharing content (being subsumed by content laws) other than broad content. Therefore, it is reasonable to expect that a notion of narrow content psychology can be constructed.' See also Perry (1986b).

# Chapter 12

# Externalism and the two-component picture

## 12.1  Can thoughts be schematic?

The major objection to the notion of narrow content concerns its alleged incoherence. There are two versions of this objection. According to the first version, there cannot be anything like a 'narrow' content (an 'M-thought', in Evans's terminology), because it would have to be schematic, and no content properly speaking can be schematic. According to the second version, there cannot be anything like a 'narrow' content, because it would have to be instrinsic to the content-bearing state (non-relational), and no content properly speaking can be instrinsic. I shall deal with these two objections in turn.

The narrow content of a thought is what we get when we abstract from the 'objective' component contributed by the environment. Like the linguistic meaning of an indexical sentence, the narrow content of a thought-episode is not a complete representation, but a schema whose contextual enrichment yields a complete representation. But, according to Gareth Evans, a schema, not being a representation, cannot be a thought-content:

> Consider a specification of a thought involving indexical expressions: say 'I am miserable, and it is too hot here with that candle spluttering away....' But consider it as a schema, with the indexicals not used to refer to anything. Now the same schema would serve in the specification both of one's Doppelgänger's M-thoughts and of one's own.
> The methodological solipsist wants M-thinking to be recognizably *thinking* – which requires at least that it be a representational state –

but he wants to think of the object of the state as a schema. The content of the state is to be given in schematic terms, so that the criterion for being in the same representational state can be given in terms that are purely inner and accessible to consciousness.

However it is hard to see how there can be a representational state that meets this condition.

The objection is simple. It is of the essence of a representational state that it be capable of assessment as true or false. If a state is a representational state, it represents something other than itself as being thus and so, with the consequence that the state is true if and only if the thing concerned is thus and so. This is reflected in the form in which representational states are ascribed: 'S Φs that $p$'. But a schema is not assessable as true or false, nor is any state whose 'content' can be given only in schematic terms assessable as true or false. So, since an M-state has a 'content' which is strictly specifiable only in schematic terms, the M-state is not assessable as true or false; hence it is not a representational state. (Evans, 1982, p. 202)

It seems to me that on a certain understanding this objection begs the question against the two-component picture. On this understanding Evans postulates that only complete representations – representations assessable as true or false – deserve to be called mental contents; this entails that there cannot be narrow contents, since narrow contents are schematic rather than fully representational. But, precisely, the two-component theorist denies that *only* complete representations deserve to be called mental contents. He holds that there are two types of mental content: the complete thought itself, and the 'internal' or narrow component which it involves.

Evans's objection can be understood differently, however. For he suggests that the two-component theorist himself is committed to the view that narrow contents must be complete representations. The two-component theorist, Evans says, 'wants M-thinking to be recognizably *thinking* – which requires at least that it be a representational state.' In other words, the two-component theorist wants narrow thinking to conform to the phenomenology of thinking, and phenomenologically our thoughts *do* represent the world as being thus and so. This, McDowell says, is 'the most perspicuous phenomenological fact there is' (McDowell, 1986, p. 152). Phenomenologically speaking, there are no 'schemas' among the immediate objects of our thought.

I am not sure that phenomenological considerations such as these constitute a real difficulty for the two-component theorist. He may say that it is our *complete* thoughts which we are conscious of, but that we are conscious of them in such a way that different thoughts may appear to us indistinguishable. Two complete thoughts such that one's consciousness of them registers no qualitative difference between them are, by definition, two thoughts which instantiate the same narrow type, the same schema. This view does not entail that our consciousness is consciousness *of* a schema, hence, as far as I can see, it does not conflict with the phenomenological facts. Be that as it may, I find it hard to take the schema objection very seriously, because it is not mandatory, but merely convenient, to represent narrow contents – or, for that matter, the meaning of indexical sentences – as schemas. As Stalnaker and Perry both pointed out, narrow content and linguistic meaning can be given propositional rather than schematic representations.[1]

## 12.2 The externalist objection

The second version of the objection is much more serious. It purports to show that the notion of narrow content is inconsistent if a certain doctrine about content, namely Externalism, is true. Here is the objection:

> The alleged 'narrow' content is, by definition, independent of the external environment; the external world 'is relevant to [narrow] content only to the extent that it impinges on sensory surfaces' (Baker, 1987, p. 198). Thus a person who perceives an apple and a *Doppelgänger* who perceives (or merely hallucinates) a qualitatively indistinguishable apple are said to entertain the same narrow content. But *what makes (or gives) an internal state of the subject a content precisely is the relation between that state and something in the world.* If the relation is severed or abstracted from, what remains can no longer be called a content: it is at best a putative *bearer* of content, that is, a syntactic object. Narrow contents are not contents, on this view: at best they are (mental or neural) *sentences*. These sentences get interpreted – they acquire a content – only through their relations to objects and states of affairs in the external world. The relations in question are constitutive of the contents of thoughts, and there is no content, however narrow, which is not constituted by these relations.

This argument rests on two premisses:

*Definition of 'narrow'*: A thought-content is said to be 'narrow' if it is internal to the individual and independent of the external environment.
*Externalism*: Content essentially involves relations to objects in the external world; hence there can be no 'content' which is independent of the external environment.

Given these two premisses, it seems to follow that the very idea of 'narrow content' is incoherent. What about the premisses themselves? The first one seems hardly controversial, since it is a definition. The second premiss *is* controversial. Some defenders of narrow contents would reject Externalism on the grounds that the only relations which content irreducibly involves are relation between the content-bearing state and *proximal* (not *distal*) objects of experience. The proximal stimulations which cause the state to occur (rather than the distal objects which are responsible for those stimulations), together with the physical *behaviour* which the state gives rise to (rather than the object-involving *actions* of the subject) are what gives the state its intrinsic (narrow) content. The distal objects only play a role in fixing the wide content of the state (its truth-conditions). So the reply would go.

I think Externalism is right, however. If there were no distal objects but only superficial stimulations of the organism, or only behaviour falling short of constituting genuine action, there would be no content at all, however narrow. Thus I concur with those who believe that content necessarily involves relations to the external world. (I shall not argue this point in what follows; I shall merely take Externalism for granted.) The two-component theorist himself accepts Externalism as far as complete thoughts are concerned. He says that a complete thought-content involves a narrow content plus a relation between that content (or the content-bearing state) and something outside the mind; without the relation to something outside the mind, the representation would be at best a tentative representation, a tentative thought. Because it acknowledges the role of the external environment in the constitution of content, the two-component theorist is 'externalist' or 'anti-Cartesian'. It rejects Descartes's view that thoughts are subjective and 'internal', that is, world-independent.[2] But he is still Cartesian as far as narrow content is concerned, and this, according to radical externalists such as Burge, Evans and McDowell, or Putnam himself in his recent work (Putnam, 1988), is an inconsistency. We might, paraphrasing Evans, say that the two-component theorist wants narrow content to be recognizably 'content', hence something relational, while at the same time construing it as 'narrow', hence non-relational.

I shall spend the remaining sections of this chapter dealing with this objection. My strategy will be to show that, on a certain interpretation, the notion of narrow content is coherent even if we take Externalism for granted. In other words I will try to show that the two-component picture is consistent with Externalism, appearances to the contrary notwithstanding.

## 12.3 Two forms of environment-dependence: the relative notion of narrowness

Even though I accept Externalism, I think the two-component picture must be defended. For it rests on a very strong intuition, which supports the notion of narrow content. Let us call it the Cartesian intuition:

> *Cartesian intuition*:
> Different causes can produce the same effects on our sense organs and, via these effects, can induce the same subjective *experiences* in us. From the subject's point of view, the way the world is experienced is the same when she perceives an apple in front of her (and thinks that it is green) and when she merely hallucinates a qualitatively identical apple in front of her (and thinks that it is green): in both situations it seems to the subject that she is perceiving a certain apple.

Note that the state of the subject talked about here represents the world as being a certain way. Thus it is a representational state, not merely a syntactic object. Yet it is invariant under changes of the environment: the subjective state is the same, whether the subject perceives apple A or apple B or a pear mistakenly identified as an apple or nothing at all (the hallucinatory case).

Not only do we have strong intuitions supporting the notion of narrow content; there is also a powerful argument in favour of the two-component analysis (McGinn, 1982, pp. 212–3). According to this argument, mental contents (and representations in general, whether mental or not) are essentially *fallible*: there is no representation without a possibility of misrepresentation. This implies that a fundamental distinction has to be made between two independent aspects of representations: *what* is represented and what it is represented *as*.³ The latter aspect is an intrinsic property of the representation, while the former aspect is a relational, extrinsic property of the representation. *What* is represented – apple A or apple B, say – depends upon the external environment (it depends on which apple is actually being perceived), but what it is represented *as* is a feature of the narrow content understood as 'the action-guiding intra-individual role' of the representation (McGinn, 1982, p. 214).

McGinn's argument, which derives the two-component analysis of content from the essential fallibility of representations, is no less simple, direct and appealing than the externalist argument against narrow content (12.2), whose conclusion it directly contradicts. So we have a problem. One way of solving the problem consists in showing that the contradiction is merely apparent. This is what I will do in this section.

The two-component picture is based on a distinction between the narrow content, which is independent of the environment, and the wide content, which depends on the environment. Now 'independent of the environment' means 'in the head' or 'individualistic'. Hence it seems that the two-component theorist is committed to individualism with respect to at least a certain type of content; and this is inconsistent with Externalism, according to which contents are essentially non-individualistic (relational).

In what follows I will deny the crucial premiss that 'independent of the environment' means 'individualistic'. Or rather, I will show that the phrase 'independent of the environment' (like, perhaps, the phrase 'individualistic' – or 'intra-individual', as McGinn says) is ambiguous; there is a sense in which a content may be independent of the environment of the thinker – hence 'narrow' – even though it is not individualistic in the sense which is unacceptable to the externalist. The distinction between these two senses follows from a corresponding distinction between two ways in which contents may be said to depend on the environment.

Mental contents are clearly environment-dependent in the sense that the existence of a certain type of content depends on there being systematic causal relations between states of the mind/brain and types of objects in the external world. Thus a (type of) configuration in the brain is a concept of water only if it is normally tokened in the presence of water. It follows that there would be no water-concept if there were no water.⁴ This sort of environment-dependence is what Externalism is concerned with. It affects mental states considered as types: the content of a mental state *type* depends on the environment – namely, on what normally causes a tokening of the type. But there is another form of environment dependence which affects *tokens* rather than types. The 'wide' content of a particular token of the thought 'This man looks happy' is environment-dependent in the (stronger) sense that it depends on the context of occurrence of this token: it depends on the particular man who happens to cause *this tokening* of the thought. These two sorts of environment-dependence must be distinguished because, for a particular state token to have a content of type T (e.g. for a particular thought to be a thought *about water*), it is not necessary that *it* be caused by the type of object (viz. water) on whose existence the very existence of T depends.[5] Thus a state token may have the same content T as two other state tokens even though one is caused by the type of object in question, the next by another type of object, and the third one by no object at all (the hallucinatory case).

The possibility I have just alluded to, namely, that of maintaining the content T of a state constant through changes in the external environment, is one of the main implications of the notion of 'narrow content', as we have seen. What changes from one occurrence of the thought 'This man looks happy' to the next is the 'wide' content of the thought; its 'narrow' content remains constant. We may say that the narrow content is the content of the thought type – the content which is common to all tokens of the type – whereas the wide content is the content which contextually attaches to a particular token of the thought. This distinction, inspired by Kaplan's analysis of indexical utterances, is the gist of the two-component picture as I understand it and as it has been criticized by radical externalists. But if, as I claim, *that* is what the two-component theorist has in mind, then the two-component picture cannot be criticized on the grounds that content is inherently relational and environment-dependent. For the two-component theorist need not deny that this is so. Since there are two senses in which a content may be said to depend (or not to depend) on the environment, it is possible to conciliate the two-component theorist's claim that the narrow content of a state token does not depend on the environment *of the token* with the externalist's claim that the content of a state type always depends upon the *type* of context in which the state is *normally* tokened.

The distinction I have just made shows up in an interesting thought-experiment devised by Tyler Burge (1986). Suppose a thinker who perceives a pear but misidentifies it as an apple: for some reason, the pear activates not the perceptual type corresponding to pears, $PT_\pi$, but the perceptual type corresponding to apples, $PT_\alpha$. This is a case of misperception. Now suppose a world $w$ in which there is no apple and the perceptual type $PT_\alpha$ is normally activated by the perception of pears. Suppose that the same episode occurs in $w$ as in the actual world: the thinker perceives the same pear and it activates the same perceptual type $PT_\alpha$. Even though the thinker is in the same internal state in $w$ as in the actual world, there is a difference in the content of her thought: in the actual world the thinker perceives the pear as an apple, while she correctly perceives it as a pear in the possible world $w$. For the perceptual type $PT_\alpha$ is that by means of which the thinker (or more generally the species to which she belongs) discriminates pears from other objects, in $w$. When an object is perceived under that type, it is perceived as a pear in $w$, in exactly the same way and for the same reason as it is perceived as an apple in the actual world.

By this example Burge purports to show that contents cannot be individualistic: even if the internal (neurophysiological) states of the individual are fixed, including the perceptual type (e.g. $PT_\alpha$) which happens to be activated in a certain episode of thought, the content of the thought may vary if the environment is made to vary. The internal states of the subject do not change as we pass from the actual world to $w$, in Burge's example; yet the thought "This apple is F" has been transformed into the thought "This pear is F". This change in the content of thought is due merely to a change in the external environment of the thinker. And it cannot be argued that the change in question affects only the 'wide' content of the thought, while leaving its 'narrow' content intact; for the content that has been transformed bears all the hallmarks of a narrow type of content. What the person who perceives the pear as an apple thinks – namely "This apple is F" – is the same thing as she would think if the object she perceives really was an apple (or if she was hallucinating an apple and there was nothing in front of her). The content Burge is talking about is the subjective ingredient of the thought, what runs through the mind of the thinker. As Burge says in terms which McGinn might have used, it is what the perceived object (if any) is perceived *as* which is affected by changes of the external environment, not merely the object which happens to be perceived.

Burge's example cuts both ways, however. It certainly shows that there is no dimension of content which is not affected by the external environment, hence it supports Externalism. But it also shows that Externalism does not undermine the wide/narrow distinction understood in a certain way. Burge distinguishes two sorts of variations in the environment, and this entails a corresponding distinction between two sorts of 'independence from' the environment,[6] hence between two different notions of 'narrow content' – a weak one and a strong one. As Burge points out, we may vary either what normally causes (i.e. activates) a given perceptual type, or what happens to cause a particular token of the type. 'Narrow content' in the weak sense is what is invariant through changes of the latter sort (the narrow content of a psychological state is independent of what causes the state, in the sense that the state's having this content is consistent with the cause's being of this or that sort), but it need not be 'narrow' in the strong sense, that is, invariant through changes of the *former* sort (as Burge points out, the state would not have this content if it were not normally caused by an object of such and such a type). Contrary to narrow contents in the strong sense – whose existence the externalist denies – the narrow content in the weak sense depends on which relations normally hold between the content-bearing state (e.g. the perceptual type, in Burge's example) and the external world; but, once fixed by the normal relations, it is constant and common to e.g. the veridical case, the case of misperception and the hallucinatory case.[7]

Corresponding to the two notions of narrow content, there are two versions of the two-component picture. One version uses the strong, individualistic notion of narrow content, and is inconsistent with Externalism. Another one – that which I am defending – uses the weak notion and is consistent with Externalism. One may thus take content to be inherently relational, in accordance with Externalism, while maintaining that there are two types of content, a type of content which does, and one which does not, depend upon the *actual* environment of the thought-episode. The 'narrow' type of content, which does not depend upon the actual environment (but only upon the normal environment), constitutes what McGinn calls 'the action-guiding intra-individual role' of the representation as opposed to 'its referential aspect' (McGinn, 1982, p. 114). That narrow content in this sense can no more be construed individualistically than wide content can is a major finding, but it should not be overstated. In particular, it does not show that it was a mistake to distinguish between the two types of content. What must be rejected is not the two-component picture *per se*, but only that particular version of the two-component picture which is associated with individualism with respect to narrow content.

## 12.4 Second-order narrow contents: the externalist's dilemma

Let me take stock. I have shown that the two-component picture, based on the wide/narrow distinction, may be interpreted in such a way that it does not conflict with Externalism. On this interpretation 'narrow' is understood in a *relative* rather than an *absolute* sense. In the absolute sense 'narrow content' means 'solipsistic', that is, wholly independent of the environment. I agree with Externalism that there is no such thing. Yet I hold that there is room for a relative notion of narrowness. To say that a content is narrow in a relative sense is to say that there is an aspect $m$ under which it does not depend on the environment; this is perfectly consistent with its depending on the environment under some other aspect $n$. Thus a content may be said to be narrow in a relative sense if it does not depend upon the actual environment of the thought-episode, even though it depends upon the normal environment. A content would be narrow in the absolute sense if there were no aspect under which it depended on the environment. (From now on I shall always use 'narrow' in the weak, relative sense and reserve the phrase 'solipsistic' for contents that are narrow in the strong, absolute sense).[8]

If narrowness is a relative notion, it seems that there must be *degrees* of width and narrowness. Some contents are narrower (or wider) than other contents. The (relative) narrow content of the thought that this apple is green is *less* environment-dependent, hence narrower, than its wide content, even though it also depends on the environment and cannot be said to be narrow in the absolute sense. Going further, we can imagine a content that would be still narrower. Consider, for example, Putnam's famous Twin Earth thought-experiment (Putnam, 1975). Putnam claims that there is something common to my concept of water and to that of my twin on Twin Earth, even though our concepts denote different substances. This common content is supposed to be independent even of the *normal* environment: for it is the normal (not the actual) environment which varies from Earth to Twin Earth. Hence the narrow content Putnam is talking of is *narrower* than the 'narrow content' which depends on the normal environment (though not of the actual environment). Whether or not we follow Putnam in construing this 'supernarrow' content as solipsistic content, it turns

```
                    wide content of
                'This water has a strange colour'
                         /        \
        first-order narrow content    +    environment
              /        \
    second-order      +    environment
    narrow content
```

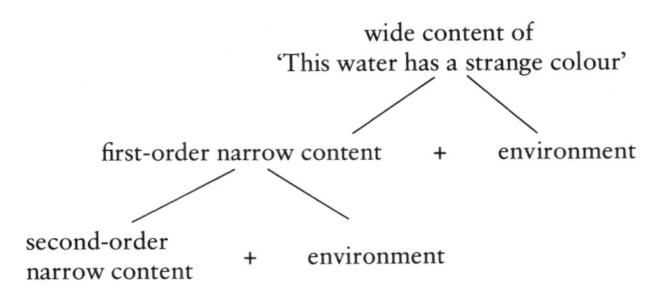

**Figure 5**

out that we have (at least) three levels to distinguish rather than merely two.

To see that it is so, let us complicate Putnam's example a bit. Suppose that, while looking at a fountain, I think: 'This water has a strange colour'; my *Doppelgänger* thinks the same thing while looking at a fountain on Twin Earth. My thought and that of my twin clearly differ in wide content: my thought refers to what flows from the fountain on Earth, while his thought refers to the different substance which flows from the fountain on Twin Earth. But, as Burge correctly points out (Burge, 1982), there is more than merely this difference between the two thoughts. Whatever it is that we are actually looking at and referring to in thought, I am thinking of it *as water* on Earth and my twin thinks of its counterpart *as t-water*. In other words, not only *what* is represented, but *how* this is represented is different on Earth and Twin Earth. Our thoughts have different *narrow contents in the relative sense*, since narrow contents in the relative sense depend upon the normal environment, and the normal environment precisely differs on Earth and on Twin Earth. Yet Putnam claims that our respective concepts of water and t-water are identical at the level of what *he* calls 'narrow content'. Putnam, in effect, provides a two-component analysis of a type of content which is *already narrow in the relative sense I have characterized* (figure 5).

Do we really need second-order narrow contents? I think we do. For the intuition in favour of second-order narrow contents is as strong as, and actually very close to, that in favour of first-order narrow contents: both notions of narrow content are supported by what I called the 'Cartesian intuition' (12.3). From the subject's point of view, the way the world is experienced is the same whether the apple she actually perceives is apple A or a qualitatively indistinguishable apple B or a hallucinatory apple or a pear misidentified as an apple. Quite similarly, the way the world is experienced is supposed to be the same for an Earthling and for her *Doppelgänger* on Twin Earth, since Earth and Twin Earth are characterized by their subjective indistinguishability. The concepts of water and t-water are certainly different, but this difference makes sense only for an external observer. Subjectively there is no difference between thinking of something as water and thinking of it as t-water: this is something which Putnam stipulates in devising his thought-experiment. Putnam's stipulation in no way seems counterintuitive; we have no trouble imagining the situation which Putnam wants us to imagine. So it seems that we cannot avoid making at least a threefold distinction between: (i) wide contents, which depend on the actual environment, (ii) (first-order) narrow contents, which depend on the normal environment, and (iii) the contents involved in Putnam's Twin Earth thought-experiment, which do not even depend on the normal environment. I shall call the latter 'PASCs', an abbreviation for 'Putnam's alleged supernarrow contents'.

The problem is that PASCs, contrary to (first-order) narrow contents, raise an apparently insuperable dilemma for the externalist. An externalist cannot accept Putnam's claim that PASCs are solipsistic contents. Given that a 'solipsistic content' is a *contradictio in adjecto*, if PASCs are contents, they cannot be solipsistic but must be environment-dependent, and if they are *not* environment-dependent, they must be conceived of as content-bearers rather than as genuine contents. Yet neither alternative seems acceptable – both conflict with the intuitions behind Putnam's thought-experiment.

Let me spell out the externalist's dilemma with respect to PASCs. If we say that PASCs are contents, we must admit that they are environment-dependent (since there is no solipsistic content, from an externalist point of view). But this seems hardly to make sense. By stipulation, PASCs are 'in the head' – they are what runs through the mind of the thinker. Being in the head, they are independent of the environment: whatever runs through the mind of someone in one environment (e.g. on Earth) also runs through the mind of her *Doppelgänger* in another environment (e.g. in Twin Earth). Thus when the Earthling thinks of water, her *Doppelgänger* entertains the same internal representation, even though what the representation denotes is water on Earth and t-water on Twin Earth. The representations differ 'objectively' or 'referentially', but subjectively everything is the same for the Earthling and her *Doppelgänger*. This solipsistic character is part and parcel of the very notion of a PASC, which corresponds to our intuitive notion of an 'internal', 'subjective' dimension of thought as opposed to its external or objective dimension. Now, in an externalist framework, this solipsistic or internal character entails that the PASC is not itself a content, nor even an ingredient of content, but merely a syntactic object, a *bearer* of content. However, *this conclusion cannot be accepted either*, for it is inconsistent with another aspect of our intuitive notion of the internal or subjective dimension of thought.

As McDowell rightly emphasized, we conceive of our subjective experiences as essentially representational and directed towards some external reality. Experience is experience *of* the world as being thus and so. This is the well-known feature of intentionality which, Brentano argued, is intrinsic to our mental life. Owing to that feature, we cannot make sense of a notion of subjective experience which would deprive it of its representational properties. 'Experience, conceived from its own point of view, is not blank or blind, but purports to be revelatory of the world we live in' (McDowell, 1986, p. 152): this, McDowell says, is 'the most perspicuous phenomenological fact there is' (ibid). There is no subjective experience without a *content* for that experience, no internal representation which is not a *representation*. It is therefore inconsistent to equate PASCs with our subjective experiences and internal representations while at the same time construing them as opaque, 'syntactic' objects deprived of representational properties.

This dilemma must be taken very seriously, because it threatens to undermine the attempt I have made to accommodate the Cartesian intuition within an externalist framework. It seems that the externalist must reject Putnam's thought-experiment as incoherent insofar as it involves the stipulation that the Earthling and her *Doppelgänger*, who live in different environments, share not only their brain states but also their subjective experiences and internal representations. Now this stipulation rests on the Cartesian intuition, on which the two-component picture is based: the intuition that different worldly causes can induce the same subjective experiences in us. Putnam's thought-experiment is nothing other than an elaboration of this basic intuition. So it seems that an externalist must reject the Cartesian intuition on which both Putnam's Twin Earth thought-experiment and the two-component picture are based.

That is not really so, however. As I made clear in 12.3, I take the Cartesian intuition, and the two-component picture which rests on it, to be consistent with Externalism. The trouble arises only when the 'internal' or 'subjective' component posited by the two-component picture is assumed to be solipsistic. For 'solipsistic' entails 'non-semantic', and this is inconsistent with the very notions of narrow *contents*, subjective *experiences* or internal *representations*. My strategy, as far as the analysis of demonstrative thoughts is concerned, has been to devise a relative notion of narrow content which is 'internal' in some sense without also being 'solipsistic'; and I think this strategy should work also in the present case. In other words, it ought to be possible to maintain both the Cartesian intuition and Externalism, provided one drops the solipsism assumption about PASCs. My suggestion, therefore, is that we get out of the dilemma not by rejecting Putnam's thought-experiment as incoherent, but by denying that the internal representations and subjective experiences involved in this thought-experiment are solipsistic. To this solution I now turn.

## 12.5  Holistic Externalism

Why does it seem so obvious that PASCs are solipsistic and do not depend even on the normal environment? Because they are common to the Earthling and her *Doppelgänger*. Since the difference between Earth and Twin Earth is a difference in the normal environment, PASCs are naturally taken to be independent of the normal environment. But this, I shall argue, is a mistake. Even though the PASC [[water]] is what we get when we *unground* the concept of water, that is, when we abstract from the environment in which it is grounded (viz. Earth, as opposed to e.g. Twin Earth), still it is part of a concept system which is *globally* grounded and environment-dependent. It thus remains grounded to some extent, via the concept system to which it belongs, and this, I shall argue, is sufficient to endow the PASC with some content, in an externalist framework.

To construct a PASC is for the thought-experimenter to abstract from the relevant aspects of the normal environment by considering only what is common to that concept and to similar concepts grounded in different environments. Now in this very process of 'ungrounding' a given concept we rely on the neighbouring concepts. Consider the way Putnam and others spell out the narrow content of 'water'. The 'narrow' concept of water (or, for that matter, of t-water) is supposed to be that of a colourless and tasteless liquid which descends from the sky as rain, which can be found in lakes and rivers, which quenches thirst, and so forth. This typical characterization of the narrow content of 'water' involves other concepts – that of a liquid, that of rain, that of a river, that of thirst, etc. This is not surprising, for concepts, in general, can be characterized along two different dimensions: the vertical dimension (that of the reference, i.e. what things in the environment the concept denotes) and the horizontal dimension (the relations between this concept and other concepts in the concept system). When we unground a concept, that is, when we sever the link between a concept and its reference, what remains are the interconceptual connections – what may be called the 'role' of the concept or (to use a different metaphor) its place in the concept system. The role thus understood is what the concepts of water and t-water, which denote different substances, have in common.

From an externalist point of view, the role is not enough to constitute content. The (formal) relations between one concept and other concepts in the concept system may be fixed even though the interpretation of the concepts (or the global interpretation of the concept system) remains undeterminate. To get an interpretation – to know what the concepts are concepts of – we need to know what those concepts denote. However, knowing the role of a concept Φ provides one with some knowledge of its content *if the concepts to which Φ is related by virtue of its role are themselves interpreted, that is, grounded in some environment*. This is precisely what happens in the case of water: in the ungrounding process we abstract from the reference and consider only the relations between that concept and other concepts in the system, *but the concepts in question are themselves interpreted*. This is why the PASC [[water]] is more than simply the formal 'role' of the concept 'water': it can itself be called a (narrow) 'concept' because it is not totally ungrounded, since it benefits from the environmental grounding of the other concepts to which it is related.

At this point it may be objected that the neighbouring concepts themselves are affected by the ungrounding process. Take for example the concept of rain, which is connected to the concept of water as well as to that of sky, of cloud, and so forth. If we unground the concept of water, that is, if we substitute the PASC [[water]] for the concept of water everywhere in the concept system, the concept of rain is thereby transformed and made 'narrower' (less dependent of the environment). Instead of the ordinary concept of rain (i.e. water descending from the sky, or something like that), what results from the ungrounding process applied to the concept of water is a 'narrow' concept of rain, namely: [[water]] descending from the sky, or something like that. Ordinary rain falls under this narrow concept, but Twin Earthian 'rain' (which is not really rain, but XYZ falling from the sky) also does. It follows that the concept of rain is ungrounded to some extent when we unground the concept of water, to which it is related. But what counts for my purposes is that the narrow concept of 'rain' remains substantially grounded, by virtue of e.g. its connections to the concept of sky which is not (or so it seems to me) significantly affected by the substitution of [[water]] for water. The concept of sky is clearly grounded: what makes it the concept of sky is its association with something in the external world, namely, the sky. Being closely related to the concept of sky, the narrow concept of rain itself is grounded to some extent, even though it is less grounded than the ordinary concept of rain.

When we unground a concept Φ, this has effects on various concepts: Φ itself if ungrounded, its close neighbours are ungrounded to a lesser extent, and so forth. All these ungroundings are nevertheless relative rather than absolute. For the concepts in question remain part of a concept system which is *globally* environment-dependent in the sense that a significant number of the concepts of the system are environmentally grounded. It follows that Φ itself, the concept that was ungrounded in the first place, is still grounded to some extent, albeit indirectly.

I conclude that the externalist's alleged argument against construing PASCs as contents in accordance with the Cartesian intuition must be rejected. The PASC [[water]] need not be construed as something purely formal and syntactic, even though it is independent of the normal environment. This is so because, although independent of the normal environment to some extent, it is not solipsistic, i.e. *absolutely* independent of the normal environment. Even the PASC [[water]] depends upon the environment via its relation to environment-dependent concepts such as 'liquid', 'lake', 'river', 'rain', and so forth. We construct PASCs by abstracting from certain aspects of the normal environment, namely, those that make the difference between Earth and Twin Earth, but there are many aspects of the normal environment which we take for granted when we induldge in this abstraction process, and they are what gives the PASC its content. If we were to abstract from *all* aspects of the normal environment, that is, if we were to unground all concepts at the same time, *then* we would be left with a network of uninterpreted symbols related to each other in various ways. But this is not what happens in the Twin Earth thought-experiment. In the Twin Earth thought-experiment, a single concept is locally ungrounded. As I hope I have shown, such a concept remains grounded to some extent via the other concepts in the system, and this is enough to make it a (narrow) 'concept' endowed with 'content', in an externalist framework.

## Notes

1. See Stalnaker (1981) and Perry (1988). See also 15.5 below. Stalnaker's 'diagonal propositions' and Perry's 'created propositions' are propositions, hence complete representations, which can be used instead of schemas to represent either the meaning of indexical sentences or the narrow content of indexical beliefs. (Actually the matter is slightly more complex than that, but I cannot elaborate here).
2. According to Descartes, we might enjoy the same thoughts as we actually entertain if the objective world was utterly different from what we think it is – even if the external world did no exist.
3. This is reminiscent of Goodman's famous distinction between a picture of a horse and a horse-picture. See e.g. Goodman, 1947, pp. 70–1.
4. This is actually too strong. It can be argued that our concept system *holistically* depends upon the environment, without every particular concept locally depending on the environment. Thus we might have a concept of water even if we had no water around, provided we had concepts of 'hydrogen' and 'oxygen' and the ability to construct the concept '$H_2O$'. In such a situation, it would be possible to entertain a concept of water which would be environmentally grounded via the neighbouring concepts, but not directly through relations to actual water. I shall deal with this holistic version of Externalism in 12.5; meanwhile I shall simplify a bit and assume (for the sake of argument) the stronger variant, local Externalism.
5. For an elaboration of this point, see Dretske, 1988, chapter 3.
6. To say that a content is independent from the environment is to say that it is not affected by changes in the environment; hence the notion of environment-independence is derivative upon that of a change (a variation) in the environment. The ambiguity of the latter notion therefore entails an ambiguity in the former one.

7 Although the narrow content is common to the veridical case, the case of misperception and the hallucinatory case, nevertheless the veridical case has an obvious primacy over the other cases since it is the 'normal' case and the normal case is *constitutive* of narrow content. As McDowell admits (1986, p. 152), this primacy given to the veridical case is *sufficient* to undermine the Cartesian picture.

8 In introducing this new sense for the wide/narrow distinction, I take advantage of the fact that 'narrow' and 'wide' are relative terms, like 'tall' and 'thin'.

# Part II
# The pragmatics of direct reference

# Introduction

As I indicated at the beginning of this book, direct reference comes in two varieties. On the one hand there are expressions which *are* referential; on the other hand there are expressions which can be *used* referentially even though they are not intrinsically referential. So far I have considered only the former, that is, expressions whose linguistic meaning includes the semantic feature which I called REF. But something has to be said about the referential use of expressions which are not intrinsically referential, e.g. definite descriptions.

Something has also to be said about non-referential (or non-purely-referential) uses of referential expressions. Attributive uses of indexicals, demonstratives or proper names are less commonly acknowledged and discussed in the literature than referential uses of definite descriptions, but they exist and must be accounted for. Consider the following example, due to Geoff Nunberg. In the context of a discussion about the difference between French and American culture, an American says: 'We (Americans) are incapable of understanding the European concept of laicism.' As Nunberg points out:

> In this case the pronoun *we* does not refer 'directly' to the 250 million particular people who are in fact Americans; it is not claimed that *they* can never understand laicism. Rather . . . we evaluate the utterance by asking whether it could be the case that someone should be an American and understand laicism. (Nunberg, 1990, p. 9)

A similar example, due to Steven Schiffer, was discussed in chapter 10 ('He must be a giant', uttered with reference to a gigantic footprint in the sand).¹ Such 'attributive' uses of indexicals and demonstratives raise a serious problem for the theory of direct reference. According to the latter an utterance including a referential term (for example a pronoun) expresses a singular proposition. But intuitively it seems that 'We are incapable of understanding laicism' (Nunberg) and 'He must be a giant' (Schiffer) are true only if *whoever is an American* has trouble understanding laicism and *whoever caused that footprint* is a giant; in other words, the propositional constituent corresponding to the referential term seems to be a concept or mode of presentation rather than the referent itself, as the theory of direct reference would predict.

We face the same sort of problem with belief sentences. The theory of direct reference seems to entail that 'John believes that Cicero was a Roman orator' and 'John believes that Tully was a Roman orator' express the same proposition (since 'Tully' and 'Cicero' directly refer to the same person), but it is intuitively clear that one may be true and the other false. This shows that, in such a context, a referential expression contributes more to propositional content than merely its reference, and this raises an obvious problem for the theory.

In the chapters which follow I will show how referential uses of non-referential terms and non-purely-referential uses of referential terms can be handled within pragmatics. That they are to be handled within pragmatics is fairly commonplace, but the sort of pragmatics that has been appealed to in the literature on direct reference is much too rudimentary for the task at hand. Since that is so, I will spend two chapters – chapters 13 and 14 – talking about methodological issues in pragmatics, so as to prepare the way for what follows. The next chapters deal with the referential/attributive distinction (with respect both to definite descriptions: chapter 15, and to indexicals: chapter 16) and with belief reports (chapters 17–20).

## Notes

1  To my knowledge, the first explicit mention of descriptive uses of indexicals is to be found in Loar's classical paper on the semantics of singular terms, where he says: 'Personal pronouns ... have a sort of "attributive" as well as a referential use. For example, upon our discovery of the murdered Smith I might say "*He* is insane", meaning that Smith's murderer, whoever that may be, is insane' (Loar, 1976, p. 356).

# II.1
# Methodological preliminaries

# Chapter 13

# Truth-conditional pragmatics

## 13.1 Enriching the Gricean picture: two sorts of pragmatic explanation

Most contemporary philosophers of language accept something which I call the 'Gricean picture'. In this section I will present the picture and show that it embodies a dubious assumption – an assumption which must be brought to light and criticized before we can confidently use the pragmatic apparatus set up by Grice and his followers.

*The Gricean picture*
The meaning of a sentence conventionally determines what is literally said by uttering the sentence – the literal truth-conditions of the utterance; for example, the meaning of the sentence 'I have not had breakfast today' determines that, if S utters the sentence on a certain day, what he thereby says is that he has had no breakfast on that day. The meaning of the sentence also determines other, non-truth-conditional aspects of utterance meaning, like those responsible for the difference between 'and' and 'but'. Grice calls them 'conventional implicatures'. Conventional implicatures are to be distinguished from the 'conversational' implicatures of the utterance, which are also distinct from, and external to, what is said. Conversational implicatures are part of what the utterance communicates, but they are not *conventionally* determined by the meaning of the sentence; they are pragmatically rather than semantically determined. For example, in saying that he has had no breakfast, S may convey to his audience that he is hungry and wishes to be fed. As Grice pointed out, the generation of these 'conversational implicatures' can be accounted for by connecting

them with certain general principles or 'maxims' of conversation that participants in a talk-exchange are mutually expected to observe. In the Gricean framework, conversational implicatures are contextual implications of the utterance act – they are the assumptions that follow from the speaker's saying what he says together with the presumption that he is observing the maxims of conversation.

Since what is communicated includes a pragmatic, non-conventional element, viz. the conversational implicatures, the fact that a given expression receives different interpretations in different contexts does not imply that it is semantically ambiguous. The intuitive difference in meaning can be accounted for at the semantic level, by positing two different literal meanings, but it can also be accounted for at the pragmatic level, by positing a conversational implicature which in some contexts combines with what is literally said. Take, for example, the sentence "P or Q". It can receive an inclusive or an exclusive interpretation. Instead of saying that 'or' is ambiguous in English, we may consider it as unambiguously inclusive and account for the exclusive reading by saying that in some contexts the utterance conversationally implicates that "P" and "Q" are not both true. When there is such a conversational implicature, the overall meaning of the utterance is clearly exclusive.

When an intuitive 'ambiguity' can be accounted for either at the semantic level, by positing two different literal meanings, or at the pragmatic level, by positing a conversational implicature, the pragmatic account is to be preferred, according to Grice. This is the substance of the methodological principle he called 'Modified Occam's Razor': *Senses are not to be multiplied beyond necessity* (Grice, 1989, p. 47). This is a principle of theoretical parsimony, like Occam's Razor. Pragmatic explanations, when available, are to be preferred because they are economical, in the sense that the principles and assumptions they appeal to are very general and independently motivated. By contrast, positing a semantic ambiguity is an *ad hoc*, costly move – a move which the possibility of a pragmatic analysis makes entirely superfluous.

The Gricean picture which I have just presented has been enormously influential, and rightly so; but it raises a problem which has been recognized only recently. The problem is connected with the notion that sentence meaning conventionally determines what is said. Grice is aware that what is said depends not only on the conventional meaning of the words but also on the context of utterance. What is said by uttering 'I have not had breakfast today' depends on who is speaking and when. That is why there is a difference between the conventional meaning of words and what is said by uttering the words. The conventional meaning of the words only determines, or helps to determine, what is said, according to Grice. But what does this mean? A common answer is that sentence meaning is a 'function' from context on to propositions; it is a rule that determines, for every context, what is said by uttering the sentence in that context. Similarly, the meaning of a word like 'I' is a function that takes us from a context of utterance to the semantic value of the word in that context, which semantic value (the reference of 'I') is what the word contributes to the proposition expressed by the utterance. On this view, made popular by Kaplan's work on the logic of demonstratives, what is said by an utterance depends not only on the conventional meaning of the words but also on the context of utterance; however, recourse to the context of utterance is guided and controlled by the conventional meaning of the words. The meaning of 'I' tells us what to look for in the context of utterance for a full identification of what is said; once the context is given, what is said can be automatically decoded.

Neat and attractive though it is, this view of the matter is quite unrealistic. In general, even if we know who is speaking, when, to whom, and so forth, the conventional meaning of the words falls short of supplying enough information to exploit this knowledge of the context so as to secure understanding of what is said. Consider a simple example, 'He has bought John's book'. To understand what is said, one must identify the intended referent of 'he'. At most, the conventional meaning of 'he' imposes that the referent be male, but this allegedly necessary condition is certainly not sufficient and does not uniquely identify the referent in the context of utterance. The meaning of the word 'he' provides no 'rule', no criterion enabling one to identify the reference. The meaning of the sentence, in this case as in many others, seriously underdetermines what is said. (More on this in 18.3.) Nor is this underdetermination limited to the reference of referring expressions. To understand what is said by 'He has bought John's book', one must identify the referent of 'he', of 'John' and (perhaps) of 'John's book'. But one must also identify the relation that is supposed to hold between John and the book. According to Kay and Zimmer (1976, p. 29), 'genitive locutions present the hearer with two nouns and a metalinguistic instruction that there is a relation between these two nouns that the hearer must supply'. 'John's book' therefore means something like 'the book that bears relation x to John'. To understand what is said by means of a sentence in which the expression 'John's book' occurs, this meaning must be contextually enriched by instantiating the variable 'x'. In other words, not only the reference but the descriptive sense of the expression 'John's book' is context-dependent. Moreover, as in the case of 'he', there is no rule or function taking us from the context to the relevant semantic value. The only constraint linguistically imposed on the relation between John and the book is that it be a relation between John and the book.

The purpose of this chapter not being to review the literature on context-dependence, I will not proceed with further examples. I will simply assume (1) that context-dependence extends far beyond reference assignment, and (2) that it is generally 'free' rather than 'controlled', in the sense that the linguistic meaning of a context-sensitive expression constrains its possible semantic values but does not consist in a 'rule' or 'function' taking us from context to semantic value.

Up to this point we need not depart from the Gricean picture, but simply enrich it. We have three levels of meaning: sentence meaning, what is said, and what is communicated. What is communicated includes not only what is said but also the conversational implicatures of the utterance.[1] The mechanism of implicature generation suggested by Grice is intended to account for the step from what is said to what is communicated. But how are we to account for the step from sentence meaning to what is said? What bridges the gap instituted by there being a 'free' type of context-dependence pervasive in natural language? Grice does not address this issue. However, as many people have suggested (e.g. Katz, 1972, p. 449; Walker, 1975, p. 157; Atlas, 1979, pp. 276–8; Wilson & Sperber, 1981, p. 156), the pragmatic apparatus by means of which Grice accounts for conversational implicatures can also be used to account for the determination of what is said on the basis of sentence meaning. In the interpretation process, the referent of 'he' and the relation between John and the book in 'He has bought John's book' are selected so as to make what the speaker says consistent with the presumption that he is observing the maxims of conversation. The speaker might have meant that Jim has bought the book written by John or that Bob has bought the book sought by John. The hearer will select the interpretation that makes the speaker's utterance consistent with the presumption that he is trying to say something true and relevant.[2]

Once the Gricean picture is enriched in the manner indicated, a problem arises. Implicit in the Gricean picture is the assumption that there are two, *and only two*, ways of accounting for *prima facie* ambiguities: the semantic approach, which posits a multiplicity of literal meanings, and the pragmatic approach, which posits conversational implicature.[3] Modified Occam's Razor provides a reason to prefer the latter approach, when it can be implemented, to the former. These two approaches correspond to the two basic levels of meaning that are distinguished in the Gricean picture: sentence meaning, which determines what is literally said, and the utterance's overall meaning, which comprises not only what is said but everything that happens to be communicated, including the conversational implicatures. The semantic approach locates the ambiguity at the level of sentence meaning, while the pragmatic approach considers that it is generated only at the level of what is communicated. But in the enriched Gricean picture, there are three basic levels of meaning rather than two: sentence meaning, what is said, and what is communicated. A pragmatic process is involved not only to get from what is said to what is communicated but also to get from sentence meaning to what is said. It follows that there are three ways of accounting for *prima facie* ambiguities rather than only two. Besides the semantic approach, which locates the ambiguity at the first level, that of sentence meaning, there are two pragmatic approaches, corresponding to the second and third levels of meaning (what is said and what is communicated). The classical Gricean approach considers that what is said is the same on all readings of the 'ambiguous' utterance, the difference between the readings being due to a conversational implicature which, in some contexts, combines with what is literally said. The other pragmatic approach considers that the difference is a difference in what is said, even though the sentence itself is not ambiguous; this is possible owing to the semantic underdetermination of what is said.[4]

The important point is that Modified Occam's Razor does not support the approach in terms of conversational implicature as against the other pragmatic approach; it only says that a pragmatic approach is to be preferred, *ceteris paribus*, to a semantic approach. Hence, enriching the Gricean picture in the manner indicated has the result that the classical Gricean approach to multiple readings in terms of conversational implicature can no longer be justified by appealing to Modified Occam's Razor, as it could when it was assumed to be the only pragmatic alternative to a semantic approach. The classical Gricean approach is threatened by the appearance of a pragmatic rival.

Consider, as an example, Donnellan's distinction between two uses of definite descriptions. Donnellan held that what is said by an utterance of 'Smith's murderer is insane' is different according to whether the description 'Smith's murderer' is used attributively or referentially. On the attributive interpretation, what is said is true if and only if there is one and only one person who murdered Smith and he or she is insane. But if the description 'Smith's murderer' is used to refer to a certain person, Jones, who is known to have murdered Smith, rather than in general to whoever murdered Smith, then the utterance is true if and only if *Jones* is insane: Jones's being the murderer of Smith is no more part of the truth-condition of what is said, on this 'referential' interpretation, than my being the speaker is part of the truth-condition of what I say when I utter the sentence 'I am insane'. This was Donnellan's view. (In chapter 15, I shall refer to this view as 'the Naive Theory' – a theory which I will set out to defend.) Now a large number of competent philosophers have used the Gricean picture to argue against this view. In doing so, they have taken for granted that there are only two possible approaches to Donnellan's distinction: a semantic approach, according to which the literal meaning of the sentence and, therefore, what is said, is different on the referential and the attributive reading, and a pragmatic approach, according to which what is said on both readings is the same thing (viz., that there is a unique murderer of Smith and that he or she is insane), the referential reading being only distinguished at the level of what is communicated. Using Modified Occam's Razor as an argument for the pragmatic approach, they concluded that Donnellan was wrong to locate the difference between the two readings at the level of what is said. This argument against Donnellan's view will be criticized in chapter 15; it relies on the mistaken assumption that there are only two possible accounts, a semantic account and a pragmatic account in terms of conversational implicature. But this is not so: another type of pragmatic account is possible, which incorporates Donnellan's view, according to which the difference between the referential and the attributive reading is a difference in what is said. On this approach, to be developed in chapter 15, the sentence 'Smith's murderer is insane' is not ambiguous, yet it can be used to express either a general or a singular proposition, depending on the context of utterance. Modified Occam's Razor provides no reason to prefer to this account an account in terms of conversational implicature; on the contrary, as I tried to show elsewhere (Recanati, 1989b, para. 8), considerations of theoretical economy tend to favour the pragmatic account that incorporates Donnellan's view.

Another example is provided by Carston's pragmatic analysis of conjoined utterances (Carston, 1988). In some contexts, a conjunctive utterance "P and Q" conveys the notion that the event described in the second conjunct occurred after the event described in the first conjunct; thus 'They got married and had many children' is not intuitively synonymous with 'They had many children and got married'. In Grice's framework this intuition can be accounted for along the following lines:

> What is *strictly and literally said* is in both cases the same thing. The temporal ordering, which is responsible for the intuitive difference between the two examples, is *conversationally implicated* rather than part of what is said. This sort of implicature is easy to account for: since the speaker is presumed to observe the maxim 'Be orderly', it is implicated that the event which is described first occurred first, and that the event which is described last occurred last. Modified Occam's Razor dictates that this approach be preferred to a semantic approach ascribing to 'and' a temporal sense to account for this type of example and a non-temporal sense to account for other examples in which the implicature is not generated (e.g. 'Jane had three children and Mary two', in which no temporal ordering is suggested).

However, as Robyn Carston has shown (Carston, 1988), another pragmatic account is possible, according to which the temporal ordering *is* part of what is said by means of 'They got married and had many children', even though 'and' is ascribed a single, non-temporal sense at the semantic level.[5] Modified Occam's Razor provides no reason to prefer to this account the classical Gricean account in terms of conversational implicature.[6]

To sum up: Enriching the Gricean picture to take the semantic underdetermination of what is said into account implies rejecting an assumption implicit in the Gricean picture, namely the assumption that there are two, and only two, possible approaches to *prima facie* ambiguities, the semantic approach and the pragmatic approach in terms of implicature. Once this assumption is abandoned, the classical Gricean treatment of *prima facie* ambiguities in terms of implicature is considerably weakened; instead of enjoying the privileges of monopoly, it has to compete with another pragmatic approach. This raises a central issue: that of the criteria that can be used in adjudicating between the different pragmatic approaches. When should a pragmatically determined aspect of utterance meaning be considered as a conversational implicature, and when should it be considered as constitutive of what is said? In what follows, I shall consider various possible answers to this question, i.e. various criteria that could be used to decide whether a given aspect of meaning is a conversational implicature or a pragmatic constituent of what is said.

## 13.2 Three minimalist principles

The first criteria that come to mind deserve to be called 'minimalist' because they work by minimizing the aspects under which what is said can go beyond the meaning of the sentence. Following Carston (Carston, 1988, pp. 163–4), I shall make a distinction between two minimalist criteria: the Linguistic direction principle and the Minimal truth-evaluability principle. I shall also mention a third criterion, which is a mixture of the other two. Let us start, then, with the Linguistic direction principle:

> *Linguistic direction principle:* A pragmatically determined aspect of meaning is part of what is said if and only if its contextual determination is triggered by the grammar, that is, if the sentence itself sets up a slot to be contextually filled.

Context-sensitive expressions, such as 'he' or the genitive, set up such slots, which in some cases at least can be represented as variables in need of contextual instantiation. It follows, by the Linguistic direction principle, that the pragmatic determination of the referent of 'he' and of the relation between John and the book contributes to determining what is said by uttering the sentence 'He has bought John's book'.

There is a problem with this version of the principle. According to some accounts (Jakobson, 1957, para. 1.5; Ducrot, 1973, 1980), a word such as 'but' is like an indexical in that it sets up a slot to be contextually filled. In Ducrot's argumentation-theoretic framework, a sentence "P but Q" indicates that there is a conclusion $r$, to be contextually identified, such that (i) "P" supports (or 'is an argument for') $r$, (ii) "Q" supports *not-r*, and (iii) "Q" is stronger than "P" so that "P but Q" also supports *not-r*. Yet the contextual value of the variable '$r$' cannot be considered as part of what is said, for the notion of 'what is said' is essentially tied to that of truth-conditional content, and "P but Q" is true merely iff "P" and "Q" are both true.

Non-truth-conditional aspects of utterance meaning, such as the conventional implicature associated with 'but', are not part of what is said, as Grice insisted. It follows that being the contextual value of a variable set up at the level of sentence meaning is not a sufficient condition for being part of what is said; the truth-conditional nature of what is said has to be taken into consideration.

The next criterion takes the close link between what is said and the truth-conditions of the utterance into account:

> *Mixed minimalist principle:* A pragmatically determined aspect of meaning is part of what is said if and only if: (i) its contextual determination is triggered by the grammar, that is, the sentence itself sets up a slot to be contextually filled, and (ii) the slot in question needs to be filled for the utterance to be truth-evaluable and express a complete proposition.

In the case of conventional implicatures, the second necessary condition is not satisfied: contextually determining the value of '$r$' is not necessary for the utterance "P but Q" to be truth-evaluable. (To be sure, it is necessary for understanding the utterance, but that is another matter.) This version of the principle captures Grice's intuition that conventional implicatures are external to the propositional (truth-conditional) content of the utterance, even though they are an aspect of utterance meaning.

But there is a problem with this second version of the principle too. Perry has shown that, in some cases, a pragmatically determined aspect of meaning *is* necessary for truth-evaluation, and therefore constitutes an integral part of the truth-conditional content of the utterance, *without* being grammatically triggered by an 'indicator' or a variable set up at the level of sentence meaning. When this happens, Perry claims that what is said involves an 'unarticulated constituent'.

> It is a rainy Saturday morning in Palo Alto. I have plans for tennis. But my younger son looks out the window and says, 'It is raining'. I go back to sleep.
> What my son said was true, because it was raining in Palo Alto. There were all sorts of places where it wasn't raining: it doesn't just rain or not, it rains in some places while not raining in others. In order to assign a truth-value to my son's statement, as I just did, I needed a place. But no component of his statement stood for a place. The verb 'raining' supplied the relation *rains (t,p)* – a dyadic relation between

times and places, as we have just noted. The tensed auxiliary 'is' supplies a time, the time at which the statement was made. 'It' doesn't supply anything, but is just syntactic filler. So Palo Alto is a constituent of the content of my son's remark, which no component of his statement designate; it is an *unarticulated* constituent. (Perry, 1986c, p. 138)

Perry's notion of unarticulated constituent enables one to capture the difference between 'It is raining' and 'It is raining here'. In both cases the second argument of the relation *rains (t,p)* is supplied by the context, but this pragmatic constituent of meaning is 'articulated' in the latter case (it is grammatically represented by a device that sets up a slot to be contextually filled) and 'unarticulated' in the former. Yet, in both cases, it seems to be part of the proposition expressed by the utterance. It follows that the first necessary condition in the mixed principle is not necessary after all. This suggests that we turn to a third (and last) minimalist criterion, the Minimal truth-evaluability principle:

*Minimal truth-evaluability principle:* A pragmatically determined aspect of meaning is part if what is said if and only if its contextual determination is necessary for the utterance to be truth-evaluable and express a complete proposition.

By this principle, conversational implicatures are clearly *not* part of what is said, because the utterance expresses a complete proposition without them. (Since conversational implicatures follow from the speaker's saying what he says, the generation of a conversational implicature presupposes that something has been said.)

What are we to think of this last minimalist criterion? Some authors have argued that it should be rejected (Sperber & Wilson, 1986; Carston, 1988). The case against the Minimal truth-evaluability principle rests on examples such as 1 and 2:

1  It will take us some time to get there.
2  I have had breakfast.

Once the identity of the speaker and hearer, the time of utterance and the reference of 'there' is determined, then, arguably, no further slot needs to be filled for an utterance of 1 to express a complete proposition. The proposition we get at this point is the proposition that there is a lapse of time (of some length or other) between our departure, or some other point of reference, and our arrival at a certain place. But, according to Carston, who borrows this example from Sperber and Wilson (1986, pp. 189–90), this is not the proposition actually expressed; to get the latter, we need to go *beyond* the minimal proposition expressible by the sentence and enrich it by pragmatically specifying the relevant lapse of time as rather long (longer than expected, perhaps). This contextual specification is constitutive of what is said, yet it is not necessary for the sentence to express a definite proposition. It follows that the Minimal truth-evaluability principle must be rejected. In the same way, according to Sperber and Wilson, once the identity of the speaker and the time of utterance has been fixed, 2 expresses a proposition, viz. the proposition that the speaker has had breakfast at least once before the time of utterance. This proposition, which would be true if the speaker had had breakfast twenty years earlier and never since, does not correspond to what the speaker means to say when he utters 'I have had breakfast'. What the speaker says goes beyond the minimal proposition expressible, contrary to what the Minimal truth-evaluability principle predicts.

In the framework laid down by Sperber and Wilson and Carston (henceforth 'SWC'), two sorts of pragmatic processes are involved in getting from sentence meaning to what is said. The first type of process, which I call 'saturation' (Recanati, 1989a), is involved whenever a slot must be contextually filled for the utterance to express a complete proposition. The second type of process is non-minimalist; I call it '(free) enrichment'. According to SWC, free enrichment is involved in e.g. the determination of the length of the lapse of time mentioned in 'It will take us some time to get there'. The enrichment of 'some time' into something more specific is not needed for the utterance to express a complete proposition, but for the proposition expressed to correspond to what the speaker means. The input to this second type of process is a complete proposition (that which results from the first type of process), and the output is a richer proposition, i.e. one that entails the input proposition. SWC's claim that the proposition expressed is obtained from the disambiguated meaning of the sentence not only by saturation but also by free enrichment is inconsistent with the doctrine I call Minimalism, according to which the proposition expressed – what is said – *is* the 'minimal' proposition expressible by the utterance, i.e. what results from simply saturating the disambiguated meaning of the sentence.

If Sperber-Wilson and Carston are right, we must reject Minimalism altogether; for none of the three minimalist criteria can be maintained. In chapter 14 I shall argue that the rejection of Minimalism is indeed justified. However, it must be realized that examples 1 and 2 *per se* are not sufficient to dispose of the Minimal truth-evaluability principle. Additional assumptions are needed to get rid of this principle, and of Minimalism in general. To see that, let us consider a possible defence of the Minimal truth-evaluability principle.

## 13.3 The Implicature Analysis

Examples 1 and 2 do not, in and by themselves, require giving up the Minimal truth-evaluability principle. One obvious way to handle them consistently with the latter would be to adopt an analysis in terms of conversational implicature, according to which the person who utters 2 'says' the he has had breakfast (at least) once, and 'implicates' that this – his having breakfast – happened on the very day of utterance. In the same way, it might be claimed that the person who utters 1 'says' that there is a lapse of time (of some length or other) between departure and arrival, and 'implicates' that the lapse of time in question is rather long. On this analysis (henceforth the 'Implicature Analysis'), the pragmatically determined constituents of meaning which are *not* necessary for truth-evaluability are *ipso facto not* part of what is said, but are only implicated.

The Implicature Analysis enables one to salvage the Minimal truth-evaluability principle in the face of *prima facie* counter-examples such as 1 and 2 . Note that the same strategy would also permit to salvage the Linguistic direction principle in the face of Perry's counter-example. For we might analyse 'It is raining' in such a way that the unarticulated constituent (i.e. the *place* concerned by the rain) is not a constituent of *what is said*, but merely an 'implicated' aspect of utterance meaning. On such an analysis, the speaker who utters 'It is raining' *says* that it is raining in some place (left indeterminate at the level of what is said), and 'implicates' that this is happening *here, in Palo Alto* (Perry's example). Such an analysis supports the Linguistic direction principle: the pragmatically determined constituents of meaning which are *not* grammatically 'articulated' are considered as *not* part of what is said, but as mere conversational implicatures.

The Implicature Analysis, then, can be used to defend Minimalism in its various forms. But I do not think this defence is acceptable, for the following reason. There is no *intuitive basis* for saying that the speaker of 'It's raining' expresses the proposition that it's raining *somewhere* (indeterminate), or that the speaker of 'I've had breakfast' expresses the proposition that his life was not entirely breakfastless: neither the speaker nor the hearer is aware that *this* is the proposition expressed. To be sure, most implicature theorists are unlikely to be moved by such an objection, for they think the proposition expressed ('what is said') need not be consciously accessible. What is consciously accessible, according to them, is only 'what is communicated', i.e. the result of combining the proposition literally expressed with various extra elements such as the conversational implicatures.[7] But this is precisely something which I deny. In Recanati (1989a) I made the opposite claim: that we are conscious of what is said. More precisely, I claimed that we have *distinct conscious representations* for 'what is said' and for 'what is implicated' by a given utterance: both are consciously accessible, and are consciously accessible *as distinct*. Note that the inferential connection between these representations is as consciously accessible as the representations themselves. Let us consider a typical example: the utterance 'I have not had breakfast this morning', which (in some easily accessible context) implicates that the speaker is hungry and wishes to be fed. Both the speaker and the hearer are aware that the speaker *says* that he has had no breakfast this morning and *implies* that he is hungry; and both are aware of the inferential connection between what is said and what is implied. This was one of the constraints on implicatures raised by Grice himself. Grice said that 'the presence of an implicature must be capable of being worked out' (Grice, 1989, p. 31). For an implicature to be worked out, two conditions must be satisfied: (i) both what is said and what is implied must be grasped, and (ii) the inferential connection between them must also be grasped. Many followers of Grice have (wrongly) interpreted this as requiring that *the theorist* be capable of working out whatever conversational implicature is posited to explain a given semantic phenomenon; but Grice clearly had in mind the participants in the talk-exchange themselves: it is the speaker and hearer who must be capable of working out the implicatures, and this entails that they have conscious access both to what is said and to what is implied. As we shall now see, this provides us with a criterion for distinguishing genuine implicatures from pragmatic

```
                    what is communicated
                   /                  \
          what is said        what is conversationally
            /      \                    implicated
           /        \
    sentence      contextual ingredients
    meaning         of what is said
```

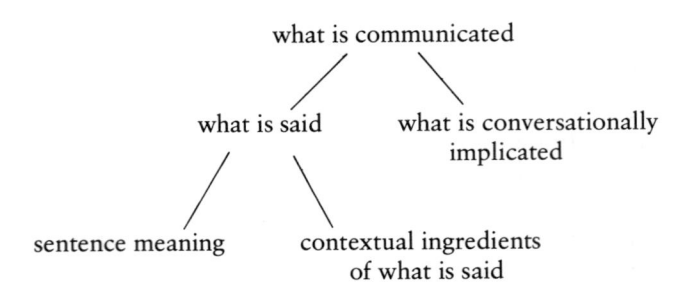

**Figure 6**

constituents of what is said – a criterion which enables us to dispose of the Implicature Analysis.

## 13.4 The Availability Principle

Let's try to make more explicit the claim concerning the accessibility of what is said (the 'availability hypothesis', as I called it in my first article on the subject). Consider figure 6. Starting at the top, this figure shows the various steps that lead, by analytical abstraction, from what is communicated to the meaning of the sentence. The analysis thus displayed is intended to mirror the actual process of understanding the utterance, this corresponding to a bottom-up reading of the diagram. At the top (i.e. the root) of the inverted tree, 'what is communicated' is the intuitive datum we, as analysts, start from; it is also the consciously accessible output of the process of pragmatic understanding. At the bottom of the tree, we find sentence meaning, a theoretical construct representing both the output of the process of semantic decoding and the input to the process of pragmatic understanding. Of sentence meaning we can assume only tacit (unconscious) knowledge on the part of the speaker who utters the sentence. To be sure, users of the language claim to have intuitions concerning what the sentences in their language mean; but these intuitions are not directly about their purported objects – linguistic meanings. They do not bear on the linguistic meanings of sentences, which are very abstract and inaccessible to consciousness, but on what would be said or communicated by the sentence were it uttered in a standard or easily accessible context.

*What is communicated*:     what is said     conversational
(top level,                                   implicatures
consciously accessible)

*sub-doxastic level*:        sentence         contextual ingredients
                             meaning          of what is said

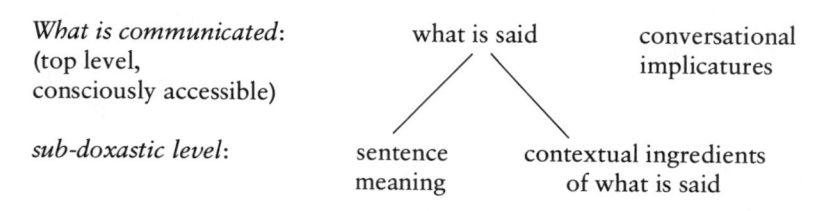

**Figure 7**

Being located at an intermediate level in the diagram, distinct from the top level where the consciously accessible output of pragmatic processing is located, 'what is said' is generally considered as no less sub-doxastic and unconscious than sentence meaning. We are supposed to be conscious only of 'what is communicated', which is distinct from what is said. But this is the picture which I reject. I claim that we are conscious of what is said (and, also, of what is implicated). To make sense of this hypothesis, I suggest a slight modification of figure 6. As it is, it implies that what is communicated – the object of our intuitions – is something over and above what is said and what is conversationally implicated: what is communicated is seen as the output of a specific cognitive process (the last step in the general process of pragmatic understanding) whose inputs are what is said and what is implicated. One way of understanding the claim concerning the availability of what is said is by rejecting this view altogether, considering that what is communicated *consists of* what is said and what is implicated instead of being something *over and above* what is said and what is implicated. Instead of locating what is communicated at one level and what is said (as well as the implicatures) at another, I suggest that we consider 'what is communicated' as simply a *name* for the level at which we find both what is said and what is implicated – the top level, characterized by conscious accessibility (figure 7). On this view, the conscious availability of what is said no longer is a mystery: if what is communicated, which is consciously accessible, consists of what is said and what is implicated, then what is said cannot but be consciously accessible. In the new diagram, it is no longer suggested that there is a specific process merging what is said and what is implicated. They constitute the final output of the general process of pragmatic understanding, not an intermediate output, as figure 6 suggests. What is said and what is implicated thus remain distinct, and are consciously available as distinct.[8]

From the availability hypothesis, according to which what is said and what is implicated are consciously accessible (and accessible as distinct), we can easily derive a criterion for telling when a pragmatically determined aspect of meaning is part of what is said and when it is not. This criterion I call the Availability Principle:

> *Availability Principle:* In deciding whether a pragmatically determined aspect of utterance meaning is part of what is said, that is, in making a decision concerning what is said, we should always try to preserve our pre-theoretic intuitions on the matter.

This principle can be appealed to in a number of cases to show that a tentative analysis is misguided. Consider the utterance 'Everybody went to Paris'. Under ordinary circumstances, what a speaker would mean by this is not that everybody in the absolute sense, i.e. every person in the world, went to Paris, but that everybody in some (contextually identifiable) group went to Paris. Suppose, for example, it is established that what the speaker means is that every member of the Johnson & Johnson staff went to Paris. Still, the utterance can be analysed in two ways. The first analysis is quite straightforward: it identifies what the speaker says with what he means, i.e. with the proposition that every member of the Johnson & Johnson staff went to Paris.[9] But there is another possible analysis. We may consider that what is literally said is that everybody in the world went to Paris, even though this is clearly not what the speaker means. A proponent of this analysis has only to assume that what the speaker says is different from what he means, i.e. that he speaks non-literally, as in metaphor. Such an analysis has been put forward in Bach (1987) and extended to many examples, including the whole class of utterances in which an incomplete definite description occurs. Thus, Bach identifies the proposition literally expressed by the utterance 'The door is closed' with the Russellian proposition that the only one door there is in the world is closed, this proposition not being what the speaker means to communicate when he utters the sentence. The Availability Principle militates against this type of analysis, which assumes a counterintuitive identification of what is said. When the speaker says 'Everybody went to Paris', or 'The door is closed', it is counterintuitive to identify what he says with the propositions that every person in the world went to Paris, or that the only door in the universe is closed. The speaker himself would not recognize those propositions as being what he said. The 'non-literal' analysis must therefore be rejected, by virtue of the Availability Principle.[10]

One important consequence of the Availability Principle is that some of the most often cited examples of conversational implicature turn out not to be conversational implicatures after all. So-called 'scalar implicatures' – or, perhaps, a subgroup of them – are a case in point. Suppose the speaker utters 'John has three children', thereby communicating that John has exactly three children. It is customary to say that the proposition literally expressed by 'John has three children' is the proposition that John has at least three children, even if what the speaker means to communicate by this utterance is that John has exactly three children. What is communicated (viz. that John has exactly three children) is classically accounted for by positing a conversational implicature that combines with the proposition allegedly expressed (viz. that John has at least three children). This proposal has great merits; it accounts for the 'ambiguity' of 'John has three children' (which may sometimes mean 'at least three' and sometimes 'exactly three') without positing several distinct lexical senses. The proposal, however, does not pass the availability test, for the speaker himself would not recognize the proposition that he has *at least* three children as being what he has said in the cases in which the intended reading is 'exactly three'. Not being consciously available, the proposition which the classical account takes to be literally expressed cannot be identified with what is said, if we accept the Availability Principle. The latter dictates that we consider the aspect of meaning which Griceans (rightly) take to be pragmatically determined (viz. the implicit restriction: no more than three children) as part of what is said rather than as a conversational implicature external to what is said.[11]

Another important consequence of the Availability Principle is that the counter-examples to the Linguistic direction principle and to the Minimal truth-evaluability principle *cannot* be disposed of by treating the relevant pragmatic constituents of meaning as 'implicatures' external of what is said. The spatial location of the rain in Perry's example ('It is raining') and the temporal location of the relevant breakfast in Sperber and Wilson's example ('I've had breakfast') must be treated as (pragmatic) constituents *of what is said*, if the availability hypothesis is correct. For it would be counterintuitive to identify what is said by these utterances with the proposition that it's raining somewhere and the proposition that the speaker has had breakfast once, respectively. I conclude that Minimalism cannot be defended by appealing to the Implicature Analysis. (I shall return to the issue of Minimalism in chapter 14.)

## 13.5 Conclusion

Not many people have observed that Grice's theory departs from our intuitions when it is applied to examples such as 'John has three children', which Griceans take to express the proposition that John has at least three children and to implicate that he has no more than three children. However, there is an important difference between this example and e.g. 'I've had no breakfast today', which implicates that the speaker is hungry and wishes to be fed. In the latter example, the implicature is intuitively felt to be external to what is said; it corresponds to something that we would ordinarily take to be 'implied'. In the former case, we are not pre-theoretically able to distinguish between the alleged two components of the meaning of the utterance – the proposition expressed (that John has at least three children) and the implicature (that he has at most three children). We are conscious only of the result of their combination, i.e. of the proposition that John has exactly three children. In this case as opposed to the other one, the theoretical distinction between the proposition expressed and the implicature does not correspond to the intuitive distinction between what is said and what is implied.[12] If I am right, this intuitive difference between the two types of example points to an important theoretical distinction, between genuine implicatures and pragmatic constituents of the proposition expressed.[13]

As we saw at the beginning of this chapter, one only has to realize that sentence meaning largely underdetermines what is said, to be forced to the conclusion that such a distinction must be made. But where must the boundary be drawn? Grice's 'tests' for conversational implicature (cancellability, non-detachability, and so forth) test the presence of a pragmatically determined aspect of utterance meaning, but they do not tell us whether it is a genuine implicature or a constituent of what is said. New criteria have to be devised to make this decision possible. In my view, the Availability Principle is the fundamental criterion we must use in this connection. Other criteria have been put forward in the literature, but they are either inadequate (like Carston's Independence Principle, criticized in Recanati, 1989a) or presuppose the Availability Principle (like the Scope Principle, discussed in the appendix pp. 269–74).

## Notes

1  The opposition between what is said and the conversational implicatures survives the claim that what is said is conventionally determined by the meaning of the sentence. *Qua* assumptions following from the speaker's saying what he says, conversational implicatures are, by definition, external to what is said.
2  Larry Horn once made the fairly surprising claim that if 'pragmatic principles – including the familiar Gricean implicata – may (contra Grice) influence propositional content and hence help determine truth-conditions..., no straightforward distinction between what is implicated and what is said... will survive' (Horn, 1989, p. 433). But as I said in note 1, conversational implicatures are, by definition, external to what is said: their being assumptions following from the speaker's saying what he says is sufficient to make them distinct from what is said, even if what is said is, to a large extent, pragmatically determined. On Horn's current position, see note 11 below.
3  This is the 'dubious assumption' which I mentioned at the beginning of this section.
4  It may be argued that there are not only different pragmatic approaches to *prima facie* ambiguities, but also different semantic approaches. Thus Cohen opposes to the standard 'insulationist' semantics an 'interactionist' semantics in terms of which, he says, those *prima facie* ambiguities which Grice handles within the implicature framework can be accounted for in a way that is immune to Modified Occam's Razor (Cohen, 1971, p. 56; for a recent statement of the interactionist point of view, see Cohen, 1986). I shall not address this issue in this chapter; the Gricean picture will be questioned only as far as the pragmatic approach is concerned.
5  Carston's pragmatic account is, roughly, the following. To determine what is said by means of the sentence 'They got married and had many children', the hearer must assign a reference to each of the referring expressions, *including the past tense 'got married' and 'had'*. Just as pragmatic principles are employed in ascertaining the referent of 'they', so, Carston says, they are used in assigning temporal reference. The hearer goes beyond the strict semantic content of the sentence uttered, and on the basis of contextual assumptions and pragmatic principles recovers from 'They got married and had many children' a representation such as 'John and Mary got married at $t$ and had many children at $t+n$'. '$t$ is

some more or less specific time prior to the time of utterance and $t+n$ is some more or less specific time, later than $t$. The temporal ordering of the events described in the conjuncts is thus treated as a by-product of the reference assignment process involved in determining [what is said]' (Carston, 1988, p. 161). This analysis raises some problems when the past tense is replaced by the present perfect, as in example 1 in the Appendix, because the present perfect can hardly be considered as referring to a specific time. (In familiar terms, the present perfect is used to express general propositions of the type: 'There is a time $t$, prior to the time of utterance, such that blah blah', while it makes sense to say that the past tense is 'singular' and refers to a specific time $t$ which must be contextually identified – with more or less precision – for the utterance to express a complete proposition.) I shall not discuss this issue in this chapter; I am concerned only with the *type* of analysis Carston puts forward – a pragmatic analysis at the level of what is said. Whether or not the details of her analysis are correct is another matter.

6 In the light of Carston's suggestion concerning 'and' we may reconsider Grice's use of Modified Occam's Razor against ordinary language philosophers, to whom he ascribed the semantic view, i.e. the notion that 'and', 'or', etc. are multiply ambiguous in English. The main reason why this view was ascribed to ordinary language philosophers like Strawson is the following: they held that what is said by uttering a sentence such as "P or Q" or "P and Q" varies according to the context of utterance; they considered that the truth conditions of an utterance of one of these sentences were not invariant under contextual change. Thus, "P and Q" is sometimes true if the event described in the second conjunct occurred before (or simultaneously with) that described in the first conjunct, and sometimes not; "P or Q" is sometimes true if "P" and "Q" are both true, and sometimes not. This way of putting the matter is certainly inconsistent with the classical Gricean approach, which assumes that what is said is the same on all readings, the difference being located at the level of implicatures. It was therefore natural to ascribe to ordinary philosophers the semantic approach, on the assumption that there are only two possible approaches, the semantic approach and the approach in terms of conversational implicature. However, this assumption must be abandoned, and the possibility of a pragmatic approach in terms of what is said acknowledged. Once this is done, Modified Occam's Razor no longer provides any reason to reject the claim that sentences such as "P and Q" can be used to say different things in different contexts; for this claim no longer implies that sentences such as "P and Q" are semantically ambiguous, and that 'and' has a range of different senses in English. (For a fuller defence of ordinary language philosophers along these lines, see Travis, 1985.)

7 As Richard says in an eloquent passage (on behalf of Salmon), 'we do not come equipped with a meter that reliably distinguishes between

semantic and pragmatic implications. Examples like that concerning 'and' and temporal order help make the point that what seems for all the world like a truth-conditional implication may turn out not to be one' (Richard, 1990, p. 123). Unfortunately for those who hold this position, most pragmaticians nowadays seem to accept the view that the temporal order associated with 'and' *is* a truth-conditional implication, albeit a pragmatically based one, and they do so on essentially intuitive grounds. (Even Horn holds this view, despite his earlier assertion quoted in note 2. See below, note 11.) More on this in chapter 17.

8   For simplicity's sake, the fact that the derivation of implicatures presupposes the identification of what is said (and other things as well) has not been represented in the diagram. It could have been represented by distinguishing two sub-levels within 'what is communicated', what is said being input at the first sub-level and the implicatures output at the second one.

9   Such an analysis is supported by the view that, in a quantified sentence like 'Everybody went to Paris', the relevant domain of quantification has to be contextually specified for a definite proposition to be expressed. See below, 14.2.

10  Bach (1987, chapter 4) points out that the non-literal use of sentences such as 'The door is closed' is their *standard* use; he speaks of 'standardized non-literality'. He might therefore try to avoid the objection I have just raised by arguing as follows: The speaker is not conscious of having said something different from what he communicates because the sentence he uses is *standardly* used to communicate something different from the proposition literally expressed. After all, the same phenomenon occurs in cases of 'standardized indirection' (Bach & Harnish, 1979, p. 192ff): when an indirect speech act is standardly performed by means of a certain type of sentence, the participants in the talk-exchange may not be conscious of the speech act directly performed (e.g. of the question in 'Can you pass me the salt?'). I shall briefly discuss this type of account in note 13 below.

11  As he made clear during a workshop held in Paris in May 1991, Larry Horn, one of the main theorists of scalar implicatures (Horn, 1972, 1989), now accepts this point with respect to cardinality implicatures (e.g. the implicature from 'eight' to 'exactly eight') or the temporal and consequential implicatures of conjoined sentences, but not with respect to other cases such as the inference from 'some' to 'not all'. He agrees that our intuitions are to be accounted for, this entailing the necessity of a distinction between implicatures which are and implicatures which are not part of what is said. The account he favours is that in terms of *conventionalized* implicatures: conventionalized implicatures get incorporated into what is said. This type of account is similar to Bach's account in terms of standardized non-literality; see note 13 below.

12  At this point, one might protest that it is a *good* thing from a scientific point of view when a theory's domain of application is extended beyond its intuitive basis. (As far as Grice's theory is concerned, the intuitive basis was the everyday distinction between what is said and what is implied.) This I do not wish to deny; I agree that scientific theorizing is to be freed from, rather than impeded by, intuitions and common sense, which provide only a starting point. Thus there is a sense in which it was a good thing to go beyond our intuitions and to show, as Grice and the Griceans did, that in many cases the meaning of an utterance results from an unconscious process of 'meaning construction'. Still, I believe there was something to worry about when the theory of implicatures was extended to examples which we would not ordinarily consider as cases of implied meaning This does not mean that I reject the 'scientific' attitude toward common sense. We may at the same time accept this attitude and recognize that human cognition is a very special field: in this field, our intuitions are not just a first shot at a theory – something like Wittgenstein's ladder, which may be thrown away after it has been climbed up – but also *part of what the theory is about*, and as such they cannot be neglected. In the case at hand, it was a mistake to ignore our intuitions, which tell us that there is a difference between standard cases of implied meaning and the other type of alleged implicatures.

13  My account of the difference between conscious and unconscious 'implicatures' relies on the claim that the latter are *not* implicatures. Now there is another type of account, which uses Grice's notion of 'generalized' implicature, or a related notion of 'short-circuited', 'standardized', or even 'conventionalized' implicature. Using these notions, one may argue that when an implicature is generalized (or standardized, or conventionalized), one is no longer conscious of its being external to what is said. This type of position I earlier ascribed to Bach (note 10) and to Horn (note 11).

The problem, with this (otherwise plausible) type of account is that it is not general enough. To get an implicature in the first place, we need a proposition expressed; but in chapter 14 I will argue, following Searle, that no proposition *could* be expressed without the context supplying unarticulated constituents. It follows that at least some of the pragmatic constituents of what is said cannot be treated as (generalized, standardized or conventionalized) implicatures. We need pragmatic constituents of what is said over and beyond those implicatures which arguably get incorporated into what is said.

# Chapter 14

# Primary pragmatic processes

## 14.1 Introduction

Minimalism is the doctrine according to which a pragmatic, contextual aspect of meaning should not be considered part of what is said *praeter necessitatem*. In other words, it is only in case of necessity that we must incorporate something contextual into what is said. Two minimalist principles were discussed in chapter 13, the Linguistic direction principle and the Minimal truth-evaluability principle.

> *Linguistic direction principle:* A pragmatically determined aspect of meaning is part of what is said if and only if its contextual determination is triggered by the grammar, that is, if the sentence itself sets up a slot to be contextually filled.
> *Minimal truth-evaluability principle:* A pragmatically determined aspect of meaning is part of what is said if and only if its contextual determination is necessary for the utterance to be truth-evaluable and express a complete proposition.

As I pointed out, both principles have counter-examples. Perry's example, 'It is raining', is a case in which a pragmatic constituent of what is said (the place where it is raining) is not grammatically 'articulated'; and 1 and 2 below are examples in which a pragmatic constituent of what is said (the temporal location of the breakfast I had, or the length of the time it will take to get there) is not necessary for truth-evaluability.

 1  It will take us some time to get there.
 2  I have had breakfast.

At the end of chapter 13, I used the Availability Principle to show that these counter-examples to the Linguistic direction principle and to the Minimal truth-evaluability principle cannot be disposed of by treating the relevant pragmatic constituents of meaning as 'implicatures' external to what is said. Does this mean, as I suggested, that Minimalism must be given up? I think so, but the issue is fairly delicate and deserves a fuller treatment than I have been able to provide so far.

## 14.2   Can Minimalism be defended?

Since the Implicature Analysis of 'It's raining' fails (13.3–4), I think we cannot avoid the conclusion that the Linguistic direction principle has to be given up. In other words, Perry's point has to be granted: there are unarticulated constituents of what is said. That the spatial *location* of the rain is an *unarticulated* constituent is shown by the contrast between 'It's raining' and 'It's raining here'; that it is a constituent *of what is said* is a consequence of the Availability Principle, which precludes construing it as an implicature external to what is said (for then what is said would be the proposition that it's raining somewhere, contrary to our intuitions).

What about 1 and 2, the counter-examples to the Minimal truth-evaluability principle? The Implicature Analysis fails in this case also. It would be counterintuitive to identify 'what is said' by these utterances with the proposition that it will take some time or other to get there or with the proposition that the speaker's life was not entirely breakfastless.[1] Yet I do not think the failure of the Implicature Analysis commits us to giving up the Minimal truth-evaluability principle, for the Implicature Analysis of 1 and 2 is not the only way to dispose of these counter-examples to the Minimal truth-evaluability principle.

Carston and Sperber and Wilson reject the Minimal truth-evaluability principle because they believe that a pragmatically determined aspect of the meaning of 1 and 2 possesses the two following properties:

(a)   it is constitutive of what is said; yet
(b)   its contextual determination is *not* necessary for the utterance to express a complete proposition.

This conjunction of (a) and (b) is inconsistent with the Minimal truth-evaluability principle, which says that a pragmatically determined aspect of the meaning of an utterance is part of what is said if and only if its contextual determination is necessary for the utterance to express a complete proposition. However, the Minimal truth-evaluability principle is not inconsistent with (a) or (b) taken separately. Defenders of the Implicature Analysis accept (b) but reject (a); they are thus able to maintain the Minimal truth-evaluability principle. We have seen that the Implicature Analysis of 1 and 2 cannot be accepted, because the rejection of (a) conflicts with the Availability Principle. But there is another treatment of these examples, consistent with the Minimal truth-evaluability principle: one may accept (a) but reject (b), i.e. consider that the relevant aspect of the meaning of 1 and 2 is constitutive of what is said (and therefore not a conversational implicature), while insisting that its contextual determination *is* necessary for the utterance to express a complete proposition. Let me briefly sketch this minimalist treatment of examples 1 and 2.

Both 1 and 2 can be analysed in terms of quantification. 1 quantifies over durations (it says that there is a duration $t$ such that it will take us $t$ to get there) and 2 quantifies over events (it says that there is a past event which is the speaker's having breakfast). Now, quantification involves a certain amount of context-dependence, because, in general, the domain of quantification has to be contextually specified. For example, it can be argued that the sentence 'Everybody went to Paris', by itself, does not express a complete proposition – not even the proposition that everybody in the world went to Paris: what it says is that everybody in some domain x went to Paris, and the context helps to instantiate the variable 'x'. (On this view, the variable 'x' may be contextually instantiated so as to make 'everybody in the world' the right interpretation, but this interpretation is no less contextual than any other interpretation.) Suppose we accept this view. Then, in the case of 1, 2 and other utterances involving quantification, there is a slot to be filled for the utterance to be truth-evaluable, corresponding to the domain of quantification. It follows that the specific interpretations of 1 and 2, which SWC present as counter-examples to the Minimal truth-evaluability principle, are consistent with the latter – one merely has to define the domain of quantification in an appropriate way. In the case of 1, we might say that the domain of quantification is a set of durations, *contextually restricted to those that are long enough to be worth mentioning in connection with the process of our going there.* (In this framework, the proposition that it will take us 'some time or other' to get there corresponds to the unlikely interpretation in which the domain of quantification is contextually identified with the set of all possible durations, including milliseconds.) In the case of 2, we might say that the domain of quantification is a time interval, or rather a collection of events defined by a time interval. This allows us to account for the intuitive difference between 'I've had breakfast' and 'I've been to Tibet' (Sperber & Wilson, 1986, pp. 189–90). In both cases, what is conveyed by virtue of linguistic meaning alone is that, in some temporal domain *d* prior to the time of utterance, there is a certain event, viz. the speaker's having breakfast or his going to Tibet; but in the first case, the time interval is contextually restricted to the day of utterance, while in the second case the relevant interval is more extended and covers the speaker's life (up to the time of utterance).

According to the view I have just outlined, it is a mistake to hold that 1 and 2 express complete propositions once the obvious indexical variables (identity of the speaker and hearer, time of utterance, reference of 'there') have been instantiated; a slot remains to be filled, which corresponds to the domain of quantification. It follows that the Minimal truth-evaluability principle can be retained even though one accepts thesis (a) above, i.e. even though one considers that what is said by means of (1) and (2) is that it will take us a *long* time to get there or that the speaker has had breakfast *on the day of utterance*. Far from being added to an already complete proposition, the pragmatic specifications I have just italicized result from filling a slot, a slot that must be filled in some way or other for the utterance to express a complete proposition.

## 14.3 Giving up Minimalism

Even though I think the Minimal truth-evaluability principle could be retained in the face of examples such as 1 and 2 above, still there are other examples which are much harder to handle without giving up the principle and having recourse to free enrichment. Carston mentions the following examples (for which she gives credit to Diane Blakemore):

3  He ran to the edge of the cliff and jumped.
4  I went to the exhibition and ran into John.

5   She took the gun, walked into the garden and killed her mother.
6   I had a holiday in Austria and did some cross-country skiing.

As Carston says, 'the interpretation of 3 in most contexts of utterance will include the understanding that he jumped over the cliff although there's no linguistic expression there telling us this or requiring us to fill in a prepositional phrase... Similarly, in 4 we would most likely assume that the place where I ran into John was the exhibition, in 5 that the killing of the mother was with the gun and took place in the garden, and in 6 that the skiing referred to took place in Austria, although, again, the linguistic content of the utterances does not supply this information or direct its retrieval' (Carston, 1988, p. 165). The important point is that the unarticulated constituent, in each example 3–6, is *optional* from the standpoint of truth-valuation. Thus 4 would still be truth-evaluable if the location of the unexpected meeting with John was left indeterminate. In other words, if we extract (or substract) the unarticulated constituent from what is said, what remains is a less specific proposition, to the effect that the following two facts obtain: I went to the exhibition, and I met John (i.e. I met him in some place or other). This is still a proposition, and it might have been the proposition expressed by 4.[2] Had it been the proposition expressed, no specific place would have been mentioned as that in which I ran into John. It would be fairly artificial to hold that on that interpretation also an unarticulated constituent would be involved, albeit a 'general' one standing for an indeterminate location. It is much more natural to hold that on that reading no unarticulated constituent corresponding to a place would be provided. This shows that the unarticulated constituent which is actually provided is optional,[3] hence that the Minimal truth-evaluability principle must be given up: something like free enrichment *is* involved in getting from sentence meaning to what is said.

It must be realized that non-minimalist pragmatic processes such as free enrichment are not contingent but essential to the constitution of what is said: although optional, unarticulated constituents of the sort I have just mentioned are *ineliminable* in some sense. When I say 'He went to the cliff and jumped', the situation I describe or refer to is a situation in which he jumped *over the cliff* even though nothing in my utterance indicates this particular feature of the situation referred to. This unarticulated feature is part of the truth-conditions of the utterance, part of the described situation. Now there are many other features which, although unarticulated, are part of the situation which the utterance purports to describe; too many, arguably, for all of them to be articulated at the same time. For example, it's part of the situation I intend to describe, that gravitation is not suspended during the jumping. Or consider SWC's example, 'I have had breakfast'. SWC consider that an unarticulated constituent corresponding to a time (or a time interval) is contextually provided. But, as John Searle pointed out to me, there are many more unarticulated constituents at play in that example:

> We take an utterance of that as saying that I have *eaten* breakfast, but of course that is not included in the literal meaning of the sentence. Furthermore, even if I had said I had eaten breakfast, we take that as meaning that I have eaten it by putting it in my mouth, chewing it, etc., as opposed to, say, stuffing it in my left ear or digesting it through the soles of my shoes. But there is nothing whatever in the semantic content of 'eat' that precludes these interpretations. I could easily tell you a story where they would be the natural interpretation. (John Searle, personal communication)

Given that such 'default' features concerning gravitation or the way eating normally proceeds *are* part of the described situation, on an ordinary understanding of 'I have eaten breakfast' or 'He jumped over the cliff', it is clear (I hope) that we could not provide a wholly *explicit* description of the situation in question, that is, a description without unarticulated constituents. That this is so has been quite convincingly suggested by Searle in various articles (Searle, 1978, 1980) and in his book *Intentionality* (Searle, 1983), with examples more or less like the above.[4] I fully agree with Searle and other 'contextualists' on this issue and conclude that 'what is said' – the situation our utterance intends to describe – necessarily involves unarticulated constituents. No proposition could be expressed without *some* unarticulated constituent being contextually provided.[5]

## 14.4 Primary and secondary pragmatic processes

The abandonment of Minimalism under its various guises has important consequences. It enables us to introduce a number of 'primary' pragmatic processes, that is, of pragmatic processes which play a role in the very constitution of what is said. Primary pragmatic processes[6] are to be contrasted with secondary pragmatic processes, which presuppose that something has been said (some proposition expressed). From the point of view of Minimalism, only one type of primary pragmatic process is allowed: *saturation*, which is involved in the contextual determination of the proposition expressed by indexical utterances. I already mentioned another, non-minimalist type of primary pragmatic process, namely *free enrichment*, and a third type of process will be introduced later in this section.

The notion of a primary pragmatic process is closely tied to that of 'pragmatic ambiguity', often used but seldom defined in the pragmatic literature. I suggest the following definition: There is *pragmatic ambiguity* whenever a sentence which is not semantically (i.e. linguistically) ambiguous can nevertheless express different propositions in different contexts, owing to some primary pragmatic process involved in the contextual determination of what is said. One particular form of pragmatic ambiguitys – that which characterizes indexical utterances – is recognized by all theorists. This particular pragmatic ambiguity is generated by a particular primary pragmatic process, namely saturation. But there are other primary pragmatic processes, and other forms of pragmatic ambiguity, as we shall see.

To begin with, it must be noted that two sorts of free enrichment have been mentioned in the pragmatic literature, only one of which corresponds to the description I have given. *Strengthening*, or logical enrichment, takes a proposition as input and yields as ouptut another proposition which entails it. Thus according to SWC 'It will take us some time' is enriched into 'It will take us a long time', 'I have had breakfast' is enriched into 'I have had breakfast this morning', and so forth. In all such cases, the enriched proposition entails the input proposition: if I have had breakfast this morning, then I've had breakfast, and if something takes a long time, then it takes some time. But another type of enrichment is sometimes evoked in the literature, namely *expansion* (Bach, 1987). It takes a proposition as input, but the proposition it yields as output does not necessarily entail the input proposition. It is a 'syntactic' rather than a 'logical' sort of enrichment. Bach gives the following examples: 'I have nothing to wear' is expanded into 'I have nothing suitable to wear to tonight's party', 'The door is open' is expanded into 'The door in this room is open'. The notion of expansion is less restrictive than that of strengthening; every case of strengthening (such as 'I have eaten', an example also discussed in Bach, 1987) can be treated as a case of expansion, but not the other way round. That I have nothing suitable to wear to tonight's party does not entail that I have nothing at all to wear; hence the enrichment of 'I have nothing to wear' into 'I have nothing to wear to tonight's party' cannot be treated as a case of strengthening.

The notion of strengthening has one advantage over that of expansion: it is well-defined, while expansion is not (or so it seems to me).[7] On the other hand, it is clear that the notion of expansion has a much wider range of application than strengthening. One major problem with explanations in terms of the latter notion is that they seem to lack generality. Consider, for example, the sentence 'One boy came'. It can be used to say something quite specific, namely that *one of the boys in the class* came. This seems to be a typical case of strengthening: 'One boy came' might be said to express the 'minimal' proposition that at least one boy came, which minimal proposition is entailed by the richer proposition 'At least one of the boys in the class came' (if one of the boys in the class came, then one boy came); the notion of strengthening therefore applies in a straightforward manner. But this account is not general enough, as can be seen by considering other cases, which look very similar but are far more difficult to handle in terms of strengthening. Thus, the sentence 'Every boy came' can be used to say that every boy in the class came; the problem here is that the output proposition, i.e. the proposition that every boy in the class came, does not entail the input proposition, viz. the 'minimal' proposition that every boy (i.e. every boy in the world!) came. Because of this problem, the account in terms of strengthening seems less attractive than an account in terms of expansion (or than a minimalist account in terms of a contextually variable domain of quantification: see 14.2).

We observe the same sort of limitation with respect to negation. We can explain the ordinary understanding of 'I have had breakfast' using the notion of strengthening, for 'I have had breakfast this morning' entails that I have had breakfast; but we cannot explain the ordinary understanding of 'I have not had breakfast' in terms of strengthening, for 'I have not had breakfast this morning' (the enriched proposition) does not entail that I have not breakfast *simpliciter* (the input proposition); I may well have had breakfast on some other occasion, even if I had no breakfast this morning.

I shall not try to adjudicate between the two notions of enrichment here. Let me simply note a possible defence of the notion of strengthening against the above criticism. Strengthening, it may be argued, can be understood as operating *locally*. For example, in the case of 'Every boy came', we might say that it is the predicate 'boy' that is strengthened into 'boy in the class', rather than the proposition 'Every boy came' into 'Every boy in the class came'. This seems to work because the predicate 'boy in the class' somehow 'entails' the predicate 'boy'. In the same way, we might say that the strengthening in 'I have not had breakfast' applies not to the global proposition but, within the latter, to the proposition that is negated: 'I have had breakfast' is strengthened into 'I have had breakfast this morning', and *this* is negated.

This remark is important because, it seems to me, primary pragmatic processes in general *must* be conceived of as operating locally: they come into play at the sub-propositional level. This is what distinguishes primary from secondary pragmatic processes. The latter cannot operate unless a primary proposition – what is said – has been identified, but primary pragmatic processes, whether minimalist or non-minimalist, do not presuppose the prior computation of some basic propositional value. If I am right, then what I earlier called the 'minimal' proposition expressible by an utterance (13.2), i.e. that which results *simply* from saturation, is a theoretical artefact, in the sense that it *need not be computed* and has no psychological reality.[8]

By way of illustration, let us consider a third type of primary pragmatic process which I have not mentioned so far, and which it is time to introduce. I have in mind the (non-minimalist) process of *transfer*. In saturation and enrichment, a propositional constituent is contextually provided either to fill a slot in semantic structure or for purely pragmatic reasons; in transfer an already available constituent is mapped into another one which replaces it. Although transfer comes in two main varieties, analogical transfer and metonymical transfer, here I shall consider only the latter sort, extensively studied by Nunberg (1978, 1979) and Fauconnier (1985). They give examples like the following:

(M) The ham sandwich is getting restless

As Nunberg and Fauconnier point out, (M) can be used in certain contexts to say of the person who ordered the ham sandwich that he is getting restless. In this particular case there is *metonymical transfer* from the primary semantic value of the linguistic expression 'the ham sandwich', namely the ham sandwich, to a secondary or derived semantic value, namely the orderer of the ham sandwich. This looks like a standard example of divergence between what Kripke (1977) and Donnellan (1978) call 'semantic reference' and 'speaker reference'; however, as Ivan Sag (1981) noticed, this sort of phenomenon can hardly be handled within a classical Gricean framework contrasting the proposition literally expressed, which includes the semantic reference, and what is communicated, which includes the speaker's reference. Such a treatment would be counterintuitive, as Sag pointed out in the following passage:

> What is the role of context in examples such as (M)? Is this a case of an absurd literal meaning (an attribution of restlessness to a culinary object) rescued from pragmatic absurdity by the Cooperative Principle augmented by some ancillary principle which guides Gricean inferencing? Or is the shift from ham sandwich to ham sandwich orderer somehow more directly involved in the semantics of such utterances? Perhaps the shift from ham sandwich to individual who is in some relation to a ham sandwich (possibly different from context to context) is like the shift in denotation that accompanies indexical expressions as they are uttered in various contexts. (...) This approach, rather than one of the first kind, where all examples like (M) are pushed off to pragmatic theory and are abstracted away from in semantic analysis, is intuitive on the grounds that these transfers seem very different in kind from the kind of inferential operations that lead one from *It's hot in here* to the sense of 'Please open the window', which clearly deserve treatment of the first type. (Sag, 1981, pp. 275–6)

The Gricean treatment would be counterintuitive, because it does not seem that the sandwich itself is (absurdly) said to be restless. Whether or not we trust our intuitions on this matter, we must account for them and especially for the intuitive difference between this type of example and other examples to which the Gricean treatment obviously and intuitively applies. Sag mentions a standard example of implicature ('It's hot in here'), but it would have been more relevant to mention examples of irony in which the speaker actually says something absurd to convey something else. As Sag emphasizes, this does not seem to be what happens in the Nunberg-Fauconnier type of example; it does not seem that the speaker says something absurd in order to convey something different. Treating metonymical transfer as a primary pragmatic process both satisfies our intuitions with respect to examples such as (M) and accounts for the difference between this sort of case (in which a primary pragmatic process is involved) and standard cases of Gricean inferencing (in which a secondary pragmatic process is involved.)

There is an obvious sense in which transfer operates locally. At no point in the interpretation process need we entertain the absurd proposition that the sandwich itself is getting restless. We do not go from that absurd proposition to the communicated proposition that the person who ordered it is getting restless; we go from the primary semantic value (sandwich) to the secondary semantic value (sandwich orderer)[9] and it is the latter which goes into the global interpretation of the utterance. In other words, there is no need to compute the global interpretation of the utterance at an intermediate stage before transfer and other non-minimalist processes occur. That is another way of saying that transfer is a primary pragmatic process, rather than a secondary one presupposing the identification of a proposition at some prior level.

One might object (indeed, Kent Bach has objected to me) that the absurdity of the 'literal' interpretation is what triggers the transfer from ham sandwich to ham sandwich orderer. So the literal interpretation has to be somehow computed, Bach suggests. I deny that this is so. Consider another example: 'John was arrested by a policeman yesterday. He had just stolen a wallet'. The pronoun 'he' is interpreted as referring to John, not as referring to the policeman. Why? Because the former interpretation is far more plausible than the latter. Does this mean that one must first consider the less plausible interpretation ('the policeman had just stolen a wallet'), realize that it is not plausible, and turn to the other interpretation? Obviously not. One need not even *consider* the less plausible interpretation. In the same way, the description 'the ham sandwich' is interpreted as referring to the ham sandwich orderer in (M) because that interpretation – accessible through a process of metonymical transfer – is much more plausible than the so-called literal interpretation of the description as referring to the ham sandwich itself. This does not mean that one must first consider the less plausible interpretation (the attribution of restlessness to a culinary object, as Sag puts it), realize that it is not plausible, and turn to the other interpretation. In this case as in the other one, the context constrains the interpretation of the referring expression (pronoun or description) so as to eliminate irrelevant interpretations, but this does not mean that the latter must be considered in order to be rejected. Irrelevant interpretations are simply *not selected*.

To be sure, the literal interpretation of 'the ham sandwich' has to come first since it provides the input to the process of transfer. But *that literal interpretation is not selected as a possible interpretation in that context*: it serves only as input to a transfer process which yields a satisfactory interpretation ('the ham sandwich orderer'), and it is the latter which goes into the interpretation of the utterance and undergoes a composition process with other semantic values associated with other sub-expressions in the utterance. In other words, we do not have a 'global' transfer from the absurd proposition that the sandwich itself is getting restless to the more plausible proposition that the ham sandwich orderer is getting restless, as Bach and many others claim, but a local transfer from the literal interpretation of the description to a non-literal interpretation, only the latter going into the interpretation of the utterance in that context and undergoing the composition process which yields the semantic value of the whole on the basis of the semantic values of its parts. On the picture I am advocating, the composition process takes place 'after' various primary pragmatic processes, including transfer, have applied locally. The latter do not presuppose the prior computation of some basic propositional value for the utterance; on the contrary, it is the process of propositional composition which presupposes the prior operation of primary pragmatic processes, since they provide the (relevant) semantic values of the parts on which the composition process operates to yield the semantic value of the whole.[10]

That transfer operates on a 'primary' semantic value means that we have a number of levels to distinguish. The primary value on which transfer operates may itself result from the operation of another primary pragmatic process, e.g. saturation, at a prior level. This shows that primary pragmatic processes are primary only in a relative, not in an absolute sense. They are primary in the sense that they do not presuppose the identification of a proposition at some prior level, contrary to secondary pragmatic processes. They are constitutive of what is said and do not presuppose that something has been said. But they are not, or not necessarily, 'primary' in the sense of being first to operate. A primary pragmatic process which takes as input the output of another primary pragmatic process is clearly not 'primary' in this second sense, in contrast to a primary pragmatic process whose input is provided directly by the meaning of the expression type.[11]

## Notes

1. The Implicature Analysis is not only counterintuitive, it also suffers from a further defect, namely its lack of generality. For it does not (or not easily) apply to examples such as 'I have not had breakfast', which could hardly be analysed into the proposition that the speaker has never had breafkast plus some implicature. The only possibility for someone who does not consider the feature 'today' as a pragmatic constituent of what is said is to consider this example as a case of non-literality, in which there is a contradiction between what is said and what is meant. This commits one to giving two different sorts of analysis for 'I've had breakfast' and for 'I have not had breakfast'.
2. By this I mean that we can imagine a context in which the sentence in 4 would be used to express the proposition in question.
3. It might be argued – contrary to what was suggested earlier – that *every* unarticulated constituent (including the location of the rain in Perry's example) is optional from the truth-valuation point of view. With respect to a context in which the location of the rain is irrelevant, 'It is raining' might express the proposition that it's raining somewhere, in the same way as 'John is eating', in many contexts, expresses the proposition that John is eating something. Here too it would be artificial to hold that an unarticulated 'location' constituent is involved, of a 'general' or 'indeterminate' nature. It seems to me much better to hold that no unarticulated constituent corresponding to a place would be provided on this interpretation. (In examples such as 1 and 2 above, the unlikely 'general' interpretation presumably results from contextually providing an unarticulated constituent corresponding to the domain of quantification. The situation is therefore different.) In any case, this is a difficult issue, one that I can only mention *en passant*.
4. Charles Travis holds similar views: see Travis, 1975, 1981, 1985 and 1989. See also Waismann's classical paper on 'Verifiability' (Waismann, 1951) – not to mention Austin and Wittgenstein.
5. 'Contextualism' is my name for the doctrine that no proposition could be expressed independent of context. I am aware that contextualism must be argued for rather than merely assumed, as I do here. But this is a very large issue, whose discussion must be postponed to a later work.
6. In later chapters primary pragmatic processes will be called 'p-processes' for ease of expression.
7. The problem with expansion is this. What is enriched is not a natural language sentence but a semantic representation. Since expansion is a syntactic operation, the expansion theorist must treat semantic representations as syntactic entities – as mental 'sentences'. This is OK, but to make the proposal precise (and to apply it to particular

examples) we would need to know much more than we do about the 'language of thought'.

8   Although it has no psychological reality, it has a role to play in the theory: it corresponds to what in chapter 16 I will call 'the proposition Normally expressed' (16.6).

9   Nunberg (1991) offers a different analysis in which transfer operates from the *property* 'being a ham sandwich' to the *property* 'being the orderer of a ham sandwich', rather than from the sandwich itself to the person who ordered it, as in Fauconnier's or Sag's framework. This issue will not be addressed here.

10  Among the primary pragmatic processes which play a role in the determination of what is said is the providing of 'unarticulated constituents' (a particular form of free enrichment). Now unarticulated constituents are semantic values which correspond to no 'part' in the sentence. It follows that the Compositionality Principle must be rejected: the semantic value of the whole is not determined solely by the semantic values of the parts and the way they are put together. (See Crimmins & Perry, 1989.)

11  There are also primary pragmatic processes whose input is neither the meaning of the expression nor a semantic value obtained from the latter through the prior application of another primary pragmatic process. I have in mind the phenomenon of *autonymy*. When an expression is understood as 'mentioned' as in '*Cat* is a three-letter word', a primary pragmatic process is at work, whose input is the expression itself (not its meaning). I cannot elaborate here.

# Appendix

## Availability and the Scope Principle

Two sorts of criteria for distinguishing implicatures from pragmatic aspects of what is said were considered in chapter 13: various versions of the Minimalist principle, and the Availability Principle. I used the latter to argue against the former, which relies on the counter-intuitive Implicature Analysis. In this appendix, I want to consider the relation between the Availability Principle and another principle which has been put forward in the literature, the Scope Principle (Carston, 1988; Recanati, 1989a; Wilson, 1991). The latter is based on observations that various people have made on the behaviour of conversational implicatures in connection with logical operators. These observations tend to provide evidence for a distinction between two types of alleged implicatures: those that do and those that do not fall within the scope of logical operators.

Consider the following pair of examples (from Cohen, 1971):

1 The old king has died of a heart attack and a republic has been declared.
2 A republic has been declared and the old king has died of a heart attack.

In 1, it is implied that the first event described (the death of the old king) occurred before the second one (the declaration of a republic). In 2 the same events are reported in a different order, and the implication is reversed; it is suggested that the death of the old king occurred after – and, perhaps, because of – the declaration of a republic. Cohen ascribes to Grice the view that in both cases the temporal suggestion is a conversational implicature stemming from the presumption that the speaker is observing the maxim of manner: 'Be perspicuous'. In general, a narrative is more perspicuous if the events are reported in the order in which they occurred. The speaker's reporting a series of events in a certain order therefore implies that they occurred in that order, by virtue of the presumption that he is observing the maxim of manner. *Qua* conversational implicature, the temporal suggestion is not part of what is said and makes no contribution to the truth-condition of the utterance. Thus, according to Grice, what is strictly and literally said by means of 1 and 2 is the same thing, even though there is an important difference in (conveyed) meaning between these two utterances. The truth-functionality of 'and' can therefore be maintained.

Cohen (1971) raises a serious objection to the view he ascribes to Grice. If 1 and 2 really have the same truth-conditions and differ only at the level of conversational implicatures, then, in Grice's framework, 3 and 4 also should have the same truth-conditions (given the truth-functionality of 'if', in Grice's theory):

3   If the old king has died of a heart attack and a republic has been declared, then Tom will be quite content.
4   If a republic has been declared and the old king has died of a heart attack, then Tom will be quite content.

But 3 and 4 do not seem to have the same truth-conditions. What 3 and 4 say is that Tom will be content if the following conditions obtain: the old king has died, a republic has been declared, *and there is a certain temporal relation between these two events*. The temporal relation allegedly implicated by 1 and 2 is an integral part of the antecedent of the conditional in 3 and 4; it falls within the scope of the conditional. If we suppose that the antecedent of the conditional and the proposition expressed by the simple utterance 1 are identical, this entails that the alleged implicature of 1 is not really an implicature, but a constituent of the proposition expressed (Carston, 1988). In the same way, when 1 is negated, the alleged implicature falls within the scope of the negation. The negation of 1 is made true if one of the following conditions fails to be satisfied: the old king has died, a republic has been declared, *and the first event occurred before the second*. Thus, one can deny 1 and thereby mean, as in 5, that the suggested order of events does not correspond to the facts:

5  It is not the case that the old king has died and a republic has been declared; what is true is that a republic has been declared first and then the old king died of a heart attack.

Deirdre Wilson gives other examples of alleged implicatures falling in the scope of logical operators (Wilson, 1991):

6  It's always the same thing at parties: either I get drunk and no one will talk to me, or no one will talk to me and I get drunk.
7  If a manhole is left uncovered and you break a leg, sue.

In all of these examples, the fact that the alleged implicature of the simple utterance falls within the scope of the operator in the complex utterance shows that it was not a genuine implicature, but a constituent of what is said. Or at least it shows this if one accepts the crucial premiss which I call Identity: that the proposition expressed by the simple utterance is identical to that which is dominated by the logical operator. (We shall see below that this premiss can be rejected.)

These considerations suggest the following criterion for telling implicatures from pragmatic constituents of what is said:

*Scope Principle:* A pragmatically determined aspect of meaning is part of what is said (and, therefore, not a conversational implicature) if – and, perhaps, only if – it falls within the scope of logical operators such as negation and conditionals.

By virtue of the Scope Principle, 3 and 4 provide evidence that the alleged implicatures conveyed by 1 and 2 are not really implicatures, but pragmatic constituents of what is said. And so forth for the other examples.

As I understand it the Scope Principle relies on two premisses. The first premiss is (e), the conclusion of the following argument (see Anscombre & Ducrot, 1978):

(a)  Conversational implicatures are pragmatic consequences of an act of saying something.
(b)  An act of saying something can be performed only by means of a complete utterance, not by means of an unasserted clause such as the antecedent of a conditional.

(c) Hence, no implicature can be generated at the sub-locutionary level, i.e. at the level of an unasserted clause such as the antecedent of a conditional.

(d) To say that an implicature falls within the scope of a logical operator is to say that it is generated at the sub-locutionary level, viz. at the level of the clause on which the logical operator operates.

(e) Hence, *no implicature can fall within the scope of a logical operator.*

I fully accept this argument and its conclusion (e). However it is important to realize that (e) by itself does not justify the Scope Principle. (e) can be paraphrased as follows:

> For every complex utterance **u** including a logical operator D (i.e. for every utterance such as 3–7), if some aspect *m* of the meaning of **u** falls within the scope of D, then *m* cannot be an implicature of **u**.

In other words, the fact that some meaning-constituent *m* falls within the scope of a logical operator in a complex utterance shows that *m* is not an implicature *of that complex utterance*, for it is *in the complex utterance* that the alleged implicature would occur at the sub-locutionary level (contrary to premiss (c)). But this does not entail anything concerning the status of *m* in what we may call the *simple* utterance, that is, the utterance (in isolation) of the clause which, in the complex utterance, is dominated by the logical operator. Thus the suggestion concerning the temporal order of the two events (the declaration of a republic and the death of the old king) cannot be considered as an implicature of the complex utterance 5, by virtue of (e); but it may well be considered as an implicature of the *simple* utterance 1. It is perfectly conceivable that something which is an implicature at the level of the simple utterance acquires a different status when the utterance is embedded into a larger structure. To rule out its being an implicature of the simple utterance, one must have recourse to a second premiss, namely Identity:

> *Identity:* the proposition expressed by the simple utterance is identical to that which is dominated by the logical operator in the complex utterance.

If the proposition expressed by 1 is the same as that which is negated in 5, then the proposition expressed by 1, like that which is negated in 5, must include the temporal suggestion that the declaration of a republic occurred before the death of the old king; and if this 'suggestion' is part of the proposition expressed by 1, then it is no more an implicature of 1 than it is of 5.

The problem is that Identity does not necessarily hold. Thus Horn (1989, ch. 6), after Ducrot (1972, 1973), talks of a 'metalinguistic' use of logical operators, characterized by the fact that the proposition expressed by the simple utterance is not identical to that which falls within the scope of the operator. As Wilson pointed out in her first work on the topic (Wilson, 1975, pp. 151–2), it is possible to negate aspects of an utterance other than its propositional content, as in 8:

8  I'm not Mary's father; she's *my* daughter.

Here what is rejected (what falls within the scope of the negation) is not the proposition expressed by the simple utterance 'I am Mary's father' but rather the way that proposition is expressed. A similar example, mentioned by Larry Horn (in an oral presentation), is 9:

9  Their victory was not an historic event; it was a historic event.

As Horn makes clear, 'metalinguistic' negation may hinge on grammar, speech level, phonetics, or implicatures. When I say 'She is not tall – she is very tall', I do not deny that she is tall, for this is entailed by what I assert, namely that she is very tall ('very tall' entails 'tall'); what I deny is an *implicature* of the utterance 'She is tall', namely the 'scalar' implicature that she is just tall or no more than tall. As Horn also points out, the same sort of metalinguistic usage can be found in connection with other operators. In all such uses, what falls within the scope of the logical operator is *not* identical to the proposition expressed by the simple utterance.

For the Scope Principle to work, we have to assume that the logical operators are not used metalinguistically. We have to assume Identity. But how do we know when Identity holds and when it does not? We have to compare what is said by the simple utterance and what is said by the complex utterance, to see whether the proposition which falls within the scope of the operator in the complex utterance (e.g. the proposition which is negated) coincides with the proposition expressed by the simple utterance. Now this supposes that we know what is said by both the simple and the complex utterance. Since our intuitions concerning the content of these utterances must be exploited in order to put the Scope Principle to use, the latter presupposes the availability hypothesis – the conscious availability of semantic content. I conclude that the Availability Principle is a more fundamental criterion than the Scope Principle.

# II.2
## Referential/attributive

# Chapter 15

# The referential use of definite descriptions

## 15.1 Introduction

During the last twenty years, dozens of papers have been published on the distinction between two uses of definite descriptions, referential and attributive. There are, I believe, three main reasons why this has been so:

1 The distinction is not a theoretical artefact; it corresponds to some genuine phenomenon – there really are two different 'readings' of the definite description "the F" in a sentence "The F is G." The very debate that followed Donnellan's original paper provides some evidence that we do have intuitions about the referential/attributive distinction; the debate hinges on how these intuitions are to be accounted for, not on the existence of these intuitions. Indirect evidence in favour of the reality of the distinction is also provided by the fact that it has been made independently by different authors, some of them with widely different philosophical backgrounds.[1]

2 The difference between the two readings of definite descriptions greatly resembles the difference between referential and non-referential terms. (As Donnellan himself said, a referentially used description is a description used 'as if it were' a referential term.) People interested in the semantics of referential terms were thus naturally interested in the distinction between the two uses of definite descriptions.

3 The referential/attributive distinction raises an interesting methodological issue, that of the division of labour between semantics and pragmatics in the explanation of *prima facie* ambiguities.

When should a multiplicity of readings be accounted for in terms of semantic ambiguity proper, and when should it be accounted for in terms of properties of the pragmatic context? Many philosophers who wrote articles on the referential/attributive distinction were primarily concerned with this methodological issue (see e.g. Kripke, 1977).

In this chapter, I will deal with the three issues I have just listed: our intuitions concerning the referential/attributive distinction, and various ways of accounting for them; in particular, the competition between alternative semantic and pragmatic explanations; and finally the relation between the referential/attributive distinction and the semantic distinction between referential and non-referential terms. I start with Donnellan's own presentation of the referential/attributive distinction; as will soon become apparent, the account to be developed in this chapter is to a large extent an elaboration of the view which Donnellan himself sketched in his famous paper 'Reference and Definite Descriptions' (Donnellan, 1966).

## 15.2 Donnellan's presentation

There are four basic components or features in Donnellan's presentation of the distinction between referential and attributive uses of definite descriptions. Distinguishing between them will allow me to dispose of most of the objections commonly raised to Donnellan, whose account I want to defend and elaborate. These objections, as we shall see, either concentrate on a relatively minor feature of Donnellan's account (the use of 'improper' descriptions as examples) or rely on a mistaken methodological assumption.

*First feature:* Donnellan's account is an instance of what I call the 'Naive Theory' (Recanati, 1989b) – a theory adhered to also by Kaplan, Stalnaker, Wettstein, and Barwise and Perry, to mention only a few. The Naive Theory holds that the truth-conditions of an utterance of "The F is G" differ when the description is used referentially and when it is used attributively. The Naive Theory is to be contrasted which the Implicature Theory, which holds that the truth-conditions of the utterance are the same on both uses. The two competing theories can be summed up as follows:

– According to the Naive Theory, the referential/attributive distinction is a distinction between two types of proposition literally expressed by "The F is G". On the referential reading, a certain object is said to be G, and the utterance is true if and only if this object is G; on the attributive reading, what is said is that there is an object which is both uniquely F and G, and the utterance is true if and only if there is such an object.

– According to the Implicature Theory, one and the same proposition is expressed on both readings, viz. the general proposition that there is an x such that x is uniquely F and x is G. The description is said to be used 'referentially' when this general proposition owes its relevance to its contextually implying (or 'conversationally implicating') a singular proposition to the effect that a certain object, *a*, is G; on the attributive reading, the general proposition literally expressed is relevant independently of any such contextually implied singular proposition. It follows that the referential/attributive distinction in 'pragmatic' in the straightforward sense that it relates to what the *speaker* means, i.e. communicates, by his utterance, not to what *his words* literally mean.

As we have just seen, the Naive Theory holds that "The F is G" is truth-conditionally ambiguous. The *second feature* of Donnellan's account which I want to highlight is his view that the ambiguity in question is not 'semantic' but 'pragmatic' in some sense which Donnellan does not precisely characterize. Donnellan's view would be inconsistent if by 'semantic', as opposed to 'pragmatic', he meant something like 'truth-conditional'. What he means when he says that the ambiguity is not semantic is simply that it is not a *lexical* or *syntactic* type of ambiguity. The sentence type is not grammatically ambiguous, Donnellan holds, even though it can be used to express different propositions in different contexts.

The *third feature* is Donnellan's systematic use of examples in which there is a divergence between what the speaker 'has in mind' and intends to refer to and what the description actually denotes. Let us call 'improper' a use of a description characterized by such a divergence. Improper uses of definite descriptions play quite a central role in Donnellan's presentation; it seems that, for him, the most typical examples of referential uses of descriptions *are* improper uses.

The *fourth feature* is Donnellan's adherence to what I call the 'Subjective Reference View'. Suppose the definite description "the F" in an utterance "The F is G" is used to refer to a certain object *a*. The speaker makes an assertion about *a*, to the effect that it is G; in the terminology of Russell and Kaplan, he communicates a singular proposition consisting of that object and the property of being G. The question arises whether this singular proposition is literally expressed (Naive Theory) or whether it is only communicated (Implicature Theory). But there is another question, concerning the object which is a 'constituent' of the singular proposition: which object is it? There are two candidates: the 'semantic referent' of the description, i.e. the object which happens to be the F, or the speaker's intended referent, i.e. the object which the speaker 'has in mind' when he uses the definite description referentially. When they diverge – when, for example, the speaker mistakenly believes that *a* is the F, and intends to refer to *a* by means of the description "the F" – the question arises, Does the singular proposition communicated include the semantic referent or the speaker's intended referent as a constituent? Donnellan's answer to this question is that the singular proposition includes the speaker's intended referent. This is what I call the Subjective Reference View.

This fourth feature of Donnellan's own account creates a certain tension within the latter. Donnellan accepts both the Subjective Reference View and the Naive Theory; it follows that, for him, the speaker literally *says* that *a* is G, or, rather, says of *a* that it is G, when he utters "The F is G" using "the F" to refer to *a* in a context in which *a* is not actually the F. But it is not obvious that one can accept *both* the Subjective Reference View and the Naive Theory. If the singular proposition which is communicated includes the *speaker's* intended referent rather than the *semantic* referent, how could that proposition be the proposition 'literally expressed' by the utterance? One feels compelled to say that it is only the proposition which the speaker intends to communicate. In other words, the Subjective Reference View comports badly with the Naive Theory.

Donnellan's insistence on improper uses is another thing which may be felt to create a tension. In improper uses there is a divergence between what the words mean and what the speaker means. If referential uses of descriptions are, typically, improper uses, this supports the Implicature Theory as opposed to the Naive theory. For the Implicature Theory has it that the referential/attributive distinction relates to what the *speaker* means, i.e. communicates, by his utterance, not to what *his words* literally mean.

Because of these tensions (between the first feature and the third and fourth features), Donnellan's account itself has been considered as ambiguous between the Naive Theory, according to which "The F is G" is ambiguous, and the Implicature Theory according to which it is not. Donnellan's talk of 'pragmatic ambiguity' (second feature) would be merely a symptom of his own ambiguity on this question, i.e. of his incapacity to decide either in favour of the ambiguity thesis or in favour of the pragmatic thesis. This conclusion, however, is a mistake. In what follows, I will attempt to show that Donnellan's framework can be used to give a satisfactory theory of the referential/attributive distinction. I will do so by offering a version of the Naive Theory which construes the truth-conditional ambiguity of "The F is G" as pragmatic. Many people have lamented that Donnellan does not explicitly characterize his notion of pragmatic ambiguity, but the notion of pragmatic ambiguity which *I* will use has been defined in 14.4. As for improper uses, I will downplay their role in the theory; they will be ascribed a purely heuristic function, and the theory will be shown to rest on the cases in which the semantic referent and the speaker's intended referent are identical. Since, in such cases, there is no problem as to which object is a constituent of the singular proposition communicated, it will not be necessary to discuss the Subjective Reference View. This last feature of Donnellan's account will therefore be ignored in what follows.

### 15.3 Improper uses and truth-conditional irrelevance: the intuitive basis of the Naive Theory

Improper uses are characterized by a divergence between speaker's reference and semantic reference, as Kripke and Donnellan put it (Kripke, 1977; Donnellan, 1978). Kripke rightly emphasized that the same sort of divergence may arise with respect to any type of referential expression; one example he gives is the proper name 'Smith' used to refer to Jones by someone who sees Jones and wrongly believes that he is Smith. The same *sort* of thing may indeed happen in connection with any type of expression whatsoever, whether referential or not. One may be mistaken as to what a given word means, for example, and use it improperly. Improper uses, in a general sense, are characterized by a divergence between 'speaker's meaning' and 'word meaning' (Grice, 1989), and the divergence between speaker reference and semantic reference is only a particular case.

Donnellan's systematic use of improper descriptions as examples is unhappy, because improper uses of descriptions cannot provide the sort of intuitive basis we need for establishing the Naive Theory. The Naive Theory construes 'what is said' as different on the referential and the attributive reading. But we have no clear intuition of what is said when there is a divergence between the two factors which normally concur into determining what is said, namely the semantic properties of the sentence on the one hand and the intentions of the speaker on the other hand. What is being said when I point to Jones and utter 'Smith is raking the leaves'? There is no clear and definite answer to this question, except one based on stipulation. The same thing holds of improper uses of definite descriptions: our intuitions concerning what is said in such cases are far from clear and definite, and cannot be expected to provide a basis for the Naive Theory.

If the intuitive basis of the Naive Theory was provided by those improper uses of which Donnellan makes so much in his paper, then, as Evans rightly pointed out (Evans, 1982, pp. 322–3), the theory would have no firm intuitive basis. But improper uses are *not* what provides the required basis, on my interpretation of Donnellan. Let me explain why.

As many people emphasized (e.g. Loar, 1976; Recanati, 1981a), two different distinctions are mixed in Donnellan's paper. There is, on the one hand, the distinction between the 'identifying' (or 'entity-invoking') and the 'non-identifying' (or 'generalizing') uses of definite descriptions, which corresponds to that I made earlier between 'informative' and 'reference-fixing' descriptions (6.5); on the other hand, there is the distinction between 'speaker's reference' and 'semantic reference'. (Again a use of a description is 'improper' whenever the latter distinction applies, i.e. whenever there is a divergence between what the speaker refers to and what the description denotes.) But the two distinctions are mutually independent. First, we find the identifying/non-identifying distinction even if we concentrate upon proper uses of descriptions; second, even a non-identifying use can be improper.

Even though paradigm referential uses, as illustrated by Donnellan's examples, are both improper and identifying, it is clear that Donnellan did not intend the referential/attributive distinction to cover the complex distinction between uses that are *both* identifying and improper and uses that are *both* proper and non-identifying. For he explicitly acknowledges the possibility of *proper* descriptions being used referentially. Impropriety cannot therefore be conceived of as criterial of referentiality. Indeed I take it that the important distinction in Donnellan's paper – what really deserves to be called *the* referential/attributive distinction – is the distinction between identifying and non-identifying uses. Donnellan brought improper uses into the picture only to emphasize that the mode of presentation of the reference – the concept expressed by the description – is not intrinsic to what is said when the description is used referentially (i.e. identifyingly); his claim, that what is said may be true even though the description is improper, was subservient to his main point, to the effect that the referent's fitting or not fitting the description is irrelevant to the truth-condition of the utterance on the referential use. Kripke is therefore particularly wide of the mark when he insists on reducing Donnellan's distinction to the distinction between speaker's reference and semantic reference (Kripke, 1977).

If I am right, then, the basis for the Naive Theory is provided by our intuitions concerning the truth-conditional irrelevance of descriptive content in certain uses of definite descriptions (the referential, as opposed to the attributive uses). We have the intuition (i) that the descriptive content of a description is not part of what is said, not part of the truth-conditions of the utterance, and (ii) more specifically, that the truth-condition is singular and involves only the reference of the description. To elicit those intuitions it is not necessary that the description taken as example be improper; we have exactly the same intuitions when the description is proper. Moreover, *the intuitions in question are* exactly *the same which direct reference theorists such as David Kaplan invoke in connection with referential terms.* Thus Kaplan says that in 'I am bald', the property of being the speaker or, more generally, the 'agent' of the utterance is truth-conditionally irrelevant even though it is linguistically signified and helps identify the person who is said to be bald. Kaplan's central distinctions between 'content' and 'character' and between 'context of utterance' and 'world of evaluation' are based on this very intuition. Since it is the same intuition of truth-conditional irrelevance which is supposed to characterize a referential use of a description, such as e.g. 'The present speaker is bald', a direct reference theorist has no reason to doubt the Naive Theory, according to which there is a truth-conditional difference between referential and attributive uses of descriptions.

I conclude that the Naive Theory does *not* lack an adequate intuitive basis, contrary to what has often been claimed. The theory which says that there are truth-conditional differences between the referential and the attributive uses of definite descriptions is based on the same intuitions of truth-conditional irrelevance as the theory which says that there is a truth-conditional difference between referential and non-referential terms (or, rather, between referential terms and non-referential uses of non-referential terms). This said, I turn to the master argument used by Implicature Theorists in their crusade against the Naive Theory.

## 15.4  An alleged argument for the Implicature Theory

A number of philosophers think they can show the Implicature Theory to be preferable to the Naive Theory *on purely methodological grounds*. In this section, I will present their argument and use the distinctions made in chapter 13 to show that it does not work.

The argument starts with the following premise which, as it stands, seems hardly controversial:

(P) When a sentence S, for example a sentence in which a definite description occurs as subject-term, can be used to mean two different things, one may try to account for the intuitive difference in meaning either at the semantic level, by positing two different literal meanings corresponding to what is superficially the same sentence, or at the pragmatic level, by positing a conversational implicature which in some contexts combines with what is literally said, thereby modifying the utterance's overall meaning.

The second part of the argument is Grice's 'Modified Occam's Razor' (13.1). According to that methodological principle, when a pragmatic solution is available, it is to be preferred to a solution in terms of semantic ambiguity. Grice's principle is a principle of theoretical economy, akin to Occam's Razor: like theoretical entities in general, *senses are not to be multiplied beyond necessity*. Now it is unnecessary to assign a special sense to an expression in order to account for its use to convey a meaning different from its standard sense, if a pragmatic explanation of why this meaning is conveyed is available. It follows that a pragmatic explanation, when available, is to be preferred to an explanation in terms of semantic ambiguity. Of course, a pragmatic explanation is not always available; but when it is – when, for example, it can be shown that uttering a sentence expressing one of the two meanings at issue would enable one to convey the other by conversational implicature – then this explanation is to be preferred.

In the case at hand – the referential/attributive distinction – a pragmatic explanation *is* available, as we have seen. The Implicature Theory accounts for the data – the two possible interpretations of an utterance of "The F is G" – along the following lines:

> What is said by an utterance of "The F is G" is that whoever (whatever) is uniquely F is G. This is uncontroversially so when the description is used attributively, but this is also the case when the description is used referentially. To account for our intuitions in the latter sort of case, we must bring contextual factors into the picture. Suppose a context in which it is known that *a* is the F; in this context, "The F is G" contextually implies that *a* is G. Suppose further that the information literally expressed by "The F is G", viz. the information that whoever is the F is G, is not relevant *per se*, but only insofar as it contextually implies something which *is* relevant, namely that *a* is G. Clearly, in such a context, the utterance "The F is G", even if it is construed as literally expressing the general proposition that whoever is the F is G, will be understood as conveying the singular proposition that *a* is G. For the speaker claims to be communicating something relevant, and it is manifest that his utterance achieves relevance only if one of its contextual implications is understood as part of what is being communicated.² A referential use of a definite description, on this account, is simply a case in which, by saying that the F is G, the speaker means that a certain object, *a*, is G. The speaker communicates not only the general proposition which is literally expressed, but also the singular proposition which is contextually implied and which gives the utterance its point.

Since this pragmatic explanation is available, it follows, according to Modified Occam's Razor, that it is to be preferred. Thus the Implicature Theory wins, and the Naive Theory loses, if the methodological argument I have just expounded is correct.

The methodological argument, however, is clearly incorrect. I accept Modified Occam's Razor, but I do not think it follows from Modified Occam's Razor that the Implicature Theory of referential descriptions is to be preferred to the Naive Theory. What Grice's principle implies is that the Implicature Theory, *qua* pragmatic theory, is to be preferred to an account in terms of semantic ambiguity, that is, to a theory which ascribes two different literal meanings to the sentence type. To conclude that the Naive Theory must be rejected, we have to construe the Naive Theory as an account in terms of semantic ambiguity. This construal is manifest throughout the philosophical literature against the Naive Theory.

Typical in this respect is Salmon's presentation of the Naive Theory as 'the thesis that sentences involving definite descriptions are semantically ambiguous, in the sense that the proposition expressed is either singular or general' (Salmon, 1982, p. 38) – as if it was not possible for a sentence to express different propositions in different contexts without being semantically ambiguous.[3] As a result of their construing the Naive Theory in this way, Implicature Theorists are puzzled when a Naive Theorist such as Donnellan rejects the thesis that the sentence "The F is G" is semantically ambiguous. This position they take to be more or less inconsistent. But, of course, there is an inconsistency here only if the Naive Theory is construed as an account in term of semantic ambiguity.

The argument against the Naive Theory rests on a mistaken identification of the Naive Theory with what I will henceforth refer to as the Ambiguity Theory. The Ambiguity Theory consists of three theses:

(a) The *sentence* at issue is semantically ambiguous, i.e. it has two different literal meanings.
(b) The (literal) truth-conditions of an *utterance* of this sentence are different on the two readings.
(c) What is strictly and literally said is different on the two readings.

The Naive Theory consists of theses (b) and (c); it says that the proposition expressed by "The F is G" is not the same when the description is used referentially and when it is used attributively. Grice's Modified Occam's Razor implies that the Implicature Theory is to be preferred to the Ambiguity Theory, but it does not imply that the Implicature Theory is to be preferred to a weaker theory embodying theses (b) and (c) but not thesis (a). *It is thesis (a) which 'multiplies senses beyond necessity'* and is therefore unwelcome by Gricean standards. So the question is: is it possible to hold (b) and (c) without holding (a)? Is it possible to be a Naive Theorist without being an Ambiguity Theorist? To this question, I answer positively. A Naive Theorist is not necessarily an Ambiguity Theorist, contrary to what has constantly been assumed in the philosophical literature against the Naive Theory. As we saw in chapter 14, there are several pragmatic processes (e.g. saturation, enrichment, and transfer) which operate in the very constitution of what is said; such processes generate 'pragmatic ambiguity', that is, a form of 'ambiguity' which affects truth-conditions even though it is pragmatic (in the sense of contextual) rather than semantic (in the sense which ties semantics to sentence meaning). An explanation in terms of pragmatic ambiguity is no less pragmatic than an explanation in terms of implicature, hence it does not violate Modified Occam's Razor; it does not multiply linguistic meanings without necessity.

At the beginning of this section, I said of premiss (P) that it seemed hardly controversial as it stood. (P) says that there are two possible theories, the Implicature Theory and the Ambiguity Theory. Interpreted at face value, this is hardly controversial. But the argument against the Naive Theory rests on a *special* interpretation of (P) – and this is where the fallacy lies. On this special, restrictive interpretation, (P) says that there are two, *and only two*, possible theories, the Implicaure Theory and the Ambiguity Theory. From (P) thus interpreted, together with Modified Occam's Razor, it does follow that the Implicature Theory, when available, is the correct theory. But I deny (P) on this interpretation. I believe there are more theories than just the Ambiguity Theory and the Implicature Theory. It may be, therefore, that the Implicature Theory is not the correct one, even if it is preferable to the Ambiguity Theory.

There are many sentences which in different contexts express different propositions even though they are not semantically ambiguous. Indexical sentences such as 'I am hungry' are obvious examples. In a context C this sentence will express the proposition that Tom is hungry at time t; in another context C* it will express the proposition that Bill is hungry at time t'. As far as such examples are concerned, theses (b) and (c) hold, but not thesis (a). What this shows is that there are three basic levels to be considered rather than merely two. There is, firstly, the level of sentence meaning. At this level, we are concerned only with sentence types and their linguistic meaning. The phenomenon of ambiguity is located at this level: an ambiguous sentence is a sentence type to which two different linguistic meanings are assigned by the semantic conventions of the language. Secondly, there is the level of what is said literally by uttering (a token of) the sentence. In the case of indexical and other context-sensitive sentences, what is said depends on the context of utterance and not merely on the linguistic meaning of the sentence type. Thirdly, there is what is communicated by uttering the sentence. What is communicated may be identical with what is said, but it is also possible to communicate more than, or something different from, what is strictly and literally said.[4]

As we saw in chapter 13, when a sentence can be used to communicate two different things in two different contexts or classes of contexts, the difference may be treated in *three* different ways, corresponding to the three different levels of meaning. It may be treated as a superficial, pragmatic difference at the third level only. On this view, what is communicated, but neither what is said nor the linguistic meaning of the sentence, varies from one context to the other. The difference between the referential and the attributive uses of descriptions is such a superficial difference according to the Implicature Theory, whereas the Ambiguity Theory ascribes the difference between the two readings to the deepest level: it considers it as a difference between two senses of the sentence type. Principle (P) in its restrictive interpretation suggests that these are the only two possibilities, but there is also a third one: *to ascribe the difference to the second level, by considering it as a difference between the propositions literally expressed, without rooting this difference in a genuine ambiguity at the first level*. This amounts to construing the difference between the two readings as a form of pragmatic ambiguity generated by some pragmatic process operating in the very constitution of what is said. It is such a version of the Naive Theory, immune to Grice's methodological principle, which I want to put forward in this chapter.

## 15.5 The Indeterminacy Theory

Since I claim that the sentence "The F is G" is not ambiguous yet expresses different propositions in different contexts, I must say what the constant meaning of this sentence is. This meaning must be such as to explain how the sentence comes to express a general proposition in certain contexts and a singular proposition in other contexts. In this section, I will present the proposal I made in an earlier paper on the subject (Recanati, 1989b), which proposal I now call the 'Indeterminacy Theory'. In 15.6 I will present an alternative proposal which I now favour.

In the first two chapters of this book I said that the meaning of a sentence partly consists in indications concerning the conditions under which an utterance of the sentence expresses a true proposition. These conditions are not to be confused with the truth-conditions of the utterance, i.e. the conditions under which the proposition actually expressed by the utterance is true. What the sentence indicates are the conditions under which *any* utterance of this sentence would express a true proposition – the conditions which must be satisfied in a world $w$ for an utterance of the sentence in $w$ to express a proposition true with respect to $w$. These conditions are invariant under contextual change, while the proposition expressed by the utterance, and therefore its truth-conditions, generally depend on the context.

Let us take an example. By virtue of its meaning, the sentence 'I am French' indicates that: for every token t of this sentence, t expresses a true proposition iff there is a person who utters t, and this person is French (at the time of utterance). Let us suppose that a token T of the sentence is actually produced. By virtue of knowing the meaning of the sentence, we automatically know what I will call the *external truth-conditions* of T – even if we don't know what the context of utterance looks like. A token T of 'I am French' expresses a true proposition if and only if *someone utters T and he or she is French (at the time of utterance)*. The italicized right-hand size of the conditional represents what I call the external truth-conditions of the utterance, or the proposition 'externally' associated with the utterance – or, for short, the external proposition.

The external proposition is different from the proposition expressed by T. If we abstract from the context and rely only on the linguistic meaning of T, we cannot say which proposition is expressed. Indeed, without a context, no proposition is expressed: the proposition expressed is essentially context-dependent. Once the context is taken into account, it turns out that T expresses the proposition that, for example, Giscard d'Estaing (whom we may suppose to be the utterer of T) is French – a proposition that can be described as the set of worlds in which Giscard d'Estaing is French. Now, consider the external proposition associated with T: as I said, we need not know the context of utterance in order to identify this proposition. By virtue of its linguistic meaning alone, T tells us which conditions must be satisfied for it to express a true proposition; it tells us that it expresses a true proposition if and only if there is an $x$ who utters T and who is French (at the time of utterance). The external proposition is just that: the proposition that there is an $x$ such that $x$ utters T and $x$ is French.

The distinction between the proposition expressed and the external proposition associated with the utterance is reminiscent of that drawn by Stalnaker between the proposition expressed and the 'diagonal proposition'.[5] Stalnaker defined the diagonal proposition associated with an utterance E as the proposition which has the following property: for any world $w$, this proposition is true with respect to $w$ if and only if E, uttered in $w$, would express a proposition true with respect to $w$ (Stalnaker, 1978, p. 318). What I am calling the external proposition can be equated with Stalnaker's diagonal proposition if we decide to ignore the worlds in which the meaning of the sentence is different from what it actually is. One may easily check that the external proposition associated with T (viz. the proposition that there is an $x$ such that $x$ utters T and $x$ is French) *is* the proposition that is true with respect to a world $w$ linguistically similar to ours if and only if the proposition expressed by T in $w$ is true with respect to $w$.

In the case of 'eternal sentences', the proposition expressed and the external proposition are identical. As I have just said, the external proposition is the proposition which is true with respect to any world $w$ linguistically similar to ours if and only if the proposition expressed when the utterance occurs in $w$ is true with respect to $w$. Now, an eternal sentence expresses the same proposition no matter in which world the utterance takes place (provided the world in question is linguistically similar to ours). It follows that the external proposition associated with an eternal sentence is true if and only if the proposition expressed by that sentence is true. The proposition expressed and the external proposition therefore coincide. But when a sentence is context-sensitive, there is a difference between the proposition expressed and the external proposition. For example, the external proposition associated with T is clearly different from the proposition actually expressed by T. The former can be described as the set of worlds in which someone utters T and is French, the latter as the set of worlds in which Giscard d'Estaing is French. Obviously, there are many possible worlds in which Giscard d'Estaing is French but no Frenchman utters T, or in which the utterer of T is French but Giscard d'Estaing is not.

Since there is this difference, for context-sensitive sentence, between the proposition expressed and the external proposition, we need not be embarrassed by the question, 'What is the meaning of "The F is G"?' We may concede to the Implicature Theorist that the meaning of this sentence is or involves a general proposition, viz. the proposition that that there is a unique F and that it is G, and insist that this proposition is not the proposition expressed, contrary to what the Implicature Theorist holds, but only the external proposition.

If we assume that, at the first level, the sentence "The F is G" externally expresses the (general) proposition that there is a unique F and that it is G, it is easy to explain why, at the second level, this sentence can express either a general or a singular proposition. In my paper 'Referential/Attributive' (Recanati, 1989b) I put forward the following account, reminiscent of Kaplan (1978, p. 233) and Stalnaker (1970, p. 285). The external proposition globally indicates the conditions under which the utterance expresses a true proposition, but it does not tell us which of these conditions are contextual conditions, i.e. conditions which must be contextually satisfied for the sentence to express a definite proposition, and which are truth-conditions proper, i.e. conditions which must be satisfied for the proposition expressed to be true. (For example, in the case of 'I am French', the condition that there be a person $x$ who utters T is a contextual condition, and the condition that this person be French is a truth-condition.) The external proposition associated with "The F is G" tells us that the utterance expresses a true proposition if and only if there is an $x$ such that $x$ is uniquely F and $x$ is G, but it does not tell us whether the condition that there be an $x$ such that $x$ is uniquely F is a contextual condition or a truth-condition proper. It follows that there are two possible interpretations, according to the context: in one type of context, the condition that there be an $x$ such that $x$ is uniquely F will be interpreted as a contextual condition, and the proposition expressed will be a singular proposition, true if and only if $a$ (the object which satisfies the contextual condition) is G. In another type of context, the condition that there be an $x$ such that $x$ is uniquely F will be considered as a full-blooded truth-condition, and the utterance will express the general proposition that there is an $x$ such that $x$ is uniquely F and $x$ is G.

To conclude, let me indicate how the semantic distinction between referentially used descriptions and referential terms can be drawn in this framework. Suppose Giscard d'Estaing utters 'The present speaker is French', using the description referentially. He might also have said, 'I am French'. According to the Indeterminacy Theory, both utterances express the singular proposition that Giscard d'Estaing is French. The difference, therefore, cannot be located at the level of what is said, since in both cases what is said is that Giscard d'Estaing is French. Apparently it can't be located at the level of sentence meaning either, for at this level each utterance indicates that it expresses a true proposition if and only if there is an x such that x is producing this very utterance and x is French. How, then, is the Indeterminacy Theory going to account for the semantic difference between the two sentences?

The solution to this problem is simple. We must allow (indeed, we have allowed) that there is more to the meaning of a sentence than just the indications it gives concerning the conditions under which an utterance of this sentence expresses a true proposition. Consider, again, an utterance T of the sentence 'I am French'. By virtue of its linguistic meaning, T indicates that T is true if and only if someone utters T and is French; but this indication does not exhaust the linguistic meaning of T. *T also indicates that the first condition, namely: that there be an x who utters T, is a contextual condition and not a truth-condition proper.* This indication is conveyed by the pronoun 'I' *qua* referential term. It is this indication which is responsible for the difference between 'I am French' and 'The present speaker is French'.

Referential terms have the following property: their meaning includes a special feature, which I dubbed 'REF', by virtue of which they indicate that there is an object, the referent of the term, such that the utterance in which they occur in subject-position is true if and only if this object satisfies the predicate. Referential terms therefore indicate that the utterance in which they occur expresses a singular proposition, with the referent of the referential term as a constituent. For example, the pronoun 'I' in T indicates that there is an x such that T is true if and only if x is French. In most cases and perhaps all, the meaning of a referential term also includes a 'mode of presentation', i.e. a descriptive condition which the referent of the term must satisfy (in the case of 'I' this descriptive condition is: being the speaker); but the effect of REF is to present this condition as merely a contextual condition, external to the proposition expressed. The mode of presentation associated with the referential term makes a certain object contextually identifiable, and the utterance is presented as true if and only if this object has the property expressed by the predicate in the sentence. Thus, by virtue of its linguistic meaning, an utterance in which a referential term occurs indicates not only the conditions under which it expresses a true proposition, but also which condition is a contextual condition and which a truth-condition proper. Owing to this further indication, the indeterminacy which characterizes description-sentences and makes them capable of two readings does not transfer to sentences in which a referential term occurs instead of a description.

## 15.6 The Synecdoche Theory

The Indeterminacy Theory raises the following objection. Even though, on this theory, sentences of the form "The F is G" are ascribed a linguistic meaning which does not wholly specify the logical form of the *utterance* – i.e. the type of proposition (singular or general) which an utterance of the sentence contextually expresses – still the Indeterminacy Theory says something quite specific about the logical form of the *sentence* "The F is G": the external proposition which the Indeterminacy Theory uses to characterize the meaning of this type of sentence is itself analyzed along the lines of Russell's theory of descriptions. Now there are uses of definite descriptions which this Russellian framework makes very hard to handle. For this reason, it would be better if our account of the referential/attributive distinction did *not* commit us to the Russellian theory even at the level of external propositions.

The uses of descriptions which I have in mind are those which Barwise and Perry (1983, pp. 158–9) dubbed 'functional'. Examples of functional uses of descriptions include 'The President changes every four years' or 'The temperature is rising.' When I utter the sentence 'The President changes every four years' I am not saying of the person contextually identifiable as 'the President' that *he* changes every four years, nor am I saying that *whoever is the President changes* every four years: rather, I am saying of the function 'President' that its value changes every four years. This is a different type of use altogether, and it is hard to see how we could account for it within the framework of the Indeterminacy Theory – the Russellian semantics which underlies the latter does not allow one to account for functional uses in any straightforward manner.[6] Since that is so, I will try to sketch an alternative account of referential uses of descriptions which is less committal than (though in the same spirit as) the Indeterminacy Theory and does not rely on Russell's theory. My strategy will be the following. Rather than assuming Russell's theory of descriptions and its characteristic analysis of the "The F is G", I will merely assume that a description "the F" expresses a descriptive concept, the concept of a unique F. I will stick to this minimal and, I hope, fairly uncontroversial basis, *without* providing an analysis of the complete sentence "The F is G" and, in particular, without saying how the concept of a unique F is related to that expressed by the predicate G at the level of sentence meaning.

How, then, does one go from the descriptive concept *the F* expressed by a definite description to the object which satisfies that concept and which, in referential uses of the description, figures in the propositional content of the utterance? Fauconnier (1985, p. 42) suggests that the step from concept to object can be understood as a particular case of metonymical transfer. As we saw in 14.4, metonymical transfer enables us to account for cases in which an object (e.g. the orderer of the ham sandwich) is referred to by means to an expression denoting another object (the ham sandwich itself). Since Fauconnier treats 'roles' – i.e. the functions or concepts expressed by definite descriptions – as objects[7] in an essentially non-Fregean manner, his extending the metonymy account to such cases in rather natural. But I do not want to be committed to this particular approach, and Fauconnier's suggestion is much less natural if we work within a Fregean framework, with a sharp distinction between concepts and objects. Nevertheless I think the notion of transfer can still be used, although not in the direct way Fauconnier favours.

I suggest that we consider referential uses of descriptions as involving a metonymical (or rather, synecdochic) transfer from the concept expressed by the definite description to *another* concept – a *de re* concept, in my terminology – rather than directly to an object. The relation between the two concepts is, I suggest, that of containment, i.e. the part – whole relation: the concept literally expressed by the definite description is part of the content of the *de re* concept. In chapters 6–7 I described *de re* concepts as dossiers containing whatever information is gained from (or about) the object which the dossier concerns, i.e. that from which it causally derives. Qua dossier, a *de re* concept contains many descriptive concepts as part of its content. Thus my *de re* concept of George Bush is a dossier containing many concepts such as: 'has a wife called Barbara', 'was Vice-President under Reagan', and so forth. Such constituent concepts may be expressed either by definite or by indefinite descriptions, depending on whether or not they may be thought of as uniquely satisfied. Thus both 'A man whose wife is called Barbara' and 'The man who succeeded Reagan at the American presidency' express descriptive concepts which are part of my *de re* concept of George Bush and which, I suggest, can call up the latter if they are activated in a suitable context. This accounts for the referential use of descriptions, whether definite or indefinite[8]: expressing a descriptive concept *the F* (e.g. *the President*) triggers the activation of a *de re* concept containing it (e.g. my concept of George Bush) through a primary pragmatic process of synecdoche – a variety of 'transfer'. This process is what Grice described in his own, very similar account of the referential/attributive distinction (Grice, 1969, pp. 141–4):

> A schematic generalized account of the difference of type between examples (1) [= attributive uses] and (2) [= referential uses] might proceed along the following lines. Let us say that *X has a dossier for a definite description* δ if there is a set of definite descriptions which includes δ, all the members of which X supposes ... to be satisfied by one and the same item. In a type (2) case, unlike a type (1) case, the speaker intends the hearer to think (*via* the recognition that he is so intended) (a) that the speaker has a dossier for the definite description δ which he has used, and (b) that the speaker has selected δ from his dossier at least partly in the hope that the hearer has a dossier for δ which 'overlaps' the speaker's dossier for δ (that is, shares a substantial, or in some way specially favoured, subset with the speaker's dossier). (Grice, 1969, pp. 141–2)

The transfer from descriptive concept to *de re* concept provides only the first half of our account. The second half concerns the step from *de re* concept to the object which figures in the proposition expressed by an utterance with a referentially used description. This part of the account is provided by my earlier characterization of *de re* concepts (chapter 6).

One of the fundamental properties of *de re* concepts is the truth-conditional irrelevance of their content. By this I mean that whatever descriptive material the dossier contains, a thought which includes a *de re* concept (that is, a thought which contains a 'pointer', 'label' or 'address' for the relevant dossier of information) represents a singular state of affairs, with the object from which the dossier causally derives as a constituent. As I said at the end of chapter 7, the thought in which a *de re* concept occurs is intended to characterize the reference itself independently of its satisfying the very concept which is used to think of it. Thus, even though my concept of George Bush includes the property 'has a wife called Barbara', my thought that George Bush is President is true iff *he* is president, whether or not he has a wife called Barbara. By virtue of this property of truth-conditional irrelevance, which we might also call 'self-bracketing', *de re* concepts point to some reality outside thought; they are those constituents of thought which endow it with its characteristic feature of intentionality. Be that as it may, the truth-conditional irrelevance of *de re* concepts has the following consequence: an utterance which is taken to express the speaker's *de re* thought about an object is necessarily taken to represent a singular state of affairs with this object as a constituent. In that way we account for the fact that an utterance with a referentially used definite description expresses a singular proposition with the reference of the description, not the descriptive concept which it expresses, as a constituent.

To sum up, let me characterize *de re* communication as it works when the speaker uses a definite description referentially. The speaker entertains a thought with a *de re* concept R as a constituent. He utters a description δ which expresses a descriptive concept belonging to the content of R, in the expectation that his hearer will recognize that the descriptive concept in question stands for some more inclusive, *de re* concept about the referent of δ. The hearer need not identify, let alone entertain, the particular *de re* concept entertained by the speaker. Understanding the utterance, for him, consists simply in (i) recognizing that the speaker expresses a *de re* thought, that is, a thought representing a singular state of affairs, and (ii) identifying the state of affairs in question. Now identifying the singular state of affairs involves identifying the object which it includes as a constituent (i.e. the referent of the description) and this in turn involves, on the part of the hearer, forming a *de re* thought about that object. As Evans (1982) puts it, the hearer must think something along the following lines: 'That object is G. This is what the speaker is saying.' However, not any old mode of identification will do on the hearer's side. A constraint has to be satisfied: like the speaker's *de re* concept about the object, the hearer's *de re* concept must include the descriptive concept expressed by the description as part of its content.

It is instructive to compare this particular type of *de re* communication – *de re* communication with non-referential terms – with the other type we have considered, viz. *de re* communication with referential terms. Like descriptions, referential terms such as indexicals or even proper names have a descriptive meaning, namely what I called the 'linguistic mode of presentation' of their reference. The difference with definite descriptions is that referential terms also convey the feature REF as part of their meaning. REF forces the hearer to interpret the utterance as representing a singular state of affairs with the reference of the referential term as a constituent. As in the case of referentially used descriptions, understanding the utterance requires identifying the object in question, hence forming a *de re* thought about it. On the hearer's side, then, REF can be seen as triggering the process of synecdochic transfer from descriptive concept to *de re* concept. When a description is used rather than a referential term, this process is optional and depends on context, rather than being linguistically triggered.

What I have just said sheds some light on the distinction which I made in chapter 4 between two sorts of mode of presentation associated with referential terms is general and indexicals in particular: the linguistic mode of presentation and the psychological mode of presentation (i.e. the concept which occurs in the thought associated with the utterance). To show that these modes of presentation are distinct, I pointed out that the linguistic mode of presentation is a *descriptive* concept such as 'the utterer' or 'the addressee', while the psychological mode of presentation is a *de re* concept, for example an egocentric concept such as **Ego**. I spent a couple of sections talking about the relation between the two sorts of mode of presentation. Now, I believe, the situation is much clearer. The linguistic mode of presentation is a descriptive concept *the F* (or *an F*) associated with the referential term as part of its linguistic meaning. This descriptive concept is part of the content of the *de re* concepts under which the speaker and the addressee respectively think of the reference of the referential term. Thus the speaker thinks of himself under the egocentric concept **Ego**, which includes as part of its content the descriptive concept 'utterer of this utterance' (i.e. the speaker is conscious of being the utterer). The *hearer* also thinks of the speaker under a *de re* concept, say **That guy**, which also includes the descriptive concept 'utterer of this utterance' as a constituent (i.e. the hearer believes of the speaker, demonstratively identified, that he is the utterer). The inclusion of the descriptive concept which constitutes the linguistic mode of presentation within the *de re* concept which constitutes the psychological mode of presentation enables the former to stand for the latter, both from the point of view of the hearer and from that of the speaker. This is also the case with referentially used descriptions: the descriptive concept linguistically expressed is part of the content of the *de re* concepts under which speaker and hearer think of the reference of the description, and this is what makes the synecdochic transfer from descriptive concept to *de re* concept possible. What characterizes referential terms as opposed to descriptions is that one *must* go beyond the descriptive concept, because of REF. REF imposes the step from the linguistic mode of presentation, which is descriptive, to the psychological mode of presentation, which is not, by signalling the truth-conditional irrelevance of descriptive content, hence the *de re* character of the thought expressed by the utterance. By contrast, when a non-referential term such as a description is used, the truth-conditional irrelevance of descriptive content is only imposed by the contextual supposition that the speaker expresses, and intends to be recognized as expressing, a *de re* thought about the reference of the description.

## Notes

1. The distinction dates back to the 17th century (Dominicy, 1984, pp. 124–6). On the history of the distinction, see Neale, 1990, pp. xii–xiii.
2. The pragmatic terminology used here is borrowed from Sperber and Wilson (1986).
3. Salmon defends himself retrospectively by distinguishing two senses of 'semantically ambiguous': the ordinary sense, and an 'artificially broad sense' which covers 'both ordinary ambiguity and the distinct phenomenon of *indexicality*' (Nathan Salmon, 1991, p. 95). (It is certainly not possible for a sentence to express different propositions in different contexts without being semantically ambiguous in the *broad* sense.) Salmon claims that, in the quotation above, he had used 'semantically ambiguous' in the broad sense. Still, I find that most authors who, like Salmon, describe the Naive Theory as 'the thesis that sentences involving descriptions are semantically ambiguous' seem to be using 'semantically ambiguous' in the *ordinary* sense, as is shown by the exceedingly common claim that the Naive Theory posits 'an ambiguity in the English word "the"' (Evans, 1982, p. 325).
4. To illustrate the three levels, consider the sentence 'It is cold'. The sentence type has a certain meaning, but this meaning is not a fully determinate proposition. As Forguson put it, the meaning of the sentence is something determinable; by contrast, the meaning of the utterance – what is said – is determinate (Forguson, 1973, pp. 163–4). To go from the sentence's determinable meaning to the utterance's determinate meaning the interpreter must rely on the context of utterance. Depending on the context, the sentence 'It is cold' will express either the proposition that the pie is cold at time t or the proposition that the temperature in the room is low at time t', or whatever proposition falls under the semantic potential of the sentence. Although it depends on the context, the determinate meaning of the utterance is literal, in the sense that it is nothing but an enrichment, a determination of the sentence's determinable meaning. But the utterance may also convey something different from a mere determination of sentence

meaning. For example, by saying that it is cold in the room the speaker may implicate that the hearer is to close the window. This implicature is part of what the utterance communicates, but it is not part of the utterance's (literal) meaning, let alone of the linguistic meaning of the sentence type.

5   A similar distinction is also made by Perry, who sometimes talks of 'created proposition' and sometimes of 'pure truth-conditions' or 'non-incremental truth-conditions' – meaning in both cases something very close to my 'external proposition'. See e.g. Perry, 1988, pp. 7–8.

6   In his otherwise careful defence of Russell's theory of descriptions (Neale, 1990) Stephen Neale surprisingly does not mention functional uses.

7   Both individuals and roles are what Fauconnier calls 'elements'. He attempts to provide a unified theory of 'elements', thereby playing down Frege's distinction between concept and object. The following passage is revealing of the non-Fregean nature of Fauconnier's enterprise: 'The elements we have talked about until now [i.e. ordinary individuals] have a fixed identity, but their other properties can change. Roles are also elements, but such that their identity (i.e. role value) can change, while one particular property (e.g. president, house) is fixed; for such elements, as opposed to others, identity is a variable property. This view has the advantage of yielding a unified analysis of verbs like *change*: if "X changes" entails that some property of X is added, lost or replaced, then that property can be identity in the case of roles (as in "The president changes at each election"), but will be a property other than identity for values ("Reagan has changed during the last two months")'. (Fauconnier, 1985, pp. 41–2)

8   On referential uses of indefinite descriptions, see Chastain, 1975, pp. 206–14; Read, 1978; Wilson, 1978; Stich, 1983; and Fauconnier, 1985.

# Chapter 16

# The descriptive use of indexicals

## 16.1  Introduction

As I said in chapter 15, descriptions are not referential terms, even though they can be *used* referentially. Their referential use is a matter of fact, whereas demonstratives, indexicals and proper names are linguistically 'marked' as referential. This is the difference between 'type-referentiality' and mere 'token-referentiality'. An expression which is type-referential can only be used referentially, to express a singular proposition, while an expression which is not type-referential can be used either referentially or non-referentially, depending on the context of utterance.

In his recent paper 'Indexicals and Descriptions in Interpretation', Geoff Nunberg summarizes the view I have been defending as follows: 'The distinction between [referentially used] descriptions and indexicals boils down to a distinction between semantics and pragmatics. What we may do with the former, we must do with the latter' (Nunberg, 1991, p. 6). And he offers what he takes to be decisive counter-examples to the view in question, namely examples of *descriptively used* indexicals. These examples serve to substantiate two objections to the theory of direct reference. First, the theory of direct reference is taken to make wrong predictions, since it entails that indexicals and other directly referential expressions can only be used referentially; second, the asymmetry which the theory postulates between referential terms and non-referential terms such as descriptions is shown not to exist: indexicals and other 'referential terms' can be used either descriptively (attributively) or referentially, exactly like definite descriptions. As Nunberg concludes, 'Indexicals

*The descriptive use of indexicals* 301

can have the same kinds of interpretations as descriptions, either singular or general as the case may be' (Nunberg, 1991, p. 10).

Nunberg's objections are supported by a wealth of examples, and they are the most serious which the theory of direct reference has ever faced, in my opinion. In this chapter I will deal with his examples and show that direct reference theory, suitably weakened and supplemented with the right sort of pragmatics, can handle even the hardest cases mentioned by Nunberg.

## 16.2 Nunberg's counter-examples: *de re* concepts in interpretation

Let us consider the following examples first:

1 Suppose that Jim introduces himself to Melanie, saying, 'Hi, I am Jim'. . . . The information which Melanie gets, and which Jim intends to convey, is not that Jim is Jim, but that *the person talking* to Melanie is Jim. (Barwise & Perry, 1983, p. 200; emphasis mine)
2 I once called a colleague at his home at a time when he was expecting a call from his mother. He was surprised to hear my voice: 'Oh, I thought *you* were my mother.' . . . It is clear that my colleague did not hold a *de re* belief of me that I was his mother; the content of *you* can be paraphrased as '*the person calling*.' (Nunberg, 1990, p. 38)
3 In the movie *The Year of Living Dangerously*, Mel Gibson plays a reporter in Sukarno's Indonesia who is looking for a shipment of arms destined for the local communists; who will kill him if they find out he is on to them. He is interviewing a warehouse manager, who tells him, 'I have seen no such shipment. And you should be careful; *I* might have been a communist' . . . The content of *I* . . . is '*the person to whom you are addressing these questions (whoever that may be)*'. (ibid.)

Nunberg makes two claims with respect to examples such as these. First, he points out that the interpretation of these utterances involves a concept, not an object. The pronoun in every example stands for a certain concept. Secondly, Nunberg holds that the concept in question is a descriptive concept – e.g. the concept of 'the person talking'. (In Nunberg's own terminology, the pronoun contributes a 'property'.) Now I accept the first claim but I reject the second one. It seems to me, contrary to what Nunberg suggests, that a *de re* concept is involved in each example 1–3; or at least, a *de re* concept is involved in the thought the thinking of which constitutes the hearer's understanding of the utterance.

In 1 the hearer – Melanie – is intended to think the (informative) thought '*That guy is Jim*' (rather than the uninformative thought 'Jim is Jim'), and in the thought in question what occurs is a *de re* concept, namely that under which Melanie thinks of the man who is talking to her. Melanie's understanding of 'I am Jim' consists in her feeding the information 'is Jim' into that *de re* concept. The concept in question is not identical to the descriptive concept 'the person talking', even though it *includes* the descriptive concept 'person talking' (as well as many other concepts which Melanie thinks the person talking to her satisfies).

The hearer of 3 is also intended to think of the reference under a particular sort of *de re* concept. This *de re* concept presumably is a demonstrative concept based on the reporter's current perceptual relation to the man he is interviewing, and it contains information such as 'is a warehouse manager', 'has a big nose', 'is being interviewed by me', 'can provide me with useful information concerning recent shipments', etc. When the man in question says 'I might have been a communist', the hearer's understanding of this utterance consists in his entertaining the thought: '*That man* might have been a communist'. The hearer is intended to think that thought, that is, to realize that his *de re* concept (his dossier) concerning the man in question might have had a communist as reference.

The case of 2 is more complex, for in 2, two *de re* concepts are involved, this time on the speaker's side. Let us consider the mental episode which the speaker is reporting. The speaker reports a change in his beliefs. Before realizing that Nunberg was calling him, he thought his mother was. This change of belief can be accounted for as follows. When the phone starts ringing, say at $t_1$, a dossier 'maker of this phone call' is opened, which contains the tentative information 'is my mother' (on the basis of the speaker's expectations); after the voice of the caller has been heard, at $t_2$, the information 'is Nunberg' is substituted for the information 'is my mother'. Note that both 'Nunberg' and 'my mother' are encyclopedia entries, hence *de re* concepts. To say that the *de re* concept 'maker of this phone call' contains the information 'is Nunberg' is to say that it contains the *de re* concept '*Nunberg*' as a constituent.

Now my suggestion is this: in 2 the pronoun 'you' straightforwardly expresses the speaker's *de re* concept of Nunberg (i.e. the *de re* concept under which the speaker thinks of the addressee), and indirectly expresses the *de re* concept 'maker of this phone call', which includes it.¹ It is the latter concept which goes into the interpretation of the utterance,² in the sense that the speaker intends the hearer to recognize this concept as being expressed by the pronoun 'you'.

Since the concepts which occur in the interpretation are *de re* concepts rather than descriptive concepts, I would not consider these uses of indexicals as genuinely descriptive. Still, one must account for the fact that it is a concept, not (or not merely) an object, that goes into the interpretation. One possibility for the direct reference theorist faced with such examples consists in *denying* that the concepts in question are part of the interpretation of the utterance, part of its semantic content. Thus Barwise and Perry draw a distinction between interpretation and information; the interpretation of an utterance is the proposition it expresses, but the information which one can derive from an utterance is not necessarily located in the proposition expressed. To construe examples such as 1 as counter-examples to the theory of direct reference is to fall prey to the 'Fallacy of Misplaced Information', according to Barwise and Perry. For 'I am Jim' and 'Jim is Jim' may well express the same singular proposition even though they do not convey the same information to the hearer.

I agree with Barwise and Perry that an utterance conveys much more information that can be located in the proposition expressed – for example an utterance of 'I am Jim' may convey the information that the speaker speaks English fluently. Like Barwise and Perry, I also think that the theory of direct reference is not threatened by examples such as 1–3 above: at least as far as 1 and 3 are concerned, it can be maintained that the utterance expresses a singular proposition with the reference as a constituent.³ But I believe these examples comport badly with the strong version of the theory of direct reference, according to which the semantic content (the interpretation) of an utterance including a referential expression is nothing other than a singular proposition. For, it seems to me, the modes of presentation involved in 1–3 are actually part of the *interpretation*, part of the *semantic content* of these utterances. They are not merely aspects of the 'information' conveyed by these utterances.⁴

The strong version of the theory of direct reference, according to which the semantic content of an utterance including a referential expression is nothing other than a singular proposition, was criticized in chapter 3. In 3.4 I pointed out that modes of presentation are genuine constituents of semantic content even when the utterance at issue includes referential terms. Thus I mentioned Loar's 'stockbroker' example, in which a mode of presentation is 'essential to what is being communicated' (Loar, 1976, p. 357) despite the use of a directly referential expression. This is consistent with the claim that an utterance including referential terms expresses a singular proposition, for the modes of presentation associated with referential terms are truth-conditionally irrelevant, while the proposition expressed is individuated on a truth-conditional basis. Thus an utterance of 'He is a stockbroker' (Loar's example) presents its truth-condition as singular, hence it expresses a singular proposition with the reference of 'he' as a constituent, even though the referent in question must be thought of under a particular mode of presentation for the utterance to be correctly understood (i.e. in accordance with the speaker's intentions). On this view, the semantic content of a referential utterance includes the singular proposition it expresses *plus* whatever (truth-conditionally irrelevant) modes of presentation are essential to what is being communicated. In most cases the modes of presentation are left very much unspecified at the level of semantic content: it is only required that the reference be thought of under some *de re* mode of presentation including the linguistic mode of presentation as constituent. But in some cases, as I pointed out in 3.4, it is contextually clear that the hearer is intended to think of the reference in a specific manner.

Nunberg, I think, would reject even the weak theory of direct reference I have just put forward, according to which the semantic content of an utterance containing a referential term consists of a singular proposition plus some mode of presentation. For he denies that a singular proposition is expressed in either 2 or 3, to the effect that *Max* (the warehouse manager) might have been a communist, or that *Nunberg* was thought by his colleague to be his mother. Let us consider, and try to explain, the intuitions behind his denial.

As far as 2 is concerned, I think Nunberg is right to a certain extent, even though I maintain that a *de re* concept is involved in that example as in the others. The thought episode which 2 reports is the speaker's thinking 'This must be my mother' while hearing the phone ring. Now the thought 'This must be my mother' is arguably not a *de re* thought about Nunberg, the actual caller, but a descriptive thought about 'the person making that phone call' (and at the same time a *de re* thought about the phone call). This much I concede. The descriptive concept in question, however, is 'almost' a *de re* concept: it is a *tentative de re* concept, analogous to the concepts associated with 'descriptive names' such as 'Julius' (10.4) or with 'descriptive indexicals' of the sort involved in Schiffer's giant footprint example and Loar's demonstrative variant of the Smith's murderer example.[5] *De re* concepts are dossiers of information, as we have seen (chapters 6–7); now a dossier or information *is* involved in the thought episode which 2 reports, namely the dossier 'maker of this phone call' which is opened at $t_1$ when the phone starts ringing. That dossier is still empty at $t_1$ (though the speaker expects it soon to be filled with information such as 'is my mother'); that is why it is only a 'tentative' *de re* concept. But it becomes a genuine *de re* concept are soon as information is fed into it. From the point of view of the speaker at the time when he utters 2, the concept in question, which he indirectly expresses by saying 'you', is a genuine *de re* concept.

It turns out that in example 2 four different concepts are associated with the word 'you': (i) the descriptive concept 'person to whom this utterance is addressed', conventionally expressed by 'you'; (ii) the *de re* concept 'Nunberg', which includes (i) as a constituent; (iii) the *de re* concept 'maker of this phone call', which includes (ii) as a constituent; and finally (iv) the ancestor of (iii), namely the tentative *de re* concept 'maker of this phone call' which occurred in the speaker's thought at $t_1$. It is the latter concept which the speaker ascribes (to his former self) in 2. What is so peculiar in 2 is the fact that, in the terminology to be introduced in chapter 20, the speaker 'exercises' the full-fledged *de re* concept 'maker of this phone call' (which includes the information 'is Nunberg') in order to 'ascribe' a thought including an *earlier stage* of that very concept.

I shall consider the special problems raised by belief sentences such as 2 later (chapters 17–20). Let us turn to example 3, which is less problematic. Nunberg insists that 'the warehouse manager's use of I... contributes a property, not an individual; he isn't saying of himself that he could have been a communist, but rather that someone who had the property he exemplifies could have been a communist' (Nunberg, 1991, p. 17). But why assume that the manager does not say of himself that he might have been a communist? Of course he is not saying of himself that there is a metaphysically possible world in which he would be a communist. This is clearly not the intended reading. As Nunberg rightly points out (1990, p. 38), 'whether the warehouse manager himself might have been a communist (say if he had had a different upbringing) is clearly irrelevant to the conversational purposes.' But why not accept that he is saying of himself that in some *epistemically* possible worlds he is a communist?[6] The utterance could thus be paraphrased as follows: 'In some worlds compatible with what you know about me, I am a communist', or, more simply: 'For all you know, I might be a communist'. I see no reason to insist that the manager does not refer to himself here. The distinction Nunberg legitimately draws between two readings of 'I might have been a communist' – the relevant one and the one which is clearly inappropriate – is a distinction between two interpretations of the predicate (which may express either a metaphysical or an epistemic possibility), *not* a distinction between two interpretations of the subject term (referential vs. attributive). Thus I maintain that a singular proposition is expressed in this example, with Max as a constituent. As a result, the hearer entertains (and is intended to entertain) a quasi-singular thought with a *de re* concept as constituent: 'for all I know, *that man* might have been a communist.'

## 16.3 Other alleged counter-examples

Let us turn to a slightly different sort of counter-example mentioned by Nunberg:

> 4   When we see a sign at the side of the road that says YOU ARE ENTERING BEDFORD FALLS, for example, we take the token of *you* as equivalent to a description of the form '*whoever is reading this under certain presumptive conditions*'. (Nunberg, 1991, p. 18)

Nunberg flatly denies that this utterance expresses a singular proposition with the addressee as a constituent. One reason for that denial is that the speaker, not knowing the reference (not being acquainted with the addressee), could not even grasp that singular proposition.[7] But this, as Evans pointed out, is no objection. The speaker may express a singular proposition even if he or she is unable to grasp that proposition: what matters for deciding whether or not a singular proposition is expressed is *what is required for understanding the utterance* (Evans, 1982). In the case at hand, the addressee must understand that *he* is entering Bedford Falls; he must therefore grasp a singular proposition (by entertaining a quasi-singular, first-person thought).

Of course, not every reader of the sign is an addressee. As Nunberg says, 'the character of *you* in this case is not simply "reader or this token"; it picks out only such readers as sight the token *under appropriate circumstances* – that is, people with normal vision who approach the sign from the road. The pronoun does not refer to someone who is looking over his shoulder on the way out of town, someone who sees the sign from the window of his house just outside the town limits, or someone on a distant mountaintop who glimpses the sign through a telescope' (Nunberg, 1990, p. 28). So a reader of the sign must determine first whether or not he satisfies the conditions that make him into an addressee. But *these conditions are not part of the proposition expressed*.[8] In Kaplan's terms, the conditions for being the addressee 'should not be considered part of the content of what is said but should rather be thought of as contextual factors which help us interpret the ... utterance as having a certain content' (Kaplan, 1978, p. 228). The descriptive concept associated with the pronoun in this example ('whoever is reading this sign under such and such conditions') does not provide a counter-example to the theory of direct reference because it does not occur in the proposition expressed, but at another level in the interpretation of the utterance. What occurs in the proposition expressed is the addressee himself or herself, i.e. whoever turns out to be reading the sign under the relevant conditions.

Nunberg's next sort of counter-example looks closer to being a genuine descriptive use of an indexical:

5  Suppose that the New Yorker at the cocktail party, on learning that his addressee comes from Montana, goes on to say (X):

(X) You [plural] are incapable of understanding why somebody would want to live in a big city.

The most reasonable interpretation of (X) is one in which the pronoun contributes a property ... exemplified by the addressee – say of being a Montanan or Westerner or hick or whatever. And to evaluate (X), we look at the people that this property applies to in all circumstances, *including those in which the addressee himself is from New York*. (Nunberg, 1991, p. 10; emphasis mine)

Here it seems that what occurs in the interpretation is the descriptive concept 'being a Montanan' rather than an object or even a *de re* concept. Nunberg gives another, very similar example which I already mentioned: when an American says, 'We are incapable of understanding the European concept of laicism', 'the pronoun *we* does not refer "directly" to the 250 million particular people who are in fact Americans; it is not claimed that *they* can never understand laicism. Rather... we evaluate the utterance by asking whether is could be the case that someone should be an American and understand laicism' (Nunberg, 1990, p. 9).

Note that these examples are in the plural. Now in the case of plural indexicals like 'we' and 'you', a distinction has to be made between what Nunberg calls the *index* and the *referent* (Nunberg, 1990, 1991). The referent is determined as bearing a certain relation to the index, and the index is a feature of the context of utterance. In the case of 'we', the index is the speaker or the 'agent' of the utterance, but 'we' does not (or not only) refer to the speaker: the referent is a certain *group* of people which includes the speaker, for example the group of sausage-eaters, or the group of Melanie's brothers and sisters, or the group of Americans (or Montanans). In the case of 'you' (plural), the index is the addressee, and the referent is, again, a group which includes the addressee. Singular indexicals such as 'I' or 'you' do not call for such a distinction between index and referent: the index of 'I' (i.e. the agent of the utterance) is also its referent.

That being so, Nunberg's point concerning the descriptive interpretation of his examples can be rephrased as follows. The index (i.e. the speaker in the case of 'we', or the addressee in the case of 'you') is not a constituent of the proposition expressed: for the proposition expressed would be true with respect to a world in which the speaker or the addressee does *not* satisfy the predicate, provided whoever has the required property (being a Montanan, or an American) in the world in question satisfies the predicate. This point is well taken, but it *does not object to the theory of direct reference*, which says only that the *referent* is part of the proposition expressed. What is the referent in the case of 'we' or 'you?' As Nunberg himself suggests: the Montanans, or the Americans, are what 'you' and 'we' refer to in the examples under discussion.[9] Now it may well be that the utterance refers to 'the Americans' *qua* group without individually referring to the 250 million particular people who are in fact Americans. In other words, the fact that there is no direct reference to the members of the class, hence to the index *qua* member of the class, may be interpreted as entailing only that collective entities such as 'the French' or 'the Americans' or 'the Montanans' are not individuated 'extensionally' (i.e. in such a way that one can't refer to the group without referring to its members). Be that as it may, I have not dealt with plurals in this book, and the theory of direct reference I have sketched is concerned only with singular reference to particulars. I have treated neither direct reference to collective entities nor direct reference to abstract objects.

To sum up: the apparent non-referentiality of 'we' and 'you' in Nunberg's last sort of example is due only to the fact that the reference that is made is to collective entities, and that collective entities need not be extensionally individuated. But Nunberg has not shown that the referent is not part of the proposition expressed, in these examples; all he has shown is that the *index* is not part of the proposition expressed, but this is not a problem for the theory insofar as it is possible to refer to the referent (the collective entity) without referring to the index (the individual member).

So far, then, we have no reason to depart from the theory of direct reference as it has been expounded in this book – no reason to deny that a referential term serves to express a singular proposition with the reference as a constituent. I now turn to what I take to be a genuine example of descriptive use of (singular) indexical, also mentioned by Nunberg; we shall see that even that sort of example can be handled within the theory of direct reference, provided the latter is weakened so as to fit the pragmatic framework set up in chapters 13–14.

### 16.4 Nunberg's theory: the index/referent distinction generalized

The example I have in mind is the following:

6   John is giving me my first chess lesson; I have just made a dubious move. He says: 'According to Horowitz, you often get in trouble with that move.' . . . It is improbable that Horowitz has said anything about what often happens to *me* when *I* play PxP in this position . . . [The pronoun 'you'] has the interpretation '*whoever makes that move that you have just made when in this position*'. (Nunberg, 1991, p. 16)

To account for this sort of use, Nunberg argues that the index/referent distinction must be generalized to all indexicals, including singular indexicals. What corresponds to the distinction between index and referent in the case of singular indexicals is that between what Fauconnier calls the reference *trigger* and the reference *target* in cases of deferred reference (Fauconnier, 1985, pp. 3–4; on deferred reference, see also Nunberg, 1978 and 1979). Take a demonstrative as example. Pointing to a banana, I may say: 'Those are no longer imported.' Here, according to Nunberg, the banana I am pointing to is the index (the 'trigger'), but the referent (Fauconnier's 'target') is a class of bananas or a type of banana. Or, in a suitable context, I may point to the banana and say, 'He is very rich now', meaning that *the man who imports those bananas* is very rich now. In all those cases of deferred ostension, Nunberg argues that there is a divergence between the index (the demonstratum, in Kaplan's terminology) and the referent, analogous to the index/referent distinction which characterizes plural indexicals. In this framework, 6 can be interpreted as involving an index or trigger which is a particular object, namely the addressee, and a referent or target which is a *property* exemplified by the index, namely the property of being 'the person playing black who plays 5 ... *PxP* in this variation of the Sicilian defense' (Nunberg, 1991, p. 16).

In Nunberg's theory, the index of an indexical is an object, but the *referent* (what actually goes into the interpretation) can be anything: it can be the index itself, or another object metonymically linked with the index, or a property. In other words, the interpretation of an indexical need not be 'singular' – it need not be a particular object. When the referent is a property exemplified by the index (or any other property), the interpretation of the indexical is *not* singular, contrary to what the theory of direct reference predicts.

If Nunberg is right, the theory of direct reference has conflated two different things: *indicativeness* and *interpretive singularity* (Nunberg, 1991, pp. 3–4). Nunberg calls 'indicativeness' the truth-conditional irrelevance of the descriptive property conventionally expressed by the indexical – the fact that the character or linguistic mode of presentation is used only to help identify the index and has a purely 'indicative' function. Nunberg agrees that indicativeness is a property of indexicals, but it is a mistake, according to him, to say that the object which the indexical indicates *is* the interpretation of the indexical, and to conclude that the interpretation of the indexical is necessarily singular. Nunberg holds that the referent (what goes into the interpretation) is not necessarily identical to the index. Contrary to the index, the referent need not be a particular object. When the referent is a property, as in 6, the proposition expressed is general rather than singular.

There are some problems with Nunberg's theory. First, note that the use of 'you' in 6 is a variety of impersonal use, on the same footing as 7:

7  When you work for yourself, you have to be very careful about your expenses.

Now impersonal uses of pronouns do not comfortably fit in Nunberg's theory, as Nunberg himself points out (Nunberg, 1991, note 21). Nunberg construes impersonal uses such as 6 or 7 as cases in which the referent of 'you' is not the addressee, who plays only the role of 'index'. But normally, inflectional features such as gender or number, which constitute what Nunberg calls the *classificatory* content of the indexical (as opposed to the Kaplan-like reference function which constitutes its *deictic* content), are supposed to characterize the referent as opposed to the index. Yet in French, as Nunberg points out, the choice between the intimate *tu* and the formal *vous* is determined by the speaker's relationship to the addressee, *even in impersonal uses* in which the addressee is supposed to be the index and not the referent.[10] 'This problem needs further study', Nunberg concludes, 'but it doesn't cloud the important observation about sentences like 6 and 7: the pronouns are interpretively general' (Nunberg, 1991, p. 46). However, the problem in question might also be taken as evidence that the addressee *is* the referent even in impersonal uses, hence that the pronoun in such uses of the second person is interpretively *singular* rather than general, appearances notwithstanding.[11] I am not saying that this is the right sort of position to hold, only that the issue remains fairly obscure. We lack a satisfactory theory of impersonal uses of pronouns, and it would not be safe to base our semantics on examples involving them.

The main problem with Nunberg's theory, however, is the following. The distinction between trigger and target can hardly be identified with that between index and referent which was introduced for dealing with plural indexicals, because we find the former distinction at work *simultaneously with* the latter in many cases. Thus it is possible, by saying 'we', to refer to e.g. the house in which we live; in some contexts, one could say 'We are in red brick', meaning: *The house in which we live, or which we own, is in red brick* (see Nunberg, 1978, 1979 and Fauconnier, 1985 for a plethora of such examples of deferred reference). In such cases, the distinction between the trigger and the target is clearly different from the distinction between the index and the referent, for the obvious reason that the index is neither the trigger nor the target. The index of 'we' is the speaker, the trigger is the group of people (including the speaker) who own or live in the house, and the target is the house itself. Thus I would rather maintain two different distinctions, instead of identifying them, as Nunberg does. On the one hand we have the distinction between index and referent which, Nunberg insists, is necessary to provide a correct semantics for plural indexicals. On the other hand, we have the distinction between trigger and target at work in cases of deferred reference. Note that deferred reference is a phenomenon which, far from being limited to indexicals, can be illustrated with any type of referring expression whatsoever.

Despite these problems, I find Nunberg's theory and his analysis of examples such as 6 in terms of transfer from object to property fairly appealing. If Nunberg is right, indexicals and (presumably) other referential terms *can* be used descriptively to express general rather than singular propositions. This means that the theory of direct reference, in the crude form in which it has been stated so far, works only for those cases in which no process of deferred reference occurs. This constitutes an indisputable weakening of the theory, but, as I shall argue now, the weakening in question must be considered as an elaboration or sophistication of the theory rather than a threat to its basic claims.

## 16.5  The basic level of interpretation

If Nunberg is right, there are two levels in the contextual interpretation of indexicals. At one level, which I call level 2 (level 1 being that of linguistic meaning), the indexical indicates an object; the interpretation of the indexical at this level is what the theory of direct reference says it is – either an object (strong theory) or an object under a truth-conditionally irrelevant mode of presentation or type of mode of presentation (weak theory). At the next level – level 3 – the interpretation is a 'target' (possibly a role or property) reached through transfer from the object indicated at the previous level.

Level 2, I claim, is *more basic* than level 3. This is so for two reasons:

- Level 3 interpretations are *optional*. Indexical reference can, but need not, be deferred: nothing prevents the speaker from actually referring to what the indexical indicates. Level 2 interpretations, on the other hand, are mandatory. There need be no target, no level 3 interpretation, over and beyond the object indicated at level 2, but there *must* be an object indicated at level 2.
- When there *is* a level 3 interpretation, it presupposes a level 2 interpretation, since the latter provides the 'trigger' for the process of transfer.

Since level 2 is more basic than level 3, in the sense I have just characterized, Nunberg's examples refute only a crude version of direct reference theory; for the latter can be rephrased as providing a correct characterization of *level 2*, the basic level of interpretation for indexicals. Note that some authors like Crimmins and Perry, when they present the theory of direct reference, seem to have in mind the sophisticated rather than the crude version: direct reference theory, they say, holds 'that the utterance of a simple sentence containing names or demonstratives *normally* expresses a "singular proposition" – a proposition that contains as constituents the individuals referred to, and not any descriptions of or conditions on them' (Crimmins & Perry, 1989, p. 686; emphasis mine). 'Normally' in this passage is not defined, but it could be glossed by saying that the *basic level contribution* which a name or a demonstrative makes to the proposition expressed by the utterance where it occurs is the individual object referred to. This is different from the crude version of the theory, which says that a referential term's contribution to what is said necessarily is an individual.

Kaplan himself, in 'Demonstratives', acknowledges the possibility of deferred reference involving indexicals. 'I am aware', he says, 'that a background story can be provided that will make pointing at [a] flower a contextually appropriate, though deviant, way of referring to a man; for example, if we are talking of great hybridizers' (Kaplan, 1989a, p. 490 note). Nunberg has criticized Kaplan's use of 'deviant' in that passage:

> I assume that Kaplan intends 'deviant' here in a pre-theoretical, intuitive way. There *is* something strained in the flower example, but the

problem lies simply in the oddness of using a flower to identify a hybridizer – you would have to presume a context in which it was common knowledge as to who hybridized what, and which flower was which, and so on... But what of the case where somebody points at a picture of Rudolf Carnap and says, 'He was the greatest philosopher of the twentieth century'? This is unexceptionable – and not, surely, because the semantic rules that determine how indexicals are used make special provision for explicit representations like photographs. It's just that it is much easier to identify somebody by pointing at a picture of him than by pointing at a flower he hybridized. If deviance is reckoned simply by intuition, then, the objection isn't sufficient to rule examples of deferred ostension out *tout court*. (Nunberg, 1991, pp. 43–4)

Nunberg is right to point out that deferred reference is pervasive in everyday speech, and not necessarily 'deviant' in an intuitive sense; but deviance can be defined so as to vindicate Kaplan's position concerning deferred reference. For example, one might say that an interpretation of an indexical is 'deviant' if and only if it is different from the basic level interpretation of that indexical.

Once the distinction between the two contextual levels of interpretation has been made, it is easy to show that Nunberg's observation concerning the possibility of attributive or descriptive uses of indexicals does not conflict with the central thesis of direct reference theory, namely the thesis of the *asymmetry* between referential and non-referential terms with respect to their possible uses. It is true that *both indexicals and descriptions can be used either referentially or descriptively*. As Nunberg says, 'Indexicals can have the same kinds of interpretations as descriptions, either singular or general as the case may be' (Nunberg, 1991, p. 10). Yet, at the basic level, indexicals must be given a *de re* interpretation, contrary to definite descriptions. That an attributive or descriptive interpretation of indexicals becomes possible at the *next* level of interpretation does nothing to undermine the asymmetry thesis thus understood.

Let us try to give a more precise, and more general, characterization of the basic level of interpretation. The first level I mentioned (level 1) is that of sentence meaning. All other levels are generated by applying primary pragmatic processes ('p-processes', for short) to semantic representations at the previous level: level 2 representations are generated by p-processes taking level 1 representations as input, and they serve as input for p-processes generating level 3 representations. Now, among p-processes, I made a distinction between those that are mandatory because either necessary for truth-evaluation or 'marked' at the level of linguistic meaning ('minimalist' p-processes), and those that are optional. In terms of this distinction, we can provide a general characterization of the basic level of interpretation as *the level of interpretation which is reached when no optional p-process occurs*. In other words, the basic level interpretation of an expression is that which results simply from applying whatever mandatory p-processes there may be to the linguistic meaning of the expression.

REF is a linguistic marker of the synecdochic transfer from descriptive concept to *de re* concept that characterizes referential terms (15.6). Being semantically marked, that process is mandatory. The same p-process of synecdochic transfer occurs with referentially used descriptions, but it is *optional* for descriptions: definite descriptions need not (though they may) be used referentially. It follows that the notion of basic level is relative rather than absolute. Level 2 is the basic level of interpretation *for indexicals* because the p-process which takes us from level 1 to level 2 (i.e. the synecdoche from descriptive concept to *de re* concept) is mandatory, while that which takes us from level 2 to level 3 is optional. Yet for (non-indexical) descriptions, it is level 1 which is basic, because the same synecdochic p-process which takes us from level 1 to level 2 is optional in the case of definite descriptions.

To sum up, let us systematically compare descriptions and indexicals at the three levels we have distinguished. At the level of linguistic meaning, both descriptions and indexicals express descriptive concepts. But the descriptive concept (or linguistic mode of presentation) expressed by an indexical is marked by REF as truth-conditionally irrelevant. REF prompts a p-process of synecdochic transfer from that descriptive concept to a *de re* concept which includes it but whose truth-conditional significance is simply the reference of the indexical. That process being mandatory because semantically marked, the interpretation it yields (level 2) is the basic level interpretation of the indexical. The same process may occur in the interpretation of a definite description, but the interpretation it yields (the referential interpretation of the description) is not basic because the p-process in question is optional for descriptions.

From what I have just said it follows that the basic level interpretation of a description is a descriptive concept (that which is expressed at level 1), while the basic level interpretation of an indexical is – at least in part – an object (that which is indicated at level 2). To be sure, from the object which is (part of) the interpretation of the indexical at the second level we may go, through transfer, to another object or to a property. At this (third) level there occurs the possibility of a descriptive – or even attributive[12] – use of the indexical, but this is clearly not on the same footing as the descriptive use of a description. The descriptive use of the indexical presupposes a more basic, referential interpretation, whereas the attributive use of a description is basic and does not presuppose a prior referential interpretation.

It is important to realize that the distinction between basic level interpretations and other, non-basic interpretations does not correspond to that between what is literally expressed (what is said) and what is merely 'conveyed'. Non-basic interpretations such as those involved in Nunberg's examples of deferred reference themselves constitute 'what is said' by the utterances which give rise to these interpretations (14.4). Consequently, the basic level of interpretation cannot be understood as the level of the proposition expressed; it is an intermediate level between sentence meaning and the proposition expressed. (More on this below.)

## 16.6 Multi-layered pragmatics and direct reference theory

The theory we arrive at uses a rich, multi-layered pragmatics. First, the proposition expressed is pragmatically determined on that theory, as are implicatures and various aspects of meaning external to what is said (chapter 13). Second, there is an intermediate level of meaning between sentence meaning and the proposition expressed, an intermediate level which is also pragmatically determined: the 'basic level' of interpretation, with respect to which direct reference theory is to be assessed.

Two questions are raised by the use of this rich pragmatic component. First, if direct reference theory is the theory of something *distinct* from what is said, namely the basic level interpretation, what are the intuitions which support the theory? According to the availability hypothesis (13.4), we have intuitions about 'what is said', about the 'locutionary content' of the utterance (in Austin's terminology); yet the theory of direct reference, in its sophisticated version, claims to be a theory about something *sub*-locutionary, viz. the basic level interpretation. Since we have *no* intuition concerning what is sub-locutionary, abandoning the claim that direct reference theory is about the proposition expressed seems to be like abandoning all kind of intuitive support for the theory.

To the question, 'What is the intuitive support of the theory', I make a simple answer. The intuitions which support the theory concern those cases in which there is no level of interpretation over and beyond the basic level interpretation, i.e. the (admittedly central) cases in which an indexical is used to refer to the object which it indicates: the cases of *non-deferred* reference. The theory based on our intuitions concerning these cases is then extended to the other cases by means of an appropriate pragmatic mechanism which accounts for the intuitive differences between the two types of case. There is nothing intrinsically wrong about this way of extending to all cases a theory based on intuitions concerning only some of the cases. To a large extent, this is what theory-building consists in.[13]

The second question raised by the rich pragmatics I am using concerns the difference between my account and other accounts using a simpler pragmatics with only two levels: the 'proposition expressed' and 'what is communicated'. In chapter 15, for example, I criticized a theory which I called the Implicature Theory, and which uses such a simplified pragmatics. The Implicature Theory holds that the referential/attributive distinction (for descriptions) does not concern the proposition expressed but only what is communicated; I tried to show that the referential/attributive distinction *is* located at the level of what is said. But, since I am using a richer pragmatics, how can we be sure that what I call the proposition expressed is the same thing as that which an Implicature Theorist would call the proposition expressed? Could we not even consider that what Implicature Theorists call 'what is communicated' is the same thing as what *I* call 'what is said', and that what *they* call 'what is said' is what *I* call the 'basic level interpretation'? After all, the 'proposition expressed', in the framework of Implicature Theorists, is not intuitively accessible (see 13.3 and 17.3); it's something unconscious, like sub-locutionary levels of interpretation in my framework. By contrast, 'what is communicated' in their framework possesses the characteristic properties of 'what is said' in my framework: it is pragmatically determined to a large extent and it is the object of our intuitions. Given this convergence, it may be argued that my theory is equivalent to that which, in chapter 15, I unduly criticized (under the name of 'Implicature Theory').

I reply that there is one big difference which ought to prevent one from equating what I call the basic level interpretation and what Implicature Theorists call the proposition expressed. No proposition, strictly speaking, can be found at the basic level of interpretation – or at least, no proposition that plays a role in the interpretation process. At the basic level we find a collection of basic semantic values for the various expressions which make up the sentence, but no basic semantic value for the global utterance. That is so because the global interpretation of an utterance is computed only when primary pragmatic processes have freely applied, including those primary pragmatic processes which lead from the basic interpretation of a constituent to some further, non-basic interpretation. (See 14.4, on the *local* application of primary pragmatic processes.) In other words, no composition process takes place which puts together the basic interpretations of the parts to yield the basic interpretation of the whole: no compositional process takes place purely at the *basic level*. For the process of propositional combination to take place, non-basic semantic values, obtained from basic values through primary pragmatic processes, must be provided if pragmatically required, and unarticulated constituents, i.e. semantic values corresponding to no expression in the utterance, must also be provided if required (Perry, 1986c; Crimmins & Perry, 1989).

If (for convenience) we decide to call something the basic level interpretation of an utterance, it will have to be a purely counterfactual entity – something that is not actually computed and plays no role in the interpretation process as it actually occurs. Thus we may identify the basic level interpretation of an utterance as the proposition the utterance would have expressed, if no optional p-process had come into play. To make the counterfactual nature of that entity salient, let us call it 'the proposition Normally[14] expressed by the utterance', to be distinguished from the proposition actually expressed. Although still objectionable[15] that notion may be useful for descriptive purposes: whenever optional p-processes come into play, we can say that the proposition expressed is different from the proposition Normally expressed. But the latter has no psychological reality (unless, *per impossibile*, no optional p-process comes into play and the proposition Normally expressed *is* the proposition actually expressed by the utterance). By contrast, the proposition literally expressed has to be computed, in the framework of the Implicature Theory: implicatures are inferable from the fact that the speaker has 'said' something, hence something must have been said for an implicature to have been generated. Owing to that crucial difference, it should be clear that my account is not merely a notational variant of the implicature account.[16]

## Notes

1.  Note that a *double* transfer is involved here: from the linguistic mode of presentation conventionally expressed by 'you' ('the addressee of this utterance') to a *de re* concept which includes it as a constituent ('Nunberg'), and from the latter to another *de re* concept which includes it ('the maker of this phone call'). The first transfer is licensed by the speaker's belief that Nunberg is the addressee, and the second one by the speaker's belief that the maker of this phone call is Nunberg. More on this complicated example below.
2.  This will be qualified below.
3.  The case of 2 is more complex for 2 is a belief report. On the proper analysis of belief reports, see chapters 18–20.
4.  Barwise and Perry make essentially that point when they talk of 'inverse interpretation' in connection with examples like 1.
5.  On these examples see 10.4 and Introduction to Part II, note 1.
6.  I am indebted to Paul Horwich for suggesting this way of handling the example.
7.  See Nunberg, 1990, p. 33.
8.  The situation is very similar to that often discussed in the pragmatic literature: when we read 'Press here', we understand that *whoever wants to get in* must press a certain button, but this does not make the concept of 'whoever wants to get in' a constituent of the proposition expressed. *The addressee* is told to press the button – and the utterance is addressed to whoever wants to get in.
9.  In Nunberg, 1991, note 16, Nunberg says that the pronoun in 'We suffered a defeat at Waterloo', uttered by Napoleon (or even by someone who thinks he is Napoleon), refers to 'the French' or 'the class of Frenchmen'.
10. As Nunberg says, 'you would use (i) in talking to a close friend, and (ii) in talking to someone you don't know well, *even though the pronoun does not refer to the actual addressee in either case*:

    (vi) Quand tu travailles à ton propre compte, tu dois faire attention à tes frais.
    (vii) Quand vous travaillez à votre propre compte, vous devez faire attention à vos frais.' (Nunberg, 1991, pp. 45–6; emphasis mine)

11. This is the line I would take with respect to *another* case discussed by Nunberg, in which the same sort of problem arises. Nunberg notes that, in 'You shouldn't open the door to just anybody; she could have been a burglar', the gender of the pronoun characterizes what he takes to be the index (the person *actually* at the door – a woman) rather than

the referent, which Nunberg takes to be distinct from the index in this example which he construes as a case of descriptive use of an indexical. Yet I would maintain that the proposition expressed by 'She could have been a burglar' is a singular proposition, to which the pronoun 'she' contributes an individual rather than a property (as Nunberg claims). On my view, the woman at the door is the referent in this example, hence it is only normal that the gender of the indexical characterizes her.

12   I follow Nunberg in making a distinction between two sorts of case: when the interpretation of an indexical is a 'property' (or 'role'), the indexical is said to be used descriptively, and it can be said to be used attributively if the role or property in question is that which the indexical conventionally expresses, i.e. the property which an object must contextually possess in order to be the referent (linguistic mode of presentation). Thus 'you' in 6 is used descriptively but not attributively, whereas 'I' in 3 is not only descriptive but also attributive, according to Nunberg.

13   Nunberg (1990) criticizes direct reference theorists for privileging one type of example. But what's wrong with privileges? The only thing required of someone who privileges a particular type of example is that he provide a mechanism accounting for the unprivileged examples. Once such a mechanism is provided (and Nunberg himself provides such a mechanism), there no longer is any problem with the bias Nunberg observes.

14   This is an allusion to the work of Ruth Millikan, whose notion of 'teleofunction' I find of some use in pragmatics. See Millikan, 1984.

15   The notion is still objectionable because, if Searle and Travis are right (and I think they are), no proposition could be expressed without appeal to unarticulated constituents (14.3).

16   The fact that, on my theory, no composition process takes place which puts together the basic interpretations of the parts to yield the basic interpretation of the whole ruins Nunberg's objection to my account of descriptive uses of indexicals (Nunberg, forthcoming). Nunberg says that, if I were right to claim that the basic level interpretation of an indexical like 'I' is or includes the speaker – a particular object – even on descriptive readings, then we could not properly account for utterances such as:

> 8   *Condemned prisoner*: I am usually allowed to order whatever I like for my last meal.
> 9   Tomorrow is always the biggest party night of the year.

That is so, Nunberg says, because 'the adverbs *usually* and *always* must be understood as involving quantification over instances, but these readings are not possible if the subjects of the sentences are interpreted singularly.' Granted, but precisely because of this discrepancy between the basic level interpretation of the indexical and the interpretation of the adverb, the basic level interpretation of the indexical is *not* selected as a possible interpretation in the context of 8 or 9; it does not go into the interpretation of the global utterance. Nunberg's critique would be justified only if the basic level interpretation of the global utterance had to be computed and constituted a 'coherent level' of interpretation. On my view, however, no coherent, integrated interpretation of the global utterance must be sought at the basic level. This is what distinguishes my view from a Gricean type of analysis. A Gricean analysis would construe the transfer at issue, e.g. that from the person who speaks to his property of being a prisoner condemned to death, as taking us from the proposition literally expressed to what is communicated. In that framework, the proposition literally expressed, viz. the (absurd) proposition that the speaker – a particular person – is usually allowed to order his last meal, would have to be somehow entertained in the process of interpreting 8. I agree with Nunberg that this consequence is unwelcome. But the transfer at issue is local, not global, on my theory. It's the level 3 interpretation of the indexical, not its basic level interpretation (level 2), which combines with the interpretation of the adverb and other constituents of the sentence to yield a complete, coherent proposition. Nunberg's examples therefore provide no reason to reject my 'thesis that the general readings of indexicals arise through a kind of pragmatic transfer', but only a particular, Gricean interpretation of that thesis in terms of global transfer.

# II.3

# Belief reports

# Chapter 17

## Belief reports and conversational implicatures

### 17.1 Accounting for opacity

According to the theory of direct reference, a referential term's contribution to the proposition expressed by the utterance in which it occurs is its reference. The theory therefore entails the Strong Substitutivity Principle (henceforth to be called 'the Substitutivity Principle' or 'Substitutivity'):

*Substitutivity:*
If two directly referential terms are coextensive (have the same reference) they can be intersubstituted *salva propositione*, hence *salva veritate*.

An obvious counter-example to that principle, and to the theory of direct reference which entails it, is provided by belief contexts. "A believes that P" and "A believes that Q" may differ in truth-value even though the only difference between "P" and "Q", hence the only difference between the two utterances in which they are respectively embedded, is the occurrence in them of two different but coextensive referential terms t and t'.

To deal with this sort of counter-example, one may opt for various strategies. A first strategy consists in *restricting* the theory of direct reference and the Substitutivity Principle which it entails by excluding from its range of application those sentential contexts in which an expression does not behave in the normal way.[1] In quotation contexts, for example, an expression does not make its normal semantic contribution; it is used autonymously and refers not to its (ordinary) reference, but to the type of which it is a token. As Carnap, Quine and many others emphasized, belief contexts are somehow comparable to quotation contexts. In "A believes that P", the proposition that P is *mentioned* as the object of A's belief. This may be thought to provide a starting point for explaining why substitution fails in belief contexts, as it does in quotation contexts.

This line may be pursued in a more or less radical fashion. The radical view has it that a directly referential expression does *not* refer to its (ordinary) reference at all when it occurs within the embedded part of a belief sentence. This was Frege's view, but, as Brian Loar pointed out, 'it is a most implausible claim' (Loar, 1972, 43). I certainly refer to Cicero if I say 'John believes that Cicero was poor and had to earn his living by writing pleas.' This utterance describes a relation between John and Cicero: it says that the former has certain beliefs concerning the latter. Still the phenomenon of opacity (failure of substitutivity) manifests itself here: From 'John believes that Cicero was poor' it does not follow that John believes that Tully was poor. It is possible for John, who believes that Cicero was poor, to believe that Tully was rich, or to entertain no Tully-related belief whatsoever, even though Cicero is Tully.

The less radical view, defended by Brian Loar, ascribes a 'dual role' to referential terms in belief contexts (Loar, 1972; see also Hornsby, 1977). Such a term refers to its (ordinary) reference, but it does more: it also specifies a way of thinking, a mode of presentation which characterizes the believer's thought about the object in question. Thus when I say 'John believes that Cicero was poor', I refer to Cicero, but I do not simply say of him that John believes that he was poor: I say of Cicero that John believes of him *under the concept 'Cicero'* that he was poor. The term 'Cicero' makes a dual contribution to the proposition expressed: it provides the reference – the object which the belief concerns – and *also* the mode of presentation of the reference, i.e. the way that object is thought about by the believer.[2] This dual role is similar to that of 'Giorgione' in Quine's famous example: 'Giorgione was so-called because of his size'. The word 'Giorgione' is at the same time used to refer to Giorgione and mentioned or referred to. In the same way, 'Cicero' in 'John believes that Cicero was poor' refers to Cicero, enabling the speaker to state a relation between him and John, and also refers to 'Cicero', the concept under which John thinks of Cicero. It is because of this latter function (the autonymous function, as we may call it) that 'Cicero' cannot be replaced by 'Tully' although they are coextensive. For, although coextensive, 'Cicero' and 'Tully' are not associated with the same concepts. Cicero is Tully but the concept 'Cicero' is different from the concept 'Tully' (or at least the two concepts are different for someone like John who does not know that Cicero is Tully).[3]

Following Quine, let us call 'opaque' those sentential contexts in which a term has an autonymous function which prevents it from being replaceable *salva veritate* by a coextensive term. According to the restriction strategy, the theory of direct reference holds for referential terms in simple sentences such as 'Cicero was poor' but *not* for referential terms in opaque contexts such as 'John believes that Cicero was poor.' The restriction strategy therefore entails giving up the principle of Innocence:[4]

> *Innocence:*
> The semantic behaviour of a referential term is the same whether the term occurs in a simple sentence or in the embedded part of a complex utterance such as "John believes that P".

Innocence is lost because referential terms are said to behave differently in simple sentences and in the embedded parts of belief sentences. In simple sentences a referential term's contribution to the proposition expressed is its reference; the Substitutivity Principle therefore applies. But belief sentences are opaque contexts for which the Substitutivity Principle does not apply.

Although the issue is fairly delicate, it would seem desirable to *preserve* the principle of Innocence since, other things being equal, a semantic theory which conforms to it is simpler and more elegant than one which does not.[5] Now preserving Innocence is certainly possible, if we adopt another strategy than that I have just discussed (the restriction strategy).

An alternative strategy, widespread among direct reference theorists, consists in *denying* that belief contexts constitute a counter-example to the Substitutivity Principle. They are supposed to be a counter-example because, arguably, John can believe that Cicero was poor without believing that Tully was poor: apparently, one cannot replace 'Cicero' by 'Tully' *salva veritate* in a belief sentence. But this fact can be denied. It can be argued that 'John believes that Cicero was poor' and 'John believes that Tully was poor' actually express the same proposition — say the same thing. This is what the theory of direct reference would seem to entail, through the Substitutivity Principle. Appearances to the contrary can be explained away by invoking the *implicatures* of 'John believes that Cicero was poor' and of 'John believes that Tully was poor' respectively. The two utterances express the same proposition, but what they convey is different, because of a difference in conversational implicature, and this is what accounts for the appearance of opacity: replacing one term by the other affects what is communicated by the utterance. But it does not affect 'what is strictly and literally said'. Hence the theory of direct reference, and the Substitutivity Principle which it entails, can be maintained.

In this chapter I shall discuss and criticize the Implicature Theory which has just been sketched; in the next one I will present a theory which explains (rather than denies) failures of substitutivity without being inconsistent with the principle of Innocence. Both theories have an essential feature in common: they take opacity (failure of substitutivity) to be a pragmatic phenomenon. I shall start by giving the reasons one has to construe opacity that way.

## 17.2   The Implicature Theory

I said that, from 'John believes that Cicero was poor', it cannot be inferred that John believes that *Tully* was poor, for John may believe that Tully was rich (and Cicero poor). This is a standard example of opacity, or failure of substitutivity, in belief sentences. Now the first thing to notice about this sort of example is that *there is* an interpretation of 'John believes that Cicero was poor' on which Substitutivity holds. Such an interpretation is generally referred to as 'the transparent reading' of belief reports. Suppose, for example, that I say: 'John believes that the wealthy Cicero was poor! He obviously does not know much of ancient history.' In this report the words 'the wealthy Cicero' are to be read transparently: they give us the reference of John's belief (the man the belief is about), but are not intended to characterize his way of thinking of the reference (rather, they express *the speaker's* point of view). What allows me to use the words 'the wealthy Cicero' to refer to the man John's belief is about also allows me to use any coextensive expression to that effect, including 'Tully' or 'your favourite Roman orator'. If, during one of my travels through time, I meet Cicero, I am also allowed to tell him

'John believes that *you* are poor.' All this, which is well-known, shows that belief sentences have two interpretations: a transparent interpretation, which licenses substitution, and an opaque interpretation, which prevents it. Which interpretation is intended depends on the context.[6] This suggests that opacity may be a pragmatic phenomenon rather than a semantic property of a certain type of sentence.

In *Logic and Conversation* Paul Grice put forward a couple of tests for distinguishing contextual suggestions or 'conversational implicatures', as he called them, from the semantic entailments of sentences. The first test is the cancellability test: conversational implicatures are supposed to be cancellable, whether contextually or implicitly.

> A putative conversational implicature that $p$ is explicitly cancellable if, to the form of words the utterance of which putatively implicates that $p$, it is admissible to add *but not p*, or *I do not mean to imply that p*, and it is contextually cancellable if one can find situations in which the utterance of the form of words would simply not carry the implicature. (Grice, 1989, p. 44)

We have just seen that one *can* find situations in which a belief sentence such as 'John believes that Cicero was poor' would not carry the suggestion that John thinks of Cicero as 'Cicero'. In such a context, the sentence would be interpreted transparently rather than opaquely; the term 'Cicero' would be understood as providing only the reference – the object the belief is about – not as indicating the way the believer himself thinks of the reference. In Grice's terminology, this shows that the latter indication, which is responsible for the failure of substitutivity, is *contextually cancellable* rather than part of the semantic entailments of the utterance. Note that it is also *explicitly* cancellable. As Barwise and Perry made clear, in a context in which the opaque interpretation of a belief sentence seems natural, it can be cancelled by an explicit denial that such a reading is intended:

> Some arguments for referential opacity seem based on a confusion between conversational implicatures and semantic entailments. 'Smith believes Cicero was an orator' does not imply, but at most suggests, that Smith would check 'Cicero was an orator' true. The suggestion is clearly cancellable: 'Smith believes that Cicero was an orator, but only knows to call him "Tully."' (Barwise & Perry, 1981, p. 394)

The cancellability test therefore suggests that the proposition strictly and literally expressed by an utterance of a belief sentence such as 'John believes that Cicero was poor' corresponds to the transparent reading of that utterance; the opaque reading results from contextually combining the proposition expressed with the (cancellable) implicature that the believer thinks of the reference (e.g. Cicero) in a certain way (e.g. as 'Cicero').

The Implicature Theory of belief sentences incorporates something like Loar's notion of a dual role for referential terms. A referential term occurring in a belief sentence (opaquely understood) refers to its ordinary referent and also indicates the way that object is thought of; but the latter implication is pragmatic, according to the Implicature Theory. It is *suggested* that the believer thinks of Cicero as 'Cicero', not as 'Tully', but this is not part of what is said. 'John believes that Cicero was poor' and 'John believes that Tully was poor' literally express the same proposition (with Cicero as a constituent) but these utterances implicate different things on their 'opaque' interpretations – that Cicero is thought of as 'Cicero' in one case, as 'Tully' in the other; this is what accounts for the *appearance* of non-substitutability. From a logical point of view, however, Substitutivity holds: as far as the proposition literally expressed is concerned, one *can* infer 'John believes that Tully was poor' from 'John believes that Cicero was poor' and 'Cicero = Tully'. This inference sounds invalid on the opaque interpretation only because the opaque interpretation goes well beyond the proposition literally expressed and incorporates a conversational implicature.

At this point, it could be objected that sentences such as 'John believes that Cicero was poor' may also be construed as *semantically ambiguous* between the transparent and the opaque interpretation. This is consistent with the cancellability test. Disambiguation, like cancellation, can be either explicit or implicit and contextual. Thus the allegedly implicature-cancelling denial (in 'John believes that Cicero was poor but only knows to call him "Tully"') can be conceived of as a way of *disambiguating* the utterance by excluding one of the two readings. In the same way, what looks like the contextual cancelling of an implicature may also be seen as the contextual disambiguation of an ambiguous utterance.

To settle the question, we may appeal to Grice's second test – the non-detachability test. The alleged ambiguity, presumably, would be syntactic rather than lexical. For it is the *construction* 'X V's that *p*', which quite systematically gives rise to two interpretations, not a particular lexical item (like 'believe') occurring in one of the slots. But if the construction in question were semantically ambiguous, it ought to be possible to remove the ambiguity by changing the construction. Indeed, many philosophers have suggested that this can be done by replacing the 'believe that...' construction by the 'believe of...' construction. Whereas 'John believes that Cicero was poor' can be interpreted either opaquely or transparently (depending on the context), 'John believes of Cicero that he was poor' has been thought to give rise only to the transparent interpretation. It that were true, that would perhaps argue against a treatment of opacity in terms of conversational implicature. For implicatures — and this is Grice's second test — are essentially *non-detachable*, in the following sense: when an utterance with a certain content carries a given implicature, 'it will not be possible to find another way of saying the same thing, which simply lacks the implicature in question, except where some special feature of the substituted version is itself relevant to the determination of an implicature (in virtue of one of the maxims of Manner)' (Grice, 1989, p. 39). So it should not be possible, simply by changing the construction, to remove the 'ambiguity' of belief sentences if the latter resulted from a process of implicature generation instead of being a genuine semantic ambiguity.

The non-detachability test, however, supports the Implicature Theory as opposed to the Ambiguity Theory. Kent Bach has shown that even the 'believe of...' locution can be interpreted opaquely, in a suitable context (Bach, 1987, p. 198). Thus it does not seem to be possible simply by changing the wording of a belief report to prevent opacity from arising: opacity (or at least, the possibility of opacity) seems to be 'non-detachable' from belief reports.

To be sure, this test is not decisive either. The ambiguity could be located at a fairly deep level of syntactic analysis, and the two constructions ('believe that' and 'believe of') might differ only at a more superficial level. Thus many philosophers think the ambiguity is a scope ambiguity in logical structure, and one might take 'logical structure' to correspond to some hidden syntactic level. There are several reasons not to accept this proposal, however. Firstly, as Bach (1987, pp. 207–8) rightly emphasizes, it is a *non sequitur* to assume that, because the difference between two utterances, or two interpretations of a given utterance, *can* be represented by a scope difference in logical form, the utterances in question *have* the 'forms' in question at some level of syntactic analysis. To license the inference one would have to provide independent syntactic evidence of the alleged scope difference. But such evidence does not seem to be available (Cole, 1981, p. 9); it does not seem that the alleged scope differences can be ascribed a syntactic basis. As Bach says, 'these logical forms serve to represent what speakers can mean in using sentences', but they lack 'the syntactic basis that the claim of scope ambiguity requires' (Bach, 1987, p. 210). Secondly, the relevant differences cannot even always be *represented as* scope differences in logical form, as Fauconnier has convincingly demonstrated in his rich and detailed study of the subject (Fauconnier, 1985). I conclude that the prospects of an analysis in terms of syntactic ambiguity are bleak.

Let us return to Grice. The cancellability and non-detachability tests, he says, provide only 'a more or less strong prima facie case in favour of the presence of a conversational implicature... Any such case would have to be supported by a demonstration of the way in which what is putatively implicated could have come be to implicated (by a derivation of it from conversational principles and other data)' (Grice, 1989, p. 43). What I am calling the Implicature Theory of belief contexts precisely offers such a demonstration.

The first one, to my knowledge, to have shown how the opacity-generating component of the meaning of a belief report can be derived from conversational principles is J.O. Urmson in a symposium which took place in 1968, shortly after Grice delivered the William James Lectures at Harvard University (Urmson, 1968). Similar accounts were later put forward by Christopher Peacocke (1975, pp. 126–8) and especially Tom McKay (1981), both of whom concentrated on proper names in belief contexts and used the Implicature Theory to defend a version of the theory of direct reference. Jennifer Hornsby also had (limited) recourse to the theory, in her paper on belief contexts (Hornsby, 1977, pp. 38–9). Besides Barwise and Perry, who followed Urmson (Barwise & Perry, 1981, p. 394; 1983, pp. 258–64), the next writer to be mentioned is George Bealer, who developed the Implicature Theory without reference to earlier attempts (Bealer, 1982, pp. 166–74). Later proponents of the theory are too numerous to be listed; I shall mention only Nathan Salmon, who devoted a whole book to its defence (Salmon, 1986a).

Implicature Theorists typically invoke a conversational principle or maxim of faithfulness which says roughly this:

*Maxim of faithfulness:*
In reporting a belief about an object, and especially in referring to that object, use an expression which the believer himself would use (insofar as differences of language or context permit), or at least, try to be faithful to the believer's own point of view, unless there are reasons not to do so.

This maxim can perhaps be seen as related to Grice's maxim of Quantity ('Make your contribution as informative as is required'). There are two aspects in a belief content: '*what* is represented and *how* it is represented' (McGinn, 1982, p. 214) – the truth-conditional content of the belief and its narrow content, in the terminology of chapter 4. A belief ascription is more informative if it specifies not only the former but also the latter. Now respecting the maxim of faithfulness is a very economical way of providing the latter sort of information. In stating what the truth-conditional content of the belief is, a speaker observing the maxim of faithfulness at the same time shows or displays the intrinsic or narrow content of the belief, for the expressions he uses to express the truth-conditional content of the belief mirror the believer's own point of view and (sometimes) correspond to expressions which the believer himself could use in expressing his own belief. A speaker who, in stating the truth-conditional content of a belief, respects the maxim of faithfulness is therefore more informative than a speaker who does not respect that maxim.[7]

To be sure, there are contexts in which the *how* is irrelevant – contexts in which the only thing that matters is the truth-conditional content of the belief. Consider, for example, the report I mentioned earlier, 'John believes that the wealthy Cicero was poor.' The report is intended to underline the discrepancy between John's belief and known facts of ancient history. In this context, the speaker does not try, and is not expected, to be as specific as possible concerning the internal aspects (the narrow content) of John's belief, since he is concerned, rather, with the relation between John's belief and external facts which falsify it. In contexts of this type, faithfulness is not required. But when information concerning the narrow content of the belief is particularly relevant, the speaker will be expected to observe the maxim of faithfulness, *ceteris paribus*.[8]

Using the maxim of faithfulness, it is easy to derive the opacity-generating implicature considered as responsible for the *prima facie* failure of substitutivity in opaque belief reports. In some contexts, the speaker will be expected to conform to the faithfulness requirement; this expectation being mutually manifest, the addressee will feel entitled to assume that the speaker actually conforms to the maxim of faithfulness and phrases his belief report so as to match the believer's own point of view. From this presumption, together with the speaker's saying e.g. 'John believes that Cicero was poor', the addressee will infer that the embedded sentence 'Cicero was poor' closely resembles a sentence which the believer himself would accept and could use in expressing his own belief.[9]

Like conversational principles in general, the maxim of faithfulness may clash with other maxims and be overriden by considerations derived from the latter (Grice, 1989, p. 30; Urmson, 1968, pp. 117). Other maxims relevant to the interpretation of belief reports include, for example, Urmson's maxim of successful reference (Urmson, 1968, p. 116): 'Use the referring expression most likely to secure successful identification by the person(s) to whom the communication is addressed'. It is easy to imagine a clash between that maxim and the maxim of faithfulness, that is, a case in which the referring expression most likely to secure successful identification by the addressee would not be an expression which the believer himself would we prepared to use (see Urmson, 1968, pp. 117–18). Another maxim put forward in the literature is the maxim of charity (Barwise & Perry, 1983, p. 258): 'Assume that people are cognitively coherent'. In the 'wealthy Cicero' example, the presumption that the speaker respects that maxim prevents one from assuming that he is being faithful to the believer; for if he were, he would be (uncharitably) ascribing an incoherent belief to him, viz. the belief that someone is both wealthy and poor. In general it is clear, in context, which consideration overrides the others, given the speaker's overall purpose in reporting the belief.

The central feature of the Implicature Theory – that which distinguishes it from other pragmatic accounts, like the account to be offered in chapter 18 or those to be discussed in chapter 19 – is its claim that the indication which an opaque belief report conveys concerning the *how* (the narrow content) of the belief is not part of the proposition expressed by the belief report and does not affect its truth-conditions. The truth-conditions of an opaque belief report are exactly the same as the truth-conditions of the same report transparently interpreted, according to the Implicature Theory. The difference between the two interpretations of the report lies entirely at the level of conversational implicatures – that is, at a level distinct from that of 'what is said'. Even in a context in which faithfulness is required, that is, in a context in which the narrow content of the reported belief is clearly relevant to the addressee, a speaker who violates the maxim of faithfulness does not utter a falsehood provided his report would count as true, transparently interpreted. The speaker's conversational contribution in such a context suffers from various interrelated defects: it is inappropriate or 'inept' (Urmson), *qua* belief report it is 'poor' (McKay), and, above all, it is 'liable to mislead' (Grice) since the addressee expects the speaker to be faithful and therefore interprets the embedded clause as somehow mirroring a sentence which the believer himself would accept; but, despite all these defects, the utterance cannot be said to be *false*. This is so because, according to the Implicature Theory, the only thing which a belief report *states* is the obtaining of a relation between the believer and the proposition expressed by the embedded sentence, such that the believer has a belief whose truth-conditional content is that proposition. What may be iconically suggested concerning the narrow content of the belief is not part of what the utterance states, and does not affect its truth-conditions. It follows that opaque belief reports constitute only *prima facie* violations of the Principle of Substitutivity; once conversational implicatures and other contextual suggestions are put aside, it turns out that Substitutivity holds: despite appearances, if Lois Lane believes that Superman is Superman, it follows that she believes that Clark Kent is Superman. To be sure, 'Lois Lane believes that Clark Kent is Superman' would be inappropriate as a belief report, for it would misleadingly suggest (through the maxim of faithfulness) that Lois Lane would accept the sentence 'Clark Kent is Superman.'[10] Yet, inappropriate and misleading though it would be, such a belief report would be strictly and literally true, according to the Implicature Theory.

## 17.3 What's wrong with the Implicature Theory (1)

The Implicature Theory has strikingly counterintuitive consequences. Consider, again, the Superman legend. It is stipulated as part of this legend that Lois Lane does *not* realize that Clark Kent is Superman. In other words, 1 is false, and 2 is true, in the context of the Superman legend:

1  Lois Lane knows that Clark Kent is Superman.
2  Lois Lane does not know that Clark Kent is Superman.

Yet, as we have just seen, the Implicature Theory entails that 1 is true and 2 is false. 1 is said to be true because (i) Lois Lane knows that Superman is Superman, (ii) Clark Kent = Superman, and (iii) Substitutivity holds even in attitude contexts, according to the Implicature Theory. 2 is said to be false because it is the negation of 1, which is true.

Far from capturing our intuitions concerning the truth-conditions of belief sentences, it is clear that the Implicature Theory severely distorts those intuitions. Salmon and other defenders of the Implicature Theory acknowledge this point, but they think it does not refute the Implicature Theory, for the latter is about the proposition literally expressed by utterances such as 1 and 2, while our everyday intuitions concern what is communicated by these utterances. What is communicated by an utterance involves not only what is strictly and literally said (the information semantically encoded, as Salmon puts it), but also the implicatures of the utterance and other pieces of 'pragmatically imparted information'. Thus, even though 1 is literally true, what it communicates is false, according to Salmon; for it communicates a proposition richer than that which it literally expresses. This accounts for the divergence between our intuitions and what the theory predicts, without threatening the theory.

According to Salmon, the proposition literally expressed by 1 is the proposition that Lois Lane has a belief the truth-conditional content of which is a certain singular proposition (the proposition that Clark Kent is Superman, or, equivalently, the proposition that Clark Kent is Clark Kent or the proposition that Superman is Superman). Now to say that Lois Lane believes this proposition is to say that *there is a mode of presentation under which she believes it*. 1 is literally true precisely because there is such a mode of presentation: Lois Lane believes the singular proposition in question when she grasps it through the sentence 'Superman is Superman' (but of course she does not believe it when she grasps it through the sentence 'Clark Kent is Superman'). 1 communicates more than that, however; 1 communicates not only that *there is* a mode of presentation under which Lois believes the singular proposition in question, but, more specifically, that she believes that proposition *when it is presented to her through the very sentence which occurs in the 'that' – clause*. 1 therefore *communicates* that Lois Lane would assent to 'Clark Kent is Superman', and *this* is false. But this, which is false, is not part of what the utterance strictly and literally says. Our intuition that 1 is false can therefore be explained away as the intuition that what 1 *communicates* is false; and this is consistent with the Implicature Theory, which says that the proposition literally expressed by 1 is true.

To sum up, although the Implicature Theory does not *trust* (nor, therefore, try to preserve) our intuitions concerning the truth-conditions of belief sentences, it cannot be accused of *ignoring* these intuitions, since it accounts for them: it explains why we have them. That is the standard defence of the Implicature Theory. In what follows, I shall argue that this defence is not successful. The Implicature Theory indeed accounts for some of our intuitions, but there are intuitions which it leaves unexplained. As I shall argue, the best way to account for those unexplained intuitions is by giving up the Implicature Theory.

The Implicature Theory accounts for our intuitions concerning the truth-conditions of belief reports by claiming that we are not pre-theoretically conscious of the distinction between what is strictly and literally said and what is implicated or conveyed by our utterances. Not being conscious of that distinction, we tend to confuse semantically encoded and pragmatically imparted information. We are conscious only of what is communicated, that is, of the *output* of the process merging together the two types of information – what is said and what is implicated. Mark Richard (on behalf of the Implicature Theorist) makes this claim very explicit in the following passage:

> The Russellian's explanation of our anti-Russellian intuitions is that we mistake a common, important, pragmatic implication about the how of the belief for truth-conditional content. Should someone suggest that Hammurabi believed that Hesperus was Phosphorus, we would (probably rightly) take him to be getting across that Hammurabi held the belief under a certain sentence, one we are certain he did not believe it under. When we insist that his claim is strictly and literally false, we are (wrongly) confusing the implication with what was strictly and literally said.
>
> This manœuvre is perfectly cogent. Although it is a primitive fact about attitude ascriptions that they convey information about the way in which attitudes are held, it is arguably not a *primitive* fact that this information is relevant to the truth-conditions of attitude ascriptions. We do not come equipped with a meter that reliably distinguishes between semantic and pragmatic implications. Examples like that concerning 'and' and temporal order help make the point that what

seems for all the world like a truth-conditional implication may turn out not to be one. (Richard, 1990, p. 123)

I already quoted the last sentences of that passage in chapter 13, for the claim that we are not pre-theoretically conscious of the distinction between what is said and what is implicated is precisely something which I rejected, when I put forward the Availability Principle. As I have argued in chapter 13, we *are* pre-theoretically equipped for distinguishing between what is said and what is only 'implied' or 'suggested'; this is quite obvious when we consider a standard example of implicature, e.g. the implication from 'It's cold in here' to 'You should close the window.' Grice's theory of implicature was meant to capture an *everyday distinction* between two components of meaning; so it's not true that 'the general masses', as Salmon says (Salmon, 1986a, p. 85), are not aware of the distinction. Ordinary users of the language have fairly strong intuitions concerning the distinction between what is said and what is implied, and the Implicature Theory is guilty of ignoring *those* intuitions, when it claims that we have no conscious access to what is strictly and literally said as opposed to what is globally communicated by an utterance.[11]

The Implicature Theorist may reply that, *in some cases* at least, we are not pre-theoretically conscious of the distinction. Implicature Theorists typically mention the case of 'and' and temporal order (see 13.1 and the appendix to chapters 13–14). This suggests that there are two sorts of cases: the cases (like 'It's cold in here') in which we are conscious of the distinction between the two components of meaning, and the cases in which we are pre-theoretically unable to make that distinction. Salmon makes that point, in his reply to Schiffer's criticism:

> Schiffer describes a particular mechanism that allows speakers to use a sentence to convey ('implicate') what it does not literally mean by means of a mutual recognition that what is conveyed cannot be what the sentence literally means. I had in mind an alternative mechanism that allows speakers to use a sentence to convey something stronger than what it literally means, thereby creating a mutual misimpression that what is conveyed is precisely what the sentence literally means ... Surely there can be such a mechanism that, when employed, sometimes has the unintended and unnoticed consequence that speakers

mistake what is conveyed ('implicated') for the literal content. Consider, for example, the conjunction 'Jane became pregnant and she got married', which normally carries the implicature that Jane became pregnant before getting married. Utterers of this sentence, in order to employ it with its customary implicature, need not be aware that the sentence is literally true even if Jane became pregnant only after getting married. Some utterers may well become misled by the sentence's customary implicature into believing that the sentence literally means precisely what it normally conveys – so that, if they believe that Mary became pregnant only after getting married, they would reject the true but misleading conjunction as literally false... It is this general sort of situation, or something very similar, that I impute to propositional-attitude attributions. (Salmon, 1989, pp. 252–3)

In a footnote, Salmon recognizes that the situations he had in mind in connection with propositional-attitude attributions do not qualify as cases of standard, particularized conversational implicature, but 'better fit one or the other of Grice's two contrasting notions of *generalized conversational implicature* and *conventional* (non-conversational) *implicature*':[12]

> Surely a great many speakers may be confused by the conventional [sic] or generalized conversational implicature of a sentence into thinking that the sentence literally says (in part) what it in fact only implicates. Grice's notion of particularized conversational implicature apparently precludes the possibility of this sort of confusion. (Salmon, 1989, pp. 275–6)

I think Salmon is right to hold that there is a special case of 'pragmatically imparted information' (as he would say) characterized by *its intuitive indistinguishability from truth-conditional content*. This is indeed connected to the issue of 'generalized conversational implicatures'. A number of linguists and philosophers have investigated this topic in general, and the classic example of 'and' and temporal order in particular. Their conclusions, however, do not support the Implicature Theory. The general tendency among these researchers is to treat the alleged implicatures which turn out to be pre-theoretically indistinguishable from truth-conditional content as *actually part of* truth-conditional content rather than as *mistakenly confused with* truth-conditional content.[13]

The only reason to insist, as Salmon does, that the pragmatic aspects of utterance meaning which are intuitively indistinguishable from truth-conditional content are *not* part of truth-conditional content seems to be the widespread confusion between the literal meaning of the sentence (what is *encoded*) and the truth-conditional content of the utterance (what is *expressed*). *Qua* pragmatically imparted information, it is clear that the sort of implicature Salmon is concerned with does not belong to the meaning of the sentence. But this is no way shows that it cannot be constitutive of the proposition literally expressed by the utterance. As I said in Chapter 13, there are three levels to be distinguished rather than merely two: the linguistic meaning of the sentence type, the proposition literally expressed by an utterance of the sentence, and what is communicated, which includes whatever manifestly follows from the fact that the speaker expresses that proposition in that context. The latter component of meaning consists of pragmatically imparted information, but the proposition expressed too is context-dependent and may incorporate pragmatically imparted information. Pragmatic processes are involved not only to get from what is said to what is implied, but also to get from sentence meaning to what is said. Grice's tests (cancellability, non-detachability, etc.) show that a component of meaning results from a pragmatic process, hence does not belong to the first level – that of sentence meaning – but the component in question may well be constitutive of the proposition contextually expressed by the utterance. In other words, there are two sorts of pragmatic components of meaning: those that are constitutive of what is said and those that are external and additional to what is said. As I pointed out in chapter 13, the most salient difference between them precisely lies in the fact that *the former, contrary to the latter, are intuitively indistinguishable from truth-conditional content.*

The considerations which I put forward in chapter 13 for treating the type of pragmatic information Salmon has in mind as integral to what is said seem to me quite powerful. I any case, the theory then sketched is supported by considerations independent of the present topic. So I suggest that we extend this treatment (argued for at length in chapter 13) to Salmon's type of example, and admit that the type of pragmatic information Salmon talks about is actually part of the proposition expressed by the utterance and affects truth-conditions. This move, I believe, is both necessary and sufficient to dispose of the major objection raised by Salmon's pragmatic approach – an objection which it is time to consider.

## 17.4 What's wrong with the Implicature Theory (2)

Belief ascriptions serve a variety of functions or purposes, which cannot be ignored in theorizing about the content of belief ascriptions. For example, in ascribing beliefs to A we may be primarily interested in pointing out that A agrees (or disagrees) with B. (A particular case is that in which A *is* B and we want to demonstrate A's own consistency or inconsistency.) In that context it would be artificial to follow the Implicature Theory and take the belief content literally being ascribed to be a bare singular proposition, to the exclusion of any particular mode of presentation of that proposition, for we *do* take modes of presentation into account when we are interested in assessing inter-individual or intra-individual consistency. We would not consider someone guilty of any logical inconsistency on the grounds that she both assents to and dissents from a given singular proposition, provided she does so under distinct modes of presentation; nor do we consider that two persons disagree in any strong sense if they respectively hold and deny a given singular proposition which they manifestly apprehend under different modes of presentation.

Another use of belief reports which tells against the Implicature Theory occurs within explanations of actions. As Mark Richard says:

> There is an enormous, easily delineated body of attitude ascriptions that can reasonably be said to have as their *primary* purpose conveying information about the how of the belief, not just information about the Russellian what. Among these are ascriptions used in the attempt to explain action, as in 'Randi waved because he wanted Hesperus to rise, and he thought that if there was waving, Hesperus would rise.' It is clear that, if these do explain behaviour, they don't do so because of what they tell us about Russellian objects of belief. That Randi wants
> &lt;Rising, Venus&gt;
> and believes
> &lt;Implication, &lt;the Russellian proposition that there is waving, &lt;Rising, Venus&gt;&gt;&gt;
> doesn't suggest in the least that Randi is disposed to wave. (Suppose he holds his wish under 'Hesperus rises' and his belief under 'If there is waving, then Phosphorus will rise', and is ignorant of the truth of 'Hesperus is Phosphorus'.) (Richard, 1990, p. 126)

The point of the objection, then, is that the Implicature Theory, as William Taschek says, 'severs the intimate connection' between the sort of content being ascribed and the general enterprise (logical appraisal, or action explanation) in which the belief ascription plays a certain function.[14] This makes the Implicature Theory rather unattractive. So far, that is not a decisive objection; but the objection becomes decisive when we realize that the Implicature Theory cannot properly account for the larger discourse structures in which belief ascriptions play the role which they do.

Let us consider a simplified version of Richard's example, 'Randi waved because he thought that, if there was waving, then Hesperus would rise.' The belief report occurs within a larger semantic unit, namely "Randi waved because...". If we follow the Implicature Theorist, how are we to account for the truth-conditions of the larger structure? Shall we say that the implicature of the belief report (i.e. the information about the mode of presentation under which Randi is supposed to believe the singular proposition <*Implication, <the proposition that there is waving, <rising, Venus>>>*) occurs within, or without, the scope of the sentential connective 'Randi waved because' which dominates the belief sentence? If the former, we capture our intuitions concerning the truth-conditions of the global utterance: the cause of Randi's waving is taken to be his believing the singular proposition *under a certain mode of presentation*. But the Implicature Theorist must explain why the mode of presentation, which is not an aspect of the proposition expressed by the embedded belief sentence "Randi thought that...", *becomes* an aspect of the proposition expressed by the larger sentence "Randi waved because he thought that...". On the other hand, if we hold that the mode of presentation in question is external not only to the proposition expressed by the embedded belief sentence but also to the proposition expressed by the larger, embedding sentence, then we must account for our intuitions concerning the truth-conditions of the latter. Whatever horn of the dilemma he chooses, I think the Implicature Theorist faces insuperable difficulties.

The problem I have just raised is fairly general. It arises whenever a belief sentence falls within the scope of a logical connective. A typical example, which I will consider in some detail, is 2, in which a belief sentence is negated. Nor is the problem restricted to belief sentences. The same problem arises, for example, in connection with Grice's Implicature Theory of the temporal suggestion conveyed by 'and'. As Jonathan Cohen pointed out, the so-called temporal implicature of 'Jane became pregnant and got married' affects the *truth-conditions* of the larger sentence 'If Jane became pregnant and got married, her father must be unhappy'; the Implicature Theory therefore turns out to be viable only with respect to a restricted class of examples, but cannot account for more complex examples (Cohen, 1971). That is one of the reasons for considering the temporal suggestion conveyed by 'and' as a pragmatic constituent of what is said rather than as an implicature external to what is said (Carston, 1988). Note that Cohen himself saw the analogy between the problem raised by Grice's account of 'and' and Urmson's account of belief sentences. In his contribution to the symposium in which Urmson first presented the Implicature Theory of belief reports, he wrote: 'Troubles emerge for Mr Urmson's theory, as for many other theories (theories of truth, probability, implication, etc.) that invoke characteristics of speech performance or rules of conversational etiquette in the analysis of logical or epistemological problems, as soon as one moves on from considering assertoric propositions of the simplest type in question to considering more complex examples' (Cohen, 1968, p. 133).

Let us consider example 2 again, to illustrate the dilemma I have talked about in connection with Richard's example:

2   Lois Lane does not know that Clark Kent is Superman.

There are two options for the Implicature Theorist. Either he says that what is negated in 2 is only the proposition strictly and literally expressed by 'Lois Lane knows that Clark Kent is Superman', or he says that what is negated in 2 is what, according to the Implicature Theory, would be *communicated* by an utterance of 'Lois Lane knows that Clark Kent is Superman.' The latter solution captures our intuitions concerning the truth-conditions of 2 – hence I will call it the 'intuitive solution', as opposed to the 'counterintuitive solution – but it amounts to conceding what the Implicature Theory insists on denying, namely, that the mode of presentation which constitutes the narrow content of the belief talked about is an aspect of the proposition expressed. At this point, there are again two options: either one gives up the Implicature Theory and admits that the mode of presentation was an aspect of the proposition expressed since the very beginning, i.e. not only in 2 but also in 1, or one maintains the Implicature Theory concerning the simple sentence 1 and one must account for the difference between 1 and 2: why does an *implicature* of the simple utterance 1 become a *truth-conditional constituent* when 1 occurs within a larger sentence such as 2? What accounts for this change of status of a given meaning-component? The only explanation I can think of on behalf of the Implicature Theorist uses the notion of *metalinguistic negation* (see Part II.1, appendix). Thus the Implicature Theorist might argue that the negation in 2 is like the negation in 'He is not tall – he is *very* tall', in which an implicature of the simple utterance 'He is tall' falls within the scope of the negation and affects the truth-conditions of the complex utterance. But this explanation is not very convincing, for metalinguistic negation has properties which examples like 2 do not exhibit. Consider the utterance 'He is not tall'. Clearly, the *default* interpretation of such an utterance is its interpretation as an instance of descriptive (i.e. ordinary, non-metalinguistic) negation; the metalinguistic interpretation has to be specially 'marked' or indicated. Nothing of the sort is the case with 2: 2 is *normally* interpreted in such a way that the mode of presentation falls within the scope of negation, and this goes against a 'metalinguistic' treatment.

Let us now consider the other option – the 'counterintuitive solution', according to which what is negated in 2 is only the proposition which the Implicature Theory takes to be literally expressed by 1, namely the proposition that there is a mode of presentation under which Lois Lane knows the singular proposition that Clark Kent (i.e. Superman) is Superman. On this construal, 2 literally expresses the following proposition: There is *no* mode of presentation under which Lois Lane believes of Superman that he is Superman. At this point, the Implicature Theorist must explain why expressing such an (obviously false) proposition may communicate the proposition communicated. The only explanation I can think of invokes a figure of speech analogous to what occurs in irony or metaphor, but (i) Stephen Schiffer has provided an argument, which Salmon has accepted, to the effect that this cannot be the sort of mechanism involved in that sort of example, and (ii) even if an explanation along these lines were acceptable, one could object to the Implicature Theory that it used *two quite distinct mechanisms* for accounting for what is obviously the *same* phenomenon, namely the 'opaque' interpretation of the belief talked about in 1 and 2.[15]

Before closing this chapter, let me deplore that defenders of the Implicature Theory, like Salmon, have not tried to work it out in detail, as Salmon himself recognizes (Salmon, 1989, p. 253). Had they done so, they would have realized that the Implicature Theory as such must be given up: the alleged implicatures posited by the theory must be considered as full-fledged propositional constituents (pragmatic aspects of what is said), if one wants to deal with more complex examples in which belief sentences fall within the scope of logical connectives. This is as expected, since the alleged implicatures in question exhibit the characteristic property of pragmatic aspects of what is said, namely their intuitive indistinguishability from what is said.

## Notes

1  I name this strategy after the Medieval logicians who used 'restrictio' when dealing with a related sort of solution to the *insolubilia* (e.g. the Liar paradox).
2  Loar renders 'John believes that Cicero was poor' as: B (John, 'x was Cicero and x was poor', Cicero) (Loar, 1972, p. 53).
3  Loar's 'dual role' theory has recently been revived by Graeme Forbes, who also uses Quine's 'Giorgione' example as a paradigm (Forbes, 1990, pp. 535–6). The similarity between what we might call 'Giorgione sentences' and belief sentences will be dealt with in 20.3.
4  The name 'Innocence' is due to Barwise and Perry (see their article: 'Semantic Innocence and Uncompromising Situations', 1981); it was chosen in reference to Davidson who wrote: 'If we could but recover our pre-Fregean semantic innocence, I think it would be plainly incredible that the words "the earth moves", uttered after the words "Galileo said that", mean anything different, or refer to anything else, than is their wont when they come in other environments' (Davidson, 1969, p. 172).
5  As I understand it, the principle of Innocence is a principle of theoretical economy. It can perhaps be construed as a consequence of Grice's Modified Occam's Razor. (See also Jackendoff's 'Grammatical Constraint' in Jackendoff, 1983, p. 13.)
6  It is sometimes said that the duality of readings characterizes descriptions as opposed to referential terms. Indexicals, for example, are said to be necessarily transparent. That will be discussed in chapter 20. (The truth is that indexicals tend to be interpreted transparently, although they can be interpreted opaquely. More on this later.) Whatever we think of indexicals, however, proper names can be interpreted both ways, like descriptions. There *is* a difference between proper names and descriptions, though: proper names tend to be referential even on the opaque reading, while descriptions opaquely understood may well be understood non-referentially. In chaper 20 I shall consider the specific behaviour of names, indexicals and descriptions in belief sentences, and explain the differences I have just mentioned within the account to be developed in chapters 18–19.

7   Many authors, following Quine (1960, p. 219), Davidson (1969) and Stich (1983, p. 83ff), hold the view that belief ascriptions involve a form of simulation (Gordon, 1986): in ascribing a belief the speaker actually utters a sentence *similar* to that which the believer himself might utter (Jacob, 1987). On this view the very point of the enterprise is to be 'faithful' to the believer's own point of view. Does this mean that the maxim of faithfulness is superfluous, in that framework? No. There are degrees of faithfulness (as there are degrees of similarity); 'using a referring expression which the believer himself would use (insofar as differences of language or context permit)' involves a fairly high degree of faithfulness, one which cannot always be expected of an ascriber.

8   According to Barwise and Perry, the maxim of faithfulness is especially important when the belief report is used 'to explain a person's action (as opposed to using it as evidence of what the world is like)' (Barwise & Perry, 1983, p. 258).

9   In Grice's terms (Grice, 1989, p. 31), the hearer would reason as follows: 'The speaker has said: "John believes that Cicero was poor"; there is no reason to suppose that he is not observing the maxim of faithfulness; he could not be doing this unless he thought that John would accept the sentence "Cicero was poor", or something very similar; he knows (and knows that I know that he knows) that the supposition that he thinks that John would accept the sentence "Cicero was poor" is required; he has done nothing to stop me thinking that John would accept "Cicero was poor"; he intends me to think, or is at least willing to allow me to think, that John would accept "Cicero was poor"; and so he has implicated that John would accept "Cicero was poor."'

10  Perry's distinction between 'belief' and 'acceptance', which on the agent's side corresponds to the distinction between truth-conditional content and narrow content, is used by many Implicature Theorists (e.g. McKay, Barwise & Perry, and Bealer), who present their view as follows: what is encoded is the belief relation between the believer and a proposition, while the acceptance relation between the believer and a sentence is only suggested. On belief vs. acceptance, see chapter 2, notes 9 and 10.

11  In Richard's terminology, I maintain that it is a *primitive* fact – part of the intuitive data to be accounted for – that information about the way in which attitudes are held is (taken to be) relevant to the truth-conditions of attitude ascriptions.

12  Salmon, 1989, p. 275. Salmon is a bit confused in that passage, as his unhappy reference to Grice's conventional implicatures shows. Contrary to what he says in the same footnote, conventional implicatures are not cancellable, hence cannot be what is at issue here. Salmon probably

confused conventional (non-conversational) implicatures and conventionalised (short-circuited) conversational implicatures. On the latter, see Morgan, 1978. This conflation confirms that 'the issues here are quite delicate' (Salmon, 1989, p. 276). In the same article, Salmon modestly admits that he has not thoroughly explored the issues in question and that 'there is a great deal more to be investigated' (Salmon, 1989, p. 253).
13  See e.g. the references given in chapter 13 (Carston, etc.), the recent book by Atlas (Atlas, 1989), and a forthcoming piece by Steve Levinson: 'Generalized Conversational Implicatures and the Semantics/Pragmatics Interface'.
14  See Taschek's paper, 'Frege's Puzzle, Sense, and Information Content', forthcoming in *Mind*.
15  According to Salmon, the mechanism at play in 1 involves the enrichment of the proposition expressed into a more specific proposition. Salmon does not seem to realize that this mechanism cannot account for 2.

# Chapter 18

# Belief reports and the semantics of 'that'-clauses

## 18.1 Frege's Puzzle and the Relational principle

The main advantage of the Implicature Theory was that it provided us with a way out of Frege's Puzzle. Frege's Puzzle rests on three theses, one of which must go if the puzzle is to be solved.

*Frege's Puzzle:*
(A) If two referential terms t and t' refer to the same object, and if two simple sentences "P" and "Q" differ only in that t occurs in "P" and t' in "Q", then "P" and "Q" express the same proposition.
(B) If "P" and "Q" express the same proposition, then "John believes that P" and "John believes that Q" express the same proposition.
(C) Yet: In some contexts at least, "John believes that P" and "John believes that Q" do not express the same proposition even though (i) "P" and "Q" differ only in that t occurs in "P" and t' in "Q", and (ii) t and t' refer to same object.

Frege's way out consists in denying (A) and therefore rejecting the theory of direct reference. The Implicature Theory denies (C) and treats opacity as an illusion due to a confusion between the proposition expressed and what is communicated. Contrary to the Implicature theorist, I accept (C), that is, I accept that (in some contexts at least) 'Lois Lane believes that Superman is Superman' and 'Lois Lane believes that Clark Kent is Superman' do not express the same proposition. I also accept the theory of direct reference. So it seems that I must deny (B).[1]

Indeed I think (B) is unacceptable on several counts. Many philosophers are reluctant to reject (B), however, because it seems hard to do so without also rejecting the Relational principle, stated below. The Relational principle entails (B), hence it seems that it cannot be maintained if (B) is rejected.

*Relational principle:*
"John believes that P" states a relation between John and the proposition expressed by "P".

Why do I say that the Relational principle, thus formulated, entails (B)? Because, if "P" and "Q" express the same proposition, it follows from the Relational principle that "John believes that P" and "John believes that Q" state the same relation between the same *relata* (viz. John and the proposition in question), hence that "John believes that P" and "John believes that Q" express the same proposition (viz., the proposition that John is belief-related to that proposition). The Relational principle therefore entails that, if "P" and "Q" express the same proposition, "John believes that P" and "John believes that Q" express the same proposition.

The Relational principle is often said to be non-negotiable, because, as Salmon says (1986b, p. 246), it 'is supported by strong linguistic evidence [and] provides the simplest and most plausible explanation' of a certain type of inference such as the following:

John believes that S,
Peter believes everything which John believes,
therefore, Peter believes that S.

John believes the proposition to which our nation is dedicated,
our nation is dedicated to the proposition that all men are created equal,
therefore, John believes that all men are created equal.

John believes that S,
it is true that S,
therefore, there is something true which John believes.

Such inferences are supposed to show that "that P" is a referring expression and 'believes' a dyadic predicate.[2] I personally think that issue is more complex and controversial than contemporary philosophers are willing to admit,[3] but I will not address it here, for it is not in my intention to deny the view that "John believes that P" states a relation between John and the proposition or content denoted by "that P". That view is indeed supported to some extent by the sort of evidence adduced above. What I want to reject is not that view, which I call the Relational conception of belief, but the Relational principle stated above. The latter incorporates the former, but it also incorporates a dubious thesis about the semantics of 'that'-clauses. In other words, the Relational principle can be decomposed into two theses, the second of which I reject:

(RP-i) "John believes that P" states a relation between John and the content denoted by "that P". [*Relational conception of belief*]
(RP-ii) The content denoted by "that P" is the proposition expressed by "P". [*Standard semantics for 'that'-clauses*]

The only thing that is required for the above inferences to go through is that (RP-i) be true and that the content referred to by "that P" be the same throughout a given inference. Nothing more is required. It follows that (RP-ii) is *not* supported by the validity of the inferences in question. I conclude that we may reject (B) and maintain the Relational conception of belief (RP-i), if we drop thesis (RP-ii) and provide an alternative semantics for 'that'-clauses. That is what I shall do in 18.3. As for now, I want to discuss the interpretation of (RP-ii) and indicate the sort of problem it raises.

## 18.2 Rejecting the Relational principle

Taken at face value, (RP-ii) is hard to make sense of, for there is no such thing as 'the' proposition expressed by a sentence "P". As the proposition expressed by a sentence depends on the context (unless the sentence in question belongs to the mythical category of 'eternal sentences'), "P" will express different propositions with respect to different contexts. Taking the possible indexicality of "P" into account, one may identify 'the' proposition expressed by the embedded sentence "P" in a belief report as the proposition which "P" would express, were it uttered in isolation in the same surroundings.[4] On that construal, the expression "that P" as it occurs in a given belief report names the proposition which "P" would express were it uttered in isolation in the very context in which the belief report is issued. This provides us with the following interpretation of (RP-ii):

(RP-ii)  The content denoted by the expression "that P" as it occurs in a particular utterance **u** is the proposition which "P" would express, were it uttered in isolation in the same surroundings as **u**.

Thus understood, I think (RP-ii) must be rejected. It can itself can be decomposed in two theses:

(RP-ii/α)  The content denoted by the expression "that P" in a particular utterance **u** is the proposition expressed by the sentence "P" as it occurs in **u**.

(RP-ii/β)  The proposition expressed by the embedded sentence "P" as it occurs in a complex utterance **u** is the proposition it would express if it were uttered in isolation in the same surroundings as **u**.

There are objections to both theses, I think. I will start by criticizing the second one, which is the version of the Principle of Innocence offered by Crimmins and Perry.[5]

As we saw in chapters 13 to 16, which proposition a given utterance expresses does not only depend on those external features of the context of utterance (who is speaking, when, to whom, and so forth) which determine the semantic value of indexical expressions, but also on whatever optional p-processes may come into play in the interpretation process. Now optional p-processes themselves are highly context-sensitive: they (and therefore the proposition expressed) depend on the context in a way which goes far beyond mere indexicality. Changing the context in which a sentence is tokened, *however slightly*, may be sufficient to change the p-processes which apply to the meaning of the sentence to yield the proposition expressed. In particular, *embedding* a sentence into a sentence frame such as 'John believes that . . .' may be sufficient to change the semantic value of the embedded sentence, even if the external features of the context (the 'surroundings') are left unchanged. In what follows, I shall give a couple of examples in which a sentence "P", which would express a given proposition with respect to a context C if it were uttered in isolation in C, does not seem to express that proposition if we suppose it to be tokened in C only as the embedded part of a belief report. Such examples contradict (RP-ii/β), hence they cast doubt on (RP-ii), the view that 'that'-clauses name the proposition which the embedded sentence would express if it were uttered in isolation.

In 16.4 I discussed Nunberg's most striking example of descriptive used indexical; I shall modify it slightly here. John is giving me my fiftieth chess lesson; I have just made a dubious move. Now consider two sentences which John might utter in this context:

1  You often get in trouble with that move.
2  According to Horowitz, you often get in trouble with that move.

I think that if John utters 1 in that context, the sentence 'you often get in trouble with that move' will be interpreted as expressing a singular proposition about me: John will be interpreted as saying that *I* often get in trouble with that move. But if John utters 2 in the same context, the same sentence 'you often get in trouble with that move' will no longer be interpreted as expressing a singular proposition about me (a proposition that would be the content of Horowitz's reported speech act), since Horowitz has never heard of me. Rather, as Nunberg points out, the pronoun's interpretation in 2 won't be its reference, but some non-basic semantic value derived from the latter through a primary pragmatic process of transfer, namely the concept of 'whoever makes the move which has just been made'. This change of interpretation (from basic to non-basic) is due to the change of context manifested by the addition of 'according to Horowitz'. Even though the context in which we suppose 1 and 2 to be uttered is the same, the context in which the sentence 'you often get into trouble with that move' is tokened is *not* the same in both cases: the fact that the sentence occurs in isolation or as part of a more complex utterance constitutes a change of context, one that is sufficient to induce a change of interpretation.

A different sort of example, mentioned by Jean-Pierre Dupuy in conversation, involves sentences 3 and 4:

3  Mitterrand is an ass.
4  My son believes that Mitterrand is an ass.

The context is this: Dupuy and his young son live in Paris near to Notre Dame. In front of Notre Dame stands a street-seller and an ass, called 'Mitterrand', which the street-seller uses to attract the tourists around. Dupuy's son knows the ass, but has hardly heard of President François Mitterrand. Dupuy's point is that, if he (Dupuy) were to utter 3, his utterance 'Mitterrand is an ass' would express a singular proposition about François Mitterrand, but if he utters 4 instead, the same words 'Mitterrand is an ass' will no longer express that proposition: rather, they will express the proposition that the individual called 'Mitterrand' is a certain sort of animal, or more perspicuously, that the name 'Mitterrand' refers to a certain sort of animal; it is that metalinguistic proposition which is the content of the belief ascribed to Dupuy's son in 4.

In these examples, it does not seem that the 'that'-clause names the proposition which the embedded sentence would express, were it uttered in isolation in the same surroundings. Rather, it names the proposition which the embedded sentence expresses in the context of the complex utterance, and that proposition is different from the proposition which the embedded sentence would express if it were uttered in isolation.

In defence of (RP-ii), it must be acknowledged that examples like Nunberg's and Dupuy's are rather special. The indexical in Nunberg's example and the proper name in Dupuy's example are given non-referential interpretations: the indexical is given a generic interpretation in Nunberg's example, and the proper name is given a metalinguistic (autonymous) interpretation in Dupuy's example. It would not be unreasonable to set such examples aside in order to concentrate on standard examples of opaque belief reports, that is, on examples like 'John believes that Cicero was poor' (in which 'Cicero' is opaquely interpreted but nevertheless refers to Cicero). But that move would not be sufficient to save (RP-ii), for counter-examples can be found in that category also.

In 18.4 we shall consider a famous example put forward by Mark Richard (1983). In that example, as Crimmins and Perry pointed out, the same sentence 'you are in danger' embedded in various instances of the schema '. . . believe(s) that you are in danger' serves to ascribe *different* belief contents even though the external features of the context relevant to fix the semantic value of the indexical constituents of that sentence remain the same. Richard imagines a man, say Jim, talking to a woman on the phone and at the same time watching a woman in a phone booth; unbeknown to him, the two women are the same. We also suppose that he knows a man is watching the woman he is talking to on the phone, without realizing that he himself is that man. When Jim says 'I believe you are in danger' in that context, the content which he ascribes to himself includes a mode of presentation of the addressee as the person to whom he is talking on to phone. He ascribes to himself the belief

'That person to whom I am talking on the phone is in danger', or something like that. But if, in the same context, he says 'The man watching you believes that you are in danger', the ascribed content is fairly different: the belief content he ascribes to the watching man (viz. himself) is something like 'That person whom I see in the phone booth is in danger' (Crimmins & Perry, 1989, p. 708). This provides further evidence that the content referred to and ascribed to the believer in a belief report is sensitive to the embedding, hence that it cannot be equated with the proposition which the embedded sentence would express, were it uttered in isolation in the same surroundings.

In Richard's example, an optional, highly context-sensitive p-process is at work, as in Dupuy's and Nunberg's examples. The process in question is a specific process of enrichment which I call 'quasi-singularization' (19.2); it takes us from the (singular) proposition expressed by the embedded sentence to a (quasi-singular) thought-content including a contextually provided mode of presentation. Contrary to the p-processes involved in Nunberg's and Dupuy's examples, quasi-singularization arguably does not affect the proposition expressed by the embedded sentence, for the proposition expressed by a sentence is individuated on a truth-conditional basis, whereas the mode of presentation which quasi-singularization provides is truth-conditionally irrelevant.[6] Hence it can be maintained that in Richard's example the embedded sentence expresses the same singular proposition it would if not embedded (19.3). On that construal, it is (RP-ii/$\alpha$) rather than (RP-ii/$\beta$) which is in trouble. Richard's example shows that even when embedding a sentence within a belief report does not affect the proposition expressed by that sentence, the content named by the 'that'-clause and ascribed to the believer may be different from (e.g. richer than) the proposition in question.

Several authors – including Crimmins and Perry – have attempted to save (RP-ii) by drawing a distinction between the ascribed belief content and the reference of the 'that'-clause. Thus, faced with Richard's example, they maintain that the 'that'-clause names a singular proposition (that which the embedded sentence would express if not embedded) while at the same time admitting that the ascribed belief content is *not* a singular proposition but something richer. That 'dualist' strategy will be criticized in chapter 19. As for now, I want to highlight what I take to be the fundamental inadequacy of (RP-ii), and present an alternative semantics for 'that'-clauses.

## 18.3 The reference of 'that'-clauses

The similarity between 'that'-clauses and quotations is often emphasized – rightly in my view. Proponents of (RP-ii) present the similarity as follows: a 'that'-clause refers to the proposition expressed by the embedded sentence, while a sentence-within-quotes (a 'quotation', for short) refers to the sentence which occurs within the quotation marks. In other words, the reference is either the content of the words (indirect construction) or the words themselves (direct construction). But I think there is another aspect under which the two types of construction are similar, which is ignored on that construal. In both cases, it seems to me, the reference is *underdetermined* in much the same sense in which the reference of, say, a demonstrative pronoun is. What I am calling 'underdetermination' is to be distinguished from mere 'context-dependence'. The reference of words like 'I' or 'today' is context-dependent, but it does not exhibit the relevant feature of underdetermination: in a given situation, the meaning of a pure indexical like 'I' or 'today' fully determines what the reference is, in such a way that the latter does not depend upon considerations of plausibility. Not so with demonstratives. The reference of 'he' or 'that' is not determined by any rigid rule; it is determined by answering questions such as, 'Who or what can the speaker plausibly be taken to be referring to, in that context?'[7] The same thing holds, I believe, of quotations and 'that'-clauses. I do not think there is, associated with either construction, a 'rule' or 'character' which, in context, fully determines what the reference is – e.g. the rule that a 'that'-clause refers to the proposition expressed by the embedded sentence, or the rule that a quotation refers to the sentence occurring within the quotes. The reference of quotations and 'that'-clauses is determined in a much more flexible manner.

Consider quotations first: they do not necessarily refer to the sentence type which occurs within the quotation marks (Sperber & Wilson, 1986, p. 228). Suppose we are in a foreign country, whose language I happen to master. I am talking to the inn-keeper. My friend asks me: What did he say? I reply: He said, 'Why don't you have any luggage?' Clearly, I am not referring to the English sentence 'Why don't you have any luggage?' here. I am not saying that the inn-keeper uttered *that* sentence. The sentence I am referring to is a *counterpart* of that English sentence in the own language of the inn-keeper. It need not even be a single sentence: I may *summarize*, in direct speech, what the inn-keeper said in his own language. In such cases, the relation between the reference of the quotation and the sentence which occurs within the quotes is not that of identity, but a suitable resemblance relation.

In the same way, 'that'-clauses need not name the proposition expressed by the embedded sentence. Like the reference of quotations, the reference of 'that'-clauses is not determined by a rule or character which picks out a unique reference independent of any consideration of plausibility. Rather, I suggest that the reference of a 'that'-clause is contextually determined in accordance with two very general constraints:[8]

(i) a *top-down* constraint: the reference must be a plausible candidate for the status of content of the ascribed belief or speech act (or, more generally, for the status of argument for whatever predicate is involved in the sentence).[9]

(ii) a *bottom-up* constraint: the reference must be recoverable from the embedded sentence, i.e. it must be possible (and easy) to reach a content satisfying constraint (i) by 'interpreting' the embedded sentence.

The important point is that the process of interpretation mentioned in (ii) may involve *optional p-processes*, processes like enrichment or transfer which take the interpreter from the basic semantic value of a sub-expression to some further, non-basic value. In other words, the 'interpretation' mentioned in (ii) need not be 'strictly literal' (as some would say) or (as I prefer to say) 'minimalist'. Whether or not optional pragmatic processes come into play is actually determined by the first, top-down constraint, that is, on a purely pragmatic basis.[10] What the second, bottom-up constraint requires is merely that there be a (reasonably short) *interpretive path* leading from the embedded sentence, with its linguistic meaning, to the ascribed content.

We now see quite clearly why (B), the second premiss in Frege's Puzzle, must be rejected. Even if two sentences "P" and "Q", which express the same proposition in isolation, continue to express that proposition when embedded in a belief sentence such as 'John believes that...' "that P" and "that Q" need not denote the proposition in question. On the view I have sketched, a 'that'-clause may refer to a richer thought-content arrived at by enriching the expressed proposition with a contextually salient mode of presentation. That sort of enrichment, quasi-singularization, is one particular type of optional p-process likely to come into play in the interpretation of 'that'-clauses, and it may well be sensitive to those aspects under which "P" differs from "Q". Hence "John believes that P" and "John believes that Q" may express different propositions even though the embedded sentences "P" and "Q" express the same proposition.

Note that we need not give up Innocence, on that account. Firstly, I am not saying that referential terms behave *differently* when they occur in simple sentences and when they occur in the embedded parts of belief sentences. Optional p-processes may come into play when a simple sentence is uttered in isolation (even though no implicit ascription of belief is made). Secondly, the typical p-process which explains failures of substitutivity in belief contexts is quasi-singularization, and it can be maintained that the embedded sentence in such cases does express the same proposition it would if not embedded; hence even the strong form of Innocence advocated by Crimmins and Perry[11] can be preserved, on that account – or at least it can be preserved if we consider only standard examples of opaque belief reports. (I shall return to that issue in 19.3 and 20.3.)

## 18.4 The context-sensitivity of 'that'-clauses

According to the account sketched above, the reference of "that P" in a belief report may but need not be the proposition (Normally) expressed by "P". If "P" (Normally) expresses a singular proposition, still the ascribed belief content may be quasi-singular and involve a mode of presentation contextually suggested by the ascriber's use of a certain expression or by some other contextual feature (as in Richard's 'phone booth' example, to be discussed below). The ascribed content may even be a general proposition, as in some of the examples discussed above (e.g. Nunberg's example). What the 'that'-clause refers to – which content the report ascribes – is determined on a pragmatic basis; the only constraint is that the content referred to be recoverable from the embedded sentence through a process of interpretation which need not be minimalist but may involve optional p-processes such as enrichment or transfer.[12]

If I am right, the context-sensitivity of belief-reports, emphasized by many authors (e.g. Richard, 1990 and Jacob, 1990), is due to a more general phenomenon, namely the underdetermination of the reference of 'that'-clauses. Given that underdetermination, any feature of the context, including the words which the speaker actually uses, may play a role in determining the reference of a 'that'-clause, by making some interpretive hypothesis more plausible or relevant than others.[13] As an example, let's go back to the Cicero/Tully example. Suppose someone says, 'John believes that Cicero was poor.' If the hearer contextually assumes that the ascriber is being 'faithful' to the believer (17.2), he will be led to assume that the ascribed belief concerning Cicero involves a mode of presentation or encyclopedia entry which includes the descriptive concept associated (*qua* linguistic mode of presentation) with the name 'Cicero' used by the ascriber. That descriptive concept is the concept 'called "Cicero".' Hence the hearer will assume that the believer thinks of Cicero as 'Cicero'; he will construe the reference of the 'that'-clause as a quasi-singular proposition involving a certain (*de re*) concept over and beyond the reference of the term 'Cicero'. If the speaker had uttered 'John believes that Tully was poor' instead, then the same presumption would have led the interpreter to construe the reference of the 'that'-clause as a quasi-singular proposition involving a *different* concept. Failure of substitutivity is thereby accounted for. If one substitutes a term t for a co-referential term t' in the embedded clause of a belief sentence, that may be sufficient to change the reference of the 'that'-clause, and therefore to change the proposition expressed by the complex utterance. (More on this in 20.3.)

Stephen Schiffer has raised an objection to that sort of account. There is, he says, a good reason why a direct reference theorist should be wary of accepting the view that, on the opaque reading of a belief report such as 'John believes that Cicero was poor', the ascribed belief content is a quasi-singular (rather than a singular) proposition which incorporates contextually determined modes of presentation of the objects referred to (as well as those objects themselves). The direct reference theorist claims that the content of an *assertion* made by means of an utterance such as 'Cicero was poor' is a singular proposition consisting of Cicero and the property of being poor. (As usual, I ignore tenses.) According to Schiffer, that claim is hard to reconcile with the view just stated concerning belief reports. The direct reference theorist faces the following dilemma according to Schiffer. Either he provides *different* representations for the contents ascribed by 'Ralph says that Fido is a dog' (assertion report) and by 'Ralph believes that Fido is a dog' (belief report), and that 'would be worse than bizarre' (Schiffer, 1987, p. 460), or he allows 'that the report of what Ralph said can be represented in the same mode-of-presentation way as the one just considered for the report of what he believes', but 'thus to admit modes of presentation into the analysis of what is said would be to deny that the content of the utterance of "Fido is a dog" was exhausted by the singular proposition' (Schiffer, 1987, p. 461).

On my analysis, it is not bizarre, let alone 'worse than bizarre', to maintain that the content ascribed by 'Ralph says that Fido is a dog' is different from that ascribed by 'Ralph believes that Fido is a dog.' Which content is ascribed – what the 'that'-clause refers to – depends on the context in the same sense in which the reference of a demonstrative depends on the context. As I said above, any feature of the context of utterance, *including the words which the speaker actually uses in phrasing the report*, may play a role in determining the reference of the 'that'-clause, by making some interpretive hypothesis more plausible or relevant than others. The Cicero/Tully example is a case in which a difference of phrasing in the embedded sentence affects the reference of the 'that'-clause. But Crimmins and Perry have shown that other examples, such as Richard's 'phone booth' example (suitably interpreted), involve differences of phrasing which also affect the ascribed content even though they occur *outside* the embedded sentence, in the main clause of the belief report. That is clearly what happens in the case discussed by Schiffer: replacing 'believes' by 'says' in 'Ralph believes that Fido is a dog' may affect the interpretation of the 'that'-clause, or so I will argue.

Let us go back to Richard's example first. Richard (1983) imagines the following situation:

> Consider A – a man stipulated to be intelligent, rational, a competent speaker of English, etc. – who both sees a woman, across the street, in a phone booth, and is speaking to a woman through a phone. He does not realize that the woman to whom he is speaking – B, to give her a name – is the woman he sees. He perceives her to be in some danger – a runaway steamroller, say, is bearing down upon her phone booth. A waves at the woman; he says nothing into the phone. (Richard, 1983, p. 184)

Richard points out that A could utter 5 in such a situation, but not 6:

5   I believe that she is in danger.
6   I believe that you are in danger.

(It is understood, Richard says, that uses of 'she' are accompanied by demonstrations of the woman across the street, while uses of 'you' are addressed to the woman through the telephone.) The natural explanation for this fact is that 5 and 6 report different beliefs involving different modes of presentation of what is (unbeknown to the believer) the same reference. The speaker holds the first belief, but not the second one; it follows that 5 is true, while 6 is false.

Richard, however, denies that 5 and 6 diverge in truth-value. He reasons as follows. 5 is obviously true, since A believes that she (the woman he sees) is in danger. Now from the truth of 5 as uttered by A it follows that, 'if B were to utter:

7   The man watching me believes that I am in danger.

(even through the telephone) she would speak truly' (Richard, 1983, p. 185). To provide a set-up for 7 (and for Richard's next example), Crimmins and Perry suppose that B sees a man (in fact, A himself) in a building across the street waving frantically. Amused, she utters 7, thereby speaking truly. A believes her, and, echoing her, utters 8:

8   The man watching you believes that you are in danger.

The situation, then, is one in which A would deny 6 but accepts 8; he takes 6 to be false and 8 true. Now Richard (1983) assumes that the *same* belief content (viz. the proposition expressed by the embedded sentence 'you are in danger') is ascribed to the *same* believer (viz. A, alternatively referred to by 'I' and by 'the man watching you') by 6 and 8, so he thinks A is wrong to take 6 and 8 to differ in truth-value. Since 8 is demonstrably true,[14] Richard concludes that 6 is also true, even though A does not realize it.

Richard's conclusion is fairly counterintuitive. As Crimmins and Perry emphasize, 'the natural intuition ... is that a use of 6 in the described circumstances would make a false claim' (Crimmins & Perry, 1989, p. 708). To preserve that intuition, the obvious move – one which Crimmins and Perry make – consists in denying Richard's premiss that 6 and 8 ascribe the same belief content to A. Thus Crimmins and Perry hold, rightly in my view, that the content ascribed by 6 involves a mode of presentation of the person referred to which includes the concept 'person to whom I am talking on the phone', while the content ascribed by 8 does *not* include that mode of presentation. That is so even though the *same* sentence occurs embedded in 6 and 8, the only difference between 6 and 8 being a difference between the expressions used to refer to the believer in the *main clause* of the report. As Crimmins and Perry conclude, 'Richard's case is especially interesting because it shows how a contextual shift can be brought about by a change in wording outside the embedded sentence in a belief report' (Crimmins & Perry, 1989, p. 709).

In the case discussed by Schiffer, it is even more obvious that replacing 'believes' by 'says' in the main clause of a belief report may affect the ascribed content. As I repeatedly stressed, following Schiffer himself, one difference between assertions and beliefs is that the content of an assertion may well be a singular proposition, while the content – or at least, the complete content – of a belief *cannot* be a singular proposition: one cannot entertain a belief about an object without thinking of that object in a certain way or under a certain mode of presentation (Schiffer, 1978, p. 181). The content of a belief, therefore, can only be *quasi*-singular, in Schiffer's own terminology (Schiffer, 1978, p. 182). This widely recognized difference between assertions and beliefs is sufficient to account for the difference of interpretation induced by the substitution of 'says' for 'believes' in a report. If the speaker utters 'Ralph asserts that Fido is a dog', it is plausible to construe the 'that'-clause as referring to the singular proposition <Fido, doghood>, because that singular proposition is a plausible candidate for the status of content of an assertion; but an utterance of 'Ralph believes that Fido is a dog' lends itself less easily to such a singular interpretation, for a singular proposition is *not* a plausible candidate for the status of belief content.

Russell's famous example of the man who believes that a certain yacht is longer than it is can also be mentioned in connection with the issue raised by Schiffer. The self-contradictory proposition that the yacht is actually longer than it is is not a plausible candidate for the status of belief content, if the believer is assumed rational (as believers normally are). But suppose the believer is a notorious madman, and the point of the ascription is precisely to show how crazy he is. Suppose I say: 'John is really crazy. Now he believes that Russell's yacht is longer than it is, and that nothing is identical to itself!' In such a context, the self-contradictory proposition that the yacht is longer than it is is a more plausible candidate for the status of ascribed content than any other proposition recoverable from the embedded sentence. Again, it's a difference *outside* the embedded sentence which prompts this major change in the interpretation of the 'that'-clause.

One paragraph back I said that a singular proposition is not a plausible candidate for the status of belief content. That must be qualified. From the fact that the complete content of a belief can only be *quasi*-singular, since it necessarily involves modes of presentation of the objects of belief, it does not follow that it is impossible to interpret the 'that'-clause in a belief report as referring to a singular proposition. What is impossible is to interpret the 'that'-clause *both* as referring to a singular proposition *and* as specifying the complete content of the belief. Thus it is possible to interpret the 'that'-clause in a belief report as referring to a singular proposition, if that proposition is construed as only a *partial* specification of the reported belief. That is what happens in so-called transparent readings of belief sentences. The referring expression occurring in the embedded sentence is taken to give us the reference of the belief (the object the belief is about), without specifying the way that object is thought about. On that reading, the linguistic mode of presentation associated with the expression only reflects the speaker's way of thinking of the reference, but the believer's way of thinking is left indeterminate. In such cases, only the truth-conditional content of the belief is specified: the believer is said to believe a certain singular proposition, and that must be under a particular mode of presentation (since singular propositions are objects of belief only under modes of presentation), but the latter is not specified. With respect to such cases, Salmon's equivalence holds: to say that someone believes a singular proposition is to say that *there is* a mode of presentation under which he or she believes it.[15]

One advantage of the analysis of belief reports expounded in this chapter is its high degree of flexibility. Other theories on the market tend to be too rigid. Thus among those who recognize that a singular proposition can be an object of belief only under a mode of presentation, there have been two major tendencies. Some, like Salmon, have said that the mode of presentation in question is quantified over in belief reports, so that the proposition expressed by 'John believes that Cicero was poor' is the proposition that *there is* a mode of presentation under which John believes the singular proposition <Cicero, the property of being poor>. Others have said that the mode of presentation is 'contextually determined and implicitly referred to' (Schiffer, 1987, p. 460).[16] Thus Crimmins and Perry hold that modes of presentation 'are among the subject matter of belief reports (via the mechanism of unarticulated constituents), and are not merely quantified over' (Crimmins & Perry, 1989, p. 698). On my view, modes of presentation are *sometimes* quantified over and *sometimes* contextually referred to and incorporated into the ascribed contents. The first type of theory suits transparent readings of belief sentences involving referential terms; the second type of theory suits opaque readings; the right theory must suit both, and it is a merit of mine that it does.[17]

## Notes

1 My reflection on the necessity of rejecting (B) was prompted by Schiffer's presentation of Frege's Puzzle in (an ancestor of) Schiffer (1987).
2 See e.g. Bealer, 1982, p. 223ff; Salmon, 1986a, pp. 5–6; Schiffer, 1987, p. 459.
3 It is sometimes said that there is no alternative to the standard analysis of 'believes' as a dyadic predicate. But Arthur Prior is famous for having put forward such an alternative (Prior, 1963). 'That'-clauses are not the genuine semantic units, according to Prior; instead of construing 'believe' as a dyadic predicate and 'that'-clauses as singular terms, Prior takes '... believes that ...' to be a connecting phrase forming a sentence out of a singular term and a sentence. Thus we have: 'John/believes that/p' instead of 'John/ believes/that p.' Prior's parsing emphasizes the similarity between epistemic operators such as 'John believes that' and modal operators such as 'It is possible that', as well as the similarity between belief sentences and constructions such as 'According to John, p' (Fauconnier, 1985). To account for the type of inference mentioned in the text, Prior appeals to substitutional quantification. One may dislike that move, but I think the issue cannot be settled a priori; some empirical evidence has been adduced in favour of Prior's viewpoint (e.g. by Rundle, 1968, pp. 194–5), and it must at least be considered. Thus it has been shown that *even intransitive verbs* can go into the 'X Vs that p' construction. We may say "He protested that p", even though 'protest' is an intransitive verb which does not take a direct object. This and related facts must be accounted for. (For an interesting discussion of these issues, see Rundle, 1979, ch. 7.)
4 The notion of 'surroundings' is intended to capture the *external* features of the context of utterance, i.e. who is speaking, when, where, to whom, and so forth. See Recanati, 1987a, p. 60ff.
5 According to Crimmins and Perry, Innocence is the claim that 'the utterances of the embedded sentences in belief reports express just the

propositions they would if not embedded' (Crimmins & Perry, 1989, p. 686).
6   It affects the truth-conditions of the global belief report, but that is another matter. See 20.3.
7   David Kaplan himself has come to the view that the main difference between demonstratives and pure indexicals is that the reference of a demonstrative is determined by the speaker's intentions rather than as a function of external features of the context of utterance (Kaplan, 1989b; on 'external' features of the context of utterance, see note 4 above).
8   As the informed reader will notice, the two constraints in question correspond to the two sides of Sperber and Wilson's notion of 'relevance'. See Sperber and Wilson (1986).
9   That constraint is fairly similar to that which is operative for determining the reference of a demonstrative such as 'he' or 'that'. In general, plausibility – together with accessibility – is what enables interpreters to succeed in finding out what the reference is despite the underdetermination of the latter.
10  Following Sperber and Wilson, we may assume that the interpretation process obeys a principle of economy, it such a way that it stops when an interpretation satisfying (i) is found. (In Sperber and Wilson's framework, the first, i.e. most easily accessible, interpretation consistent with the pragmatic requirement of 'relevance' is retained.) Does this mean that optional p-processes come into play for any given sub-expression only if the Normal, minimalist interpretation of the expression appears not likely to contribute to any interpretation of the utterance satisfying constraint (i)? In other words, should a 'Normal' interpretation of the utterance be tried first? I do not think so. The Normal interpretation of the global utterance need not even be *considered*. In a given context, it may be that a sub-expression (e.g. a lexical item) directly calls to mind a metonymical or metaphorical interpretation, because the latter is psychologically very accessible in that context. In such situations, the transfer process occurs *locally*: a lexical item calls to mind a contextually accessible non-basic interpretation, and it is the latter which goes into the interpretation of the utterance and undergoes a composition process with other semantic values associated with other sub-expressions in the utterance. Whether or not the Normal interpretation of the utterance *would* satisfy constraint (i) is an issue which is not even raised: the Normal interpretation of the utterance is not considered first (hence it is not considered at all), because in that context it turns out to be less accessible than the actual interpretation. (I take the view just expounded to be very close to that put forward by Sperber and Wilson about metaphor when they stress that the literal interpretation is not even considered.)

11  See note 5 above.
12  As we shall see below (note 15), the reference of the 'that'-clause may also be less than fully propositional.
13  Richard (after Schiffer) talks of 'indexicality' in connection with belief reports, since the same sentence "John believes that P" can be used to ascribe different beliefs in different situations. Richard and Schiffer do not make any distinction between the two sorts of primary pragmatic process I distinguished in chapters 13–14, namely saturation on the one hand and optional or non-minimalist processes on the other. When a mode of presentation is contextually provided, we have a (non-minimalist) process of enrichment; we also have a non-minimalist process, namely transfer, in e.g. Nunberg's chess example. So it seems that the sort of context-sensitivity at play here is different from indexicality, insofar as indexicality involves a minimalist p-process, namely saturation. But in fact the situation is more complex than that: if I am right about belief reports, optional processes such as enrichment and transfer occur as part of a global (minimalist) process of saturation, namely the process of finding a suitable contextual reference for the 'that'-clause. That process is minimalist in the sense that, without it, the sentence "John believes that P" would not express a definite proposition. To that extent, one may talk of 'indexicality' in connection with belief reports. Yet there is another problem: given the distinction between the type of context-dependence associated with pure indexicals in the sense of Kaplan, and the underdetermination characteristic of demonstratives and (if I am right) 'that'-clauses, talking of indexicality might suggest, quite misleadingly, that the context-dependence at play in belief reports belongs with the former variety. That is why I prefer to talk of semantic underdetermination rather than of indexicality.
14  'If $B$'s utterance of 3 through the telephone, heard by $A$, would be true, then $A$ would speak truly, were he to utter 4 through the phone' (Richard, 1983, pp. 185–6).
15  The ascribed thought content can be left unspecified under other aspects than the mode of presentation. As we shall see in 19.4, there are cases in which (some constituent of) the *truth-conditional content* of the reported belief is quantified over rather than explicitly specified. When the indefinite description in 'John believes that *a doctor* wants to marry him' is given a 'specific' interpretation (whether opaque or transparent), it is said that there is a person $x$ such that John believes a proposition including $x$ and the property of wanting to marry John as constituents; the person in question, hence the proposition which is the truth-conditional content of John's belief, is described in general terms without being fully specified. In the standard, transparent reading of 'John believes Russell's yacht is longer than it is', John's belief content

is also underspecified: it is said that there is some length $n$, greater than the actual length of Russell's yacht, such that John believes the length of Russell's yacht to be $n$. Another interesting example, 'Most Europeans believe that they are poor', will be discussed in chapter 19, note 10.

These cases raise an apparent difficulty for the theory I have sketched, according to which the 'that'-clause in a belief report is a referential expression, or at least, has a referential role. The examples I have just mentioned show that sometimes the content ascribed to the believer is not fully specified. One might argue that in such cases the believer's thought content is not referred to in the strong sense of the term but merely *described*. Far from referring to a particular content and saying that the agent believes it, the speaker says that among the agent's beliefs *there is* one with such and such characteristics. This view I call 'thesis Q'. There is a lot to be said for it.

> Thesis Q: When the ascribed belief is underspecified (quantified over), the believer's thought content is not referred to but merely described.

I actually accept Q, but I deny that it raises a difficulty for my theory. One can hold that an underspecified ascription merely describes the agent's thought-content while maintaining that the 'that'-clause refers, in such a context. In other words, Q does *not* entail Q*:

> Thesis Q*: When the ascribed belief is underspecified (quantified over), the 'that'-clause does not refer, but merely describes.

As against Q*, one can maintain that *the 'that'-clause refers, even when the truth-conditional content of the ascribed belief is underspecified*, that is, even when some constituent of the ascribed content is quantified over. What the 'that'-clause refers to in such cases is an incomplete (schematic) thought-content. To make that suggestion consistent with Q we need only generalize Salmon's equivalence: *To say that someone believes a schematic thought-content is to say that she believes some completion of the schema.* Thus by saying that the agent believes a certain schema (referred to by the 'that'-clause), the speaker 'describes' the agent's belief as an instance of the schema. The content of the agent's belief is not referred to, on this view, but the 'that'-clause nevertheless refers to *something*, namely a schema of which the agent's belief content is an instance.

16 Schiffer's first statement to that effect is to be found in Schiffer, 1977, p. 31ff; see also Schiffer, 1978, p. 183. His latest statement is in Schiffer, forthcoming.

17 Other theories fare as well as mine in that respect. Thus Fodor (1990) acknowledges that transparency is a limiting case of opacity: the mode of presentation may be more or less fully specified, and sometimes it's not specified, but merely quantified over (see 19.3). Schiffer himself, in the early paper mentioned in note 2, mentions that possibility (Schiffer, 1977, p. 40, note 10), and in his latest paper he accounts for it by saying that the mode of presentation implicitly referred to is a *type* of mode of presentation which can be more or less fully specified and may also be left wholly unspecified (transparent readings); in the latter case we can say that the modes of presentation are quantified over. See also Stich (1983, ch. 6) and Crimmins and Perry (1989, section IV).

# Chapter 19

# Comparison with other accounts

## 19.1 Unitary vs. dualist accounts of belief reports

The account of belief reports offered in chapter 18 is very similar to recent accounts by Crimmins and Perry (1989), Jacob (1990), Fodor (1990), Richard (1990) and Schiffer (forthcoming).[1] We all accept the following theses:

(i) A belief report (opaquely understood) specifies the narrow content of the reported belief, that is, the way the believer thinks of the state of affairs that constitutes the truth-conditional content of the belief.

(ii) That component of the meaning of the utterance is 'pragmatic' in the sense that it is not part of the conventional meaning of the words used in the belief report; so it's not the belief sentence *per se*, but only the belief sentence *qua* uttered in a particular context, that conveys the relevant specification concerning the 'how' (the narrow content) of the reported belief.

(iii) Although pragmatic and contextual, the specification in question is relevant to the truth-conditions of the belief report: it's part of what the belief ascriber *says*, not merely of what she 'implicates'.

Theses (i) and (ii) are common to the above-mentioned accounts and to the Implicature Theory. Thesis (iii) is where the former depart from the latter. As Crimmins and Perry say, 'it is a mistake to relegate pragmatics to matters of felicity and implicature. In the case of belief reports, it is central to understanding content and truth' (Crimmins & Perry, 1989, p. 711). Richard and Schiffer both claim that belief sentences are 'indexical' or involve a 'hidden indexical'; this claim captures the intuition that the relevant component of utterance meaning is both pragmatic (contextual) and part of what is said by the utterance.

In this chapter I want to make clear where my own account departs from that offered by the philosophers I have just mentioned (and others who hold similar views). There are two main differences, I believe. The first difference concerns the Relational principle, which I reject (18.2). All other authors except, perhaps, Stich (1983) accept the view that what a 'that'-clause names is (and can only be) the proposition expressed by the embedded sentence – a view which, according to me, does not do justice to the high degree of context-sensitivity exhibited by the reference of 'that'-clauses. The second difference is less salient and I shall lay stress on it in this chapter. It concerns the general structure of the account. As I shall now set out to explain, the account I favour is *unitary*, while that offered by the above-mentioned authors is *dualist*.

To see what the characterization of an account of belief reports as unitary or dualist amounts to, we must consider the entities with which such an account is supposed to deal. There are three, namely:

(a) the proposition expressed by (or, rather, the semantic content of) the embedded sentence;[2]
(b) the reference of the 'that'-clause;
(c) the ascribed belief content.

An account is unitary if and only if it equates (a), (b) and (c). That is the sort of account I shall argue for in this chapter. On the view I shall defend, the report *ascribes* a certain belief content to the believer; the embedded sentence *expresses* that content, in the context of the belief report; and the 'that'-clause *refers* to the belief content thereby expressed. By contrast, a dualist account draws a distinction between (a), the proposition expressed by the embedded sentence, and (c), the ascribed belief content. Thus Fodor or Crimmins and Perry insist on distinguishing what the embedded sentence expresses from the content ascribed to the believer. The embedded sentence, they hold, expresses a singular proposition, while the content ascribed to the believer may well include a mode of presentation.[3]

There are two sorts of dualist view depending on whether we equate, or distinguish, (a) and (b), the proposition expressed by the embedded sentence and the reference of the 'that'-clause. Fodor or Crimmins and Perry, like most authors, equate (a) and (b), that is, they take the 'that'-clause to refer to what the embedded sentence expresses; but there is another possibility for a dualist: one may take the embedded sentence in an opaquely understood belief report such as 'John believes that Cicero was poor' to express a singular proposition, while maintaining that the 'that'-clause does *not* refer to that singular proposition but to something richer, viz. a belief content consisting of that singular proposition together with a particular mode of presentation. That version of the dualist view, contrary to the first one, is consistent with the semantics for 'that'-clauses offered in chapter 18 and the rejection of the Relational principle.

To sum up, there are (at least) three possible types of theory, namely the following:

*Dualist theories:*
1. (a) = (b) ≠ (c)
2. (a) ≠ (b) = (c)

*Unitary theory:*
3. (a) = (b) = (c)

By equating (b) and (c) – the reference of the 'that'-clause and the ascribed belief content – the account of belief reports presented in chapter 18 excludes the first type of dualist theory, advocated by virtually all the authors who accept theses (i)–(iii) above (Richard, Fodor, Crimmins & Perry, Jacob, and Schiffer).[4] But it remains basically neutral between the second type of dualist theory and the unitary theory. In this chapter, I want to go further and argue against dualism in general.

## 19.2 The incoherence of dualism

In this section, I would like to emphasize what I take to be a tension within the dualist account – a tension which should lead the dualist at least to adopt the second type of dualist theory instead of the first one. I shall mostly use Crimmins and Perry's lucid presentation in what follows, but what I say about them applies to other dualist proposals, such as Schiffer's, Fodor's, Richard's, or Jacob's.

These authors emphasize the context-sensitivity of belief reports, which they (rightly) think has been underestimated by previous researchers, but at the same time they perpetuate the tradition of playing down context-sensitivity, when they deal with the sentence embedded in the belief report.

The account by Crimmins and Perry makes essential use of Perry's important observation that the proposition expressed by an utterance may involve an 'unarticulated constituent', i.e. a propositional constituent to which no expression corresponds in the sentence (Perry, 1986c). Such propositional constituents are not 'marked' in the sentence – not even through some indexical variable in need of contextual instantiation. Crimmins and Perry give the following example:

> If I say, 'it is raining', you understand me as claiming that it rains at that time at some place the context supplies. It often is, but need not be, the place of utterance... The phenomenon of unarticulated constituency is similar to that of indexicality in the reliance on context. But the two phenomena should not be conflated. If we say, 'It's raining here', an expression in our statement identifies the place. The place is articulated in a context-sensitive way. In the case of indexicals, expression and context share in the job of identifying the constituent... In a case of underarticulation, there is no expression to determine the constituent in this way. (Crimmins & Perry, 1989, pp. 699–700)

Arguably, in examples such as 'It is raining', the relevant propositional constituent must be contextually provided for the sentence to express a definite proposition, that is, something truth-evaluable. But, as we saw in chapters 13–14, unarticulated constituents may also be contextually provided which are not necessary for the sentence to express a definite proposition. Robyn Carston gives a number of examples, like the utterance 'He took out his key and opened the door' which is naturally understood as meaning that he opened the door *with the key*. In that example the instrumental constituent 'with the key' is neither articulated (no prepositional phrase is present at any level of linguistic analysis, Carston argues) nor necessary for truth-evaluation (without that unarticulated constituent, the sentence would still express a definite, though less determinate, proposition, viz. the proposition that he took out his key and opened the door by some means or other).

Crimmins and Perry invoke the phenomenon of unarticulated constituency to account for belief reports. In their framework, what is explicitly stated by a belief report such as 'John believes that Cicero was poor' is that the believer, John, believes a certain singular proposition, viz. the proposition which the embedded sentence expresses; yet the statement also includes something which is not explicitly articulated but nevertheless belongs to what is said. That unarticulated constituent concerns the way John thinks of Cicero, his 'notion' of Cicero. Very often, when someone's belief about a particular object is reported, it is contextually manifest which representation (or 'notion') of that object the belief involves – how the believer thinks of that object; it is therefore possible for the speaker to ascribe a belief content which includes that notion, without explicitly specifying the notion in question, simply because the context supplies it. In such cases, Crimmins and Perry say, the notion is an unarticulated constituent of the ascribed belief. In Richard's example, discussed earlier (18.4), the same singular proposition (expressed by the embedded sentence 'you are in danger') is said to be believed by the same person $A$ (who is both the speaker and the man watching the addressee) in 'I believe you are in danger' and in 'The man watching you believes you are in danger'; yet a different unarticulated constituent is provided in each case, in such a way that the two utterances say different things: the belief content $A$ would ascribe to himself were he to utter 'I believe you are in danger' involves a certain notion of $B$ as the person to whom $A$ is talking on the phone, while the belief content $A$ ascribes to the watching man (viz. $A$ himself) when he says 'The man watching you believes you are in danger' involves a different notion, linked to the watching man's visual perception of $B$ (Crimmins & Perry, 1989, p. 708).

As I have just said, Crimmins and Perry start by pointing out that the semantic value of an utterance may depend on more than the (basic) semantic values of the sub-expressions which make up the sentence: unarticulated constituents may also go into the interpretation, they claim, if pragmatically required. That seems to be a fairly general point, not a specific one about belief reports. Belief reports are only a particular type of example in which an unarticulated constituent is supplied. But they also insist that the semantic value of the embedded sentence in e.g. 'John believes that Cicero was poor' is a singular proposition which does *not* include the unarticulated mode of presentation (e.g. John's notion of Cicero) which they say is contextually provided. That unarticulated constituent, they hold, is a constituent of the proposition expressed by the belief report but *not* a constituent of the (singular) proposition expressed by the embedded sentence. I believe there is a tension between these two claims – the general claim about unarticulated constituency, which provides the basis for their account of belief reports, and the particular claim that the embedded sentence in a belief report such as 'John believes that Cicero was poor' expresses a singular proposition uncontaminated by unarticulated constituents. If unarticulated constituents can contextually enrich the interpretation of an utterance such as 'It is raining' or 'He opened the door', why not admit that the same thing can happen with 'Cicero was poor?' Why not admit that, in the context of the belief report, the semantic value of 'Cicero was poor' is enriched with and incorporates an unarticulated constituent corresponding to John's notion of Cicero, in such a way that in that context, the sentence expresses something quasi-singular, viz. a belief content including a particular notion of Cicero, rather than merely a singular proposition including Cicero but no mode of presentation of him?

To be sure, the unarticulated mode of presentation which occurs in the belief content expressed by 'Cicero was poor' is truth-conditionally irrelevant, while the unarticulated constituents which occur in the propositions expressed by 'It is raining', 'He opened the door' or 'John believes that Cicero was poor' are full-fledged truth-conditional constituents. That difference goes a long way toward explaining why Crimmins and Perry say that the unarticulated mode of presentation occurs within the statement made by the global belief report but is no part of what the embedded sentence expresses: they use 'unarticulated constituent' in a restrictive manner, in accordance with the implicit stipulation that nothing truth-conditionally irrelevant can be a genuine *propositional constituent*, whether articulated or not. That terminological choice is consistent with my own claim that the proposition expressed by an utterance is individuated on a truth-conditional basis (more on this in 19.3). Still there is no reason, it seems to me, to view the *general* phenomenon we are talking about – whether we call it 'unarticulated constituency' or 'enrichment' – so restrictively as to exclude cases in which a truth-conditionally irrelevant meaning component is provided. The same phenomenon is involved whether what is contextually provided is truth-conditionally relevant or not, and that must be reflected in one's theory.

I conclude that the dualist view comports badly with the very picture Crimmins and Perry use to motivate that view. On that picture, 'strict compositionality' must be given up, for the semantic values of the parts and the way they are put together do not determine the semantic value of the whole (since the semantic value of the whole also depends on unarticulated constituents).[5] By insisting that the semantic value of the embedded sentence is a singular proposition determined on a strictly compositional basis out of the semantic values of its parts, rather than a complete belief content, Crimmins and Perry give the impression of not taking their own picture seriously. They seem to retreat to a much weaker position, according to which strict compositionality must be given up *for belief sentences*, but not in general (and, in particular, not for the simple sentence which is embedded within the belief sentence). That position would be fairly *ad hoc*; it would not be based on a general claim about language understanding and the role of context, contrary to the first, stronger position. But if one holds the stronger position (as Crimmins and Perry clearly do), one can hardly refuse to treat the embedded sentence accordingly. As soon as one accepts that a mode of presentation of the reference is provided through the mechanism of unarticulated constituents, one must also accept that the semantic content of the embedded sentence is thereby enriched: the embedded sentence expresses a *quasi*-singular belief content, in the context of the belief report, and it is that quasi-singular belief content which the 'that'-clause designates and which the belief report ascribes to the believer. One must, in other words, accept the unitary account of belief reports. (As I will show in the next section, that does not entail giving up dualism altogether: there is a version of dualism which is consistent with the unitary account, and to which the dualist may retreat when faced with the above objection.)

The gist of the unitary account is that *the embedded sentence itself expresses the ascribed belief content*, in the context of the belief report. As I suggested in 18.3, the embedded sentence comes to express the ascribed belief content through an optional p-process of *enrichment* which turns a singular constituent into something quasi-singular. Applied to the embedded sentence in 'John believes that Cicero was poor', that process ('quasi-singularization') operates as follows:

<Cicero> → <Cicero, '*Cicero*'>
<<Cicero>, the property of being poor> → <<Cicero, '*Cicero*'>, the property of being poor>

The singular constituent which is the name's contribution to the proposition expressed (viz. the singleton consisting of Cicero himself) is quasi-singularized through the addition of a truth-conditionally irrelevant mode of presentation, and the singular proposition consisting of that singular constituent and the property of being poor is quasi-singularized accordingly.[6]

## 19.3  The combined account

The argument which has just been given in favour of the unitary account is not sufficient to dispose of the dualist view. The latter can be defended, by appealing to a set of distinctions I made earlier.

Recall what I said in chapter 2 (2.3–4). The *proposition* expressed by an utterance is individuated on a truth-conditional basis; by contrast, the *thoughts* associated with an utterance are individuated on a cognitive rather than merely truth-conditional basis and, for that reason, they may include truth-conditionally irrelevant constituents, e.g. *de re* concepts. Thus an utterance such as 'You are in danger' expresses a singular proposition with the reference of 'you' as a constituent, but the speaker's *thought* is quasi-singular and involves a (*de re*) mode of presentation of the person in question.

There are cases in which an utterance with a referential term expresses more than merely a singular proposition; sometimes, as Loar said, a mode of presentation is 'essential to what is communicated'. In such cases at least the semantic content of the utterance (its interpretation) is richer than a singular proposition and comes close to being a complete thought.[7] Arguably, that is what happens with belief reports such as 'I believe that you are in danger': the embedded sentence in such a report expresses a complete, quasi-singular thought, involving a (truth-conditionally irrelevant) mode of presentation of the object thought about along with that object itself. That is the gist of the unitary account sketched in 19.2.

Is the unitary theory, according to which a quasi-singular thought (or type of thought) is expressed by the embedded sentence, inconsistent with the dualist's claim that a singular proposition is expressed? Not really. As we saw ealier, it is an essential property of quasi-singular thoughts that their truth-conditional content – their semantic core, as we might say – is a singular proposition; it follows that *whenever a quasi-singular thought is expressed, a singular proposition (which constitutes the truth-conditional content of the thought) is also expressed.* So the dualist need not give up his view that the embedded sentence expresses a singular proposition to which a mode of presentation is added, in the context of the belief report. He may grant that the semantic content of the embedded sentence is a quasi-singular thought or type of thought which incorporates a mode of presentation of the reference, while maintaining his own view, that the embedded sentence expresses a singular proposition; that is made possible by the distinction between the proposition expressed by the embedded sentence and its semantic content. The semantic content, or interpretation, of a sentence token including a referential term goes beyond the proposition expressed when the token expresses a complete, quasi-singular thought rather that merely a singular proposition. Thus the two views are reconciled: the embedded sentence in a belief report such as 'John believes that Cicero was bald' (opaquely understood) expresses both a singular proposition *and* a quasi-singular belief content, the latter being the interpretation or semantic content of the sentence, in that context.

Note that the version of the dualist view we come up with – that which is consistent with the unitary account and which for that reason I call the 'combined account' – is closer to the second version mentioned in 19.1 than to the first version. We now have four rather than three entities to deal with:

(a) what is expressed by the embedded sentence:
 (a-i) a singular proposition
 (a-ii) a quasi-singular thought-content
(b) what the 'that'-clause designates
(c) the ascribed belief

Like the unitary account, the combined account equates (a-ii), (b) and (c): the thought-content expressed by the embedded sentence is what the 'that'-clause designates and which the belief report ascribes. Like dualist accounts (whether of the first or the second variety), it draws a distinction between (a-i) and (c), that is, between the proposition expressed and the ascribed belief content. Finally, like the second dualist account, it draws a distinction between (a-i) and (b), that is, between the proposition expressed and what the 'that'-clause designates: what the 'that'-clause designates is the quasi-singular thought-content, not the singular proposition. Endorsing the combined account therefore entails rejecting the Relational principle

(18.1–2) and accepting the underdetermination of the reference of 'that'-clauses (which may refer either to the proposition expressed or to the associated thought, depending on the context).

Even though I find the combined account much more plausible and coherent than any other version of the dualist view, I think it remains unsatisfactory as a general account of belief reports involving referential terms. It can account for the (admittedly central) cases in which the ascribed belief content is a *de re* thought, but not for another type of case in which the ascribed belief content is a *descriptive* thought.

In 18.2 I discussed the following examples in which a referential expression is given a descriptive interpretation:

1  According to Horowitz, you often get in trouble with that move.
2  My son believes that Mitterrand is an ass.

According to Nunberg, the pronoun in 1 means something like 'whoever is in your position'; similarly, the proper name in 2 means something like 'the individual called *Mitterrand*'. The thought-content being ascribed is, in both cases, descriptive rather than *de re*.[8] How could we account for that interpretation in a dualist framework?

According to the combined account, the embedded sentence expresses a singular proposition even though its semantic content is non-singular. When the semantic content of the embedded sentence is quasi-singular, there indeed is a singular proposition which can be said to be expressed by the embedded sentence, viz. that which constitutes the truth-conditional content of the quasi-singular thought. The quasi-singular thought can be analysed into two factors, namely the singular proposition which constitutes its truth-conditional content (which the dualist takes to be explicitly specified by the embedded sentence) plus something else. But when the ascribed thought-content is descriptive, as in 1, the combined account is in trouble, for the truth-conditional content of a descriptive thought is *not* a singular proposition. In that case, it is useless to analyse the ascribed belief content into two factors, namely the truth-conditional content of the belief plus a mode of presentation contextually supplied; for one does not get a general proposition by enriching a singular proposition with a mode of presentation. One can get a quasi-singular thought in that way, but not a descriptive thought. The suggested mechanism therefore cannot account for the type of case illustrated by 1.

I conclude that a belief report whose embedded portion incorporates a referential term generally or descriptively interpreted cannot be satisfactorily handled within the combined account. The latter entails that the truth-condition of the ascribed belief must be singular (since the embedded sentence includes a referential term and therefore expresses a singular proposition which is taken to constitute the truth-conditional content of the belief), yet the truth-condition of the ascribed belief is not singular but general, when the referential term is interpreted descriptively. Faced with such cases, a dualist can only 'multiply senses beyond necessity' and argue that e.g. 'you' is ambiguous in such a way that it is not a genuine referential term (but a descriptive term homonymous with the referential term 'you') when it is given a descriptive, generic interpretation, as in 1. As Grice emphasized, that sort of 'solution' is *ad hoc* and must be avoided if possible. A dualist might be tempted to reply that there is a genuine ambiguity, as shown by the fact that a generic interpretation of the pronoun may be involved even when the sentence 'You often get in trouble with that move' is uttered in isolation. But that (correct) observation does not establish that the pronoun is ambiguous, nor does it object to what I said concerning the interpretation of the embedded sentence in 1. Whether or not optional p-processes come into play is a matter of context, and a belief context is precisely *one* sort of context (though not the *only* one) in which such processes may affect the interpretation of the utterance.

To account for descriptive interpretations of referential terms, whether they occur in belief contexts or elsewhere, we must weaken the theory of direct reference as I did in chapter 16 and admit that a sentence does not necessarily express a singular proposition even if it includes a (non-empty) referential term. The most that can be claimed is that a sentence including a (non-empty) referential term *Normally* expresses a singular proposition. In particular, the embedded sentence in a belief report does not necessarily express a singular proposition even if it includes a (non-empty) referential term; what it expresses is determined in accordance with the two constraints mentioned in 18.3, and that may well be a general proposition, if, for example, a non-minimalist p-process of transfer takes us from the basic semantic value of the referential term (viz. its reference) to a descriptive concept, as happens in 1. It follows that dualism – even on its most defensible version, the combined account – cannot be maintained.

## 19.4 Schematic belief reports

My last objection to dualism is based on cases in which the truth-conditional content of the ascribed belief is singular but incompletely specified by the ascriber. According to the dualist, the embedded sentence in a belief report expresses a proposition which is the truth-conditional content of the ascribed belief, while the 'mental sentence' or way of thinking under which the believer apprehends that content is only contextually suggested. In Fodor's and Richard's account, the believer's way of thinking is indicated through some kind of similarity relation between the believer's mental sentence and the embedded sentence used by the ascriber. It follows that the embedded sentence has two functions: it expresses the truth-conditional content (or, as Fodor says, the 'propositional object') of the belief, and it 'displays' the mental sentence, that is, the 'vehicle' of the belief (Fodor, 1990, p. 169). Now, according to Fodor, there is an important difference between these two functions which the embedded sentence plays:

> In the case of the first of the functions of the embedded formula – specifying the propositional object of the attributed belief – the matter is clear: the embedded formula must express the very proposition that the 'believes' predicate attributes. I think, however, that it is otherwise with the specification of the vehicle; here everything is slippery and pragmatic. Roughly, what is required is a degree of isomorphism to the vehicle that is appropriate to the purposes at hand; and there isn't any purpose-independent specification of how much isomorphism is enough.... To put it another way, it's not that there are *de dicto* attributions and *de re* attributions; it's rather that there is a continuum along which an embedded expression can be explicit about the vehicle of an attributed belief. If there's a rule in play, it's a rule of conversation: 'Kindly so construe my embedded formulas that my belief attributions come out plausible on the assumption that my utilities are rational'. If I say that John believes that Cicero was Tully, I *must* be trying to specify John's vehicle; what would be the point of my telling you something that would be true in virtue of John's believing that Cicero is Cicero? On the other hand, if I tell you that the English wanted to seize New York from the Dutch, I couldn't possibly be

wanting to specify their vehicle; everybody called the place New Amsterdam at the time. (Fodor, 1990, pp. 171–2)

The difference between the two functions, then, is this: being pragmatic and purpose-dependent, the specification of the vehicle varies along a continuum. The vehicle may be more or less fully specified and it may even be *un*specified (transparent readings). But the propositional object of the belief, that is, its truth-conditional content, can only be *exactly* specified: while the vehicle of the belief is only supposed to be relevantly 'similar' to the embedded sentence, the propositional object of the belief is supposed to be *identical to* the proposition expressed by the embedded sentence. No pragmatic variation is allowed here.[9]

That view entails that the truth-conditional content of the belief is always specified (unless some expression within the 'that'-clause lacks semantic value), contrary to the narrow content, which may be more or less fully specified and may even be unspecified. But that is wrong. The propositional content of the belief need not be wholly specified. Consider the following example:

3  John believes that a doctor wants to marry Bill.

Imagine that the speaker utters 3 to convey that there is a certain person, say A, such that John believes that *she* wants to marry Bill. Whether or not John thinks of A as being a doctor does not matter here: John may think of A as being a doctor, or the speaker (but not John) may think of A as being a doctor, or they may both think of A as being a doctor (Hornsby, 1977). What matters is that 3, on that reading, ascribes to John a belief whose truth-conditional content is clearly singular: John is said to believe of someone in particular, whom either the speaker or John believes to be a doctor, that she wants to marry Bill. But the identity of that person, who is a constituent of the singular proposition which is the truth-conditional content of John's belief, is not given; hence the singular proposition which is the truth-conditional content of John's belief is not wholly specified. We only know that John believes a singular proposition of a certain type, but we don't know which proposition exactly.[10]

Examples like 3 raise no problem in my framework: the reference of the 'that'-clause, in a case like that, is taken to be (or to include) an incompletely specified singular proposition. In the overall interpretation of the belief report, the missing constituent is quantified over, in the same way in which the missing mode of presentation is quantified over when the 'that'-clause in a belief sentence is interpreted as referring to a singular proposition (ch. 18, note 15). Thus 3 is naturally interpreted as meaning that there is a person (whom either the speaker or John believes to be a doctor) such that John believes that she wants to marry Bill.

By contrast, the dualist has trouble dealing with such examples. Given his equation of the proposition expressed by the embedded sentence and the truth-conditional content of the ascribed belief, the dualist must hold that the truth-conditional content of the ascribed belief is the proposition expressed by 'a doctor wants to marry Bill.' Now that sentence may express various propositions, depending on whether we interpret the indefinite description referentially or not, etc., but these propositions are all complete propositions, hence they do not capture the fact that the truth-conditional content of the ascribed belief is only incompletely specified.

One possible solution for the dualist would be to say that he is not concerned with 'relational' or '*de re*' readings of belief sentences, but only with '*de dicto*' readings. But that would be self-defeating, given that dualists explicitly (try to) account for so-called 'referential ambiguities' in belief sentences and, in particular, for the *de re/de dicto* 'ambiguity'. (See above, Fodor's quotation about *de re* and *de dicto* readings). What they can do, however, is claim that there is no such thing as 'the' *de re/de dicto* ambiguity. Different phenomena are involved, they might (plausibly) claim (Richard, 1990, p. 129). On the one hand, there is the transparent/opaque 'ambiguity', which can be accounted for along dualist lines, by saying that the required degree of similarity between the embedded sentence and the mental sentence is context-dependent and may vary along a continuum: a limiting case is that in which the speaker is not expected to be 'faithful' (17.2) and the embedded sentence is understood transparently as providing only the truth-conditional content of the ascribed belief. On the other hand, there is a quite different phenomenon, namely quantifier-scope ambiguity, as illustrated by 3 and by sentences such as 'Someday, everybody in the room will be hungry.' The latter phenomenon must be put aside in discussing the merits of dualism: we must consider only sentences in which quantifiers such as 'a doctor' are given *narrow* scope. (In the relevant interpretation of 3, the quantifier is given wide scope.) If we do so, then we can maintain that the proposition expressed by the embedded sentence captures the truth-conditional content of the ascribed belief.

It is not clear to me what exactly that defence of the dualist position would amount to. Does it mean that examples such as 3 (interpreted in the way I suggested) are *exceptions* to the claim that the proposition expressed by the embedded sentence is the truth-conditional content of the ascribed belief? Or would the defender of dualism deny that in 3, it is the sentence 'a doctor wants to marry Bill' which is embedded when the quantifier is given wide scope? Or would the dualist admit that that sentence is embedded, but deny that it expresses a proposition when the quantifier is given wide scope? I am certainly not saying that the dualist cannot find a way out of the difficulty raised by examples such as 3; I am only pointing out that there is a difficulty. Be that as it may, my objection, based on that example, is simply this: the dualist's claim that in a belief ascription the truth-conditional content of the belief is exactly specified, while the specification of narrow content is a matter of degree, seems to me downright false. Like the narrow content, the truth-conditional content of the belief need not be fully specified in a belief report. It is even possible *for both the narrow and the truth-conditional content, at the same time*, to be unspecified to some extent. Thus there are interpretations in which constituents of narrow content *and* truth-conditional content are quantified over. Suppose, for example, that 3 is interpreted in such a way that the description 'a doctor' is the speaker's way of characterizing A rather than a mode of presentation ascribed to John himself. As I pointed out above, that is a possible interpretation of 3. Thus understood, the utterance could be paraphrased as follows: *There is a person* x, *who is a doctor, and there is a mode of presentation* m, *such that John believes of* x *under* m *that she wants to marry Bill*. Here the reference of the 'that'-clause is a belief content which is partly unspecified both with respect to narrow content and with respect to truth-conditional content.

I think we are back to the issue I discussed in the previous section. The dualist acknowledges the context-sensitivity of belief reports; like the implicature theorist, he admits that the narrow content of the reported belief is pragmatically rather than semantically (conventionally) indicated, but, contrary to the implicature theorist, he recognizes that that pragmatic component of the meaning of a belief report is part and parcel of the proposition expressed by the latter. In other words, he recognizes that even the truth-conditional content of an utterance may be affected by pragmatic factors, in a way which goes far beyond standard 'indexicality'. But the dualist is not radical enough. He still thinks the content of a belief report can be analysed in two components: one which is semantically expressed and is not subject to contextual variation (except in the very limited mode having to do with indexicality), and another one with respect to which 'everything is slippery and pragmatic.' In other words, he wants to insulate some central aspect of the content of the belief report from pragmatic factors, as Fodor makes very clear in his 'Substitution arguments' paper (Fodor, 1990, pp. 172–4). In 19.2 I tried to expose the incoherence of that dualist strategy: one cannot at the same time give up and maintain strict compositionality, or acknowledge and deny the context-sensitivity of semantic content. What is true of the global belief sentence is also true of the embedded sentence: the semantic content of the latter depends not only on external features of the context of utterance (which serve to fix the basic semantic values of indexical terms) but also on pragmatic considerations of relevance or plausibility which in turn make it depend on a host of background assumptions. Fodor wants to avoid that plunge into holism at all costs, but his reasons for so doing are dubious: he apparently believes that if the contents of belief ascriptions are admitted to be determined on a pragmatic and holistic basis, then the contents of our mental states themselves will have to be individuated on such a basis, that is, in a non-realistic manner. I personally don't quite see the connection between the two claims. (Nor do I think that the radical view I have sketched entails anything like giving up 'denotational semantics': it is precisely such a semantics that I am advocating in this book.) Be that as it may, the dualist's insulation strategy does not work, as I hope I have shown in this section. It is the ascribed belief content *as a whole*, not merely the narrow aspect of it, which is determined pragmatically, in accordance with the top-down constraint mentioned in 18.3.

## Notes

1. The first one to have put forward that sort of account is Schiffer, in the paper mentioned earlier (Schiffer, 1977, p. 31ff).
2. The distinction between the proposition expressed by an utterance and its semantic content (3.4) will be appealed to below (19.3).
3. Richard (1990) might not recognize himself in that picture, since he holds that the embedded sentence expresses a RAM rather than a proposition in the traditional sense. On Richard's view, see below, note 9.
4. As I mentioned above, the only theorist who does not seem attracted by dualism is Stich (1983, ch. 6); but he never explicitly discusses that issue.

5 Crimmins and Perry, 1989, pp. 710–11. See also Fodor, 1990, pp. 170–71 for a similar point.
6 The emergence of a *truth-conditional* unarticulated constituent in the proposition expressed by the global belief report is easy to account for, in that framework (20.3). Since the belief report involves a reference to what the embedded sentence expresses, the mode of presentation itself is referred to rather than merely expressed, hence it affects the truth-conditions of the report.
7 As I suggested at the end of chapter 3, the semantic content of an utterance with a referential term can *never* be reduced to a singular proposition (even though the utterance expresses a singular proposition); it always includes at least a rudimentary (type of) mode of presentation of the reference. See 3.4.
8 In saying this, I deliberately ignore the fact that the embedded sentence in 1 contains a referential term ('that move') other than that which is descriptively interpreted.
9 Despite terminological differences, the view expounded in Richard (1990) is very close to that of Fodor (1990). Richard's view involves the notion of a RAM, or 'Russellian annotated matrix'. RAMs result from pairing off the constituents of a sentence with their Russellian interpretations; simplifying somewhat, we may think of them as pairs of sentences and propositions. Thus the RAM expressed by an utterance such as 'Cicero was poor', whether or not it is embedded in a belief report, consists of the uttered sentence together with the Russellian proposition it expresses. The ascribed content is also a RAM, consisting of a mental sentence together with its truth-conditional content. In a belief report, the RAM expressed by the embedded sentence represents the believer's RAM iff (i) 'stripped of their linguistic parts, the two RAMs amount to the same Russellian proposition' (Richard, 1990, p. 138), and (ii) the linguistic parts of the two RAMs are themselves relevantly 'similar'. Richards account is rich and detailed, and I cannot do it justice here, but the core of that account seems to me clearly along dualist lines and subject to the objections raised in this section.
10 The same sort of analysis works for examples like 'Most Europeans believe that they are poor' (an example I owe to Stephen Neale). This utterance says that for most $x$ such that $x$ is a European, there is a $y$ such that (i) $x = y$, and (ii) $x$ believes <<$y$, Ego>, the property of being poor>. Four things are to be noted in connection with that example:

> a The 'that'-clause refers to a schema (see ch. 18, note 15). But in this particular example there is a complication. The variable '$y$' is interpreted as anaphoric on 'most Europeans', through a process of enrichment. As a result we understand the utterance as saying that most Europeans think *of themselves* ($x = y$) that

they are poor. In such cases I say that the schema referred to is a *labelled chema*, involving variables *and* constraints on their interpretation.

b   Through enrichment too the mode of presentation **Ego** is contextually provided. We understand the utterance as saying that most Europeans think of themselves that *they themselves* (**Ego**) are poor.

c   Salmon's equivalence holds: to say that someone believes a schema is to say that she believes an instance of the schema. To say that most Europeans$_i$ believe the schema <<$y_i$, **Ego**>, the property of being poor> is to say that they believe an instance of the schema. For example *I* am a European and I believe that I am poor – that is, I believe <<Recanati, **Ego**>, the property of being poor>.

d   We can hardly say, as I did previously (with respect to another example), that 'we only know that [the agent] believes a ... proposition of a certain type [without knowing] which proposition exactly.' There is a sense in which we know exactly which proposition most Europeans believe. Still that proposition is described rather than referred to, insofar as one of its constituents (viz. the believer himself) is merely quantified over.

# Chapter 20

# How ambiguous are belief sentences?

## 20.1  Introduction

As I pointed out several times, one advantage of my account of belief reports is its high degree of flexibility. I have shown how, within that account, one explains cases in which the reference of the 'that'-clause is general, singular or quasi-singular, and also cases in which it is less than fully propositional. I now want to be more specific about the various ways in which a belief report can be interpreted. A number of observations were made in the recent past about the possible 'readings' of belief sentences, and I want to show how these observations can be accounted for within my framework. In particular, I want to show that the contrastive behaviour of referential and non-referential terms in belief sentences corroborate the theory put forward in this book.

I start with belief sentences containing definite descriptions. Belief sentences with referential terms (proper names and indexicals) will be considered in 20.3 (proper names) and 20.4 (indexicals).

## 20.2  Definite descriptions in belief contexts

What are the possible readings of a sentence such as 1?

1   John believes that the winner will go to Hong Kong.[1]

Several distinctions are commonly used in the literature to deal with such examples:

- relational vs. notional
- *de re* vs. *de dicto*
- transparent vs. opaque
- wide scope vs. narrow scope
- referential vs. attributive

Let us start with Quine's distinction between the notional and the relational reading of the 'believe' predicate. When 'believe' is understood notionally, the ascribed content is a complete content. In 1, for example, John is said to believe this: 'The winner will go to Hong Kong.' The description's contribution to the ascribed content is the notion or concept it expresses, namely the concept of 'the winner'. In the relational reading, however, the description's contribution to the ascribed belief content is its reference, namely the winner: John is said to believe of the winner that she will go to Hong Kong. Thus understood the report does not tell us how John thinks of the person whom he thinks will go to Hong Kong; the thought-content is not completely specified. As Quine puts it (Quine, 1956), the belief report ascribes to John a partial content, namely the predicate '.... will go to Hong Kong', and an object, namely the reference of the description 'the winner', such that John's belief is about that object (and involves some – unspecified – representation of that object). The two readings can be represented as follows:

1a  $B^n$ (John, 'the winner will go to Hong Kong')
1b  $B^r$ (John, '... will go to Hong Kong', the winner)

Many philosophers apparently believe that the five distinctions listed above do the same job in slightly different ways. The *de re/de dicto* distinction is supposed to be particularly close to Quine's distinction, except that it applies to the object of belief rather than to the 'believe' predicate itself. When 'believe' is understood notionally, the object of belief is a complete *dictum*: John is said to have in his belief box a mental counterpart of the sentence 'The winner will go to Hong Kong.' When 'believe' is understood relationally, the object of belief is a pair consisting of a partial content (viz. the predicate '... will go to Hong Kong') and an object the belief is about: hence the ascribed belief is *de re* – it involves a particular object. The other distinctions can also be seen as notational variants of Quine's. Instead of taking the verb 'believe' to be lexically ambiguous, as

Quine does, we may equivalently say that the scope of 'believe' is either wider or narrower than that of the description. (That move is not open to Quine himself, since he rejects quantifying in.) When the description takes wide scope, as in 1b, it is 'transparent': the concept which it expresses is not part of the ascribed content. When the description takes narrow scope, as in 1a, it is 'opaque': the concept it expresses is part of the ascribed content. That seems also to correspond to the referential/attributive ambiguity, since a referentially used description's contribution to content is its reference, while an attributive description's contribution to content is the concept which it expresses.

That syncretic view is utterly misguided, however. There is not one but *several* distinctions at play, as shown by the fact that sentences such as 1 are more than two-ways 'ambiguous'. Consider the case in which the description 'the winner' is opaque and expresses a notion which is an integral part of the believer's thought-content, that is, the case in which John is said to believe 'The winner will go to Hong Kong.' That is still ambiguous, it seems to me, depending on how the description in the latter sentence is interpreted. The believer may think 'The winner, whoever she is, will go to Hong Kong', or he may believe of someone in particular, whom he takes to be the winner, that she will go to Hong Kong. What this shows is that the description may be used to ascribe a *de re* belief, that is, a belief involving a particular object, even though it is given an *opaque* interpretation. (As an example of that sort of reading, Jennifer Hornsby mentions the sentence, 'Bill thinks that the bank-manager was rude, but it actually was a clerk about whom Bill reached that conclusion'.)[2] It is therefore a mistake to contrast 'opaque' with *de re*, as many philosophers have done after Quine. There is a useful distinction between two sorts of beliefs, namely those that are *de re* in the sense that they involve a particular object and those that are *de dicto* or, better, 'descriptive' in the sense that they are purely general, but that distinction is distinct from, and cannot be reduced to, that between transparent (wide scope) and opaque (narrow scope) readings of the description in the belief sentence. It can perhaps be said to correspond to the referential/attributive distinction as applied to opaquely used descriptions, but then it must be noticed that the referential/attributive distinction also applies to transparently used descriptions: like 1a, 1b allows two distinct readings – the speaker may say either that the winner, whoever she is, is such that John believes she will go to Hong Kong, or he may say of someone in particular, presented as the winner, that John believes she will go to Hong Kong.

So far, then, we have two basic 'ambiguities' generating four rather than two different readings for 1:

> *Transparent vs. opaque:* The definite description expresses a certain (descriptive) concept – the concept of 'the winner'. That concept may be either *exercised* by the speaker in order to identify some object John's belief is about (transparent reading), or *ascribed* to John himself as a constituent of his belief (opaque reading).
> 
> *De re vs. descriptive:* Although the concept expressed by the definite description is a descriptive concept, it may, through the process of synecdoche described in 15.6, stand for a *de re* concept including that descriptive concept. That is the referential or *de re* reading of the description, as opposed to its descriptive or attributive reading.

The latter ambiguity combines with the former one, in the sense that there are two possibilities *both* when the concept is exercised (transparent reading) and when it is ascribed (opaque reading). When the concept is exercised, it may be interpreted as purely descriptive or as *de re*; in both cases, it is taken to specify some object the ascribed belief is about. When the concept is ascribed, it may also be interpreted as purely descriptive or as *de re*, that is, the speaker may be interpreted as ascribing a descriptive concept or a *de re* concept to the believer. This gives us four readings:

Transparent uses
{
[1] The concept is exercised and interpreted as purely descriptive. On that reading, the speaker does not specify the object the ascribed belief is about in a referential way but in an attributive manner: he says that the winner, whoever she is, is such that John thinks she will go to Hong Kong. (*Attributive use.*)

[2] The concept is exercised and interpreted as *de re*. On that reading, the speaker expresses a *de re* thought about a particular person, say Mary; the speaker's *de re* concept of Mary includes the descriptive constituent 'the winner' (i.e. the speaker believes Mary is the winner), and he uses the latter to represent the former through a process of synecdoche (15.6). He says of the person whom he takes to be the winner, viz. Mary, that John thinks she will go to Hong Kong. (*Referential use.*)
}

|              | [3] The concept is ascribed to the believer and interpreted as purely descriptive. In that case, the ascribed belief itself is descriptive. The believer is said to believe this: 'The winner, whoever she is, will go to Hong Kong.' (*Oblique-attributive use*.) |
|---|---|
| *Opaque uses* | [4] The concept is ascribed to the believer and interpreted as *de re*. In that case, the believer is held to believe of someone in particular, thought of as the winner, that she will go to Hong Kong. (*Oblique-referential use*.) |

These are the main interpretations, but of course there are others. First, various optional p-processes may come into play besides the synecdoche which takes us from a descriptive concept to a more inclusive *de re* concept. Thus there might be a p-process of transfer taking us from the descriptive concept expressed by the description to some *other* descriptive concept (Fauconnier, 1985, p. 46ff). Second, even if we restrict ourselves to the four main readings, we observe that they are not mutually exclusive, for the concept expressed by the description may be both exercised *and* ascribed (Hornsby, 1977, pp. 36–7). This gives us two further readings, one in which the speaker and the believer both think of a particular person, say Mary, as the winner, and one in which the believer is held to have a particular person in mind as the winner but the speaker has a purely descriptive notion of the winner:

|              | [5] The speaker exercises the concept in a descriptive manner while ascribing to John a *de re* thought involving that very concept: John is held to think *of* the winner (whoever she is) that she will go to Hong Kong *and* to think of her *as* 'the winner'. (*Attributive + oblique-referential*.) |
|---|---|
| *Mixed uses* | [6] The speaker exercises the concept in a referential manner – he says of the person whom he takes to be the winner, viz. Mary, that John thinks she will go to Hong Kong – but he also ascribes that concept to John: John is held to believe of Mary that she will go to Hong Kong *and* to think of her as 'the winner' (*Referential + oblique-referential*.) |

There are no other 'mixed' readings, for two reasons. First, a belief content cannot be both *de re* and descriptive; so the only mixed readings there are arise out of the possibility for a description to be both transparent and opaque (i.e. to express a concept which is both exercised and ascribed). Second, among opaque uses, only the oblique-referential uses can be at the same time transparent uses. Oblique- attributive uses cannot, because an oblique-attributive description is used to ascribe a descriptive belief, that is, a general thought-content, and the ascribed thought-content cannot be general when the description is understood transparently. (To say that a description is transparent, or transparently used, is to say that it gives us an object for the ascribed belief to be about, so there *must* be an object in the ascribed belief – hence the latter cannot be general.) It follows that the only 'mixed' readings there are are those indicated above, the referential + oblique-referential and the attributive + oblique-referential.

Although they have a number of 'readings', sentences such as 1 need not be considered as ambiguous in the linguistic sense, i.e. as lexically or syntactically ambiguous. As we have just seen, two basic distinctions are involved: *de re* vs. descriptive and transparent vs. opaque. The ambiguity based on the first distinction is clearly pragmatic, in the sense I glossed earlier (14.4). If what I said in 15.6 is right, there is a p-process of synecdoche which makes it possible for a descriptive concept – for example, that expressed by a definite description – to stand for a *de re* concept which includes it. That process is at work whenever a description is used referentially, but it also accounts for oblique-referential uses of descriptions. As for the other distinction, it can often be represented in terms of relative 'scope', but this does not show that the ambiguity based on that distinction is structural in the sense of syntactic (17.2). Presumably, if the distinction were syntactic, it would not be possible for the concept expressed by a definite description to have *both* narrow and wide scope, as happens in the mixed readings. Be that as it may, the 'logical forms' which we distinguish when we talk of e.g. the scope of the belief operator are perspicuous representations of the various *interpretations* which belief sentences may take, but the sentences themselves need not have these 'forms' at any level of syntactical construction. In the absence of any substantive evidence supporting the thesis of syntactic ambiguity – let alone that of lexical ambiguity, which is especially unattractive – I assume that belief sentences are merely *underdetermined* as far as logical form is concerned.

Whether we take belief sentences to be ambiguous or semantically underdetermined, the interpretation process is essentially that of looking for a suitable reference for the 'that'-clause. The hearer has to make a number of decisions concerning the reference of the 'that'-clause, that is, the ascribed belief content: she must decide in context whether or not the ascribed belief content is likely to include the concept expressed by the description, whether it is most plausibly construed as *de re* or as descriptive, whether it may be considered as fully specified or as partly unspecified, and so forth. The 'ambiguities' are resolved as those interpretive decisions are made.

Let us take a closer look at the reference of the 'that'-clause on the various readings I have distinguished. As I said above, when the description is understood transparently, the reference of the 'that'-clause, normally, cannot be a general proposition. The description gives us an object for the belief to be about, so there must be an object in the ascribed belief. One might go further and claim that the reference of the 'that'-clause must be singular rather than quasi-singular when the description is transparent, since the mode of presentation associated with the description is not considered part of the ascribed content, on that reading. But the fact that the mode of presentation associated with the description is not considered part of the ascribed content does not entail that *no* mode of presentation is part of the ascribed content. Some contextually salient mode of presentation, distinct from that which the speaker exercises when specifying the reference of the belief, may be ascribed to the believer, as in Richard's example interpreted by Crimmins and Perry (18.4). Or the same mode of presentation which the speaker exercises may be at the same time ascribed to the believer, as in the mixed readings. I conclude that the transparent interpretation of the description rules out a general interpretation of the ascribed content, but not a quasi-singular interpretation. The reference of the 'that'-clause may be either singular or quasi-singular, depending on how fully specified the ascribed content is.

In the same way as a transparent interpretation of the description rules out a general interpretation of the reference of the 'that'-clause, an opaque interpretation of the description rules out a singular interpretation of the 'that'-clause: if the description is opaque, the ascribed content must include the mode of presentation associated with the description, hence it must be either quasi-singular or general (depending on whether the ascribed mode of presentation is interpreted as descriptive or *de re*).

Beside the transparent/opaque distinction and the *de re*/descriptive distinction, there is a further principle of classification for the ascribed content. As we saw in 18.4 and 19.4, the latter may be a fully specified thought-content or a partly unspecified thought-content. When the reference of the 'that'-clause is interpreted as singular, the believer's thought-content is not wholly specified: the mode of presentation under which the believer thinks of the object his belief is about is merely quantified over (18.4). That happens when the description is transparent and no contextually salient mode of presentation is supplied. The truth-conditional content of the ascribed belief may also be unspecified to some extent, as we saw in 19.4. That happens in particular when the description is attributive (that is, transparent and descriptive). A transparent description gives us an object for the belief to be about rather than a concept for the belief to include, but that object, which is *posited* whenever a transparent description is used, is not necessarily *identified*: When the description is attributive, the object the ascribed belief is about is posited *without* being identified. For example, we know that John believes of the winner, whoever she is, that she will go to Hong Kong, but we don't know who that person is; we have only descriptive knowledge of the object the belief is about. As a result, we can *describe* the singular proposition which constitutes the truth-conditional content of John's belief, but 'we are not acquainted with the proposition itself' (Russell, 1918, p. 218).

The same thing may happen when the description is opaquely interpreted. On the oblique-referential use of the description, the ascriber is said to think *de re* of some object, under a certain mode of presentation, that it has a certain property; but the object thus said to play a role in the believer's thought need not be identified, it may be only posited. In [4] the believer is said to believe of someone in particular, thought of as the winner, that she will go to Hong Kong, but *the speaker himself* does not make an 'identifying reference' to that individual. That is clear in Hornsby's example, 'Bill thinks that the bank-manager was rude but it actually was a clerk about whom Bill reached that conclusion.' Bill's belief is *de re*, yet the person it is about is only vaguely described as 'a clerk'. No identifying reference is made to the clerk in question. The singular constituent of the belief is merely quantified over, in that sort of case.

## 20.3 Proper names in belief contexts

In this and the next section the theory of direct reference put forward in this book will be tested by considering the main readings which a belief sentence such as 1 can take when the description is replaced by a referential term. The theory predicts a drastic reduction of the number of readings, due to the feature REF which distinguishes referential terms from definite descriptions. I shall also consider, and seek to explain, the difference of behaviour between proper names and indexicals in belief contexts. Proper names will be considered in this section, indexicals in the next one.

Being semantically marked as 'referential', a referential term is supposed to have only referential uses. That rules out all the readings in which the speaker does not make an identifying reference to the object the ascribed belief is about, namely:

(a) the reading in which the ascribed belief is about no object in particular (oblique-attributive reading, viz. [3] above);
(b) the readings in which the speaker describes the object the ascribed belief is about but does not make an identifying reference to it (attributive reading and mixed attributive + oblique-referential reading, viz. [1] and [5] above);
(c) the reading in which the speaker ascribes an identifying reference but does not make one (oblique-referential reading, viz. [4] above).

Only two readings are left, namely the referential reading ([2] above) and the mixed referential + oblique-referential reading ([6] above). That corresponds to the ambiguity discussed in chapters 17–8, namely that between what I then called the transparent and the opaque reading of a proper name in a belief sentence such as 'John believes that Cicero was poor.'

Let us recall what was said in chapter 17. When the speaker says 'John believes that Cicero was poor', his utterance may be interpreted in two ways, depending on whether or not John himself is supposed to think of Cicero as 'Cicero'. On the 'transparent' reading the mode of presentation associated with the proper name 'Cicero', viz. the concept 'called *Cicero*', is exercised by the speaker in order to identify the object John's belief is about, but it is not ascribed to John himself as characterizing his own way of thinking of Cicero. On the 'opaque' reading the concept 'called *Cicero*' (or, rather, a *de re* concept including it) is ascribed to John himself. We now realize, in light of the discussion in 20.2, that it was (slightly) improper to call this the transparent/opaque ambiguity for proper names. It is rather a distinction between transparent uses and *mixed* uses (that is, uses that are both transparent *and* opaque). When the proper name in 'John believes that Cicero was poor' is understood 'opaquely', it is still transparent in the sense that *the speaker himself presents Cicero as 'Cicero', while at the same time ascribing to John an identifying reference to the same man through the same mode of presentation.* That is not a purely opaque use in the sense of the above taxonomy (i.e. a use such as [4]), but a mixed use. It is very easy to overlook that distinction when discussing the behaviour of proper names in belief contexts, for mixed uses corresponding to [6] in the above taxonomy are the only opaque uses that are not ruled out by the semantic feature REF which proper names convey as part of their meaning. (Being semantically referential, a proper name can only be used referentially; in particular, the name 'Cicero' can only be used to refer to Cicero. But a purely opaque use, that is, a use corresponding to [4] in the above taxonomy, would be a use of 'Cicero' which did *not* refer to Cicero. Recall that, in [4], the speaker himself does not refer to the object the belief is about, but merely posits such an object. A purely opaque use of 'Cicero' would be such that the speaker would not refer to Cicero, but would rather ascribe to John a belief about some man thought of by John as 'Cicero'.)

There is an obvious objection to the claim I have just made, that mixed uses corresponding to [6] in the above taxonomy are not ruled out by the semantic feature REF which proper names convey as part of their meaning. For, according to my criteria, a proper name behaves in accordance with REF only if its truth-conditional contribution is (nothing other than) its reference. It would seem to follow that an interpretation like [6] ought to be ruled out when the description in 1 is replaced by a proper name, for the name on such an interpretation contributes *more* than its reference: it indicates not only the object the ascribed belief is about, but also the manner in which that object is thought about.

My answer to that objection proceeds in two steps. First, let us consider what exactly is ruled out by virtue of the feature REF which distinguishes referential terms from definite descriptions. It would be misleading to say that REF rules out all interpretations except singular interpretations. What the feature REF does is constrain the truth-condition of any utterance including a term that conveys that feature. By virtue of REF, the truth-condition of the utterance must be singular. It follows that the proposition expressed by a sentence such as 'Cicero was poor' must be a singular proposition, consisting of Cicero and the property of being poor (2.1). But the utterance may also express something richer than that proposition, namely a complete, quasi-singular thought-content: REF does not object to the utterance's expressing such a content, since an utterance which expresses a quasi-singular thought *eo ipso* expresses a singular proposition, namely the proposition which constitutes the truth-conditional content of the thought (19.3). The important point is that *the mode of presentation which is a constituent of a quasi-singular thought is truth-conditionally irrelevant, hence it does not prevent the truth-condition of the utterance from being singular.* It follows that the interpretation of a referential term may well be quasi-singular without infringing the constraint set up by REF. (By contrast, a general or descriptive interpretation is ruled out because it would infringe the constraint.)[3]

Still, the objector will pursue, the modes of presentation which are ascribed to the believer on the interpretations corresponding to [6] in the above classification are far from truth-conditionally irrelevant: *pace* Salmon, they do affect the truth-conditions of belief reports (17.3–4). Hence the constraint set up by REF is infringed, on such an interpretation: the *truth-conditional* contribution of the proper name goes beyond its reference, in violation of REF.

The second step in my response consists in denying the latter claim by pointing out the similarity between belief reports and 'doubly referential' utterances such as Quine's 'Giorgione' example (Quine, 1943, 1961). That similarity has already been emphasized by various authors, as I mentioned earlier (17.1). Let me consider Quine's example first and analyse it as I think it should be. In 'Giorgione was so-called because of his size', the name 'Giorgione' behaves in accordance with REF: the contribution it makes to the truth-condition of the utterance is its reference, *and nothing more*. It is true that something about the name 'Giorgione' is said, in such a way that the identity of the name itself affects the truth-condition of the utterance; so one is tempted to conclude that the name's contribution to the truth-condition goes beyond its reference. But that conclusion is too hasty. What happens is this: there are two referring expressions in the sentence, the name 'Giorgione' on the one hand and the demonstrative adverb 'so' in 'so-called' on the other hand. The former refers to Giorgione, the latter to the name 'Giorgione'. Given that there are two referring expressions, we can maintain that the truth-conditional contribution made by the name 'Giorgione' is merely its reference. Reference *to* the name 'Giorgione' is achieved not by that name itself, but by means of another referring expression,

## How ambiguous are belief sentences? 397

namely the demonstrative adverb. The failure of substitutivity is explained by the fact that replacing the name in the sentence changes the reference of the *other* referring expression. (As far as the name's own semantic contribution is concerned, Substitutivity holds.)

In the same way, in 'John believes that Cicero was poor' (on the 'opaque' interpretation, that is, the mixed reading corresponding to [6] in the classification of 20.2) the semantic contribution of the name 'Cicero' satisfies REF: it is quasi-singular and involves the reference of the name together with a truth-conditionally irrelevant mode of presentation. The constraint set up by REF is not violated, since the only contribution made by the name to the truth-conditions of the utterance is its reference (the mode of presentation being truth-conditionally irrelevant). But the 'that'-clause itself is a referring expression, which refers to the content expressed by the embedded sentence, as the demonstrative adverb refers to the name 'Giorgione' in Quine's example. Hence the truth-conditionally irrelevant mode of presentation which is a constituent of that content is itself referred to and becomes a (truth-conditionally relevant) constituent of the proposition expressed by the belief report. Still, I maintain that the name's own contribution satisfies the constraint set up by REF. For the mode of presentation which is a (truth-conditionally relevant) constituent of the proposition expressed by the belief report is no part of the semantic contribution made by the proper name to that proposition:[4] it is part of the semantic contribution of the *other* referring expression, namely the 'that'-clause.

In conclusion, we can maintain the view that REF rules out all readings of a belief sentence except those corresponding to [2] and [6] in the classification of 20.2. Belief sentences with proper names are therefore only singly 'ambiguous', contrary to belief sentences containing definite descriptions, which are multiply ambiguous. On one reading, the mode of presentation associated with the proper name reflects both the speaker's and the believer's way of thinking of the reference, while on the other reading it is exercised by the speaker without being ascribed to the believer.

### 20.4 Indexicals in belief contexts

From the fact that proper names, like definite descriptions, can be interpreted opaquely or transparently in belief contexts, some philosophers were tempted to conclude that proper names and descriptions behave in the same way in belief contexts, in contrast to indexicals, which can only be used transparently. This was supposed to cast doubt on the view that proper names and indexicals are referential terms while definite descriptions are not. The possible opacity of proper names in belief contexts was taken to demonstrate that proper names are *not* directly referential, but have a 'sense' or 'connotation', like definite descriptions. That line of argument is clearly mistaken. I have shown that there is a major difference between proper names and definite descriptions, a difference which does not disappear in belief contexts. Owing to the feature REF, proper names can only be interpreted referentially, so that only two readings remain possible out of six possible interpretations for belief sentences with definite descriptions. That is what the theory of direct reference predicts, and that also corresponds to our intuitions.

Let us be slightly more precise. As I said in chapter 2, there are *two* types of intuition which the theory of direct reference is intended to account for — one about the necessary identification of the reference of a referential term, the other about the truth-conditional irrelevance of whichever mode of presentation is used to identify the reference (2.5). Concerning the first point, we do have the intuition that 'John believes that Cicero was poor' *identifies* the object John's belief is about, whereas the description in 1 does not necessarily identify the object John's belief is about. When a description is used, as in 1, there may be no object for John's belief to be about, and when there is such an object, it may not be identifyingly referred to; by contrast, when a proper name is used, REF demands that there be an identifying reference to the object the ascribed belief is about. That constraint holds whether we interpret the name 'transparently' or 'opaquely' (in the improper sense of chapter 17). The behaviour of proper names in belief contexts therefore conforms to the first intuition supporting the theory of direct reference.

With respect to the second intuition, the behaviour of proper names in belief contexts seems to conflict with the theory of direct reference, for the mode of presentation ascribed to the believer on the 'opaque' reading of a belief sentence is relevant to the truth-condition of the belief report. However, I have shown that the semantic contribution of the proper name is as predicted by the theory of direct reference, appearances notwithstanding (20.3). The mode of presentation which affects the truth-conditions of opaque belief reports is not contributed by the proper name which occurs in the belief sentence; the latter does contribute a mode of presentation through the p-process of quasi-singularization (a particular case of enrichment), but that mode of presentation is truth-conditionally irrelevant.

If the behaviour of proper names in belief contexts conforms to the theory of direct reference, how can we account for the alleged difference between proper names and indexicals in belief contexts? Indexicals are often said to be necessarily transparent, in contrast to proper names. In a sense, proper names themselves are necessarily transparent, for, as we have seen, their so-called 'opaque' use actually is a mixed use in which the name is used both transparently and opaquely. But the transparency of indexicals is supposed to be something stronger: even the mixed use illustrated by [6] in the classification of 20.2 seems to be ruled out for indexicals. Thus if I say to the winner:

2   John believes that you will go to Hong Kong.

there is only one possible reading, namely that corresponding to [2] in the classification of 20.2. The mode of presentation associated with the pronoun 'you' is certainly not part of the belief content ascribed to John, hence a reading such as [6] is ruled out. And that seems to be quite generally the case for indexicals: they tend to be purely transparent, in contrast to both proper names and definite descriptions. That fact about indexicals seems hard to accommodate within the theory I have developed in this book, for, according to that theory, indexicals and proper names are semantically very similar. In both cases the linguistic meaning of the expression consists of the feature REF together with a (linguistic) mode of presentation.

I think it can be maintained that indexicals and proper names are very similar from a semantic point of view. Their different behaviours in belief contexts can be accounted for in purely pragmatic terms, as Tom McKay pointed out (McKay, 1981, pp. 293–4). The psychological mode of presentation associated with an indexical expression, as we have seen, is a *de re* mode of presentation (a dossier) linguistically constrained as containing the descriptive concept which constitutes the character (or linguistic mode of presentation) of the indexical. For example, the mode of presentation associated with a particular token of 'you' addressed to Paul is a *de re* concept having Paul as reference and including the information 'is the addressee'. One cannot think of Paul under that mode of presentation unless one has access to the information that it is Paul who is being addressed. Now only participants in the speech situation have access to that piece of information. It follows that the mode of presentation associated with 'you' – and, in general, the mode of presentation associated with an indexical – is tied to the particular context in which that indexical is used. Only someone in that context can think of the reference under that mode of presentation. So the mode of presentation associated with the indexical can hardly occur outside the thoughts of the speaker and his addressee, who are both in the right context; in particular, there is no reason to suppose that the mode of presentation in question is also a constituent of the *believer's* thought, since the believer is generally not one of the participants of the speech episode.

Let me give an example. When Tom says to Cicero, 'John believes that you are poor', both Tom and Cicero think of Cicero (the reference of 'you') under a *de re* mode of presentation which includes the concept 'addressee': Tom thinks of Cicero as (*inter alia*) the person he is talking to, while Cicero thinks of himself as (*inter alia*) the person whom Tom is addressing. But John, to whom the thought about Cicero is ascribed, is not participating in the speech episode and there is no reason to suppose that his notion of Cicero includes the concept 'being now addressed by Tom'. That is why an indexical is interpreted transparently: the mode of presentation associated with the indexical is tied to the speech situation, hence it cannot plausibly be attributed to the believer, since the latter is not one of the participants in the speech situation.

To check that that is the right account, let us consider two sorts of test cases. Let us first imagine a belief report situation in which the proper name that is used to refer to the object the ascribed belief is about is mutually believed to figure only in the repertoire of the actual participants in the speech situation. Thus suppose that Tom and Sam share a 'code' which only they employ when talking about persons: they use secret names rather than the ordinary, public names. Let us further imagine that, for contingent reasons, their friend Max has two different names in their code, namely 'Orecic' and 'Yllut'. Whether Tom says 'John believes that Orecic is poor' or 'John believes that Yllut is poor', it will not be plausible to suppose that John's concept of Max includes the constituent 'called *Yllut*' or 'called *Orecic*', since those names are not in John's repertoire. We may suppose that John has only one name for Max in his repertoire, namely 'Max'. In such a situation, the two utterances 'John believes that Orecic is poor' and 'John believes that Yllut is poor' will ascribe the same belief to John: they will be transparently interpreted. (See McKay, 1981, p. 294 for further examples of the same type.) Now the reason why, in that particular context, these utterances would be given the transparent interpretation is the same why indexicals, in general, are transparently interpreted in belief reports.

The second test case I want to consider is that in which the believer himself is one of the participants in the speech situation. Let us suppose that, in the course of a conversation between John, Sam and Cicero, Sam says to Cicero, 'John believes that you are poor.' In that context, a mixed use of the sort corresponding to [6] in the taxonomy of 20.2 turns out to be possible: not only do Sam and Cicero think of the reference of 'you' (namely Cicero) under a *de re* concept containing the concept 'person being addressed', the belief ascribed to John may also be construed as involving such a concept. A trivial illustration of that sort of case is provided by self-ascriptions of belief. If John says to Cicero, 'I believe that you are poor', the ascribed belief will be construed as including the *de re* concept under which the speaker thinks of his addressee, simply because the speaker is the believer, in that case. Something corresponding to [6] is the most natural reading for such an utterance.

I conclude that the observed difference between indexicals and proper names is essentially pragmatic. It arises out of the context-boundedness of the modes of presentation associated with indexicals as opposed to the modes of presentation associated with proper names. The information that a man is called by a certain name is normally less context-bound (more widespread) than the information that the man in question is now being addressed, and that is why indexicals are less likely to be interpreted opaquely than proper names. Ultimately, however, whether or not the believer can plausibly be construed as thinking of the reference under the mode of presentation associated with the referential term depends on the context, as the above examples show. That is not to deny that there are regularities due to the difference between the linguistic modes of presentation characteristic of proper names and indexicals respectively. Owing to those regularities, we can say that, in general, indexicals tend to be interpreted purely transparently, in contrast to proper names.

## Notes

1. I borrow this example from Fauconnier (1985). The taxonomy which follows is similar to those offered by Fauconnier (1985), Hornsby (1977), Stich (1983), and Bach (1987).
2. Hornsby, 1977, p. 34.
3. This does not mean that they are (factually) impossible – they *are* possible, if enough background assumptions and p-processes are brought into play.
4. Arguably, the name 'Cicero' in 'John believes that Cicero was poor' makes no *direct* contribution to the proposition expressed by the complex utterance; rather, it contributes to the content expressed by the embedded sentence (in the context of the belief report), and the 'that'-clause contributes that content to the proposition expressed by the global belief report.

# Bibliography

Adams, F., Drebushenko, D., Fuller, G. and Stecker, R. 1990: Narrow Content: Fodor's Folly. *Mind and Language*, 5:213–29.
Anscombe, E. 1975: The First Person. In S. Guttenplan (ed.), *Mind and Language*, Oxford: Clarendon Press, 45–65.
Anscombre, J.-C. and Ducrot, O. 1978: Echelles argumentatives, échelles implicatives et lois de discours. *Semantikos*, 2:43–67.
Atlas, J. 1979: How Linguistics Matters in Philosophy: Presupposition, Truth and Meaning. *Syntax and Semantics*, 11:321–36.
Atlas, J. 1989: *Philosophy without ambiguity*. Oxford: Clarendon Press.
Austin, J.L. 1971: *Philosophical Papers*. 2nd ed., Oxford: Clarendon Press.
Bach, K. 1970: Part of what a picture is. *British Journal of Aesthetics*, 10:119–37.
Bach, K. 1981: What's in a name? *Australasian Journal of Philosophy*, 59:371–86.
Bach, K. 1987: *Thought and Reference*. Oxford: Clarendon Press.
Bach, K. and Harnish, M. 1979: *Linguistic Communication and Speech Acts*. Cambridge, Mass.: MIT Press.
Baker, L. 1987: Content by Courtesy. *Journal of Philosophy*, 84:197–213.
Barwise, J. and Perry, J. 1981: Semantic Innocence and Uncompromising Situations. *Midwest Studies in Philosophy*, 6:387–403.
Barwise, J. and Perry, J. 1983: *Situations and Attitudes*. Cambridge, Mass.: MIT Press/Bradford Books.
Bealer, G. 1982: *Quality and Concept*. Oxford: Clarendon Press.
Benveniste, E. 1956: La nature des pronoms. Reprinted (1966) in his *Problèmes de linguistique générale*, Paris: Gallimard, 251–7.
Block, N. 1986: Advertisement for a Semantics for Psychology. *Midwest Studies in Philosophy*, 10:615–78.
Brody, B. 1977: Kripke on Proper Names. *Midwest Studies in Philosophy*, 2:64–69.

Burge, T. 1977: Belief De Re. *Journal of Philosophy*, 74:338–62.
Burge, T. 1979: Individualism and the Mental. *Midwest Studies in Philosophy*, 4:73–121.
Burge, T. 1982: Other Bodies. In A. Woodfield (ed.), *Thought and Object*, Oxford: Clarendon Press, 97–120.
Burge, T. 1986: Cartesian Error and the Objectivity of Perception. In P. Pettit and J. McDowell (eds), *Subject, Thought, and Context*, Oxford: Clarendon Press, 117–36.
Carston, R. 1988: Implicature, Explicature, and Truth-Theoretic Semantics. In R. Kempson (ed.), *Mental Representations: The interface between language and reality*, Cambridge: Cambridge University Press, 155–81.
Castañeda, H.-N. 1966: 'He': a Study in the Logic of Self-Consciousness. *Ratio*, 8:130–57.
Castañeda, H.-N. 1967: Indicators and Quasi-Indicators. *American Philosophical Quarterly*, 4:85–100.
Chastain, C. 1975: Reference and Context. In K. Gunderson (ed.), *Language, Mind, and Knowledge*, Minneapolis: University of Minnesota Press, 194–269.
Chomsky, N. 1986: *Knowledge of Language*. New York: Praeger.
Chomsky, N. 1988: *Language and Problems of Knowledge: the Managua Lectures*. Cambridge, Mass.: MIT Press.
Church, A. 1956: *Introduction to Mathematical Logic, vol. 1*. Princeton, N.J.: Princeton University Press.
Cohen, L.J. 1968: Criteria of Intensionality (symposium with J.O. Urmson). *Aristotelian Society Proceedings, Supplementary Volume*, 42:123–42.
Cohen, L.J. 1971: Some Remarks on Grice's Views about the Logical Particles of Natural Language. In Y. Bar-Hillel (ed.), *Pragmatics of Natural Language*, Dordrecht: Reidel, 50–68.
Cohen, L.J. 1980: The Individuation of Proper Names. In Z. van Straaten (ed.), *Philosophical Subjects: Essays presented to P.F. Strawson*, Oxford: Clarendon Press, 140–63.
Cohen, L.J. 1986: How is Conceptual Innovation Possible. *Erkenntnis*, 25: 221–38.
Cole, P. 1981: On the Origins of Referential Opacity. *Syntax and Semantics*, 9:1–22.
Cornulier, B. de 1980: *Meaning Detachment*. Amsterdam: J. Benjamins.
Cresswell, M.J. 1985: *Structured Meanings*. Cambridge, Mass.: MIT Press/Bradford Books.
Crimmins, M. and Perry, J. 1989: The Prince and the Phone Booth. *Journal of Philosophy*, 86:685–711.
Davidson, D. 1967: Causal Relations. Reprinted in his *Essays on Actions and Events*, Oxford: Clarendon Press, 149–62.
Davidson, D. 1969: On Saying That. In D. Davidson and J. Hintikka (eds), *Words and Objections: Essays on the Work of W.V. Quine*, Dordrecht: Reidel, 158–74.

Dennett, D. 1982: Beyond Belief. In A. Woodfield (ed.), *Thought and Object*, Oxford: Clarendon Press, 1–95.
Descartes, R. 1647: *Les Méditations Métaphysiques*. Reprinted (1973) in C. Adam and P. Tannery (eds), *Oeuvres de Descartes*, vol. 9(1), Paris: Vrin, 1–72.
Devitt, M. 1981: *Designation*. New York: Columbia University Press.
Devitt, M. 1989: Against Direct Reference. *Midwest Studies in Philosophy*, 14:206–40.
Dominicy, M. 1984: *La Naissance de la Grammaire Moderne: Langage, Logique et Philosophie à Port-Royal*. Bruxelles: Pierre Mardaga Editeur.
Donnellan, K. 1966: Reference and Definite Descriptions. *Philosophical Review*, 75:281–304.
Donnellan, K. 1978: Speaker Reference, Descriptions and Anaphora. *Syntax and Semantics*, 9:47–68.
Dretske, F. 1981: *Knowledge and the flow of information*. Oxford: Basil Blackwell.
Dretske, F. 1988: *Explaining Behavior: Reasons in a World of Causes*. Cambridge, Mass.: MIT Press/Bradford Books.
Ducrot, O. 1972: *Dire et ne pas dire*. Paris: Hermann.
Ducrot, O. 1973: *La Preuve et le Dire*. Paris: Mame.
Ducrot, O. 1980: *Les Echelles Argumentatives*. Paris: Minuit.
Evans, G. 1981: Understanding Demonstratives. In H. Parret and J. Bouveresse (eds), *Meaning and Understanding*, Berlin: de Gruyter, 280–303.
Evans, G. 1982: *The Varieties of Reference*, ed. by J. McDowell. Oxford: Clarendon Press.
Fauconnier, G. 1985: *Mental Spaces: Aspects of Meaning Construction in Natural Language*. Cambridge, Mass.: MIT Press/Bradford Books.
Fodor, J. 1987: *Psychosemantics: the Problem of Meaning in the Philosophy of Mind*. Cambridge, Mass.: MIT Press/Bradford Books.
Fodor, J. 1990: Substitution Arguments and the Individuation of Belief. In his *A Theory of Content*, Cambridge, Mass.: MIT Press/Bradford Books, 161–76.
Forbes, G. 1990: The Indispensability of *Sinn*. *Philosophical Review*, 99:535–63.
Forguson, L.W. 1973: Locutionary and Illocutionary Acts. In I. Berlin *et al.*, *Essays on J.L. Austin*, Oxford: Clarendon Press, 141–85.
Frege, G. 1960: *Translations from the Philosophical Writings of Gottlob Frege*, by P. Geach and M. Black. 2nd ed., Oxford: Basil Blackwell.
Frege, G. 1977: *Logical Investigations*. Translated and edited by P.T. Geach and R.H. Stoothoff, Oxford: Basil Blackwell.
Gardiner, A.H. 1932: *The Theory of Speech and Language*. Oxford: Clarendon Press.
Geach, P. 1957: *Mental Acts: their Content and their Objects*. London: Routledge and Kegan Paul.

Geach, P. 1962: *Reference and Generality: an Examination of Some Medieval and Modern Theories*. Ithaca: Cornell University Press.
Gibson, J.J. 1968: *The Senses Considered as Perceptual Systems*. London: George Allen & Unwin.
Goodman, N. 1949: On Likeness of Meaning. Reprinted (1952) in L. Linsky (ed.), *Semantics and the Philosophy of Language*, Urbana: University of Illinois Press, 67–74.
Gordon, R.M. 1986: Folk Psychology as Simulation. *Mind and Language*, 1:158–71.
Grice, P. 1969: Vacuous Names. In D. Davidson and J. Hintikka (eds), *Words and Objections*, Dordrecht: Reidel, 118–45.
Grice, P. 1989: *Studies in the Way of Words*. Cambridge, Mass.: Harvard University Press.
Horn, L. 1972: *On the Semantic Properties of Logical Operators in English*. Ph.D. thesis, University of California at Los Angeles.
Horn, L. 1989: *A Natural History of Negation*. Chicago: University of Chicago Press.
Hornsby, J. 1977: Singular Terms in Contexts of Propositional Attitude. *Mind*, 86:31–48.
Inwagen, P. van 1980: Indexicality and Actuality. *Philosophical Review*, 89: 403–426.
Jackendoff, R. 1983: *Semantics and Cognition*. Cambridge, Mass.: MIT Press.
Jacob, P. 1987: Thoughts and Belief Ascriptions. *Mind and Language*, 2: 301–25.
Jacob, P. 1990: Semantics and Psychology: the Semantics of Belief-Ascriptions. In N. Cooper and P. Engel (eds), *New Inquiries into Meaning and Truth*, Hemel Hempstead: Harvester Wheatsheaf, 83–109.
Jakobson, R. 1957: *Shifters, verbal categories, and the Russian verb*. Russian Language Project, Department of Slavic Languages and Literatures. Harvard University.
Kahneman, D. and A. Treisman, forthcoming: Changing Views of Attention and Automaticity. In R. Parasumaran and J. Beatty (eds), *Varieties of Attention*, New York: Academic Press.
Kaplan, D. 1969: Quantifying In. In D. Davidson and J. Hintikka (ed.), *Words and Objections*, Dordrecht: Reidel, 206–42.
Kaplan, D. 1978: Dthat. *Syntax and Semantics*, 9:221–243.
Kaplan, D. 1989a: Demonstratives. In J. Almog, H. Wettstein and J. Perry (eds), *Themes from Kaplan*, New York: Oxford University Press, 481–563.
Kaplan, D. 1989b: Afterthoughts. In J. Almog, H. Wettstein and J. Perry (eds), *Themes from Kaplan*, New York: Oxford University Press, 565–614.
Kaplan, D. 1990: Words. *Aristotelian Society Proceedings, Supplementary Volume*, 64:93–119.

Katz, J.J. 1972: *Semantic Theory*. New York: Harper & Row.
Katz, J.J. 1977: A Proper Theory of Names. *Philosophical Studies*, 31:1–80.
Katz, J.J. 1979: The Neoclassical Theory of Reference. In P. French, T. Uehling and H. Wettstein (eds), *Contemporary Perspectives in the Philosophy of Language*, Minneapolis: University of Minnesota Press, 103–24.
Katz, J.J. 1986: Why Intentionalists Ought Not Be Fregeans. In E. LePore (ed.), *Truth and Interpretation: Perspectives in the Philosophy of Donald Davidson*, Oxford: Basil Blackwell, 59–91.
Katz, J.J. 1990: Has the Description Theory of Names been Refuted? In G. Boolos (ed.), *Meaning and Method: Essays in Honour of Hilary Putnam*, Cambridge: Cambridge University Press, 31–61.
Kay, P. and Zimmer, K. 1976: On the Semantics of Compound and Genitives in English. *Sixth California Linguistics Association Conference Proceedings*, San Diego: Campanile, 29–35.
Kneale, W. 1962: Modality, De Dicto and De Re. In E. Nagel, P. Suppes and A. Tarski (eds), *Logic, Methodology and Philosophy of Science*, Stanford: Stanford University Press, 622–33.
Kripke, S. 1971: Identity and Necessity. In M. Munitz (ed.), *Identity and Individuation*, New York: New York University Press, 135–64.
Kripke, S. 1977: Speaker's Reference and Semantic Reference. *Midwest Studies in Philosophy*, 2:255–76.
Kripke, S. 1979: A Puzzle About Belief. In A. Margalit (ed.), *Meaning and Use*, Dordrecht: Reidel, 239–83.
Kripke, S. 1980: *Naming and Necessity*. Oxford: Basil Blackwell.
LePore, E. and Loewer, B. 1986: Solipsistic Semantics. *Midwest Studies in Philosophy*, 10:595–614.
Levinson, S., forthcoming: Generalized Conversational Implicatures and the Semantics/Pragmatics Interface.
Loar, B. 1972: Reference and Propositional Attitudes. *Philosophical Review*, 81:43–62.
Loar, B. 1976: The Semantics of Singular Terms. *Philosophical Studies*, 30:353–77.
Loar, B. 1980: Names and Descriptions: A Reply to Michael Devitt. *Philosophical Studies*, 38:85–9.
Lockwood, M. 1975: On Predicating Proper Names. *Philosophical Review*, 84:471–98.
McCulloch, G. 1989: *The Game of the Name: Introducing Logic, Language and Mind*. Oxford: Clarendon Press.
McDowell, J. 1977: On the Sense and Reference of a Proper Name. *Mind*, 86:159–85.
McDowell, J. 1984: *De Re* Senses. In C. Wright (ed.), *Frege: Tradition & Influence*, Oxford: Basil Blackwell, 98–109.
McDowell, J. 1986: Singular Thought and the Extent of Inner Space. In P. Pettit and J. McDowell (eds), *Subject, Thought and Context*, Oxford: Clarendon Press, 137–68.

McGinn, C. 1982: The Structure of Content. In A. Woodfield (ed.), *Thought and Object*, Oxford: Clarendon Press, 207–58.
McGinn, C. 1983: *The Subjective View: Secondary Qualities and Indexical Thoughts*. Oxford: Clarendon Press.
McKay, T. 1981: On Proper Names in Belief Ascriptions. *Philosophical Studies*, 39:287–303.
Mill, J.S. 1947: *A System of Logic*. London: Longmans.
Millikan, R. 1984: *Language, Thought and Other Biological Categories*. Cambridge, Mass.: MIT Press/Bradford Books.
Millikan, R. 1990: The Myth of the Essential Indexical. *Noûs*, 24:723–34.
Millikan, R., forthcoming: *White Queen Psychology*.
Morgan, J.L. 1978: Two Types of Convention in Indirect Speech Acts. *Syntax and Semantics*, 9:261–80.
Morgan, M.J. 1977: *Molyneux's question: Vision, Touch and the Philosophy of Perception*. Cambridge: Cambridge University Press.
Neale, S. 1990: *Descriptions*. Cambridge, Mass.: MIT Press/Bradford Books.
Nozick, R. 1981: *Philosophical Explanations*. Oxford: Clarendon Press.
Nunberg, G. 1978: *The Pragmatics of Reference*. Bloomington: Indiana University Linguistics Club.
Nunberg, G. 1979: The Non-Uniqueness of Semantic Solutions: Polysemy. *Linguistics and Philosophy*, 3:143–84.
Nunberg, G. 1990: Indexicality in Contexts. Paper delivered at the conference on Philosophy and Cognitive Science, Cerisy-la-Salle, France, June 1990.
Nunberg, G. 1991: Indexicals and Descriptions in Interpretation. Ts.
Nunberg, G. forthcoming: On the Meaning and Interpretation of Indexical Expressions. Final version of Nunberg, 1991, to appear in *Linguistics and Philosophy*.
Peacocke, C. 1975: Proper Names, Reference, and Rigid Designation. In S. Blackburn (ed.), *Meaning, Reference and Necessity*, Cambridge: Cambridge University Press, 109–32.
Peacocke, C. 1981: Demonstrative Thought and Psychological Explanation. *Synthese*, 49:187–217.
Peacocke, C. 1983: *Sense and Content: Experience, Thought and their Relations*. Oxford: Clarendon Press.
Peacocke, C. 1989: Perceptual Content. In J. Almog, J. Perry and H. Wettstein (eds), *Themes from Kaplan*, New York: Oxford University Press, 297–329.
Perry, J. 1977: Frege on Demonstratives. *Philosophical Review*, 86:474–97.
Perry, J. 1979: The Problem of the Essential Indexical, *Noûs*, 13:3–21.
Perry, J. 1980a: Belief and Acceptance. *Midwest Studies in Philosophy*, 5: 533–42.
Perry, J. 1980b: A Problem About Continued Belief. *Pacific Philosophical Quarterly*, 61:317–32.

Perry, J. 1986a: Perception, Action, and the Structure of Believing. In R. Grandy and R. Warner (eds), *Philosophical Grounds of Rationality: Intentions, Categories, Ends*, Oxford: Clarendon Press, 333–61.
Perry, J. 1986b: Circumstantial attitudes and benevolent cognition. In J. Butterfield (ed.), *Language, Mind and Logic*, Cambridge: Cambridge University Press, 123–34.
Perry, J. 1986c: Thought without Representation. *Proceedings of the Aristotelian Society, Supplementary Volume*, 60:137–51.
Perry, J. 1988: Cognitive Significance and New Theories of Reference. *Noûs*, 22:1–18.
Perry, J. 1990a: Meaning and the Self. Paper delivered at Ecole Polytechnique, Paris, March 1990.
Perry, J. 1990b: Individuals in Informational and Intentional Content. In E. Villanueva (ed.), *Information, Semantics and Epistemology*, Oxford: Basil Blackwell, 172–89.
Perry, J. 1992: *Meaning and the Self*. Lectures delivered at CREA, Paris, March–April 1992.
Prior, A. 1963: Oratio Obliqua. Reprinted (1976) in his *Papers in Logic and Ethics* (ed. by P. Geach and A. Kenny). London: Duckworth, 147–58.
Putnam, H. 1975: The Meaning of Meaning. Reprinted in his *Philosophical Papers vol. 2: Mind, Language and Reality*, Cambridge: Cambridge University Press, 215–71.
Putnam, H. 1988: *Representation and Reality*. Cambridge, Mass.: MIT Press/Bradford Books.
Quine, W.v.O. 1943: Notes on Existence and Necessity. Reprinted (1952) in L. Linsky (ed.), *Semantics and the Philosophy of Language*, Urbana: University of Illinois Press, 77–91.
Quine, W.v.O. 1956: Quantifiers and Propositional Attitudes. Reprinted (1976) in his *The Ways of Paradoxes and Other Essays*, revised and enlarged edition, Cambridge, Mass.: Harvard University Press, 185–96.
Quine, W.v.O. 1960: *Word and Object*. Cambridge, Mass.: Harvard University Press.
Quine, W.v.O. 1961: *From a logical point of view*. 2nd edition, Cambridge, Mass.: Harvard University Press.
Read, S. 1978: Identity and Reference. *Mind*, 87:533–52.
Recanati, F. 1979: *La Transparence et l'Enonciation*, Paris: Editions du Seuil.
Recanati, F. 1981a: On Kripke on Donnellan. In H. Parret, M. Sbisà and J. Verschueren (eds), *Possibilities and Limitations of Pragmatics*, Amsterdam: John Benjamins, 595–630.
Recanati, F. 1981b: *Les Enoncés performatifs*. Paris: Minuit.
Recanati, F. 1986: On Defining Communicative Intentions. *Mind and Language* 1:213–42.
Recanati, F. 1987a: Contextual Dependence and Definite Descriptions. *Proceedings of the Aristotelian Society*, 87:57–73.

Recanati, F. 1987b: *Meaning and Force: the Pragmatics of Performative Utterances*. Cambridge: Cambridge University Press.
Recanati, F. 1988: Rigidity and Direct Reference. *Philosophical Studies*, 53: 103–17.
Recanati, F. 1989a: The Pragmatics of What is Said. *Mind and Language*, 4:295–329.
Recanati, F. 1989b: Referential/Attributive: A Contextualist Proposal. *Philosophical Studies*, 56:217–49.
Recanati, F. 1990: Direct Reference, Meaning, and Thought. *Noûs*, 24: 697–722.
Reichenbach, H. 1947: *Elements of Symbolic Logic*. London: Macmillan.
Richard, M. 1983: Direct Reference and Ascriptions of Belief. Reprinted (1988) in N. Salmon and S. Soames (eds), *Propositions and Attitudes*, Oxford: Oxford University Press, 169–96.
Richard, M. 1990: *Propositional Attitudes*. Cambridge: Cambridge University Press.
Rundle, B. 1968: Transitivity and Indirect Speech. *Proceedings of the Aristotelian Society*, 68:187–206.
Rundle, B. 1979: *Grammar in Philosophy*. Oxford: Clarendon Press.
Russell, B. 1918: Knowledge by Acquaintance and Knowledge by Description. In his *Mysticism and Logic and Other Essays*, London: Longmans, Green and Co, 209–32.
Russell, B. 1919: *Introduction to Mathematical Philosophy*. London: George Allen & Unwin.
Russell, B. 1956: *Logic and Knowledge: Essays 1901–1950*, edited by R.C. Marsh. London: George Allen & Unwin.
Sag, I. 1981: Formal Semantics and Extralinguistic Context. In P. Cole (ed.), *Radical Pragmatics*, New York: Academic Press, 273–94.
Sainsbury, M. 1985: The Varieties of Reference. *Mind*, 94:120–42.
Salmon, N. 1982: Assertion and Incomplete Definite Descriptions. *Philosophical Studies*, 42:37–45.
Salmon, N. 1986a: *Frege's Puzzle*. Cambridge, Mass.: MIT Press/Bradford Books.
Salmon, N. 1986b: Reflexivity. Reprinted (1988) in N. Salmon and S. Soames (eds), *Propositions and Attitudes*, Oxford: Clarendon Press, 240–74.
Salmon, N. 1989: Illogical Belief. *Philosophical Perspectives*, 3:243–85.
Salmon, N. 1991: The Pragmatic Fallacy. *Philosophical Studies*, 63:83–97.
Schiffer, S. 1977: Naming and Knowing. *Midwest Studies in Philosophy*, 2: 28–41.
Schiffer, S. 1978: The Basis of Reference. *Erkenntnis*, 13:171–206.
Schiffer, S. 1981: Indexicals and the Theory of Reference. *Synthese*, 49:43–100.
Schiffer, S. 1987: The 'Fido'-Fido theory of belief. *Philosophical Perspectives*, 1:455–80.
Schiffer, S., forthcoming: Belief Ascription.

Schoemaker, S. 1968: Self Reference and Self-Awareness. *Journal of Philosophy*, 65:555–67.
Searle, J. 1969: *Speech Acts*. Cambridge: Cambridge University Press.
Searle, J. 1978: Literal Meaning. *Erkenntnis*, 13:207–24.
Searle, J. 1980: The Background of Meaning. In J. Searle, F. Kiefer and M. Bierwisch (eds), *Speech Act Theory and Pragmatics*, Dordrecht: Reidel, 221–32.
Searle, J. 1983: *Intentionality*. Cambridge: Cambridge University Press.
Shepard, R. and Chipman, S. 1970: Second-Order Isomorphism of Internal Representations: Shapes of States. *Cognitive Psychology*, 1:1–17.
Smith, B.C., forthcoming: Varieties of Self-Reference. To appear in the Proceedings of the Conference on Theoretical Aspects of Reasoning About Knowledge, Monterey, California, March 1986.
Sperber, D. 1982: *Le Savoir des anthropologues*. Paris: Hermann. [English trans. 1985: *On Anthropological Knowledge*, Cambridge: Cambridge University Press.]
Sperber, D. and Wilson, D. 1986: *Relevance: Communication and Cognition*. Oxford: Basil Blackwell.
Stalnaker, R. 1970: Pragmatics. *Synthese*, 22:272–89.
Stalnaker, R. 1978: Assertion. *Syntax and Semantics*, 9:315–32.
Stalnaker, R. 1981: Indexical Belief. *Synthese*, 49:129–51.
Stich, S. 1983: *From Folk Psychology to Cognitive Science*. Cambridge, Mass.: MIT Press/Bradford Books.
Strawson, P. 1971: *Logico-Linguistic Papers*. London: Methuen.
Strawson, P. 1985: *Analyse et Métaphysique*. Paris: Vrin.
Taschek, W. 1987: Content, Character, and Cognitive Significance. *Philosophical Studies*, 52:161–89.
Taschek, W., forthcoming: Frege's Puzzle, Sense, and Information Content. To be published in *Mind*.
Travis, C. 1975: *Saying and Understanding*. Oxford: Basil Blackwell.
Travis, C. 1981: *The True and the False: the Domain of the Pragmatic*. Amsterdam: J. Benjamins.
Travis, C. 1985: On What is Strictly Speaking True. *Canadian Journal of Philosophy*, 15:187–229.
Travis, C. 1989: *The Uses of Sense*. Oxford: Clarendon Press.
Treisman, A. 1992: L'attention, les traits, et la perception des objets. In D. Andler (ed.), *Introduction aux sciences cognitives*, Paris: Gallimard, 153–91.
Urmson, J.O. 1968: Criteria of Intensionality (symposium with L.J. Cohen). *Aristotelian Society Proceedings, Supplementary Volume*, 42:107–22.
Waismann, F. 1951: Verifiability. In A. Flew (ed.), *Logic and Language*, 1st series, Oxford: Basil Blackwell, 17–44.
Walker, R. 1975: Conversational Implicatures. In S. Blackburn (ed.), *Meaning, Reference and Necessity*, Cambridge: Cambridge University Press. 133–81.

Wettstein, H. 1986: Has Semantics Rested on a Mistake? *Journal of Philosophy*, 83:185–209.
Wiggins, D. 1980: *Sameness and Substance*. Oxford: Basil Blackwell.
Wilson, D. 1975: *Presuppositions and Non-Truth-Conditional Semantics*. London: Academic Press.
Wilson, D. 1991: Pragmatics and Time. Paper delivered at the ESPRIT workshop on Pragmatics and its Boundaries, Paris, May 1991.
Wilson, D. and Sperber, D. 1981: On Grice's Theory of Conversation. In P. Werth (ed.), *Conversation and Discourse*, London: Croom Helm, 155–78.
Wilson, G. 1978: On Definite and Indefinite Descriptions. *Philosophical Review*, 87:48–76.
Wittgenstein, L. 1953: *Philosophical Investigations*. Oxford: Basil Blackwell.
Wittgenstein, L. 1958: *The Blue and Brown Books*. Oxford: Basil Blackwell.

# Index

abstract objects, *de re* thoughts about, 116, 309
acceptance, 42–3, 334–5, 346
acquaintance, 72, 109–10, 126–7, 129, 179, 183–4, 393
Adams F., 208
Almog, J., 41, 58
ambiguity, 8, 10, 143, 180, 234, 236–9, 249, 251, 252, 277–8, 279, 281, 284–8, 298, 330–2, 378, 381, 386–402; pragmatic, 261, 279, 281, 286–7
analog, vs. digital, 113–14, 117–18
Anscombe, E., 11, 120–1
Anscombre, J.C., 271
Aristotle, 188
Atlas, J., 236, 347
Austin, J.L., 30, 267, 316
autonymy *see* quotation
availability, 246–51, 256, 269, 274, 338
Ayers, M., 187

Bach, K., 16, 43, 58, 79, 99–101, 104, 116, 117, 131, 155, 165, 248, 253, 254, 261, 265, 331–2, 402
Baker, L., 210

Barwise, J., 278, 293, 301, 303, 319, 329, 332, 334, 345, 346
basic level interpretation, 312–18, 321, 378
Bealer, G., 332, 346, 363
belief, vs. acceptance *see* acceptance; vs. assertion, 21, 358–9, 361; change of, 82, 302; as cause of action *see* psychological explanation; dual structure of, 36–7, 42–3, 64–7, 77, 333, 337, 341, 346, 379 *see also* two-component analysis; reports of, xii–xiii, 23, 59, 68, 78, 302, 304–5, 319, 323–402
Benveniste, E., 185
Blakemore, D., 258
Block, N., 66
Brentano, F., 221
bridging thoughts, 124–5, 128
Brody, B., 23
buffers, 123–7, 129, 131, 171
Burge, T., 103, 145, 212, 215–17, 219

Carnap, R., 326
Carston, R., 239, 240, 242–4, 251–2, 256–61, 269–70, 347, 371

Cartesianism, 101–2, 196, 212–13, 219, 221–2, 224, 226
Castañeda, H.N., 59, 72, 78
causes, explanatory vs. producing, 204, 208
character, 17, 28–31, 33, 37, 41, 66–70, 76, 81–2, 135, 136, 139, 152, 153, 156–7, 159, 235–6, 283, 311, 355, 399
Chastain, C., 299
Chipman, S., 117
Chomsky, N., 149–52
Church, A., 155, 165
cognitive significance, xii, 34, 37, 42, 45, 63–4, 67–8, 80–94, 97, 135, 195–7
Cohen, L.J., 143, 153, 251, 269–71, 342–3
Cole, P., 332
collective entities, reference to, 308–9
communication, xiii, 20, 48–59, 76, 90–1, 152, 174, 178, 185–7, 296–8
composition, semantic process of, 266, 268, 318, 320, 374, 383
concepts, and buffers, 123–5, 126–7, 131; and categories, 93, 129, 132; *de re* see *de re* concepts; egocentric see egocentric concepts; environment-dependence of, 214, 225; as part of a system, 222–5; see also encyclopedia entries, modes of presentation, sortals
Condillac, E. de, 131
Congruence Principle, 54–5, 65, 97, 174–8, 181
conjoined utterances, pragmatics of, 239, 251–2, 253, 269–71, 337–9, 342–3
context-sensitivity see underdetermination

contextualism, 267
conversational implicatures, xii, 233–74, 278–81, 284–8, 299, 318, 328–47, 348, 368; conventionalized or generalized, 253, 254, 339, 347; testing for, 245, 250–1, 329–32, 340
Cornulier, B. de, 58
Cresswell, M., 23
Crimmins, M., 268, 313, 318, 351, 353–4, 357, 360–1, 362–3, 368–74, 384, 392

Davidson, D., 203–4, 208, 345, 346
*de re* concepts, xii, xiii, 4, 41, 79, 88, 91, 92, 97–132, 173–6, 181–7, 198–200, 294–8, 302–6, 315, 319, 358, 375, 389–93, 401; tentative, 305
*de re* thoughts, 4, 15, 21–2, 41, 45–59, 76, 97–132, 170, 194–6, 295–6, 302, 390
deferred reference, 263–5, 294, 310–14, 317
definite descriptions, xi, 3, 7–16, 22–3, 25, 103–4, 109–11, 184, 186, 237–8, 277–99, 314–15; attributive uses of, 12, 13, 38–9, 41, 107, 113, 176–7, 238, 277–99, 389–91; in belief contexts, 386–93, 397; functional uses of, 293, 299; improper, 279–83; incomplete, 248–9; informative vs. reference-fixing, 111–12, 117, 282; mathematical, 11–12, 14; in modal contexts, 8–10, 23; non-referentiality of, 3, 7, 11–12, 16, 22–3, 30–1, 38, 393–5, 398; referential uses of, 2, 24, 31, 41, 91, 229, 238, 277–99, 300, 389–91; rigid, 11–14; Russell's theory of, 248, 293, 299

# Index

demonstratives *see* indexicals
Dennett, D., 66, 208
denotational semantics, 383
Descartes, R., 165, 212, 225
description *see* acquaintance, definite descriptions, indefinite descriptions
descriptive names, 107–8, 109–12, 117, 176–80, 183, 189, 305
Devitt, M., xii, 23
diagonal proposition, 225, 289–90
digital *see* analog
division of linguistic labour, 144–6
dominance, of non-descriptive information, 126–9, 132
Dominicy, M., 298
Donnellan, K., xii, 31, 117, 237–8, 264, 277–83, 286
Drebushenko, D., 208
Dretske, F., 113, 117–18, 170–1, 225
DTHAT, 31, 107
Ducrot, O., 240, 271, 273
Dupuy, J.P., 352–4

effability, 58
egocentric concepts, 85–94, 98, 119–32, 168, 175, 181–4, 186, 189
egocentric system, 131
egocentric thoughts, 48–9, 55–6, 58, 59, 71–4, 88–90, 120–30; pure, 120–2, 125
empty case *see* hallucination
encyclopedia entries, 91, 98, 120, 125–30, 181–7, 189, 358
enrichment, 243, 258–9, 261–3, 267–8, 298, 347, 354, 356–7, 365, 371–5, 384–5, 399
eternal sentences, 78, 290, 350
Evans, G., xii, 13, 17, 38, 41–2, 43, 56, 74, 77, 78, 79, 88–9, 94, 98–103, 107–8, 115–16, 120–5, 155, 160, 165, 166, 173, 176–7, 187, 188, 194–7, 199, 201, 202–3, 207, 209–10, 212–13, 282, 296, 298, 306–7
exercising vs. ascribing *see* modes of presentation
external proposition, 289–91, 299
Externalism, 78, 207, 211–26

Fauconnier, G., 263–4, 268, 294, 299, 310, 312, 363, 390, 402
Fodor, J., 66, 155, 165, 208, 367, 368–70, 379–83, 384
Forbes, G., 345
Forguson, L.G., 298
Frege, G., 32, 34–7, 41–2, 48, 53, 63–4, 77, 78, 97, 102–3, 106, 115–17, 193, 195–7, 201, 207–8, 299, 326, 348
Frege's Constraint, 75, 82, 93, 94
Frege's Puzzle, 348, 356, 363
Fuller, G., 208
fundamental epistemic relations, 91, 92, 122–3, 126–9, 131, 182

Gardiner, A., 188
Geach, P., 25, 166, 170–2
generality constraint, 123–4, 126–7
Gibson, J.J., 130–1
*Giorgione*, 326, 345, 396–7
Goodman, N., 225
Gordon, R., 346
Granger, G., 188
Grice, P., xii, 20–2, 108, 109–10, 153, 177, 233–40, 241, 245, 250, 251, 252, 254, 264, 269–70, 281, 284–6, 288, 295, 321, 329–35, 338–40, 342–3, 346, 378
grounding, 222–5

hallucination, 98–101, 114, 195, 199–200, 206–7, 211, 213, 215–17, 220, 225

Harnish, R.M., 16, 58, 253
Horn, L., 251, 253, 254, 273
Hornsby, J., 326, 332, 380, 388, 390, 393, 402
Horwich, P., 319

iconicity, 113–14, 119, 120, 125, 335
identification, of reference; necessary for understanding, 13–15, 17, 28, 30, 193, 296, 398, see also understanding; two levels of, 171–2, 182
imagination, 113–14
immunity to error through misidentification, 87–90, 131, 173–5, 181, 188
impersonal uses, of pronouns, 311, 319, 353
implicatures; conventional, 233, 240–1, 346–7; conversational see conversational implicatures
indefinite descriptions, 185–7, 294, 299, 365–6, 380–2
index vs. referent, 308–12, 320
indexical thoughts, 58, 66, 72, 76, 78, 194–5, 209–10; see also egocentric thoughts
indexicals, xi, 7, 10, 12, 24, 63–94, 115, 135, 140–3, 155–7, 168, 185, 194, 235, 240, 242, 261, 264, 287, 289–90, 297; in belief contexts, 397–401; cognitive significance of, 48–9, 54–9, 80–94, 119–20, 131, 172–3, 175, 181–2, 186; descriptive uses of, 174, 177–8, 188, 189, 229–30, 300–16, 320, 321, 352; mental, 79, 99, 101–3; plural, 307–9; proper names as see proper names; pure indexicals vs. demonstratives, 41, 79, 81–3, 91n, 92, 93, 94, 141–2, 235–6, 364, 365

indicators, xi, 17, 19, 241
indirect speech acts, 16, 253
individualism, 214–17
initiating labels, 110, 183–4
Innocence, Principle of, 327–8, 345, 351, 357, 363–4
intentionality, 19–20, 130, 221, 295
interpretation, 48–52, 58–9, 65, 356; basic level of see basic level interpretation; vs. information, 303; inverse, 319; levels of see levels of meaning; see also semantic content
intuitions; supporting direct reference theory, 38–9, 283–4, 316–17, 398; of what is said see availability
Inwagen, P. van, 23

Jackendoff, R., 345
Jacob, P., 346, 357, 368, 370
Jakobson, R., 155, 165, 240

Kahneman, D., 171
Kaplan, D., xi, 17, 23, 29–31, 34, 36–7, 40, 41, 58, 64, 66–71, 78, 79, 81–2, 91, 106–8, 153, 156, 166, 193, 195, 235, 278, 280, 283, 291, 307, 310, 313–14, 364, 365
Katz, J.J., 58, 155, 159, 165
Kay, P., 235
kinaesthesis, 89, 121–2
Kneale, W., 155, 158, 162, 165, 236
Kripke, S., xi, 7–13, 19, 23, 24, 105, 155–67, 180, 189, 264, 278, 281, 283

languages, individuation of, 149–52
LePore, E., 79

levels of meaning, xi, 15, 19, 28, 31, 233–40, 246–7, 266, 287–91, 298–9, 312–18, 340
Levinson, S., 347
Lewis, D., 23
literal, vs. non-literal, 50, 54–5, 65, 174, 178, 248–9, 253, 265, 267, 287, 344, 364
Loar, B., 17, 53, 57–8, 155, 159–60, 230, 282, 304, 326, 345
Localness; local vs. global grounding of concepts, 222–5; local operation of p-processes, 262–6, 317–18, 320–1, 364; property of words, 146–9
Lockwood, M., 13–16, 23
Loewer, B., 79

McCulloch, G., 77
McDowell, J., 41–2, 43, 77, 98–103, 115–16, 194–9, 202, 207–8, 210, 212, 221, 226
McGinn, C., 66, 83, 85, 87, 92, 93, 99, 102, 116, 198–9, 208, 213–14, 216–17, 333
McKay, T., 332, 335, 346, 399–401
Marcus, R., 11
markedness, 91, 300, 315, 344, 371, 394
metalinguistic use; of logical connectives, 273, 344; of proper names, 169, 352–3
metaphor, 50, 65, 248, 344, 364
metonymy, 263–6, 294, 310, 364; *see also* transfer
Mill, J.S., 11, 29, 204, 208
Millikan, R., 78, 131–2, 167, 320
minimal proposition, 243, 262–3, 265–6, 268, 318, 378
minimalism, 240–5, 249–50, 255–62, 265, 269, 314–15, 356–7, 365, 378

misfit, 110–12
modes of presentation; descriptive vs. non-descriptive, 72–3, 76, 90–1, 97–118, 173–80, 294–8, 301–3, 304–5, 315, 393; exercised vs. ascribed, 305, 382, 389–92, 394–5; linguistic vs. psychological, xii–xiii, 24–5, 35–6, 55, 57, 63–94, 97, 135, 168, 172–3, 186, 297, 304–5, 315, 319, 358; types vs. tokens, 74, 77, 83–4, 92–3, 100–1, 116, 126, 132, 153, 169, 187, 198–200, 202–208, 214–17
Modified Occam's Razor, 234, 237–9, 251, 252, 284–7, 345, 378
Morgan, J.L., 347
Morgan, M.J., 131

narrow content, 64–70, 76, 77–8, 80, 92–3, 97–103, 114, 168, 194–226, 333–5, 346, 368, 380, 382; and linguistic meaning, 66–9; in psychological explanation, 64, 77, 200–5; two senses of, 65, 77–8, 214–18
Neale, S., 298, 299, 384
negation, metalinguistic *see* metalinguistic use
non-descriptiveness; and iconicity, 112–15; and relationality, 98–102; and truth-conditional irrelevance, 39–41, 103–5; two senses of, 114–15, 119
Nozick, R., 79
Nunberg, G., 229–30, 263–4, 268, 300–16, 319–21, 352–4, 357, 365, 377

Objectivity Constraint, 125, 126–7, 131
opacity, xii, 326–35, 345, 348, 353, 357, 365–6, 367, 368, 376, 380–1, 387–402

*oratio obliqua* vs. *oratio recta*, 55, 68, 78, 355
ordinary language philosophy, 252

P-processes *see* primary pragmatic processes
PASCs, 220–5
Peacocke, C., 10–11, 13, 19, 41, 42, 77, 78–9, 82, 87, 92, 93, 94, 99, 116, 117–18, 196, 201–3, 208, 332
Peirce, C.S., 114
perception, 98, 100–1, 103, 112–15, 119–32, 170–2, 182, 195, 206, 213–16
Perry, J., xii, 37, 41, 42–3, 48, 52, 56, 58, 59, 64, 66–71, 78, 79, 92, 99, 103, 116, 122–5, 129, 130, 131, 193, 195, 208, 210, 225, 241–2, 244, 249, 255–6, 267, 268, 278, 293, 299, 301, 303, 313, 318, 319, 329, 332, 334, 345, 346, 351, 353–4, 357, 360–1, 362–3, 368–74, 384, 392
pragmatic ambiguity *see* ambiguity
pragmatics, xii–xiii, 20–1, 91, 153, 230, 233–40, 277–8, 284–7, 300, 316–18, 320, 328–35, 368–9, 399–401
primary pragmatic processes, 260–8, 286, 294–5, 314–16, 318, 352–4, 356–7, 364, 365, 378, 390–1, 399
Prior, A., 363
proper names, 133–89; in belief contexts, 393–9, 400–1; descriptive *see* descriptive names; and encyclopedia entries, 131, 181–7; as indexicals, 140–3; local character of *see* localness; metalinguistic use of *see* metalinguistic use;

metalinguistic view of, 155–67; in modal contexts, 8–9, 23; in thought, 168–89
proposition normally expressed *see* minimal proposition
propositional content; and complete thought, xii, 24–5, 34–8, 46–7, 375; and implicatures, 233–54; and linguistic meaning, 26–30, 33, 233–6, 287, 288–90, 298, 340; and truth-conditions, 18, 19, 25, 28, 32, 49; *see also* availability; semantic conent
proprioception, 89, 121–2
psychological explanation, 71, 73, 77, 195–6, 197, 200–8, 341
Putnam, H., 78, 144–8, 151, 160, 166–7, 194–5, 208, 212, 218–22

quantification; domain of, 248–9, 253, 257–8, 262, 267; over modes of presentation, 362–3, 367, 382, 393; over propositional constituents, 365–6; substitutional, 363
quasi-indicators, 59
quasi-singular propositions, 31–2, 35, 39–41, 47, 196, 357–8, 361–2, 373–7, 386, 392, 396
Quasi-singularization, 354, 357, 374–5, 399
Quine, W.v. O., 11, 326–7, 345, 346, 387–8, 396–7
quotation, 49, 268, 325–7, 353, 355–6; *see also oratio obliqua* vs. *oratio recta*

Read, S., 299
Recanati, F., xi, 16, 23, 58, 81–2, 238, 243, 245, 251, 269, 278, 282, 288, 291, 363

REF, xi, xii, 17, 26, 31, 33, 91, 130, 137–40, 157, 229, 292, 296–7, 315, 394–9
referential/attributive distinction; applied to definite descriptions, 237–8, 277–99, *see also* definite descriptions; applied to indexicals, 229–30, 300–21, *see also* indexicals; and belief reports, 386–402
referentialism, critical, 58
Reichenbach, H., 70, 141
Relational principle, 349–54, 369–70, 376–7
relevance, 79, 165, 265, 266, 364
resemblance *see* similarity
Richard, M., 252–3, 337–8, 341–3, 346, 353–4, 357, 359–61, 365, 368–70, 372, 379, 381, 383, 384, 392
rigidity; ambiguity of the notion, 7; *de facto* vs. *de jure*, 12, 13, 23; and direct reference, xi, 10–16, 19, 25, 27, 28; and scope, 7–11, 19, 23; and truth-conditions, 9–16, 19–20, 27–8
Rundle, B., 152, 363
Russell, B., 10, 11, 72, 117, 155, 165, 177–9, 188, 280, 293, 299, 361, 393
Russell's Principle, 117

Sag, I., 264, 268
Sainsbury, M., 203
Salmon, N., 37, 252, 286, 298, 332, 336, 338–40, 344, 346–7, 349, 362, 363, 366, 385, 396
Salmon's equivalence, 336, 362, 366, 385
saturation, of egocentric thought by perceptual information, 93, 121, 123, 132; p-process of, 261, 263, 266, 365

Schiffer, S., 23, 32, 177–8, 189, 229–30, 338, 344, 358–9, 361, 362, 363, 365, 366, 367, 368–70, 383
Scope Principle, 251, 269–74
Searle, J., 16, 24, 43, 79, 99, 117, 166, 254, 260, 320
secondary pragmatic processes, 261, 265–6
semantic content, 45–9, 53–4, 56, 63, 303–4, 369, 375–7, 383, 384
semantic indeterminacy *see* underdetermination
semantic reference, vs. speaker reference, 264, 280, 282–3
Semi-propositional thoughts, 169
Sensory deprivation, 120–2
sentence meaning, vs. utterance meaning *see* levels of meaning
Shepard, R., 117
Shoemaker, S., 88
similarity, 49–50, 104, 206, 346, 356, 379–81, 384
simplified picture, 66–70, 78, 80, 84–5
Smith, B.C., 132
solipsistic content, 218–22, 224
sortals, 24, 25, 147, 169–72, 187–8, 189
speech act theory, xi, 16–17
Sperber, D., 24, 49–50, 58, 79, 153, 165, 169, 236, 242–4, 249, 256–8, 260, 261, 298, 355, 364
Stalnaker, R., 210, 225, 278, 289–90, 291
Stecker, R., 208
stereotype, 146–8
Stich, S., 299, 346, 367, 369, 383, 402
Strawson, P., 20, 30, 252
subjectivity, 46, 48–9, 51–7, 58, 59, 68, 72–3, 78, 101, 113,

120, 195, 212, 213, 216, 219–22; *see also* egocentric thoughts
substitutivity, 325, 327–8, 333, 335, 357–8, 397
surroundings, 350–1, 363
synecdoche, xiii, 91, 184, 186, 293–8, 315, 389, 391

Tarski, A., 24
Taschek, W., 78, 341–2, 347
teleofunction, 320
temporary files, 127–9, 131–2, 171–2, 182–3
token-referentiality *see* type-referentiality
token-reflexivity, 70, 72–3, 77, 79, 85–6, 94, 141–2
tracking, 122, 131–2, 182
transfer, 263–6, 268, 294–8, 315, 319, 321, 356–7, 378, 390
transparency *see* opacity
Travis, C., 252, 267, 320
Treisman, A., 132, 171–2, 182
truth-conditional irrelevance, xii, 40–1, 45, 47, 56–8, 64, 97–8, 103–8, 112, 113–14, 119, 130, 193, 295, 297–8, 312, 315, 354, 373, 375, 396–7, 398–9
two-component analysis, 51, 58, 64–6, 77, 78, 97, 115, 191–226, 333; *see also* narrow content

type-referentiality, vs. token-referentiality, 3–4, 16–19, 22–3, 24, 31, 300; *see also* REF

unarticulated constituents, 241–2, 244, 254, 255–6, 259–60, 267, 268, 320, 371–5; *see also* enrichment
underdetermination, 79, 235–7, 239, 246, 250, 298, 355, 357–8, 365, 377, 382–3, 391
understanding, 13–15, 17, 21, 26, 27–8, 30, 34, 43, 56, 169, 178, 188, 241, 296, 307
ungrounding *see* grounding
Urmson, J.O., 332, 334–5, 343

Waismann, F., 267
Walker, R., 236
Wettstein, H., 41, 58, 78, 79, 81, 278
Wiggins, D., 25, 170–2, 187, 188
Wilson, D., 49–50, 58, 79, 153, 165, 236, 242–4, 249, 256–8, 260, 261, 269, 271, 273, 298, 355, 364
Wilson, G., 299
Wittgenstein, L., 88, 117, 254, 267

Zimmer, K., 235